THE ELDERS OF THE CITY

THE SOCIETY OF BIBLICAL LITERATURE
MONOGRAPH SERIES

Number 55
THE ELDERS OF THE CITY
A Study of the Elders-Laws in Deuteronomy

by
Timothy M. Willis

THE ELDERS OF THE CITY
A Study of the Elders-Laws in Deuteronomy

Timothy M. Willis

Society of Biblical Literature
Atlanta, Georgia

THE ELDERS OF THE CITY
A Study of the Elders-Laws in Deuteronomy

by
Timothy M. Willis

Library of Congress Cataloging-in-Publication Data

Willis, Timothy M.
    The elders of the city : a study of the elders-laws in Deuteronomy /
Timothy M. Willis.
        p. cm. (Monograph series / The Society of Biblical Literature ; no. 55)
    Includes bibliographical references and index.
    ISBN 1-58983-013-X (alk. paper)
    1. Aged in the Bible. 2 Bible. O.T. Deuteronomy—Criticism, interpretation, etc.
3. Leadership in the Bible. 4. Jewish law. I. Title. II. Monograph series (Society of
Biblical Literature) ; no. 55.

BS680. A34 W55 2001
222'.1506—dc21   200104824

08 07 06 05 04 03 02 01   5 4 3 2 1

Printed in the United States of America
on acid-free paper

TABLE OF CONTENTS

v

ACKNOWLEDGEMENTS

This study began as a dissertation, completed a decade ago at Harvard University, which surveyed the references to Israel's "elders" (local or tribal) in pre-exilic contexts. In the end, the topic proved too broad to accommodate the kind of examination I really wanted to undertake. The members of my committee advised me at that time to "dig deeper" into certain aspects of this broad topic. In particular, Prof. James Kugel suggested that I might limit myself to the Book of Deuteronomy. Ultimately, even that proved to be too broad for two reasons. First, an investigation of references to elders in the framework of Deuteronomy must by necessity be expanded to consider references in the Deuteronomistic History as well. Second, there are two different categories of elders mentioned in Deuteronomy. The elders mentioned in the framework are "the elders of Israel," while those in the laws are city elders. I have decided to focus on the latter here.

There are several individuals whom I would like to thank for the help they have provided me in the long process of writing this book. The well-reasoned criticisms and gracious encouragement provided by Prof. Frank Moore Cross and the other members of my dissertation committee have proven invaluable. Over the past decade, I presented preliminary drafts of a couple of the chapters of the present work to the Biblical Law Group at Annual Meetings of the Society of Biblical Literature. The aid and advice of several members of the group (particularly Raymond Westbrook, Paul Dion, Carolyn Pressler, John Welch, William Morrow, and

Bernard Levinson) have been crucial in shaping many parts of the present study. Adequate thanks cannot be given to my father, John T. Willis of Abilene Christian University, who first trained me and has continually demonstrated to me what it means to be a careful scholar and a devoted family man.

Most of the manuscript was written during a sabbatical leave in the Fall of 1998; so I would like to thank Pepperdine University for graciously providing me with that time. I would also like to express my appreciation to Dr. Terence Fretheim, Dr. Dennis Olson, and the others associated with the Monograph Series for their assistance in bringing this project to its completion.

Finally, I would like to give a special word of thanks to my wife, Jan. She has had to endure far too many days with books and papers scattered around the room, and far too many nights illuminated by the glare of the computer screen. Her steady encouragement and unwavering patience inspired me to press on in the most discouraging of times. I gratefully dedicate this work to her.

ABBREVIATIONS

AB	Anchor Bible
AJSL	*American Journal of Semitic Languages*
AmAnthro	*American Anthropologist*
AmAntiq	*American Antiquities*
AnBib	*Analecta Biblica*
AnthroQ	*Anthropology Quarterly*
AOAT	Alter Orient und Altes Testament
ASAM	Association of Social Anthropologists Monographs
ASOR	American Schools of Oriental Research
BASOR	*Bulletin of the American Schools of Oriental Research*
BBB	Bonner Biblische Beiträge
BETL	Bibliotheca ephemeridum theologicarum lovaniensium
BHH	*Biblisch-Historisches Handwörterbuch*
Bib	*Biblica*
BibTr	*Bible Translator*
BibZ	*Biblische Zeitschrift*
BZAW	Beihefte zur Zeitschrift für die alttestamentliche Wissenschaft
CBC	Cambridge Bible Commentary
CBQ	*Catholic Biblical Quarterly*
CompStudSocHist	*Comparative Studies in Social History*
CurrAnthro	*Current Anthropology*
CV	*Communio Viatorum*
ÉgTh	*Église et Théologie*
EOTHR	*Essays in Old Testament History and Religion*
EphThL	*Ephemerides theoligicae lovanienses*
ErFor	Erfurt Forschungen
FRLANT	Forschungen zur Religion und Literatur des Alten and Neues Testaments
HL	Hittite Laws
HSM	Harvard Semitic Monographs
HTR	*Harvard Theological Review*

HUCA	*Hebrew Union College Annual*
ICC	International Critical Commentary
IDB	*Interpreter's Dictionary of the Bible*
IEJ	*Israel Exploration Journal*
IntJAfrHist	*International Journal of African History*
Interp	*Interpretation*
JAfrHist	*Journal of African History*
JANES	*Journal of the Ancient Near Eastern Society*
JAOS	*Journal of the American Oriental Society*
JBL	*Journal of Biblical Literature*
JCompFamStud	*Journal of Comparative Family Studies*
JESHO	*Journal of the Economic and Social History of the Orient*
JewQR	*Jewish Quarterly Review*
JModAfrStud	*Journal of Modern African Studies*
JNES	*Journal of Near Eastern Studies*
JRel	*Journal of Religion*
JRelHist	*Journal of Religious History*
JSOT	*Journal for the Study of the Old Testament*
JSOTS	Journal for the Study of the Old Testament Supplement Series
JSS	*Journal of Semitic Studies*
LCL	Loeb Classical Library
LE	Laws of Eshnunna
LH	Laws of Hammurabi
LL	Laws of Lipit-Ishtar
LU	Laws of Ur-Nammu
MAL	Middle Assyrian Laws
MAPD	Middle Assyrian Palace Decrees
MARI	*Mari, annales de recherches interdisiplinaires*
NICOT	New International Commentary on the Old Testament
OBO	Orbis biblicus et orientalis
Or	*Orientalia*
OTL	Old Testament Library
OTS	*Oudtestamentische Studiën*
PRU	*Le Palais Royales d'Ugarit*
RB	*Revue Biblique*
ResQ	*Restoration Quarterly*
SAAS	State Archives of Assyria Studies
SAOC	Studies in Ancient Oriental Civilization
SBLDS	Society of Biblical Literature Dissertation Series
SBTS	Sources for Biblical and Theological Study
SVT	Supplements to Vetus Testamentum
TDNT	*Theological Dictionary of the New Testament*
TDOT	*Theological Dictionary of the Old Testament*
TelEd	Telepinu Edict
Ug	*Ugaritica*
VT	*Vetus Testamentum*

WMANT	Wissenschaftliche Monographien zum Alten und Neuen Testaments
ZA	*Zeitschrift für Assyriologie*
ZAW	*Zeitschrift für die alttestamentliche Wissenschaft*
ZAWSup	*Zeitschrift für die alttestamentliche Wissenschaft Supplement Volume*

CHAPTER 1
"THE ELDERS OF THE CITY":
PRELIMINARY CONSIDERATIONS

There have been numerous investigations over the years regarding leadership in the Hebrew Bible. Most of these have focused on the significance of particular types of national leaders—kings, prophets, priests, savior-judges—each significant for the social, political, and religious life of Israel. Far less attention has been given to local leaders, even though experience tells us that the roles played by local leaders often would have had just as much significance (if not more) in the day to day lives of most Israelites. The present study attempts to enhance our understanding of leadership in ancient Israel by looking at one of those groups of local leaders, the city elders.

PREVIOUS STUDIES OF ISRAELITE ELDERS

Three German dissertations devoted to the broad subject of elders in ancient Israel have been published. The earliest of these, by Otto Seesemann, appeared in 1895.[1] It represents the consensus opinion of its day and stood as the only extended study of Israel's elders for the next sixty years. It was eventually

---

[1] O. Seesemann, "Die Ältesten im Alten Testament" (Diss. phil., Leipzig, 1895).

1

followed with a study by Horstklaus Berg in 1959,[2] and another by
W. A. Roeroe in 1976.[3] Each takes a traditio-historical approach to
this subject. The primary concern of each is with the role played
by elders at the national level. The major differences between
them primarily reflect changes in the theories regarding the
redactional history of the Hebrew Bible.

Seesemann lays out a broad schema for the evolution of the
institution of elders which sets the tone for most subsequent
studies. In the pre-settlement period, the elders were clan and
tribal representatives who oversaw national affairs. This strong
national role was lost when the tribes settled down, and the power
of the elders came to be restricted to local communities. The early
Hexateuchal sources preserve a recollection of the national role
that the elders played, but the depiction of elders is colored in
those sources by the authors' conceptions of elders derived from
the roles played by elders living in their own time. The depictions
of elders preserved in the laws of Deuteronomy, where only local
elders are mentioned, is considered by Seesemann to be a fairly
accurate (and complete) reflection of the roles of elders in the
monarchic period. Following the fall of Jerusalem, the national
role of elders was revitalized, remaining strong in the absence of
kings.

Berg is heavily influenced by Noth's ideas regarding a pre-
monarchic Israelite amphictyony. He focuses on the pre-monarchic
period, offering a different explanation for the origin of the notion
(reflected in writings from the monarchic period) that Israel's
elders had been a political force at the national level prior to the
rise of the kings. He points to references from throughout the
Hebrew Bible which indicate that "the elders of Israel" were
leading participants in national cultic ceremonies. In particular,
they appear in the Hexateuch in several covenant renewal
ceremonies (Exodus 19, 24; Deuteronomy 29; Joshua 23, 24). He
deduces from this that the elders had been central figures in the
"amphictyonic" cult.[4] Berg does not deal with the functions of
elders at the local level.

---

[2] H. Berg, "Die 'Ältesten Israels' im Alten Testament" (Diss. theol.,
Hamburg, 1959).

[3] W. A. Roeroe, "Das Ältestenamt im Alten Testament" (Diss. theol., Mainz,
1976).

[4] Berg, "Die 'Ältesten Israels,'" esp. pp. 129–40.

Roeroe represents something of a return to Seesemann, in that his work is more comprehensive. He differs, however, in his focus on the development of the roles of elders at the local level during the monarchic period. Elders not only retained their pre-monarchic functions at the local level throughout the monarchic period, they even assumed new roles as local officials for the state. This is represented, he argues, in the lists of local officials found primarily in Deuteronomistic and prophetic writings. For example, Josh 24:1 mentions "the elders of Israel, and its heads, and its judges, and its officers" as participants in a cultic ceremony. Roeroe believes that the first term designates the whole group of local leaders involved, while the other three identify its sub-groups. These more precise delineations of elders' roles are not found (for the most part) in writings subsequent to the destruction of Jerusalem.[5]

Another monograph-length treatment of Israel's elders was completed less than twenty years ago by Hanoch Reviv.[6] He, too, attempts to provide a traditio-historical analysis of the references to elders. His dependence on certain Israeli and Jewish critics is obvious, as he bases many of his arguments on the antiquity and reliability of Priestly sources in the Pentateuch and Chronicles. He concludes that national power was in the hands of tribal chiefs (נשיאים and ראשים) in the pre-settlement period, but that it shifted to local elders as the tribes became more sedentary. The influence of a group of local elders never exceeded a clan's territory, though. Depictions of pan-tribal gatherings are monarchic in composition and represent an idealized transposition of local structures to a national level. The powers of these elders declined as the powers of judges and, subsequently, the kings increased. Yet, the elders never lost all of their authority at the local level, and the kings eventually had to share many local administrative responsibilities with them.[7]

In addition to these lengthy investigations, several shorter studies of Israel's elders have appeared in journals and Bible

---

[5] Roeroe, "Das Ältestenamt," esp. pp. 69–70, 114–81, 190, 206–11.

[6] H. Reviv, *The Elders in Ancient Israel: A Study of a Biblical Institution*, trans. Lucy Plitmann (Jerusalem: Magnes, 1989). (The original, in Hebrew, appeared in 1983.)

[7] Reviv, *Elders in Ancient Israel*, esp. pp. 40–46, 74–75, 187–91.

handbooks and dictionaries.[8] In discussing the overall significance
of elders, these shorter studies have tended to echo the earlier
conclusions of Seesemann. The institution of elders is said to
originate in a nomadic milieu (the pre-settlement period); it is
altered by the process of sedentarization, whereby clan leaders
become community leaders; these local elders are in constant
competition with the crown (at the national level) or its local
representatives (at the community level); overall, their power and
influence diminish as the power of the central state increases;
depictions of a body of national elders in the monarchic period are
often attributed to the transference of the roles of local elders to
an idealized national body.

There are also a few general studies of Israelite society which
include extended remarks on the roles and functions of Israel's
elders.[9] These seem to assume Seesemann's basic schema as well.
They only briefly mention a national body of elders, because such
an institution is considered to be an idealization. More is said in
these studies, instead, about the functions of elders in the local
communities. Even here, however, it is the political power of local
elders vis-à-vis the power of the central authorities which is of
greatest interest.

Recent developments in theories regarding the literary
development of the Hebrew Bible point to the need for a complete
reexamination of the portrayals of Israel's elders. Noth's
amphictyonic hypothesis has been generally dismissed in the past
two decades, completely undermining Berg's assumptions and

[8] J. L. McKenzie, "The Elders in the Old Testament," *Bib* 40 (1959) 522–40
[= *AnBib* 10 (1959) 388–406]; J. Dus, "Die 'Ältesten Israels,'" *CV* 3 (1960)
232–42; J. van der Ploeg, "Les anciens dans l'Ancien Testament," in *Lex tua
veritas. Festschrift für Hubert Junker*, pp. 175–91; ed. H. Groß and F.
Mußner (Trier: Paulinus-Verlag, 1961); G. H. Davies, "Elder in the OT," *IDB*
II, pp. 72–73; D. N. Freedman, s.v., "Ältester," *BHH* I, pp. 76–77; J. Conrad,
s. v. "זקן," *TDOT* IV, pp. 122–31; Victor H. Matthews and Don C. Benjamin,
"The Elder," *The Bible Today* 30 (1992) 170–74.
    This list does not include several works and articles which contain some
brief remarks on Israel's elders as part of an investigation into the roots of
synagogue structures or early church polity (e.g., G. Bornkamm, s. v.
"πρεσβυς," *TDNT* VI, pp. 651–80).
[9] E.g., J. Pedersen, *Israel: Its Life and Culture* I–II (London: Oxford, 1926),
pp. 34–39; M. Noth, *The History of Israel*, 2nd ed. (New York: Harper and
Row, 1960), pp. 98–109; R. de Vaux, *Ancient Israel: Its Life and Institutions*,
trans. J. McHugh (New York: McGraw-Hill, 1961), pp. 8, 68–70, 138, 152–53.

conclusions. The analyses of Seesemann and Roeroe assume the conclusions of Wellhausen, but those conclusions have been seriously questioned in many recent studies. A complete reappraisal of the development of the roles of elders in Israel is therefore warranted, but the magnitude of the task makes it unlikely that one will soon be produced.

The complexity of the issue might be one of the reasons why more recent studies (including the present one) are quite restricted in scope. Surprisingly, each of these recent investigations addresses this topic in regard to the same book—Deuteronomy. Still, they primarily consider the national role played by elders. Leslie Hoppe, dissatisfied with previous proposals regarding the literary locus of the Book of Deuteronomy, argues that the elders were a force significant enough on the national scene to have composed the book.[10] Unfortunately, the types of questions regarding other proposals which make him skeptical of them completely undermine his own proposal. Two subsequent monographs resume the more traditional approach, where the elders simply represent a significant political force (the traditional tribal groups) in the national scene, to whom the laws are addressed. The question they seek to answer is, When in Israel's history were the elders likely to have the powers attributed to them in the Deuteronomic laws? The earlier study of the two is by Joachim Buchholz.[11] Buchholz's aim is to demonstrate how varying descriptions of the roles of Israel's elders in Deuteronomy support and refine reconstructions of the literary development of Deuteronomy and the Deuteronomistic History proposed by Dietrich, Smend, and others. He argues that city elders (and the traditional groups they represent) had a fairly significant role at the local level in pre-exilic Israel. That role is reflected in the stratum of Deuteronomy written early in the exilic period which preserves pre-exilic traditions. Their powers fade during the exile, however, as seen in the diminution of their responsibilities in later strata of the book, and they are fairly

---

[10] Leslie J. Hoppe, "The Origins of Deuteronomy" (Ann Arbor, MI: University Microfilms, 1978). His conclusions are summarized in "Elders and Deuteronomy: A Proposal," *ÉgTh* 14 (1983) 259–72.

[11] J. Buchholz, *Die Ältesten Israels im Deuteronomium* (GTA 36; Göttingen: Vandenhoeck & Ruprecht, 1988).

insignificant when the exiles return to Judah.[12] Buchholz's conclusions receive a serious challenge a few years later in a monograph by Jan Christian Gertz. He argues that most of the Deuteronomic laws concerning local elders reflect an early post-exilic setting, because the traditional groups enjoyed a resurgence of power during the initial stages of the return from Exile.[13] The opposing conclusions of Buchholz and Gertz reflect recent disagreements among German scholars regarding the literary development of the Book of Deuteronomy. They differ from the present study because their primary focus continues to be the national power and influence of elders and the tribal groups they represent. Explication of their local functions is of secondary importance.

THE PRESENT STUDY: ITS SCOPE AND METHODOLOGY

The present investigation is limited to the five laws in the Deuteronomic Code which refer to elders. Its primary aim is to understand more fully the roles to be played by elders in local communities, according to the laws of the D Code. My assumptions regarding the place of the D Code in the history of Israelite religion align fairly closely with the majority of American scholars of the Hebrew Bible. I assume that the core of Deuteronomic laws is a product of pre-exilic Israel, with redactions occurring in the late pre-exilic or exilic periods. Elements of these laws which tend to confirm this assumption will be mentioned. Some possible implications for redactional issues are proposed in the concluding chapter. As such, this study stands in part as a counterpoint to the studies of Buchholz and Gertz.

But the redaction-critical questions are of secondary importance here; instead, my primary focus entails a reevaluation of the Deuteronomic laws mentioning local elders in the light of an extensive cross-cultural analysis of local leaders of kinship-based societies. My primary goal is to interpret the Deuteronomic elders-laws as manifestations of the powers and functions of local elders

---

[12] Buchholz, *Die Ältesten Israels*, esp. pp. 103–105.

[13] J. C. Gertz, *Die Gerichtsorganisation Israels im deuteronomischen Gesetz* (FRLANT 165; Göttingen: Vandenhoeck & Ruprecht, 1993).

in ancient Israel. Questions regarding the national implications of my findings are only tangentially considered.

A major component of the present analysis is the extensive utilization of comparative ethnographic evidence. Conclusions drawn from comparisons with elders and other traditional leaders in other societies have sometimes been assumed in previous investigations, but concrete parallels have only rarely been noted.[14] Moreover, comparative analyses which have been conducted have typically used relatively small databases.[15] This has naturally limited the investigators' abilities to draw informed conclusions. Sweeping statements are sometimes made based on the evidence of very few examples. I have tried to remedy this situation by entering into a more thorough cross-cultural analysis of the roles and functions of elders than has been attempted previously. I will explain my ideas on this in more detail shortly. Before doing that, however, I need to set out my understanding of the phrase "elders of the city" more precisely.

---

[14] An exception to this rule is the article by McKenzie ("Elders in the Old Testament," pp. 532–34). He writes of specific similarities between Israel's elders and Bedouin shaykhs and emirs.

Even McKenzie is guilty of some methodological shortcomings, though. He, like many before him, has limited his field of comparable societies to nomadic groups. This has led to an equation between tribal structures and nomadic structures. Tribal structures and ideals in Israel are said to be attributable directly to an early "nomadic" phase in Israel's history. Further, developments in contemporary Bedouin society which have occurred as the Bedouin become more sedentary are automatically ascribed to Israel. Tribal structures are said to have been inevitably altered when Israel settled in the land (and because Israel *settled* in the land). No further explanation is deemed necessary. Many of the ethnographies utilized here demonstrate that (1) many "nomadic" notions are held by non-nomadic peoples, and (2) those notions often persist in local communities long after those communities have been absorbed by a central state. For these reasons, I am reticent to associate the notions reflected in these laws directly with nomadism.

[15] Reviv's work (*Elders in Ancient Israel*) represents a step in the right direction, as he relies heavily on recent sociological theory regarding patriarchal and tribal societies. He still compromises the helpfulness of his work, however, by consulting only a few actual field studies.

ELDERS IN THE HEBREW BIBLE: AN OVERVIEW

The primary term in the Hebrew Bible to denote an "elder" is
זָקֵן, literally, "bearded one."[16] It is used more than 120 times,
usually in the plural. It can denote old age in a general sense (Lev
19:32; Jer 6:11; 51:21–23; Ezek 9:6; Psalm 119:100; Job 32:9; Ezra
3:12), but it more commonly indicates that one is a member of "a
distinct social grade or collegiate body with certain political and
religious functions."[17]

There are three general categories of elders in the Hebrew
Bible. One category is that of senior members of a group that is
united primarily by vocation. The most prominent examples of
this category of elders are what could be called "royal elders."[18]
They are senior members of a king's servants and advisors,
designated as "the elders of his (the king's) house" (Gen 50:7; 2
Sam 12:17) or "his elders" (Ps 105:22; cp. Isa 24:23). This
designation probably arose naturally from the practice of referring
to a wealthy man's chief servants as "the elders of his house" (see
Gen 24:2). Only slightly different is the designation of leading
priests as "elders of the priests" (2 Kgs 19:2; Jer 19:1).

A second category of elders is the national or tribal elders. The
questions regarding this category abound. Overshadowing them
all is the question of historicity. In the past, it was often asserted
that the introduction of the monarchy virtually eliminated the
national political power of the tribal groups, even at the local
level.[19] There are problems with the reconstruction, though. First,

---

[16] The Hebrew term שֵׂיבָה, "old age," cognate of the Babylonian *shibu*, is
used as a designation of age rather than position in life.

[17] McKenzie, "Elders in the Old Testament," p. 522.

[18] See T. M. Willis, "Yahweh's Elders (Isa 24,23): Senior Officials of the
Divine Court," *ZAW* 103 (1991) 375–85.

[19] E. Neufeld, "The Emergence of a Royal-Urban Society in Ancient Israel,"
HUCA 31 (1960) 37–41, 48–50; Hoppe, "Elders and Deuteronomy," p. 267; N.
P. Lemche, *Early Israel* (Leiden: Brill, 1985), p. 283. This has been the
"consensus" opinion since first laid out by Otto Seesemann almost a century
ago (see Berg, "Die 'Ältesten Israels,'" pp. vii–viii).

The general notion that a centralized bureaucracy will virtually eliminate
preceding tribal structures is based on sociological theory developed in the
nineteenth century, which was derived almost exclusively from data on Greek
and Roman culture. See M. Godelier, "The Concept of the 'Asiatic Mode of
Production' and Marxist Models of Social Evolution," in *Relations of*

the significance of kinship at the local level and the power of tribal groups at the national level should be viewed separately (see below). The former often persist long after the national groups have ceased to function. Moreover, the persistence of the national strength of Israel's tribal groups is now more commonly accepted. The traditional tribal groups show their relative strength, for example, in that lineages of some of the guild cities were actually grafted into the older ones (1 Chr 4:21–23).[20] This was so, even though these cities emanated from the court. Similarly, the Davidic house in Judah never separated itself genealogically from the other tribal groups. Thus, the national strength of traditional tribal groups appears to have continued down to the destruction of Jerusalem; but a fuller study of that issue is still needed.[21]

The distinction presented in the Hebrew Bible between national elders ("the elders of Israel") and local (city) elders is primarily one of function. The only function which national elders clearly fulfill is a representative one, while city elders perform several functions within their local community. The "elders of Israel" most likely consisted of men who functioned as city elders locally, but who also happened to come from the core lineages residing in their tribal territory. Probably only the main towns within a tribal territory would produce elders that would represent the tribe at the national level; by analogy, only members of the more influential lineages of a community would stand on behalf of their community before the rest of the tribe.[22]

Production: Marxist Approaches to Economic Anthropology, ed. D. Seddon, trans. H. Lackner (London: Frank Cass, 1980), pp. 233–35.

[20] See I. Mendelsohn, "Guilds in Ancient Palestine," *BASOR* 80 (1940) 18–19.

[21] A large percentage of the studies which I have read involve tribes or tribal confederacies which exist within states without losing their tribal identities. The conclusion that the emergence of a centralized state in Israel led inevitably to the disintegration of tribal structures is overstated.

[22] B. Halpern, *The Constitution of the Monarchy* (HSM 25; Chico, CA: Scholars Press, 1981), pp. 190, 198–99, 215.

There are some obvious parallels to national elders in contemporary Middle Eastern societies in the persons of shaykhs. H. P. Smith routinely translates זקנים as "Sheikhs" (*A Critical and Exegetical Commentary on the Books of Samuel* [ICC; Edinburgh: T. and T. Clark, 1899; reprint ed. 1977]; cp. McKenzie, "Elders in the Old Testament," p. 533; van der Ploeg, "Les anciens," p. 190). Shaykhs sometimes serve alone as a village or town head, but more often there are several members of shaykhly families who serve as

Consideration of the meaning of "tribe" clarifies this to some extent. A "tribe" is understood as a combination of kinship and territory. The clearest evidence of this comes from 1 Sam 30:26–31. David gives some of his spoils "to the elders of Judah, to his friends" (1 Sam 30:26).[23] These "elders of Judah" are subsequently defined as those who come from various cities within the tribal territory of Judah. Some of these cities are mentioned individually, but others are viewed collectively according to clan groupings ("the cities of the Jerahmeelites" and "the cities of the Qenites"). Some of those individual cities are linked to specific clans in biblical genealogies (see 1 Chr 2:42–43; 4:17; cp. Shechem, Tirzah). These facts indicate that a tribe of Israel was understood as a collection of cities, but also that cities were often associated with particular clans; thus, a tribal designation has both territorial and kinship aspects to it.[24]

---

elders in their local communities; yet, there can be leading members of other (non-shaykhly) families who serve as city elders alongside them. Still, shaykhs are more likely than other local elders to represent their villages or towns at extra-mural gatherings, to other communities, and before government officials. On the roles of shaykhs in contemporary societies, see R. A. Fernea, *Shaykh and Effendi* (Cambridge, MA: Harvard University, 1970), pp. 30–33, 52–54, 66–69, 101–53; D. P. Cole, *Nomads of the Nomads: The Al-Murrah of the Empty Quarter* (Chicago: Aldine, 1975), pp. 94–96; P. Dresch, "The Positions of *shaykhs* among the Northern Tribes of Yemen," *Man* 19 (1984) 37–41; H. Goldberg, "From Shaykh to Mazkir: Structural Continuity and Organizational Change in the Leadership of a Tripolitanian Jewish Community," in *Jewish Societies in the Middle East: Community, Culture, and Authority*, ed. Sh. Deshen and W. P. Zenner (Washington, D.C.: University Press of America, 1982), pp. 139–46; M. Katakura, *Bedouin Village: A Study of a Saudi Arabian People in Transition* (Tokyo: University of Tokyo, 1977), pp. 40–41, 69–70; L. Holy, *Neighbours and Kinsmen: A Study of the Berti People of Darfur* (New York: St. Martin's, 1974), pp. 145–51.

I would caution against the use of the phrase "primus inter pares" to describe a national elder in contradistinction to his fellow city elders, because there might be more than one national elder from a given city.

[23] McCarter conjectures an original reading of "to the elders of Judah city by city," proposing the following developments: לרעיהו > לרעיו > לעריו (see LXX). P. K. McCarter, *1 Samuel* (AB; Garden City: Doubleday, 1980), p. 433. This would fit nicely into my discussion here, but I am not convinced of its validity.

[24] See Berg, "Die 'Ältesten Israels,'" pp. 28, 135–36. Many prophetic condemnations of Israelite society address a national audience by speaking of injustices performed in cities—"in the gate" (e.g., Amos 5:10–13; cp. Deut 16:18–20).

PRELIMINARY CONSIDERATIONS 11

On the surface, then, tribal/national elders might appear to represent regions rather than particular lineages; in reality, however, they most likely represent both. Their primary function is to represent the people of their city and tribe to the king and his officials and to elders of other cities and tribes at inter-tribal gatherings. Only the members of a locally powerful lineage would have the influence necessary to succeed in such a capacity. Their opinion must be well-respected by their constituents, and they must be powerful enough to influence the opinions of their counterparts in other tribes or have the ear of the king and his officials. The central city of a clan is the most likely place to produce such men, although it is possible that local conditions might warrant the inclusion of men from other communities within a clan district as well. Also, because these elders represent a geographical area (a tribe), elders of guild cities and even administrative centers might be included in the ranks of "the elders of the tribe of X." Still, kinship ties would play a major role in determining which city elders would adequately function as tribal elders.[25]

This leaves the third and final category of elders, the city elders, who are the primary focus of the present study. I give a fuller characterization of these elders in the chapters that follow, but a few preliminary comments are necessary in the present overview. First of all, it should be obvious that city elders are

---

[25] There is another distinction of some significance that should be kept in mind. Several passages refer both to "the elders" of Israel (or of a tribe or city within Israel) and to "the men" of the same place (e.g., Deut 21:18–21; 22:13–21; Jdgs 8:13–17). It is generally accepted that the latter designates the fighting men of the nation or a particular area within it, and I see no reason to contest that opinion. See H. Tadmor, "'The People' and the Kingship in Ancient Israel: The Role of Political Institutions in the Biblical Period," *Journal of World History* 11 (1968) 50–54; idem, "Traditional Institutions and the Monarchy: Social and Political Tensions in the Time of David and Solomon," in *Studies in the Period of David and Solomon, and Other Essays*, ed. T. Ishida (Tokyo: Yamakawa-Shuppansha, 1982), pp. 241–44; Z. Weisman, "Charismatic Leaders in the Period of the Judges," *ZAW* 89 (1977) 407–408; C. Schäfer-Lichtenberger, *Stadt und Eidgenossenschaft im Alten Testament* (BZAW 156; Berlin: Walter de Gruyter, 1983), pp. 292–96. Cp. Evans's interpretation of the consultations between Gilgamesh, the "elders," and the "men" (G. Evans, "Ancient Mesopotamian Assemblies," *JAOS* 78 [1958] 1–11).

more than simply the old men of the community.[26] The community has certain routine leadership tasks ("functions") which must be performed if the community is to survive and prosper. The elders are the men who possess the qualities necessary to perform those tasks best. These personal qualities are fairly predictable, going hand-in-hand with the elders' typical responsibilities. Because city elders deal with local matters, the influence and respect afforded to city elders need not extend beyond the territory controlled by the city. An elder whose influence does extend beyond the local community will have a greater voice in some matters and on some occasions, and he will probably represent his community in extra-community affairs; but this does not give him authority over the other elders. His influence is different in its application only; he has additional functions.[27]

---

[26] On this, see the remarks of M. Teitelbaum, "Old Age, Midwifery, and Good Talk: Paths to Power in a West African Gerontocracy," in *Aging and Cultural Diversity: New Directions and Annotated Bibliography*, ed. H. Strange and M. Teitelbaum (South Hadley, MA: Bergin and Garvey, 1987), pp. 39–40.

A. Kuper ("Introduction: Council Structure and Decision-Making," in *Councils in Action*, ed. A. Richards and A. Kuper, pp. 13–15) distinguishes two types of local councils—the "arena" council and the "élite" council. The former refers to councils whose members represent most, if not all, sections of the local population relatively equally. The latter type is a rudimentary oligarchy, where a small minority of a city's population dictates policy to the rest of the city. The Biblical evidence supports the view that Israelite councils were mostly "arena" councils. (See, e.g., Deut 25:5–10, where the elders cannot force a man to abide by their wishes.)

One might argue that "élite" councils existed in the large urban centers, where greater inequalities existed. Jer 26:7–19 provides the most detailed picture of a council in Jerusalem. Unfortunately, the status of each individual involved in the proceedings is not known. In particular, we would need to know the identities of "the elders of the land" (26:17) and the unspecified "people" (26:7–9, 11–12, 16–17) who are present. It seems likely, however, that these groups reflect some sort of representation by more than a few individual families of a separate class from the rest of the population. This does not appear to be an "élite" council or an "arena" council, in the purest sense of those terms, but something in between the two. Therefore, I view councils in Israel as "arena" councils, with some local variations in the larger cities.

[27] The society which Teitelbaum examines (the Jokwele Kpelle of Liberia) is a good example of what I am trying to describe. There are groups of "clan elders" among the Kpelle called the *loi namu*, who derive their prestige and influence from their pedigrees. A group of *loi namu* oversees the affairs of an area encompassing several villages. Within each village, however, there is a

Second, it now appears likely that local kinship-based political mechanisms were not altered significantly following the establishment of the monarchy.[28] Recent studies affirm the persistence of the kinship basis to most Israelite communities.[29] The Rechabites provide one example in support of this (Jer 35:6–10); the story of Jeremiah's redemption of his cousin's property (Jer 32:6–15) provides another.[30] There is also evidence that kinship ideology developed in the trade and manufacturing settlements (guild cities) which were established during the later monarchic period. Similar communities in the more "hierarchical" societies of the ancient Near East organized themselves along (fictive?) kinship lines,[31] so the same phenomenon in Israelite communities should not be surprising. In any case, proving the persistence of the national strength of the tribal groups is not a necessary prerequisite to assuming the persistence of local kinship-based institutions (i.e., "the elders of the city").

---

group of "town elders" which takes care of concerns limited to the citizens of that particular village alone. These two levels of councils are denoted by specific names, but the members of both can be designated by the more general term of "elders" (*nuu polo*; Teitelbaum, "Old Age, Midwifery, and Good Talk," pp. 43–45).

[28] A. Causse, *Du groupe ethnique à la communauté religieuse: le problème sociologique de la religion d'Israël* (Paris: F. Alcan, 1937), pp. 35–37; Halpern, *Constitution of the Monarchy*, pp. 214–15; Tadmor, "'The People' and the Kingship," p. 48.

[29] E.g., Paula M. McNutt, *Reconstructing the Society of Ancient Israel* (Louisville, KY: Westminster John Knox, 1999), especially pp. 75–98, 164ff.

[30] Causse (*Du groupe ethnique*, pp. 67–69) believes that the Rechabites demonstrate a "nomadic ideal" which persisted in Israel. I would modify this to say that they demonstrate persisting ideals of clan solidarity common in tribal societies, nomadic or sedentary.

[31] I. Mendelsohn, "Guilds in Babylonia and Assyria," *JAOS* 60 (1940) 68–72; F. Frick, *The Formation of the State in Ancient Israel: A Survey of Models and Theories* (Sheffield: Almond, 1985), pp. 128–42; M. Gibson, "Introduction," in *The Organization of Power: Aspects of Bureaucracy in the Ancient Near East*, ed. M. Gibson and R. D. Biggs (SAOC, No. 46; Chicago: Oriental Institute, 1987), p. 3.

עִיר ("CITY") IN THE HEBREW BIBLE

Local elders in Israel are usually designated as "elders of the city." The term "city" is very elastic in its application, apparently referring to any kind of settlement: an isolated town, a central settlement, a "daughter" settlement, a central settlement and its "daughters" together, an urban center, or perhaps even a ward or neighborhood ("street") within an urban center. Frick points to the military function of a settlement as that which uniquely constitutes it as a "city,"[32] but this seems too limited. An Israelite "city" (עִיר) served as a gathering-place for a particular group of people. The purposes for which they might have gathered could be military, economic, religious, or social. It was "a site ideologically apart from its environs."[33]

There probably were four types of cities in ancient Israel and Judah. Two types were present (in both the pre-monarchic and monarchic periods) within individual clans. One is a simple "city," and the other "the city of the clan." Some clans had several cities within their borders, some only one (e.g., Shechem, Tirzah).[34] Even where there were several cities within a clan, it is likely that one city served as "the city of the clan." The city in Zuph in which Saul finds Samuel (1 Samuel 9) might be one example of this. The city is not named, but there is a high place there, and the people gathered there for a sacrifice.[35] Similarly, David's clan met at a regional center (Bethlehem) for its ceremonial gatherings (1 Sam 20:6). The possibility that the inhabitants of several cities might

---

[32] Frick, *Formation of the State*, pp. 25–61. The fact that certain "cities" are specified as being "fortified cities" is sufficient reason to be wary of such a restrictive interpretation.

[33] R. Fox, *Urban Anthropology: Cities in Their Cultural Setting* (Englewood Cliffs, NJ: Prentice-Hall, Inc., 1977), p. 31. Fox even has examples of cities with no inhabitants (pp. 40–41). These are cultic sites which have been abandoned, but whose religious significance is still upheld after their abandonment.

[34] Then again, it could be that these clans simply bore the name of their central cities. This need not have precluded the existence of other lesser cities within their borders.

[35] Perhaps Ramathaim-zophim (1 Sam 1:1) and Ramah, the hometown of Samuel (1 Sam 7:17), are one and the same. Ramoth-gilead might be another example. This raises the possibility that each clan or sub-clan had its own "high place." Obviously, there is not enough evidence available to raise this suggestion above the level of speculation.

consider one central city as their common city, so to speak, is also reflected in the reference to "the cities of Hebron" (2 Sam 2:3). A third type of city served as a gathering-place for a broader spectrum of the population, one that performed a common function for several clans or tribes. These were primarily religious centers (e.g., Shiloh, Bethel, Shechem, Gilgal, Beersheba, the Transjordanian shrine).[36] The kings added a couple of wrinkles to this picture. First, they apparently incorporated these higher supra-clan centers into their administrative structure.[37] The kings also established new cities of another type, the administrative city, which controlled broader areas than the traditional clan centers. These included royal cities, fortified cities, and store-cities. At the top of these administrative cities was the national capital. Thus, the lines between these different types of settlements probably became blurred in many cases.[38]

Administrative cities are regarded as being at a "higher level" functionally, but this does not necessarily mean they were larger than most. Excavators at T. Mevorakh, along the central coastal plain, uncovered the remains of a small government center there, dating from the tenth century.[39] The settlement could not have supported many inhabitants, yet there was a great diversity in the ceramic remains found there.[40] This suggests that the site served

[36] Mizpah of Gilead and Jabesh-gilead might have been inter-clan centers, but the reason for their preeminence is not known.

[37] David placed the national shrine in his capital (2 Samuel 6), while Jeroboam appointed two cities in the North—each with a strong claim to religious importance from the past—as his national religious centers. The cultic roles of other supra-clan sites is not always retrievable, but some significance must have been retained for some of them. For example, the meeting with Rehoboam (1 Kgs 12:1–20) was convened at Shechem probably because of the cultic significance of that city.

[38] Jerusalem was a special case. It certainly served as an administrative center, but its primary role was as a "regal-ritual city" (Fox, *Urban Anthropology*, pp. 39–57; L. Stager, "The Archaeology of the Family in Ancient Israel," *BASOR* 260 [1985] 25), which would make it similar in many ways to the old cultic centers of the clans.

[39] E. Stern, *Excavations at Tel Mevorakh (1973–1976). Part One: From the Iron Age to the Roman Period* (Qedem 9; Jerusalem: The Institute of Archaeology, The Hebrew University of Jerusalem, 1978); esp. p. 85.

[40] The excavators found the remains of only one house, yet there were ceramic remains with parallels in Hazor, Beth-shan, Megiddo, Tirzah, and other central sites in Palestine, as well as several pieces from Phoenicia and Cyprus. (Stern, *Excavations at Tel Mevorakh*, pp. 48–60)

as an exchange center for the government between inhabitants of
the region, the central government, and foreign traders. Yet, other
communities in Israel with larger populations were little more
than agricultural centers for a clan.

This evidence reveals that the modern concept of a city (as
opposed to a town or village) does not necessarily correspond to
the "city" (עִיר) of ancient Israel. Most important for our purposes,
they show that it is incorrect to assume that "city" implies a large
settlement, or that every "city" was part of the state
establishment, standing in opposition to rural tribal groups. Clan
groups also organized themselves into cities (note the number of
city names that are also clan names). Still, it is possible to speak
of distinctions between rulers and ruled in cities, between "haves"
and "have-nots." The larger the city, the more likely would it be
for social distinctions to arise.[41] The upper echelons of the more
hierarchized socio-political structures which naturally developed
were not necessarily filled by government personnel or appointees,
though. The élite which emerged could have included members of
a locally powerful lineage or clan.[42]

Looking more specifically to the end of the monarchic period,
Jeremiah describes the nation of Judah of his day as "the cities of
Judah and the streets of Jerusalem" (Jer 7:17, 34; 11:12; 33:10;
44:17, 21; cp. 25:18; 44:2; Isa 40:9; 44:26; Zech 1:12). The balance
between "cities" and "streets" suggests that the latter might refer
to city districts or wards. Jeremiah also speaks of "the land of
Benjamin, the environs of Jerusalem, the cities of Judah, the cities
of the hill country, the cities of the Shephelah, and the cities of the
Negeb" (Jer 32:44; 33:13; cp. 17:26; Obad 19–20). This description
identifies the two tribes that had traditionally belonged to the
nation of Judah as a "land" and a group of "cities." Other settled
areas probably contained large numbers of refugees from the

---

[41] Investigations of cities in modern peasant societies often reveal an urban
élite minority standing in contradistinction to the large peasant majority,
who inhabit both the city and the countryside. L. Marfoe. "The Integrative
Transformation: Patterns of Sociopolitical Organization in Southern Syria."
BASOR 234 (1979) 15–16; G. Sjoberg, *The Preindustrial City* (Glencoe, IL:
The Free Press, 1960), pp. 121–23; Frick, *Formation of the State*, p. 98.

[42] Pre-monarchic Shechem provides a good example of a local lineage
forming an élite group. The family of Hamor (Gen 34:6; Jdgs 9:28) has the
upper hand there until the Israelites take over. Other examples are seen in
references to an individual as the "father" of a particular city.

tribal groups of the North who would have established new settlements in the South.[43] This reflects an acceleration in a long process of settlement, a process which began prior to the rise of kings.[44] Possible implications of such an acceleration should not be missed by the interpreter of the laws of Deuteronomy.

A good example of the fluidity of the term "city" is demonstrated in references to the "city" of Hebron. Hebron was remembered as the home of a Canaanite group (the Anakim) prior to the arrival of the Israelites (Josh 14:13; 15:13). The city and its surrounding area (שָׂדֶה and חֲצֵרִים) were given as a נַחֲלָה to the Calebites and to a Levitical clan (21:11–13; cp. 14:13–15; Jdgs 1:20). It served as a "city of refuge" at some time in its history (Josh 20:7; 21:13; on the cities of refuge, see Chapter 3),[45] and the

---

[43] The archaeological evidence on this point is impressive. Of all the settlements of Judah that appeared during Iron Age II, approximately half were founded in the seventh century alone. M. Broshi, "The Expansion of Jerusalem in the Reigns of Hezekiah and Manasseh," *IEJ* 24 (1974) 25–26; cp. I. Finkelstein, *The Archaeology of the Israelite Settlement*, trans. D. Saltz (Jerusalem: Israel Exploration Society, 1988), pp. 48–53.

[44] Cities were important structural components of the pre-monarchic tribes (see Schäfer-Lichtenberger, *Stadt und Eidgenossenschaft*, pp. 195–322; W. Thiel, *Die soziale Entwicklung Israels in vorstaatlicher Zeit* [Neukirchen-Vluyn: Neukirchener Verlag, 1980], pp. 78, 96–98, 147).

The work of Christa Schäfer-Lichtenberger is a significant corrective to the earlier theories of Max Weber (*Ancient Judaism*, trans. H. H. Gerth and D. Martindale [Glencoe, IL: The Free Press, 1952]; and *The City*, trans. and ed. D. Martindale and G. Neuwirth [New York: The Free Press, 1958]), whose work influenced Alt. Based on Weber's dichotomy between "league" (*Eidgenossenschaft*) and "ancient feudalism" (*antike Stadtherrschaft*), Alt portrays monarchic Israel as a previously egalitarian tribal society whose kings had imposed a stratified Canaanite city-state system of administration upon it ("Der Stadtstaat Samaria," *Kleine Schriften zur Geschichte des Volkes Israel*, Volume III, pp. 258–302; so Frick, *Formation of the State*, p. 16—"The Israelites were heirs of the Canaanite city-state system of administration"). Schäfer-Lichtenberger shows (1) that Canaanite cities were not all of the same type (*Stadt und Eidgenossenschaft*, pp. 202–322; in fact, most of those which existed in the hill country in Iron I were organized as oligarchies or, like their Israelite counterparts, as "primitive democracies"), and (2) that local structural changes brought on by the Israelite court affected only royal cities; the traditional tribal cities were virtually untouched (*Stadt und Eidgenossenschaft*, pp. 369–419).

[45] Josh 14:13–15 and Jdgs 1:20 mention only the Calebites, who are said to receive Hebron as their "inheritance." In Josh 21:11–12, they possess only "the field and enclosures" of the city, while the city is ascribed to the Levites.

Chronicler reports that Rehoboam made it a "fortified city" (2 Chr 11:10). Hebron served as David's Judahite capital for seven years (2 Sam 2:1–3, 11; 5:5; 1 Kgs 2:11), and the families of his men lived "in the cities of Hebron" (בְעָרֵי חֶבְרוֹן; 2 Sam 2:2–3). This final reference is the most intriguing. The most likely explanation is that "Hebron" here refers to a clan (see 1 Chr 2:42–43), but it suggests that "city of Hebron" might have referred to more than one settlement, because these "cities" are probably implied by "city of Hebron" in other passages.[46] In any case, it is obvious that this "city" was socially heterogenous. There is literary evidence of at least three distinct social groups there, each with its own peculiar sphere of influence. And yet, these groups overlapped one another because of the common territory which they shared.

To what, then, would the phrase "elders of the city" refer? The answer would depend on the nature and scope of the situation being addressed. In the case of Hebron, if a situation arose involving residents of one of its "cities," it was probably settled by elders of that particular "city" alone. If it involved inhabitants of one segment of the population (e.g., the Levites), only the elders of that segment need have been called upon to resolve it.[47] If it threatened the peace of all of "Hebron," all the elders of Hebron (the clan) might have become involved.[48] Thus, "the elders of the

---

In 21:13, the city "with its pasture lands" (מִגְרָשׁ) is designated as a city of refuge, given to Aaron and his descendants.

[46] It is possible that a metathesis has occurred (עִיר > עָרֵי), but this is unattested textually. Further, the plural must represent a lectio difficilior, and so should probably be retained.

[47] From the ancient Near East, there are at least two examples of elders of foreign ethnic communities within a large urban center—among Assyrian traders at Kanesh (T. Jacobsen, "Primitive Democracy in Ancient Mesopotamia," *JNES* 2 [1943] 160–62), and in an Egyptian ward in Babylon (M. A. Dandamayev, "The Neo-Babylonian Elders," in *Societies and Languages of the Ancient Near East: Studies in Honour of I. M. Diakanoff* [Warminster: Aris and Phillips, 1982], p. 41).

[48] There are several examples of the fluctuating sizes of local assemblies, dependent on the nature of a particular case and/or the parties involved. E.g., A. Musil, *The Manners and Customs of the Rwala Bedouins* (New York: American Geographic Society, 1928), p. 427; G. I. Jones, "Councils Among the Central Ibo," in *Councils in Action*, ed. A. Richards and A. Kuper (Cambridge: Cambridge University, 1971), p. 78; L. Mair, *African Societies* (Cambridge: Cambridge University, 1974), pp. 143–44; P. Spencer, *The Samburu: A Study of Gerontocracy in a Nomadic Tribe* (London: Routledge and Kegan Paul, 1965), pp. 176–77; A. Kuper, "Introduction: Council Structure and Decision-

city" (זִקְנֵי הָעִיר) is a catch-all phrase to refer to any or all of the elders of a city, with the extent of the "city" being determined by the immediate situation.[49]

ASSUMPTIONS REGARDING THE SOCIAL CONTEXT OF ISRAEL'S CITY ELDERS

Kinship-Based Communities

These "elders of the city" must now be situated sociologically. It has recently been demonstrated that ancient Israel's traditional social structure is best described as a "segmentary lineage system" or a "segmentary state."[50] It would seem logical, then, to look to

---

Making," in *Councils in Action* (Cambridge: Cambridge University, 1971), p. 17.

A variant to this is described by R. G. Abrahams ("Neighbourhood Organization: A Major Sub-System Among the Northern Nyamwezi," *Africa* 35 [1965] 168–86). An area of villages is overseen by a chief. There are no kin ties between the chief and the inhabitants of these villages. The chief comes from one of the few aristocratic lineages in the society. Within each village, a council of headmen (elders) takes care of whatever local matters are deemed appropriate to its jurisdiction. Matters above its jurisdiction are handled by the area chief.

[49] A specific example of this might be preserved in Ruth 4. The narrator (Ruth 4:2) says that Boaz chose "ten men of the elders of the city" to hear his negotiations with the near-kinsman; but Boaz himself refers to them as "the elders of my people" (4:4) The latter probably indicates that the actual "elders" were limited to Boaz's kinship group, that other "elders" of the city were not involved.

[50] The label "segmentary lineage" denotes a social structure based on extended lineages which are traced to a common ancestor. These lineages extend vertically through multiple generations (usually called "father," "sons," "grandsons," etc.), then segment into horizontally parallel groups (usually called "brothers"). A unified "system" might be as narrow as a single community or as broad as an entire state. The familial designations commonly used reflect the strength of the various groups, relative to one another. Not everyone in the "system" is a member of these groups, but they comprise the dominant structure of the society.

On segmentary lineage systems, see P. Bonte, "Pastoral Production, Territorial Organisation and Kinship in Segmentary Lineage Systems," *Social and Ecological Systems*, ed. P. C. Burnham and R. F. Ellen (ASAM 18; London: Academic Press, 1979), pp. 203–34; E. E. Evans-Pritchard, *The Nuer*

the institutions and practices of segmentary lineage systems in contemporary societies for analogies to Israel's social phenomena, such as city elders and local adjudicative practices. Moreover, present-day segmentary lineage systems are usually embedded within larger states with centralized state bureaucracies, whose political authority often derives from some source other than a national network of kinship ties. The situation in ancient Israel, according to the biblical text, is of a special type, in that the central authorities are said to arise from within the traditional lineages, and their basis of authority is the same as that for the lineages—kinship and religious tradition.[51]

On the other hand, comparing Israel's situation with that of full-blown segmentary lineage systems alone would be unnecessarily restrictive. The elders-laws in Deuteronomy concern

---

(Oxford: Oxford University, 1940); R. Lawless, "On the Segmentary Lineage," *CurrAnthro* 18 (1977) 114–15; C. Lindholm, "Kinship Structure and Political Authority: The Middle East and Central Asia," *CompStudSocHist* 28 (1986) 334–55; E. L. Peters, "Some Structural Aspects of the Feud among the Camel-Herding Bedouin of Cyrenaica," *Africa* 37 (1967) 263–82; M. D. Sahlins, "The Segmentary Lineage: An Organization of Predatory Expansion," *AmAnthro* 63 (1961) 322–45; P. Salzman, "Does Complementary Opposition Exist?" *AmAnthro* 80 (1978) 53–70; idem, "Ideology and Change in Middle Eastern Tribal Societies," *Man* 13 (1978) 618–37.

On the application of this model to ancient Israel, see F. Crüsemann, *Der Widerstand gegen das Königtum. Die antiköniglichen Texte des Alten Testamentes und der Kampf um den frühen israelitischen Staat*, WMANT 49 (Neukirchen-Vluyn: Neukirchener, 1978); D. Fiensy, "Using the Nuer Culture of Africa in Understanding the Old Testament: An Evaluation," *JSOT* 38 (1987) 73–83; N. Gottwald, *The Tribes of Yahweh: A Sociology of the Religion of Liberated Israel, 1250–1050 B.C.E.* (Maryknoll, NY: Orbis Books, 1979), esp. pp. 237ff.; J. D. Martin, "Israel as a Tribal Society," in *The World of Ancient Israel: Sociological, Anthropological and Political Perspectives*, ed. R. E. Clements (Cambridge: Cambridge University Press, 1989), pp. 95–117; J. W. Rogerson, "Was Early Israel a Segmentary Society?" *JSOT* 36 (1986) 17–26.

[51] There is always room for debate as to the nature of the actual political relationship between the royal families in Israel and Judah and the lineage system of the tribes. The flexible nature of genealogically-based traditions is widely recognized (see W. E. Aufrecht, "Genealogy and History in Ancient Israel," in *Ascribe to the Lord: Biblical and Other Studies in Memory of Peter C. Craigie*, ed. L. Eslinger and G. Taylor [JSOTS 67; Sheffield: Sheffield Academic, 1988], pp. 205–35). However, even if blood relationships were in reality fictive, they most likely functioned as reality in the minds of the Israelites (as is the case in segmentary societies of today), and thus had the same influence on their actions.

familial/collective responsibility for homicides (Deut 19:1–13; 21:1–9) and habitual malfeasants (Deut 21:18–21), contractual marriages and familial shame associated with extra-marital sex (Deut 22:13–21), and levirate marriage (Deut 25:5–10). Any society in which one finds situations, institutions, and practices such as those encountered in Deuteronomy's elders-laws is potentially suitable for use as an analogy for interpreting those laws. There are, in fact, numerous societies which do not technically fulfill the definition for a segmentary lineage system, yet local communities within them can appropriately be utilized as analogies for Israelite cities. What they share in common is that kinship[52] ties influence to a significant degree how local social, judicial, and political matters are addressed by community members. Thus, I have chosen the broader designation of "kinship-based communities" to designate those from which I will be drawing analogies to ancient Israel.[53]

In kinship-based communities, persons understand their "place" in their community—and, thus, interact with one another—to a large extent on the basis of blood descent. Further, they tend to conceptualize and act upon interpersonal relations according to lineages, or "descent groups." Close agnates tend to think of themselves as "brothers" in contrast to another group of "brothers" within the same lineage; but those two groups tend to think of themselves as "brothers" vis-à-vis other lineages in the community; and so forth. This is often tied to the concepts of honor and shame, particularly in many Mediterranean societies.[54] The actions of each member of a lineage influence the reputation (honor or shame) of the entire lineage in the community. That these general concepts regarding lineages and their resultant

---

[52] "Kinship" refers to bonds between persons based not simply on lineage, but also on marriages and other economic unions.

[53] Admittedly, there is some circularity to this mode of argumentation. However, there is circularity in the reasoning of those who would object on the grounds that one should use analogies from segmentary lineage societies alone. There is variety among those societies, and distinguishing absolutely between them and similar societies is not always possible. Moreover, those distinctions usually are made at the national level, not the local level.

[54] See J. G. Peristiany, ed., *Honour and Shame: The Values of Mediterranean Society* (Chicago: Chicago University, 1966).

obligations and privileges were held in ancient Israel has been demonstrated in many studies.[55]

There are numerous studies now available on kinship-based communities from all over the world. I am limiting myself for the sake of the comparisons here to societies in the Middle East and Africa. In all cases, these contain kinship-based communities and peoples which exist within the political oversight of a centralized state. In some cases, the central bureaucracy in control at the time of the sociological investigation was a foreign colonial power; in other cases, it was an indigenous power. And there are some cases in which the peoples studied can remember living successively under both situations. In addition, there are many cases in which pre-state judicial practices have been retained in the memories of local leaders and, to a lesser extent, in local judicial practices, in spite of attempts by recently-arrived central authorities to undo them. All of these have proven to be helpful to the present investigation, because they all give examples of how traditional judicial structures and practices might be affected by the intrusion of state mechanisms, which is precisely the situation one faces with ancient Israel.[56]

Antecedent to considering these findings, one must recognize the complexity involved in examining this issue within a given society. Completely isolating judicial practices, structures, and ideas in kinship-based communities like that of ancient Israel is

---

[55] See n. 29, above. For a few specific examples of rivalries between lineage groups, defense of the group's honor, and kinship obligations in biblical accounts, one might consider the actions and words of the Ephraimites in Jdgs 8:1–3 and 12:1–6, the Benjaminites in Jdgs 20:12–13, or Jeremiah in Jer 32:6–12.

[56] It must be granted that there might be some differences which depend on whether the state government is indigenous or historically "foreign" to the group being studied. However, in my investigations, such a distinction has not proved crucial to predicting how and to what extent traditional practices will be affected, especially at the local level. See K. R. G. Glavanis and P. M. Glavanis, "The Sociology of Agrarian Relations in the Middle East: The Persistence of Household Production," *Current Sociology* 31,2 (1983) 72–74; S. F. Moore, "Descent and Legal Position," in *Law in Culture and Society*, ed. L. Nader (Chicago: Aldine Publishing Co., 1969), pp. 381–82; and J. Tosh, *Clan Leaders and Colonial Chiefs in Lango: The Political History of an East African Stateless Society, c. 1800–1839* (Oxford: Clarendon Press, 1978), p. 2.

not really possible.[57] Judicial customs and mores are inextricably intertwined with other historical, social, economic, and religious matters.[58] Second, in societies in which a state is imposing itself over previously disparate peoples or a previously non-centralized society, that state can easily claim powers and authority that are not necessarily recognized by the local inhabitants. If they are not, the result is parallel structures, one "official" and one more "real." These structures might or might not function simultaneously. The central government might claim that their centrally-controlled system is the only one that is used, while researchers discover and describe how much is adjudicated outside that system. So, it is sometimes difficult to determine the "reality" of a given society's situation.

Determining the "reality" of the situation in a society of the past is even more complicated. The only direct information available to us is what was recorded, and what was recorded might give only one side (probably the "official" side) of the picture. Further, as discussion of the formation of the D Code shows, even the "official" side might seem somewhat unreliable, as it can involve several revisions and reinterpretations. Hopefully, consideration of several societies will help us make a more educated guess as to how to evaluate that recorded evidence.

It would be ideal to give an annotated summary of the ethnographic data on each society individually, but two considerations explain why this has not been done. First, the sheer number of societies surveyed makes such an approach impraticable. Second, such a survey would leave the wrongful

---

[57] This is most obvious from the fact that "non-judicial" persons (e.g., military officers, priests) often serve judicial functions. It is also seen when judicial forms are used in non-judicial contexts. In Israel, the use of the "covenant lawsuit" is an excellent example.

[58] K. S. Newman, *Law and Economic Organization: A Comparative Study of Preindustrial Societies* (Cambridge: Cambridge University, 1983), pp. 204–205; D. Tait, "The Territorial Pattern and Lineage System of Konkomba," in *Tribes Without Rulers*, ed. John Middleton and D. Tait (London: Routledge and Kegan Paul, 1958), p. 179. See Maurice Bloch, "Decision-Making in Councils Among the Merina of Madagascar," in *Councils in Action*, ed. A. Richards and A. Kuper (Cambridge: Cambridge University, 1971), p. 60; Fernea, *Shaykh and Effendi*, p. 91; G. I. Jones, "Councils," p. 64; David Parkin, *Palms, Wine, and Witnesses: Public Spirit and Private Gain in an African Farming Community* (Aylesbury: Chandler Publishing Co., 1972), p. 24.

impression that there has been more arbitrariness in the selection of ethnographies surveyed than is really the case. Probably none of the ethnographies cited records analogous cases for all the cases we will analyze from the D Code. This is because of the selectivity of the ethnographers themselves. Their choice of topics to include in their ethnographies is based on criteria which differ from our own. In other words, they did not set out simply to report on situations analogous to those in the elders-laws of the D Code. So, while almost all ethnographies touch on cases of homicide (Deut 19:1–13; 21:1–9) and adultery (Deut 22:13–29), many do not discuss levirate marriage (Deut 25:5–10). One cannot assume from this, however, that those societies do not have cases of levirate marriage. It could be that the ethnographer chose not to include those cases because they seemed minor, or perhaps they did not encounter such a situation in their limited field study.

To offset this, I have tried to support my findings with examples from across the geographical spectrum of Africa and the Middle East.[59] These are not uniform nor entirely consistent with one another; there is great variety. Still, some general or relatively common principles can be discerned. Implications for our understanding of ancient Israel's judicial institutions and practices as presented in the D Code can then be set forth, but only as probabilities, not as certainties.[60]

---

[59] See Robert Wilson, *Genealogy and History in the Biblical World* (New Haven: Yale University, 1977), p. 17.

[60] "Comparative analysis is used as a heuristic aid, not as 'evidence,' for clarifying the literary and archaeological information." Paula M. McNutt, "The Kenites, the Midianites, and the Rechabites as Marginal Mediators in Ancient Israelite Tradition," *Semeia* 67 (1994) 110–11.

There have been several essays written regarding the use of cross-cultural comparisons to interpret archaeological remains (ethnoarchaeology). Since the biblical text itself is, in some sense, an artifact of ancient Israel, the principles set forth in those essays can also be employed profitably as one seeks to interpret the biblical text. See L. R. Binford, "Smudge Pits and Hide Smoking: The Use of Analogy in Archaeological Reasoning," *AmAntiq* 32 (1967) 1–12; R. A. Gould, "Beyond Analogy," in *Living Archaeology* (Cambridge: Cambridge University, 1980), pp. 29–47; P. J. Watson, "The Idea of Ethnoarchaeology: Notes and Comments," in *Ethnoarchaeology: Implications of Ethnography for Archaeology*, ed. C. Kramer (New York: Columbia University, 1979), pp. 277–88.

Using this "general comparative" approach rather than a "direct historical" one is desirable, I believe, for another important reason. It is better to talk in generalities than in specifics in this type of study for the very

Robert Wilson delineates six guidelines for how to go about collecting and utilizing comparative data for such an enterprise, and I have tried to follow these guidelines.[61] They can be summarized as follows:

(1)   use data that have been "systematically collected by a trained observer;"

(2)   try to interpret data concerning a particular phenomenon within the overall societal matrix;[62]

(3)   use a wide variety of societies;

(4)   concentrate on the raw data, not on interpretations of that data;

(5)   be sure that the biblical phenomenon being considered is truly comparable with the ethnological data which are being utilized; and,

(6)   the ethnological data can be used to create an hypothesis, but the proof for the hypothesis must come from the biblical data.

The analyses offered here are based to a significant degree on more than three dozen ethnographies describing contemporary communities of the Middle East and Africa, along with specialized studies concerning the treatment in those societies of the situations addressed in the Deuteronomic elders-laws. Some of these are studies of an entire ethnic group, while others involve a single village or town. Most deal with groups which are now controlled by state governments. These studies are then coupled with evidence provided by written records from Israel's geographical neighbors, particularly cuneiform law codes. Taken as a whole, these bodies of evidence provide a solid and

---

reason that each society is unique. If one were to try to base one's arguments on just one or two "good" examples, then one would have to demonstrate a direct relationship between them and ancient Israel. That is not the goal here. The goal is to establish what is "natural" or "likely." This leaves room then for the unique aspects which are going to exist in Israel, as in any society.

[61] Wilson, *Genealogy*, p. 16.

[62] See C. R. Hallpike, "Some Problems in Cross-Cultural Comparison," in *The Translation of Culture*, ed. T. O. Beidelman (London: Tavistock, 1971), pp. 137–38.

sufficiently diverse set of analogies that are used to evaluate and interpret the biblical laws.

It is not enough, though, to know how groups and institutions tend to act in a given situation; one must also consider why they act as they do. "Satisfactory causal explanations cannot be formulated unless the intentions, motives and reasons of the actors themselves are taken into account."[63] This is a difficult requirement to fulfill when one is dealing with an ancient society, because it is impossible to go back to a place like ancient Israel to interact with and interview "the actors themselves" so that one can know their "intentions, motives and reasons." The best that one can do is assume that contemporary peoples who live within a social milieu (kinship-based communities) and under ecological constraints which have the most in common with those found in ancient Israel will also possess "intentions, motives and reasons" for their actions which are most similar to those held by ancient Israelites.[64] Additional considerations can help in this procedure. The primary one is to look within the biblical records themselves to see whether a rationale is given there for a particular action. If not, then analogies which can be drawn from societies that are closest to ancient Israelite society both temporally and geographically should be deemed the most pertinent.[65]

---

[63] L. Holy and J. Blacking, "Explanation through Comparison," *JCompFamStud* 5 (1974) 59.

[64] See the remarks of P. J. Watson, "The Theory and Practice of Ethnoarchaeology with Special Reference to the Near East," *Paléorient* 6 (1980) 55. Although her remarks are directed toward the interpretation of archaeological remains, what she says about making comparisons also holds true for investigations like the present one.

H. J. M. Claessen ("The Early State," in *The Early State*, ed. H. J. M. Claessen and Peter Skalník [New York: Mouton, 1978], p. 536) speaks of "facet-comparison," i.e., the comparison of a particular aspect of an institution in various societies, rather than looking for a perfect match in every respect. The latter is impossible. Yet, one must always keep in mind that a particular phenomenon reveals something about only one facet of the thing being considered, and that other facets inevitably influence that one.

[65] Sometimes only one rationale (or one kind of rationale) is given, even though a wide variety of societies are being consulted. If that is the case, then the likelihood increases that that is the rationale to be used to explain the similar biblical phenomenon or situation. At other times there are several rationales provided. In that case, the rule of temporal and geographical proximity should be invoked.

Beginning from that basis, I try to follow a general four-part process in my investigations. First, I identify the situation or practice assumed in the law being considered. Second, I describe ethnographic examples of similar situations or practices in contemporary kinship-based communities and ancient Near Eastern societies. Third, I consider what rationales are given (by participants themselves, whenever possible) to explain why certain actions are taken in those situations. Fourth, I return to the biblical law to see what rationale is given there or, in the absence of that, what rationales given elsewhere provide the most adequate explanation of the actions described in the law. The result normally is that the rationale is discovered to have been contained in the biblical records all along, sometimes recognized by modern interpreters, sometimes not. In the end, the use of cross-cultural comparisons in the study of Israel's city elders sets in relief the ancient Israelites' own understanding of who elders were, what they did, and why.

Kinship Ideology and Power Struggles in Ancient Israel

Finally, I need to lay out my understanding of typical ideas of kinship held by members of kinship-based communities and how those ideas are likely to have affected life in Israel. It is sometimes asserted that relations between Israel's central administration and members of the traditional kinship groups would have amounted to a class struggle. The "upper classes" have been associated with wealthy urbanites who are said to have adopted "Canaanite" ideas and therefore felt free to take advantage of their fellow Israelites; the "lower classes" are equated with rural tribal folk who held to old Yahwistic ideals.[66] Besides over-

---

[66] Neufeld, "Emergence of a Royal-Urban Society," pp. 31–53. The most throughgoing reconstruction which supports this idea was formulated by Alt ("The Monarchy in the Kingdoms of Israel and Judah," *EOTHR*, pp. 239–59; idem, "Der Stadtstaat Samaria," pp. 258–302). He argues that Jerusalem and Samaria were, in fact, city-states, modeled after Canaanite predecessors which had a strong class system. See H. Donner, "The Separate States of Israel and Judah," in *Israelite and Judaean History*, ed. J. H. Hayes and J. M. Miller (OTL; Philadelphia: Westminster, 1977), p. 403. Schäfer-Lichtenberger (*Stadt und Eidgenossenschaft*, pp. 381–417) gives a detailed refutation to each of Alt's arguments.

generalizing Canaanite society, such a model misses the subtle complexities of day to day life in a traditionally kinship-based society like Israel's. Analogies suggest that there would have been significant social inequalities even in pre-monarchic Israel, and these would have widened and been hierarchized as a result of political centralization and urbanization. Nevertheless, it is inappropriate to describe the struggle in monarchic Israel as a class struggle (in the modern-day sense of that term). Rather, it is more appropriate to conceive of this struggle as an extension of traditional segmentation principles.

A deep-seated notion held by members of kinship-based communities is that one is obligated (to lessening degrees) to one's extended family, lineage, clan, and tribe. At the same time, there is a competing desire for segmental autonomy and preeminence.[67] Each segment wants to elevate its own status within the broader structure.[68] A nuclear family strives to rise above its "brothers" in the lineage and become a lineage in its own right; a lineage strives

---

[67] There are at least two sayings from the Middle East which have been quoted to illustrate this idea. The more common is, "I against my brother, I and my brother against my cousins, I and my cousins against the world." (Cited by Salzman, "Does Complementary Opposition Exist?" p. 53.) Another saying is, "We are brothers, yet when we evaluate the inventory, we are enemies." (Cited by Lindholm, "Kinship Structure and Political Authority," p. 349.)

There are several examples of intra-lineage conflicts in the Hebrew Bible. One is in the story of Jephthah. Jephthah's brothers force him out of his inheritance (Jdgs 11:1–3), an inheritance which they share with him. A second is the hypothetical story of the Tekoite widow (2 Sam 14:4–11). This involves first a dispute between two brothers, and then a conflict between the surviving brother and his clan mates. (Even though the story is fictitious, the scenario obviously is a plausible one.) David is asked to step in on behalf of one nuclear family against the others of its lineage and clan. Moreover, the story itself points to another lineage in which intra-family disputes commonly arise, viz. the royal family.

[68] Consider the following observation of W. R. Smith: "There cannot be a greater mistake than to suppose that Arab society is based on the patriarchal authority of the father over the sons; on the contrary there is no part of the world where parental authority is weaker than in the desert, and the principle of uncontrolled individualism is only kept in check by the imperious necessity for mutual help against enemies which binds together, not individual families but the whole *hayy*, kinsmen within certain degrees but the whole circle of common blood." *Kinship and Marriage in Early Arabia* (Boston: Beacon, 1885; reprint ed., 1967), p. 68. Similarly, see Evans-Pritchard, *Nuer*, pp. 198–99, 216–17.

to rise above its brother-lineages and become a clan; each clan strives to become a tribe. Rivalries between brother-segments inevitably exist.[69] There is a constant threat that these conflicts will develop into permanent divisions.

Two mechanisms typically work to counter the threat of such divisions. One, usually broader in effect, is any significant external threat (military, political, or ecological).[70] The presence of a common "enemy" leads to cooperative defensive responses. This often involves several communities. For example, some of the stories of the Book of Judges (Jdgs 8:1–7; 12:1–6; 19:1–21:24; cp. Joshua 22) paint a picture of pre-monarchic Israel in which inter-tribal rivalries threatened to dissolve a tenuous confederacy; but these were overshadowed by external threats (foreign incursions) which prompted clan, tribal, and inter-tribal cooperation behind various charismatic leaders. Similarly, the initial calls for a king are portrayed as primarily motivated by a desire to regularize responses to external military threats (1 Sam 8:19–20; 12:6–13).[71]

The other social mechanism that should have deterred divisiveness at the local level was the group of local elders. But this was not always the case. The struggle between obligations to one's kin and the desire for lineage autonomy and preeminence would have been felt most keenly by traditional community leaders (like the elders). On the one hand, they would have promoted traditional lineage and clan structures, because their power was derived from those structures. On the other hand, these leaders could have been among those who could most easily take advantage of the opportunities for personal enrichment afforded by the presence of a centralized government. From their

---

[69] The stories of the patriarchs contain several examples of sibling rivalries which split (or, at the least, threatened to split) families into separate groups. The dispute between Jephthah and his brothers (Jdgs 11:1–3) and the fictitious plight of the Tekoite woman (2 Sam 14:4–7) illustrate the same potentiality.

[70] Such external threats have collectively been called "environmental circumscription." R. L. Carneiro, "A Theory of the Origins of the State," *Science* 169 (1970) 733–38.

[71] It is to be expected—based on analogies—that a primary force in promoting this cooperation at the supra-tribal level would have been the cult. Demonstrating this would require a full-length study of its own.

positions as community leaders, they could have manipulated affairs to the advantage of their own kinship groups.[72]

Some traditional leaders (including elders) probably moved into the larger administrative centers, particularly Jerusalem and Samaria, for the purpose of elevating their own kinship group above others. From this position they walked a tightrope of loyalties. They probably continued to feel a sense of obligation to their home community,[73] and they were the most likely candidates to serve as representatives of the interests of their fellow clansmen before the king. On the other hand, they might sometimes have wished to gain additional wealth and power by cooperating with the court (see, for example, Mic 2:1–5). This fact, coupled with the physical distance between these individuals and their hometowns, could have led to a certain callousness toward the needs of more distant clansmen and neighbors.

Similar situations are common today where kinship-based communities interact with centralized governments. There is a constant strain between loyalties to one's home community and economic opportunities in the larger cities. Some independently wealthy members of a village even move permanently into a city, particularly the capital, yet they will often maintain a house and fields in their hometowns.[74] This reveals the tension of loyalties

---

[72] See Fernea, *Shaykh and Effendi*, pp. 136–47; Parkin, *Palms, Wine, and Witnesses*, pp. 19–29; Holy, *Neighbours and Kinsmen*, pp. 128–30.

[73] A major reason for this sense of loyalty would have been the belief that one's home-town was still the home of one's ancestors. To abandon it would be to dishonor one's father and mother. See H. C. Brichto, "Kin, Cult, Land and Afterlife—A Biblical Complex," *HUCA* 44 (1973) 6–24. This is why David's explanation of returning to his hometown for a religious feast would have seemed plausible (1 Sam 20:6).

[74] S. Amanolahi-Baharvand, "The Baharvand, Former Pastoralists of Iran" (Ph.D. Diss, Rice University; Ann Arbor: University Microfilms, 1975), p. 221; G. R. Garthwaite, *Khans and Shahs: A Documentary Analysis of the Bakhtiyari in Iran* (Cambridge: Cambridge University, 1983), p. 45; D. Grossman, "The Bethel Hills—An Unusual Rural Development," *Israel—Land and Nature* 1,1 (1975) 25–26; J. Gulick, *Social Structure and Culture Changes in a Lebanese Village* (New York: Wenner-Gren Foundation for Anthropological Research, 1955), p. 171; F. I. Khuri, *Tribe and State in Bahrain: The Transformation of Social and Political Authority in an Arab State* (Chicago: University of Chicago, 1980), pp. 45–50; H. Rosenfeld, "Social and Economic Factors in Explanation of the Increased Rate of Endogamy in the Arab Village in Israel," in *Mediterranean Family Structures*, ed. J. G. Peristiany (Cambridge: Cambridge University, 1976), pp. 130–33. The

which these people feel. They pursue individual opportunities for their own lineages, yet they still feel some loyalty toward their hometowns and the need to maintain a presence there. Abuses of the system occur when the desire for lineage preeminence outweighs the sense of obligation to other members of one's hometown.[75] The overall psychological effect of political centralization on local affairs, then, is an inclination to reduce the strength of one's kinship-based obligations, so that only the core members of one's kin group are considered;[76] the needs of peripheral members of a community are often ignored.

For these reasons, I regard the typical power struggle in monarchic Israel and Judah not as a class struggle, but as a sort of "sibling rivalry" felt most profoundly by the wealthier members of the society, among those affiliated with the court and among traditional community leaders. The struggle involved kinship-based obligations, on the one hand, and the inherent desire for family autonomy and preeminence over one's more distant kin, on the other. Prophetic critiques of monarchic society reveal the reality that the latter often prevailed. One outcome of the present study should be a clearer picture of how the laws of Deuteronomy address these natural struggles at the local level.

---

widespread phenomenon of commuter workers which exists today could not have existed in ancient Israel.

[75] Ibn Khaldûn, *The Muqaddimah: An Invitation to History*, trans. Franz Rosenthal; abridged ed. (Princeton: Princeton University, 1969), pp. 102–103; Fernea, *Shaykh and Effendi*, p. 31.

[76] J. Ginat, *Blood Disputes among Bedouin and Rural Arabs in Israel: Revenge, Mediation, Outcasting and Family Honor* (Pittsburgh: University of Pittsburgh, 1987), pp. 20, 83, 125, 137, 152. In some areas local leaders find themselves losing influence with their villagers because of changes brought on by the central government, and they look for ways to reverse this situation. See Amanolahi-Baharvand, "Baharvand," pp. 194, 209–10, 224; Fernea, *Shaykh and Effendi*, pp. 147–53.

Rosenfeld describes marriage patterns which also point in this direction. In times of social transition brought on by the presence of economic opportunities generated from outside the local village, lineage members tend to turn inward—as evidenced by the increase in endogamy—to insure the survival of the lineage. One negative consequence of this is the avoidance of obligations to those outside one's own lineage. Consequently, members of smaller lineages tend to be forced out of the community. Rosenfeld, "Social and Economic Factors," pp. 117–30.

CHAPTER 2
THE JUDICIAL SYSTEM OF THE
DEUTERONOMIC CODE

Students of the history of Israelite law have long recognized that developments in ancient Israel's judicial system probably occurred in concert with broader developments in Israelite society.[1] The general outline reflected in the biblical narratives—illuminated in many ways by sociological models and supported by archaeological findings—is that Israel evolved from a conglomeration of extended families and clans in Iron Age I into a monarchic state (or better, dual states) in Iron Age II. The judicial system early on in such a society would have consisted of adjudication by the "father" of a family or, if the situation demanded, by town or clan elders (i.e., a collection of "fathers" in a community). This would have changed with or by the time of the emergence and growth of the monarchies, as the central authorities would take on various judicial responsibilities in the governing of the nation. Then, the exile of the Israelites by the Assyrians and Babylonians would have greatly altered or even eliminated many existing socio-political structures, including the judiciary. There is overwhelming sociological evidence that such

---

[1] This aspect of the question is not considered by P. Bovati, *Re-Establishing Justice: Legal Terms, Concepts and Procedures in the Hebrew Bible*, trans. M. J. Smith (JSOTS 105; Sheffield: JSOT Press, 1994). His descriptions of Israel's judicial practices are usually excellent, but the fact that he assumes a seamlessness and uniformity for these over the centuries is a significant weakness to the study as a whole.

developments are common in kinship-based societies, and there is sufficient archaeological evidence from ancient Israel to suggest that such developments occurred there as well. Most scholarly discussions, then, are not concerned with proving whether these general developments took place, but with ascertaining what particular developments are suggested by a given text, and when and to what extent they actually occurred in Israel.[2]

The core laws of the Deuteronomic Code (Deuteronomy 12–26) provide more information about the later stages in the development of Israel's judicial practices and institutions than any other section of the Hebrew Bible. Of particular interest in the present investigation are the laws which identify those who are to adjudicate certain cases. These include "judges and officers," priests, and city elders. Two laws speak to the importance of "witnesses" (Deut 17:2–7; 19:15–21). Most agree that one cannot underestimate the significance of these data for understanding Israel's judicial system, but they disagree strongly over what that significance is. These disagreements are the result of another discussion: the discussion of the redaction of the Book of Deuteronomy.[3]

Many redaction critics attribute the D Code's relative wealth of information on adjudicative practices to a multiplicity of sources and redactional layers which they see in the book. They analyze

---

[2] There are several treatments of judicial procedures in Israel, some of which only briefly touch on the evidence in the D Code. These primarily attempt to reconstruct how the emergence of the state affected judicial institutions. See L. Köhler, "Justice in the Gate," in *Hebrew Man* (trans. P. Ackroyd; New York: Abingdon Press, 1956), pp. 127–34; D. A. McKenzie, "Judicial Procedure at the Town Gate," *VT* 14 (1964) 100–104; G. C. Macholz, "Die Stellung des Königs in der israelitischen Gerichtsverfassung," *ZAW* 84 (1972) 157–58; H. J. Boecker, *Law and the Administration of Justice in the Old Testament and Ancient East* (trans. J. Mosier; Minneapolis: Augsburg, 1980), pp. 27–40; R. Wilson, "Israel's Judicial System in the Preexilic Period," *JewQR* 74 (1983) 229–48.

[3] I will give a more expanded discussion of my opinions on the redaction of the book in Chapter 3. I need to clarify how I am using a few terms here, though. I use the term "Deuteronomic" to refer to literary elements that are typical of the D Code (essentially, Deuteronomy 5–28), and "deuteronomistic" to refer to elements that are typical of the Deuteronomistic History (Deuteronomy 1–4 + 29–34; Joshua–Kings). It is often difficult to distinguish between these two, and in those cases I use the hybrid designation "Deuteronom(ist)ic."

the text of the D Code with the intent of unraveling those various layers in order to propose a cogent reconstruction of the history of the D Code and what it reveals about broader developments in the nation's socio-political institutions (including the judiciary) in the late monarchic and early exilic periods. They then can work back from these conclusions to scattered references in other texts in order to elaborate on earlier stages in the evolution of Israel's judicial system.[4]

But redaction critics do not approach the D Code empty-handed. They come armed with various assumptions about what to expect in the development of Israel's judicial system. In particular, many assume that traditional judicial authority (held in Deuteronomy by city elders and, perhaps, priests) and professional judicial authority (held by appointed "judges and officers") are mutually exclusive. It is my contention, however, based on analogies from societies similar to that of ancient Israel's, that these supposedly incompatible judicial institutions were actually complementary. The remaining chapters of this study deal with only half of that picture in this study, the half concerning the judicial roles of city elders. The other half of the picture—the judicial roles of others—will be addressed briefly (and somewhat indirectly) in the present chapter. This should be sufficient, however, to demonstrate that the laws of the D Code regarding adjudicative responsibilities can be read as a consistent whole. Such a conclusion will necessitate reevaluations of what the D Code's judicial legislation reveals regarding the redactional process of the entire book; but that will have to be saved for a separate study.

---

[4] The passages most closely related to those of the D Code are Exod 18:13–27; Num 11:10–30; Deut 1:9–18; 2 Chr 19:4–11. Most other passages touch on the judicial functions of Israel's kings in the early monarchic period. For a thorough treatment of those texts, see Macholz, "Die Stellung des Königs," pp. 157–82; and K. Whitelam, *The Just King: Monarchical Judicial Authority in Ancient Israel* (JSOTS 12; Sheffield: JSOT Press, 1979).

Herbert Niehr provides a fairly thorough survey of the scholarly discussion of the broader question of Israel's judicial system ("Grundzüge der Forschung zur Gerichtsorganisation Israels," *BibZ* 31 [1987] 206–27). He divides his survey into three categories. Two of these concern treatments of historical developments which would have occurred long before the composition of the D Code. For that reason, and because the evidence examined in those studies comes from outside the D Code, we will not review most of that evidence here.

PREVIOUS STUDIES

There are nine laws in the D Code in which the judicial personnel involved are noted. In four laws, the only judicial functionaries mentioned are city elders (Deut 19:1–13; 21:18–21; 22:13–21; 25:5–10; in two of these, "the men of the city" execute the elders' decision). In one passage, elders are mentioned along with "judges" and "priests, the sons of Levi" (Deut 21:1–9). One passage calls for the appointment of "judges and officers" (שֹׁפְטִים וְשֹׁטְרִים) in all the "gates" of Israel (Deut 16:18–20), while three others speak of bringing disputes before a "judge" or "judges" (Deut 25:1–3), before a "judge" and one or more "(levitical) priests" (Deut 17:8–13)[5], or before a multiplicity of both "priests and judges" (Deut 19:15–21). There are, of course, numerous other laws which would have required adjudication by the appropriate judicial functionaries; however, the specific functionaries involved are not identified.[6]

---

[5] This passage is especially problematic because it is inconsistent regarding what officials are to be consulted. In 17:9, one approaches "the levitical priests and the judge." But in v 12 one is to listen to "the priest standing to serve the Lord your God there or the judge." For recent examinations of this passage, see U. Rüterswörden, *Von der politischen Gemeinschaft zur Gemeinde: Studien zu Dt 16,18–18,22* (BBB 65; Frankfurt am Main: Athenäum, 1987), pp. 39–49; and B. M. Levinson, *Deuteronomy and the Hermeneutics of Legal Innovation* (New York/Oxford: Oxford University, 1997), pp. 127–37.

[6] There are only scattered references elsewhere in the Hebrew Bible to legal proceedings and the appointment of certain groups of individuals to legal tasks. For example, Boaz seeks out ten elders to serve as legal witnesses to his acquisition of the property of Elimelech and his sons, and of Ruth (Ruth 4:1–12); Naboth is falsely accused and executed with the judicial complicity of the "elders and nobles" of Jezreel (1 Kgs 21:8–14); Jeremiah is brought by "priests and prophets" to a trial before "the officials and the people," a trial for which "some of the elders of the land" provide legal precedents (Jer 26:7–19). Cases like these might reflect changes over time; but they are so few and the provenance of the written sources for each is so much debated that scholars cannot seem to reach more than a very general consensus regarding these developments. In sum, these examples do little more than demonstrate the variety possible in Israel's judicial affairs over several centuries, and their significance for elucidating judicial institutions and procedures in Deuteronomy is minimal. The remaining cases tend to be those brought before the king (e.g., 2 Sam 12:1–6; 14:1–11; 15:1–6; 1 Kgs 3:16–28; 2 Kgs 8:1–6). On these, see Macholz, "Die Stellung des Königs," pp. 160–75.

Several interpretations have been given over the years regarding what these various laws reveal about the judicial system envisioned by the Deuteronomic writer(s). In my mind, these interpretations fall into three groups: (1) those who see these laws legitimating and/or furthering prior royal reform(s) of the judiciary; (2) those who see these laws as introducing something new, as part of the centralization program; and (3) those who see these laws primarily as part an exilic writer's future (utopian) program envisioned for a post-exilic Israel.

Association with Prior Royal Reform

Attempts to link the D Code's judicial practices to judicial reforms mentioned elsewhere in the Hebrew Bible can be traced back at least to W. F. Albright in 1950. He argues that the story of Jehoshaphat's judicial reform, recorded in 2 Chr 19:4–11, is historically reliable. This reform is reflected in the call for the appointment of judges in all towns in Deut 16:18–20. In this reform, Albright sees the removal of city elders from all judicial responsibilities, due to their replacement by centrally-appointed professional judges. The laws of the D Code which call for adjudication by elders are thus seen as relics from the days before Jehoshaphat, preserved (supposedly) because the judges are expected to adjudicate such cases in the same way as elders had previously adjudicated them.[7]

A few subsequent studies have accepted Albright's thesis basically as is,[8] while others have developed it further in studies

---

Seen as most pertinent to the laws in Deuteronomy has been the account of Jehoshaphat's judicial reform of the mid–ninth century B.C.E. (2 Chr 19:4–11). This passage mentions the judicial appointments of "judges, ... [then] Levites and priests and heads of families (lit. 'fathers') of Israel." This is similar in many ways to the prescriptions given in Deut 16:18–17:13.

[7] W. F. Albright, "The Judicial Reform of Jehoshaphat," in *Alexander Marx Jubilee Volume*, ed. Saul Lieberman (New York: Jewish Publication Society, 1950), pp. 75–79.

[8] "It can therefore be deduced that Jehoshaphat abolished the local jurisdiction of the elders, and instead appointed royal officials to the fortified cities who were responsible to the king for the administration of justice in the districts under their control... The law of Deuteronomy is meant to be read on the understanding that the local administration of justice was in the hands of

of Exod 18:13–27 and Deut 1:9–18.[9] Still others have gone another step, revising the thesis in some key areas. The most thoroughgoing treatment is that of G. C. Macholz.[10] He argues that Deut 1:9–18 (along with Exod 18:13–27) and the account of Jehoshaphat's reform in 2 Chr 19:4–11 represent—from the perspectives of different written traditions—a single historical event: the royal appointment of military personnel to judicial positions at military settlements only ("fortified cities"). Whether this was actually the work of Jehoshaphat or of some other king (e.g., Josiah) is not certain.[11] The judiciary laws of Deuteronomy (especially 16:18–20) take this further, then, by calling for the appointment of judges in all towns (not just military

---

professional judges (16:18)." A. Phillips, *Ancient Israel's Criminal Law: A New Approach to the Decalogue* (London: Basil Blackwell, 1970), pp. 18–19.

See also R. Gordis, "Democratic Origins in Ancient Israel—The Biblical 'EDAH," in *Alexander Marx Jubilee Volume*, ed. Saul Lieberman (New York: Jewish Publication Society, 1950), pp. 376–77 n. 16; J. M. Salmon, "Judicial Authority in Early Israel: An Historical Investigation of Old Testament Institutions" (Th.D. Diss., Princeton University; Ann Arbor, MI: University Microfilms, 1968), pp. 378–79, 423–26; A. D. H. Mayes, *Deuteronomy* (Grand Rapids: Eerdmans, 1979), pp. 263–64; V. H. Matthews, "Entrance Ways and Threshing Floors: Legally Significant Sites in the Ancient Near East," *Fides et Historia* 19 (1987) 27–28.

[9] See esp. R. Knierim, "Exodus 18 und die Neuordnung der Mosaischen Gerischtsbarkeit," *ZAW* 73 (1961) 146–71. For a survey of this view, see Niehr, "Grundzüge," pp. 215–19; also Rütersworden, *Von der politischen Gemeinschaft*, pp. 10–38.

[10] G. C. Macholz, "Zur Geschichte der Justizorganisation in Juda," *ZAW* 84 (1972) 314–40. Macholz's conclusions are adopted for the most part by Boecker (*Law*, pp. 28–31) and by Wilson ("Israel's Judicial System," pp. 229–48).

Henoch Reviv links each of these passages (Exod 18:13–27; Num 11:10–30; Deut 1:9–18) with a different judicial reform. H. Reviv, "The Traditions Concerning the Inception of the Legal System in Israel: Significance and Dating," *ZAW* 94 (1982) 566–75; idem, *Elders in Ancient Israel*. Unfortunately, he does not address passages in the D Code which would challenge some of his conclusions.

[11] For example, Wilson ("Israel's Judicial System," pp. 243–48) believes that the appointment of professional judges preceded the composition of the D Code, yet he argues that the Chronicler's account of Jehoshaphat's reform has been thoroughly redacted in the fifth century.

settlements)[12] and by omitting any explicit reference to the judicial role for the king.

The resulting reconstruction suggests three developmental stages: (1) the laws containing adjudication by city elders alone represent the earliest stage; (2) 2 Chr 19:4–11 represent an intermediate stage, when Jehoshaphat (or some other king) established a centralized judicial system for military settlements ("fortified cities"), but without altering adjudicative procedures elsewhere;[13] and (3) Deut 16:18–17:13 represent a late monarchic stage, when the previously-constituted central tribunal (2 Chr 19:4–11) was reformed (Deut 17:8–13) and all local judicial responsibilities were wrested from city elders and placed in the hands of professional judges (Deut 16:18–20).

There are a couple of items which make me question this reconstruction as it touches on Deuteronomy. First, it is not at all certain that the laws of Deut 16:18–17:13 come from a literary stratum later than that of 2 Chr 19:4–11[14] or Exod 18:13–27 or, especially, Deut 1:9–18. Those three seem to link the judiciary to the military, while Deut 16:18–17:13 does not.[15] Since it is most likely that Deut 1:9–18 comes from a later redactional layer than 16:18–20, it would seem that the association with the military could be a development subsequent to that of Deut 16:18–20,

---

[12] Rütersworden (*Von der politischen Gemeinschaft*, p. 16) challenges this interpretation by arguing that "gates" (Deut 16:18) would refer to fortified cities only, because gates would exist only in cities with walled fortifications. However, this line of reasoning would lead one to conclude that adjudication could only take place in settlements with walls. This seems unlikely; so, "gates" probably refers to any place where public judicial, legal, and business matters were ordinarily handled, as they were "in the gates" of walled cities.

[13] In this reconstruction, it is possible that the laws involving elders could have been written in the years between Jehoshaphat and the composition of the D Code.

[14] See Niehr, "Grundzüge," p. 220; and Wilson, "Israel's Judicial System," pp. 247–48.

[15] Exod 18:13–27 and Deut 1:9–18, Moses selects "officers" (שֹׁרִים) and "heads... and officers" from among the people to be adjudicators. Knierim ("Exodus 18," pp. 170–71) argues that this term betrays a military association for these appointees (cp. Macholz, "Zur Geschichte," pp. 322–24, 333–34). J. Buchholz concludes that שֹׁרִים is merely a pre-exilic term for royal appointees, which is replaced by שֹׁפְטִים in the Exile (*Die Ältesten Israels*, pp. 99–101).

rather than it being a prior situation which the D Code is revising.[16]

Second, this reconstruction does not explain how to correlate the many late monarchic passages in DtrH and elsewhere which seem to support the active involvement of Israel's kings in judicial matters. For example, G. Gerbrandt cogently argues that Josiah is presented as a "covenant administrator" in a pre-exilic redaction of DtrH.[17] "Since Israel's continued existence as a people on the land was dependent on her obedience to the covenant, and since the king's ultimate responsibility was to insure this continued existence, the king's role was then to make sure that the covenant was observed in Israel."[18] It would have been difficult for a king "to make sure that the covenant was observed in Israel" unless that king played an active role in the administration of the judicial system. Thus, it would be logical to conclude that the Deuteronomistic Historian expected the king to oversee the judiciary. But Deut 16:18 says that "you"—not the king—will appoint judges in all the towns. The usual conclusion drawn from

---

[16] It is possible that Deut 1:9–18 represents a pre-exilic (Josianic) deuteronomistic renewal of a prior situation. It seems unlikely, however, that it would be an exilic or post-exilic law, as Israel did not have a standing army during those eras. In any case, the point I am wishing to make is simply that the evidence for a development of judicial appointments in military settlements only to appointments in all settlements is not firmly proved.

[17] G. E. Gerbrandt, *Kingship According to the Deuteronomistic History* (SBLDS 87; Atlanta: Scholars Press, 1986), pp. 61–64, 96–102. Critical to this dating is 2 Kings 22–23. Gerbrandt provides a brief survey of research on this subject (pp. 195–200). For a more thoroughgoing redaction-critical analysis which demonstrates the pre-exilic nature of this passage, see N. Lohfink, "Die Bundesurkunde des König Josias. Eine Frage an der Deuteronomiumsforschung," *Bib* 44 (1963) 261–88, 461–98; idem, "Recent Discussion on 2 Kings 22–23: The State of the Question," in *A Song of Power and the Power of Song: Essays on the Book of Deuteronomy*, ed. D. L. Christensen (SBTS 3; Winona Lake, IN: Eisenbrauns, 1993), pp. 36–61. [Translated by L. M. Maloney from "Zur neueren Diskussion über 2 Kön 22–23," in *Das Deuteronomium: Entstehung, Gestalt und Botschaft* (ed. N. Lohfink; BETL; Louvain: Louvain University Press, 1985), pp. 24–48.]

For an overview of Jewish traditions regarding Moses as a royal figure, see D. J. Silver, "Moses Our Teacher was a King," *Jewish Law Annual* 1 (1978) 123–32. For another example of judicial expectations connected with Israel's kings, see H. A. Kenik, *Design for Kingship: The Deuteronomistic Narrative Technique in 1 Kings 3:4–15* (SBLDS 69; Chico, CA: Scholars Press, 1983).

[18] Gerbrandt, *Kingship*, p. 99.

this passage is that the D Code is taking the responsibility of judicial appointments away from the central administration and placing it in the hands of the local citizenries.[19] On the other hand, it seems clear that the king and his administration were expected to be involved in judicial matters during the careers of Isaiah (Isa 11:1–5; 32:1–8) and Jeremiah (Jer 22:1–5, 13–17; 26:10–19).

This compels us to speculate about when there might have been a time that an author would mistrust Israel's kings and call for the people to appoint judges. Assuming that Isaiah and any deuteronomists who might have lived at that time were in

---

[19] Dean McBride tries to maintain a precarious balance on this issue, emphasizing the judicial responsibility of the general populace while not eliminating the king's role entirely. He writes: "Most important of all for the preservation of political stability is the judicial system legislated in 16:18–17:13. It needs to be stressed that this system is expressly grounded in the responsibility of the *whole* society to maintain justice: hence officers of the city courts in each tribal jurisdiction are both chosen by and act on behalf of the population at large (16:18–20)...

...The *only* positively accepted task of the Israelite monarch is to study the written polity throughout his reign and to serve as a national model of faithful obedience to its stipulations (17:18–20)... But he may be involved implicitly in its official interpretation as well as enforcement, for it is not unlikely that the king was supposed to function as the national 'judge' who, according to 17:9–12, convened or otherwise sat with the judicial council of levitical priests." S. Dean McBride, Jr., "Polity of the Covenant People: The Book of Deuteronomy," *Interp* 41 (1987) 240–41.

Lohfink gives essentially the same view, saying that the king administrates and models the reading of the Law, but that the judiciary is "an autonomous authority, no longer under the king and his governors in the garrison cities." ("Distribution of the Functions of Power: The Laws Concerning Public Offices in Deuteronomy 16:18–18:22," *A Song of Power and the Power of Song* [ed. D. L. Christensen; Winona Lake: Eisenbrauns, 1993], p. 349; originally in "Die Sicherung der Wirksamkeit des Gotteswortes durch das Prinzip der Schriftlichkeit der Tora und durch das Prinzip der Gewaltenteilung nach den Ämtergesetzen des Buches Deuteronomium (Dt 16,18–18,22)," in *Testimonium Veritati: Festschrift Wilhelm Kempf* (ed. H. Wolter; Frankfurter Theologische Studien 7; Frankfurt: Knecht, 1971), p. 52; trans. R. Walls in *Great Themes from the Old Testament* (Chicago: Franciscan Herald, 1981), pp. 71–72.) Cp. Boecker, pp. 35–49; Mayes, *Deuteronomy*, pp. 268–69; Rütersworden, pp. 50–66, 89–93.

Levinson locates the king further out of the judicial realm. "Indeed, the depiction of the functions of the king in this unit serves far more to hamstring him than to permit him to exercise any meaningful authority whatsoever." Levisnon, *Deuteronomy*, p. 141.

agreement, it would be plausible to posit a date for the composition of Deut 16:18–20 prior to Isaiah's time (i.e., among northern Yahwists, opposed to the idolatrous regimes there, who eventually migrated south to avoid the Assyrian armies). Or, if one were to insist that "deuteronomism" did not emerge until the seventh century, then a date of composition during the reign of Manasseh (a king who could not be trusted to uphold the demands of the D Code) might be preferable. Finally, it is possible that this law should be attributed to an exilic author or redactor, who envisioned a very limited kingship after the Exile as the way of preventing a repeat of the conditions which precipitated the Exile.[20]

All that this implies is that the discussion regarding the diachronic reconstruction proposed by Albright, Macholz, and others is far from over. These issues obviously merit a much fuller treatment. Their resolution would require analyses of many texts, most of which are outside the D Code and contribute nothing different to our understanding of the elders as adjudicators beyond what is suggested by passages within the D Code. I hope to be able to address these issues elsewhere, but for now let us shift to another interpretation of the judiciary laws of the D Code.

Association with the Centralization of the Cult

M. Weinfeld sees the judiciary laws of the D Code as a necessary corollary of the cult centralization program. That program prohibited local priests from performing their traditional sacral duties away from the central sanctuary. Those duties had included judicial functions (e.g., oaths and the ordeal).[21] Prohibiting the exercise of those judicial functions "created a

---

[20] One's interpretation of Deut 17:14–20 is crucial to investigating this question. Recent treatments of that passage lean toward a combination of Deuteronomic and deuteronomistic elements. But scholarly opinions vary greatly as to when to date those respective layers. I am inclined toward Cross's school of thought on the broader question of deuteronomistic literary activity, but the variations within this school of thought still allow for any of the three general proposals given here, although the third would be possible only in regard to a final redaction. Also, see below on my criticisms of those who see the D Code as a utopian reform program of the exilic period.

[21] See Boecker, *Law*, pp. 35–36.

judicial vacuum in the provincial cities, and the law providing for the appointment of state judges in every city was apparently designed to fill it (Deut 16:18–20)."[22] Thus, the professionalization of the judiciary did not arise until the implementation of the D Code. The role played by these judges did not negate the judicial role of city elders, though. The sacral judicial functions formerly carried out by priests had been supplementary to the elders' secular judicial functions, and the judges merely fill the gap left when the priests are restricted to the central sanctuary.[23]

B. Levinson goes a step further than Weinfeld, saying professional judges would displace both the priests and the city elders in their judicial functions. However, he does not really attempt to justify this position. He simply states, "It is doubtful that the two systems of judicial administration—that of the elders and that of the professional judicial appointees of Deut 16:18–20—ever coexisted historically... What the text here presents as simple installation [of professional judges] actually involves the replacement of one system of justice with another, as the elders are silently evicted from their customary place of honor."[24] Levinson explains why the coexistence of elders with judges is "doubtful" simply by saying it "strikes me as harmonistic: Deut 16:18 installs the professionalized judiciary precisely at the site where the elders would exercise their public function."[25] But this exposes an as yet unproved assumption: that elders and judges carried out identical judicial functions.

The problem with both of these proposals is that they are apparently contradicted by subsequent laws in the D Code. The "polemical silence" (also called "exegetical silence") which Levinson attributes to Deut 16:18–20 is effectively broken in the laws which call for adjudication by city elders. The way out of this dilemma, of course, is to attribute the elders-laws to earlier

---

[22] M. Weinfeld, *Deuteronomy and the Deuteronomic School* (Oxford: Clarendon, 1972), p. 234.

[23] Weinfeld, *Deuteronomy and the Deuteronomic School*, pp. 233–36; idem, "Judge and Officer in Ancient Israel and in the Ancient Near East," *Israel Oriental Studies* 7 (1977) 65–88.

[24] Levinson, *Deuteronomy*, pp. 124–26.

[25] Levinson, *Deuteronomy*, p. 125 n. 70. However, the writer of Lam 5:14 still expects to find elders in the gate, and Jeremiah speaks of the king sitting in the gate (Jer 38:7). It seems there might be room for all the leaders in the gate.

literary layers, as many have done.[26] But again, this is based on the prior assumption that the introduction of something new to the judicial system eliminates the need for (or even prohibits the possibility of) the continuation of what already existed. For some, it might be just as logical to argue that the laws calling for adjudication by elders were written later than Deut 16:18–20, and that those laws use "polemical silence" to prohibit continued adjudication by professional judges.[27] Thus, Levinson's interpretation is based on an *argumentum e silentio*, but one which is inconsistently applied.

Weinfeld's proposal at least has the advantage of explaining the continuing presence of laws involving elders as adjudicators, but he faces a problem similar to Levinson's with the law of Deut 21:1–9. That law calls for priests to carry out a sacral function away from the central sanctuary. Moreover, in its present form, it calls for judges and priests to function simultaneously in a legal matter. This should not be, if the judges are appointed for the purpose of filling a void created by the removal of priests from local sanctuaries. Weinfeld, like others before him, argues that the references to priests and/or judges are secondary in this passage. But this implies that a deuteronomistic redactor has created a situation which, according to Weinfeld, the lawgiver tries to prevent in 16:18–20—the involvement of priests in local judicial matters. Also, this redactor confuses the situation by having judges work alongside priests, rather than replacing them. What is most curious about this is that this is the only instance in which the redactor causes this confusion. But if a redactor could add a reference to judges, it would seem that he could also delete a reference to priests, eliminating any confusion. We shall return to 21:1–9 in Chapter 3. For now, it is enough to see that this interpretation cannot be sustained without recourse to textual emendation at some point, which leaves it open to question.

---

[26] See above.

[27] For example, Gertz (*Die Gerichtsorganisation Israels*) argues that most of the elders-laws are exilic in origin. Cp. Hoppe, "The Origins of Deuteronomy."

Association with Utopian Ideals

Redaction critics who hold to a predominantly exilic date for Deuteronom(ist)ic writings tend to interpret the socio-political system assumed in the D Code's laws—and thus the laws themselves—as more utopian than real. From this perspective, the judiciary laws do not reflect past or current judicial institutions; rather, they reflect the status of influence groups among the exiles and ideals of what should inhere in the post-exilic community. For example, J. Buchholz attributes the contents of the judiciary laws in the D Code primarily to the early exilic period. They preserve some local judicial practices from the monarchic period, but they also contain some hypothetical reconstruction by exilic redactors. That the elders adjudicate more than any other functionaries in the D Code Buchholz attributes to the resurgence of the importance of clan elders among the exiles following the dismantling of state mechanisms by the Babylonians. Subsequent legislation gives more judicial responsibility to priests and judges, because those clan elders quickly fell out of favor with the Deuteronomists in the exile.[28] A more radical proposal has recently been made by J. C. Gertz, who attributes the elders-laws in which the elders serve as adjudicators (Deut 21:18–21; 22:13–21; 25:5–10) entirely to the later exilic period. To him, they represent an Exilic resurgence of the prominence of the clans and a preference for them to oversee the execution of the Torah (see Deut 27:1; 31:9).[29]

My reservations about this perspective on the D Code are based on two assumptions which I hold regarding ancient Near Eastern law codes in general. First, these law codes typically reflect existing practices and institutions, rather than being hypothetical.[30] Every ancient Near Eastern law code of which I am

---

[28] See Buchholz, *Die Ältesten Israels*, esp. pp. 103–105. Rütersworden's analysis produces similar conclusions (*Von der politischen Gemeinschaft*, pp. 94–111), but he says very little directly about adjudication by elders.

[29] Gertz, *Die Gerichtsorganisation*, pp. 28–97, 173–225.

[30] The codes are inherently hypothetical in one sense: that the laws they contain would be observed appropriately by the populace. But it is quite another thing to say that the very socio-political background of a law code is hypothetical. This lands us squarely in the middle of current discussions regarding the redactional history of Deuteronomy. How one proceeds depends largely on his/her assumptions about what is "likely" or "unlikely" in the

aware assumes the prior existence of the basic social and judicial mechanisms mentioned in its individual laws.[31] To predicate the implementation of a collection of laws on the ability and success of a subjugated people to gain its independence and set up the socio-political structures assumed by the laws would seem to undermine their authority entirely. If conditions prevented the Israelites from setting up the kind of socio-political structure assumed by the D Code, then they could not expect to implement the laws of the D Code. In fact, this socio-political structure never did materialize following the Exile, and proponents of this third line of interpretation say that the D Code was never actually implemented. According to this school of interpretation, this people regularly altered and sculpted this collection of laws (and others equally hypothetical) during the Exile in anticipation of what they thought the socio-political situation would be once they returned. But then, once they had returned and were living in their land again—but in a setting different from anything they had anticipated—they felt they were prohibited from altering those never-before-used laws any further. Instead, they could only try to reinterpret them for use in this unanticipated socio-political situation.[32] I simply find this whole reconstruction to be harder to accept than a reconstruction which envisions the co-existence, at some time, of the various laws of the D Code and the socio-political setting which they assume.[33]

---

process of a work's composition. See below, and Chapter 3, for my own assumptions.

[31] Certainly there would be local variations for which an adjudicator might have to make allowances, but those local variations would be similar enough that any adaptations deemed necessary would seem "natural" to anyone involved.

[32] A major component of the Book of Deuteronomy is the prophetic-like promise that Yahweh would make this socio-political structure possible. If such a possibility never existed after the composition of the D Code (in some form), then it would leave the impression that Yahweh had not been able to fulfill his promise. If Yahweh's side of the covenant had never been realized, then when would the people ever develop the sense that their side of the covenant could or should be realized?

[33] This does not rule out the possibility that some laws might reflect one time, while others come from another time. But to say that both "times" are hypothetical and yet the laws on which they are based are so authoritative that they preclude further redaction in a "real" setting pushes the envelope of credulity, in my mind.

Second, I am skeptical about this perspective because it assumes that the laws are being composed and redacted in something of a vacuum. For example, Gertz bases his redactional reconstruction of Deut 22:13–29 on the assumption that certain individual laws (esp. v 29) existed first, all alone, and then others were written over the years to supplement them and clarify their application. This line of thinking ignores the possibility of any external influence on the composition of Israel's laws.

Some recent studies raise serious questions about such an assumption. George Mendenhall and Moshe Weinfeld challenge this assumption in a general way by pointing to possible parallels and influences between Assyrian treaties and the Book of Deuteronomy. If the general structure of the latter has been influenced by the former, then perhaps there are contacts between individual pieces as well. Eckart Otto contends that the legal scribes of Mesopotamia and Judah share certain "redactional techniques" in common when they put together groups of laws on a particular topic, but he denies any actual influence from one to the other.[34] Raymond Westbrook addresses this question more broadly and proffers a compelling theory for the composition and redaction of all ancient Near Eastern law codes. He argues that other scholars have made too much of the differences between various law codes by assuming that each code is exhaustive in its coverage of offenses and punishments. Among other things, this assumes that each code is composed "from scratch." The reality, according to Westbrook, is that none of these law codes is complete on its own. Instead, they each assume an existing broad corpus of commonly-known laws regarding various crimes and offenses.

> Because these law codes could only have a fraction of their discussion committed to writing, each code contains no more than a few aspects of a given scholarly problem, sometimes overlapping with the aspects preserved in other codes, sometimes not. Moreover, a given system may pursue the discussion in a particular direction, considering variants not discussed elsewhere.

---

[34] E. Otto, "Aspects of Legal Reforms and Reformulations in Ancient Cuneiform and Israelite Law," in *Theory and Method in Biblical and Cuneiform Law: Revision, Interpolation and Development*, ed. B. M. Levinson (JSOTS 181; Sheffield: Sheffield Academic, 1994), pp. 190–91.

It is by combining the similar and not-so-similar provisions of the various codes that the whole problem and thus the underlying law may be revealed and any peculiarities of the individual systems disclosed. This approach is, to be sure, in some sense an argument from silence, but it is a positive argument, that refuses to see contradictions in mere omissions from sources that are by nature incomplete, when in all other respects they are complementary.[35]

We will return to this point in our discussions of some of the elders-laws. For now, it is enough to recognize that law codes of the ancient Near East typically were composed by persons who were familiar with other codes. We should assume the same for the D Code.

Thus, it seems that those who hold to a multiple exilic composition and redaction of the D Code err in two ways. First, they are wrong to assume that a collection of laws would be composed and redacted for a hypothetical Israelite society, and then left basically untouched in "the real world" following the Exile. Second, they are wrong to ignore the likely influences—direct or indirect—from a long history of law-writing in the ancient Near East. It is more likely to assume that the laws of the D Code were written at a time when Israel controlled her land, and that they reflect some knowledge of legal traditions and law codes commonly known to the peoples of the ancient Near East.

In sum, these three groups of interpretations of the judiciary laws in D represent one component of their respective proponents' broader theories regarding the compositional history of the D Code. Albright, Macholz, and others believe that the D Code represents the preservation and adaptation of old legal materials in a late monarchic document. Weinfeld and Levinson represent those who see the D Code as a religio-political program, introduced in pre-exilic Jerusalem, probably during the seventh century. Buchholz and Gertz represent those who see the D Code as a product of repeated exilic redaction of scattered pre-exilic legal materials, giving a utopian view of life in a post-exilic Israel which never became a reality. My own assumptions cause me to be

---

[35] R. Westbrook, "Adultery in Ancient Near Eastern Law," *RB* 97 (1990) 548.

inclined toward one of the first two interpretations. However, regarding how the judiciary laws of the D Code fit into those interpretations, I see the need for some revisions. In particular, most of these interpretations share a significant misconception, in my opinion. This misconception is that the adjudicative functions of elders and the adjudicative functions of appointed judges described in the D Code are mutually exclusive functions.[36]

The main argument to support this assumption is that most of the laws which call for elders to adjudicate do not mention appointed judges (Deut 19:1–13; 21:18–21; 22:13–21; 25:5–10), and laws calling for adjudication by judges do not mention city elders (Deut 16:18–20; 17:8–13; 19:15–21; 25:1–3). The crucial text in this discussion is Deut 16:18. It prescribes the appointment of judges "in all your gates." Elders traditionally judged "in the gate;" so, if judges are placed "in the gate" to "judge the people," they must be taking the place of those elders. Since they are not mentioned in the laws referring to adjudication by elders, it is argued that those laws must come from a time when judges did not yet sit "in the gate." This is an argument from silence, but a very efficacious silence, according to scholars such as Levinson.

I question the consistency of this argument. If the omission of a reference to "judges" in some laws means that they did not yet function judicially, and if the omission of a reference to "elders" in other laws mean that they had been replaced, then, to be consistent, we should conclude that laws which mention neither elders nor judges reflect a time when individual men ("you") rather than these groups carried out judicial functions. This seems highly unlikely. Similarly, the deuteronomistic redactors would be shown to be inconsistent in the application of their own reform. If

---

[36] Of those surveyed above, only Weinfeld does not assume this exclusivity. See also Ze'ev Weisman, "The Place of the People in the Making of Law and Judgment," in *Pomegranates and Golden Bells: Studies in Biblical, Jewish, and Near Eastern Ritual, Law, and Literature in Honor of Jacob Milgrom* (ed. D. P. Wright, D. N. Freedman, and A. Hurvitz; Winona Lake, IN: Eisenbrauns, 1995), p. 420. His position seems to be similar to my own; however, he does not set forth any arguments to explain it.

In this investigation, I am not concerning myself with resolving the debate over when priests and/or Levites were introduced into the mix. I will argue that their participation in the judicial process could logically run parallel to that of judges, but this does not prove their participation nor their exact identity (i.e., that they are Levites).

they wished for judges to replace elders in all judicial matters, as Albright, Macholz, Levinson, and others contend, then it would seem incumbent upon them to mandate such a change specifically in those cases which had previously called for the elders to exercise that judicial authority; yet, they redact those laws without altering the identity of the adjudicators. Or, if the elders-laws were inserted or redacted secondarily, then the redactor should eliminate or revise those laws which prescribe adjudication by professional judges; yet, those have been left intact. In either case, the D Code as a whole is inconsistent in itself regarding how its various laws are to be administered (i.e., the diachronic reading prevents any possibility of a synchronic reading).

I believe that the consideration of cross-cultural analogies opens the door to a viable alternative to these interpretations. It seems that much of what is said regarding developments in Israel's judicial system is based on assumptions about sociological developments supported by evidence drawn from a very few examples (particularly Greco-Roman ones). However, by taking in a broader swath of examples—examples both ancient and modern—which are similar to that of ancient Israel, one finds that another reconstruction of what might have happened in Israel is possible. We can then reevaluate the judiciary laws of Deuteronomy in light of what we find in those analogies.

CROSS-CULTURAL ANALOGIES TO ISRAEL'S JUDICIAL SYSTEM

I will begin with some general observations derived from a perusal of ethnographies of several contemporary societies which include kinship-based communities. These are especially helpful because they reveal more than just judicial structures and practices. Researchers are able to live among and interview members of these societies and discuss not only what is done, but why (i.e., the rationales for social phenomena such as judicial practices).[37] So, I will first present an overview of judicial

---

[37] One must acknowledge that, even in this regard, there are circumstances which prevent a totally objective description of a society. Ethnographers inevitably import some of their own presuppositions into their work, they cannot describe nor investigate an entire society, and the cultural differences

practices and ideas among contemporary kinship-based societies, and then I will shift to analogies from the ancient Near East. The rationales for judicial structures and practices in ancient societies are usually left unsaid (they felt no need to explain why they did what they did) and must be deduced by the modern investigator. Hopefully, the possibilities raised in the overview of contemporary societies will be a better guide to possible explanations for the practices and ideas in ancient Israel reflected in the biblical text. Also, the temporal and geographical proximity of ancient Near Eastern societies to Israel provides the investigator with fairly direct (though still general) cultural influences upon Israel (i.e., Israelites could have been influenced by judicial ideas they encountered through interaction with many neighboring peoples). All of this information will then be used to consider anew the significance of the laws of the D Code which touch on judicial practices in ancient Israel.

Judicial Systems in Contemporary Kinship-Based Societies

Judicial Structures

Judicial systems in kinship-based societies usually consist of multiple tiers. By "tiers" I mean a recognized hierarchy of locations and persons to which individuals may go for judicial matters. There is some variety in this, but some basic principles tend to underlie the judicial structure of every society. Three factors are mentioned most often as significant: the "social distance" between the persons involved in the legal matter, the seriousness of the offense in the eyes of the community, and the nature of the offense (whether sacral or profane, whether civil or criminal). "Social distance" is in turn based on several factors, such as (a) how closely related the parties are by blood descent and/or marriage, (b) geographical proximity, and (c) relative social status (e.g., landowner or client, chiefly lineage or "commoner").

---

between a Western ethnographer and the non-Western society being investigated can never be fully bridged. On these inherent problems, see P. Bohannan, "Ethnography and Comparison in Legal Anthropology," in *Law in Culture and Society*, ed. L. Nader (Chicago: Aldine Publishing Co., 1969), pp. 401–18; cp. Hallpike, "Some Problems," pp. 137–38; Holy and Blacking, "Explanation through Comparison," pp. 57–60.

Also, the perceived seriousness and nature of an offense will vary from society to society, dependent on the mores and religious beliefs of the society (e.g., adultery might be "winked at" in one society, but deserving of death in another).[38]

"Social distance" is often the first consideration made when deciding on the venue for a trial or hearing.[39] Cases involving and affecting persons within a single lineage or village community are often resolved by a local headman and/or group of lineage elders, in reflection of the political institutions of the local community.[40]

---

[38] For example, Abrahams, "Neighbourhood Organization," pp. 181–84; J. C. Buxton, *Chiefs and Strangers: A Study of Political Assimilation among the Mandari* (Oxford: Clarendon Press, 1963), p. 120; E. Cotran, "Tribal Factors in the Establishment of the East African Legal Systems," in *Tradition and Transition in East Africa: Studies of the Tribal Element in the Modern Era*, ed. P. H. Gulliver (Berkeley and Los Angeles: University of California Press, 1969), p. 129; I. Cunnison, *Baggara Arabs: Power and the Lineage in a Sudanese Nomad Tribe* (Oxford: Clarendon, 1966), p. 154; J. S. Eades, *The Yoruba Today* (Cambridge: Cambridge University, 1980), pp. 113–14; Holy, *Neighbours and Kinsmen*, pp. 130–37; S. F. Nadel, *The Nuba: An Anthropological Study of the Hill Tribes in Kordofan* (London: Oxford University, 1947), pp. 501–503; Peters, "Some Structural Aspects," pp. 261–69; J. Roscoe, *The Baganda: An Account of their Native Customs and Beliefs* (New York: Barnes and Noble, 1966), pp. 262–63; I. Schapera, "Law and Justice," in *The Bantu-Speaking Tribes of South Africa: An Ethnographical Survey* (ed. I. Schapera; London: Routledge and Kegan Paul, 1959), p. 218; Spencer, *Samburu*, pp. 176–77; Tosh, *Clan Leaders*, p. 66; and A. A. M. Zeid, "Honour and Shame among the Bedouins of Egypt," in *Honour and Shame*, ed. J. G. Peristiany (Chicago: University of Chicago, 1966), p. 246.

[39] Some ethnographers wrestle with designating some relatively informal, local legal proceedings as "trials" and the location for legal gatherings as "courts." However, they usually justify these designations by saying that the persons in the community use the same designation for such informal gatherings as they do for "official" court matters held at a centrally-identified site and overseen by centrally-appointed adjudicators. See R. G. Abrahams, *The Political Organization of the Unyamwezi* (Cambridge: Cambridge University, 1967), pp. 101, 159; Buxton, *Chiefs and Strangers*, pp. 128–29; Nadel, *Nuba*, p. 459; and A. Richards, "The Conciliar System of the Bemba of Northern Zambia," in *Councils in Action*, ed. A. Richards and A. Kuper (Cambridge: Cambridge University, 1971), p. 111.

[40] Most of my examples come from rural, agricultural societies. However, the principles being brought out are found in large cities as well, at the district or ward level. The main difference between villages and city wards would seem to be geographical proximity between communities. For examples of "traditional" peoples in urban settings, see W. Bascom, *The Yoruba of*

This was true in stateless societies, and it is generally maintained when such societies are incorporated into a state.[41] In the latter case, the central authorities will often accept the perpetuation of traditional adjudicative procedures and persons at the local level, although they might wish to moderate or modify the severity and types of punishment employed.[42] Moreover, ethnographers have found that traditional judicial practices and institutions tend to continue surreptitiously, even when the state authorities order

---

Southwestern Nigeria (New York: Holt, Rinehart and Winston, 1969), pp. 38–41; and B. G. Dennis, *The Gbandes: A People of the Liberian Hinterland* (Chicago: Nelson-Hall Co., 1972), p. 251; Gulick, *Social Structure*, p. 171; and J. Middleton, "Home-Town: A Study of an Urban Centre in Southern Ghana," *Africa* 49 (1979) 246–57.

[41] See A. S. Ahmed, *Social and Economic Change in the Tribal Areas [Pakistan], 1972–1976* (Karachi: Oxford University, 1977; Amanolahi-Baharvand, "Baharvand," pp. 139–40; Bascom, *Yoruba*, pp. 38–39; T. O. Beidelman, *The Kaguru: A Matrilineal People of East Africa* (New York: Holt, Rinehart and Winston, 1971), p. 86; Buxton, *Chiefs and Strangers*, pp. 127–32; Cotran, "Tribal Factors," pp. 127–33; Cunnison, *Baggara Arabs*, pp. 181–82; Dennis, *Gbandes*, pp. 264–65; N. Dyson-Hudson, *Karimojong Politics* (Oxford: Clarendon Press, 1966), pp. 209–10, 220; Eades, *Yoruba Today*, pp. 53–54, 113–25; J. Ensminger, "Co-Opting the Elders: The Political Economy of State Incorporation in Africa," *AmAnthro* 92 (1990) 662–63; M. Fortes, "The Structure of Unilineal Descent Groups," *AmAnthro* 55 (1953) 26; Goldberg, "From Shaykh to Mazkir," pp. 139–49; P. B. Hammond, *Yatenga: Technology in the Culture of a West African Kingdom* (New York: The Free Press, 1966), pp. 144–52; G. I. Jones, "Councils," pp. 64–65; Katakura, *Bedouin Village*, pp. 60–61, 155–56; H. Kuper, *The Swazi: A South African Kingdom* (New York: Holt, Rinehart and Winston, 1963), p. 37; B. A. Lewis, *The Murle: Red Chiefs and Black Commoners* (Oxford: Clarendon Press, 1972), pp. 43–45, 72–76; Mair, *African Societies*, pp. 105–106; Nadel, *Nuba*, pp. 159–62, 255, 312, 469–72; S. Noland, "Dispute Settlement and Social Organization in Two Iranian Rural Communities," *AnthroQ* 54 (1981) 194–99; Rosenfeld, "Social and Economic Factors ," pp. 120–27; and J. van Velzen, *The Politics of Kinship: A Study in Social Manipulation among the Lakeside Tonga of Malawi* (Manchester: Manchester University, 1971), pp. 294–95, 309–11.

[42] See Bascom, *Yoruba*, p. 40; Katakura, *Bedouin Village*, p. 156; J. C. Mitchell, *The Yao Village: A Study in the Social Structure of a Nyasaland Tribe* (Manchester: Manchester University, 1966), p. 54; Nadel, *Nuba*, p. 160; J. G. Peristiany, "Law," in *The Institutions of Primitive Society*, ed. E. E. Evans-Pritchard (Glencoe, IL: The Free Press, 1954), p. 44. In these cases, there is a sort of double indemnity for the offender. The central government imposes a fine or prison sentence on a wrongdoer, but then the local people insist that the guilty party also pay a traditional fine or undergo a traditional "cleansing" procedure after the official punishment has been completed.

their suspension and recognize the legality of proceedings in centrally-mandated courts only.[43]

Legal matters which extend beyond the local village (or ward, in a larger city) are also addressed in ways which reflect the political structures of the broader area.[44] If a case involves members of more than one village, it can be resolved—if the parties involved seek resolution—with the adjudicative services of

---

[43] Among the Ibo, matters are "quietly" settled by local leaders for the stated reason that they do not wish the state authorities to become involved. G. I. Jones, "Councils," p. 74. Observers among the Bemba commented that, despite "direct orders" from colonial rulers, the tribesmen were carrying on legal "business as usual" some thirty years after the orders were given. Richards, "Conciliar System," pp. 101–102, 113–14.

See also Abrahams, *Political Organization*, p. 159; Amanolahi-Baharvand, "Baharvand," pp. 139–40, 215; Beidelman, *Kaguru*, p. 88; L. Bohannan, "Political Aspects of the Tiv Social Organization," in *Tribes Without Rulers*, ed. J. Middleton and D. Tait (London: Routledge and Kegan Paul, 1958), p. 53; Ginat, *Blood Disputes*, pp. 95–152; Hammond, *Yatenga*, p. 144; Katakura, *Bedouin Village*, p. 156; A. Kuper, "The Kgalagari Lekgota," in *Councils in Action*, ed. A. Richards and A. Kuper (Cambridge: Cambridge University, 1971), pp. 84–85, 90–94; Lewis, *Murle*, p. 80; E. Marx, *The Social Context of Violent Behaviour: A Social Anthropological Study in an Israeli Immigrant Town* (London: Routledge and Kegan Paul, 1976), p. 15; Teitelbaum, "Old Age, Midwifery, and Good Talk," pp. 43, 47–48; E. Winter, "The Aboriginal Political Structure of Bwamba," in *Tribes Without Rulers*, ed. J. Middleton and D. Tait (London: Routledge and Kegan Paul, 1958), pp. 159–60; and Zeid, "Honour and Shame," pp. 253–54.

[44] For example, among the Tiv, there are three areas of judicial activity. These areas can be delineated according to the scope of the adjudicators' "authority" and the nature of the case. The primary social unit is the "compound" (a minimal lineage). In cases involving members of only one compound, the senior male of that compound has "definite authority over specified fields." Matters which concern a broader swath of the village than a compound are brought before the village "elders" and/or "leaders." Bohannan stresses that these "higher officials" do not possess "authority" over their village in the way that a senior male holds authority over his compound. The people involved in a dispute must request the aid of the elders or leaders for them to become involved. They cannot assume it for themselves because of their "authority" (because such authority is not acknowledged by the people). Moreover, only the elders (and never the "leaders") are asked to deal with matters involving magic or religion (ancestor worship), because those powers are exercised by elders only. L. Bohannan, "Political Aspects," pp. 53–58.

See also Abrahams, "Neighbourhood Organization," p. 177; Cotran, "Tribal Factors," p. 128; Dresch, "Positions of *shaykhs*," p. 40; Hammond, *Yatenga*, pp. 141–52; Nadel, *Nuba*, pp. 469–70, 499–500; M. Read, *The Ngoni of Nyasaland* (London: Frank Cass and Co., 1970), p. 91.

the lineage elders or headmen of the respective communities and/or a local chief who is recognized as being "over" both communities.[45] The desire for resolution between the disputants is based on the existing socio-political situation between their respective villages, and the success of the case's outcome will probably influence their future socio-political relations. This basic pattern can be extended outward, always reflecting the general socio-political situation of the people(s) involved and of the nation-state which they inhabit.[46]

As the social distance between disputants increases, so increases the likelihood that they will look to a centrally-appointed adjudicator—if anyone—to judge or mediate a resolution to the case. This is so for a simple reason: local communities are often self-sustaining, while central governments are dependent on the cooperative efforts of many communities for their continued existence. If two communities can prosper (or at least maintain their current life) in spite of animosity between each other, and if they do not share some personal or religious mandate to interact peaceably, then they will not "bother" with the peaceful resolution of a dispute between them. If they feel the

---

[45] Buxton, *Chiefs and Strangers*, p. 119; Cunnison, *Baggara Arabs*, pp. 154–56; E. Gellner, *Saints of the Atlas* (London: Trinity, 1969), pp. 108–109; Hammond, *Yatenga*, p. 144; Holy, *Neighbours and Kinsmen*, p. 131; A. Kuper, "Kgalagari Lekgota," p. 89; Nadel, *Nuba*, p. 250; Noland, "Dispute Settlement," p. 194; and E. V. Winans, *Shambala: The Constitution of a Traditional State* (Berkeley and Los Angeles: University of California Press, 1962), p. 115.

[46] See M. Abélès, "In Search of the Monarch: Introduction of the State among the Gamo of Ethiopia," in *Modes of Production in Africa: The Precolonial Era*, ed. D. Crummey and C. C. Stewart (Beverly Hills, CA: Sage, 1981), pp. 51–52; Amanolahi-Baharvand, "Baharvand," p. 126; L. Bohannan, "Political Aspects," pp. 53–58; Evans-Pritchard, *Nuer*, pp. 151–69; Fernea, *Shaykh and Effendi*, pp. 93, 145–47; S. E. Greene, "Land, Lineage and Clan in Early Anlo," *Africa* 51 (1981) 454–55; G. I. Jones, "Councils," pp. 68, 78; Mair, *African Societies*, pp. 34, 103–106, 144; Peristiany, "Law," pp. 44–46; Richards, "Conciliar System," pp. 100–101, 111–15; Spencer, *Samburu*, pp. 63–65, 176–80, 206; Tosh, *Clan Leaders*, pp. 66–105; G. Wagner, "The Political Organization of the Bantu of Kavirondo," in *African Political Systems*, ed. M. Fortes and E. E. Evans-Pritchard (London: Oxford University, 1940), pp. 211, 220–21; and Winter, "Aboriginal Political Structure," pp. 142–44.

need to resolve their differences, then they will seek out a mediator/adjudicator to facilitate that resolution.[47]

This "need" to maintain peace can arise naturally due to local environmental circumstances, or it can be artificially imposed due to the existence of central bureaucracies. The latter is more obvious in Western-oriented states, but it is not limited to them. The determining factor will be the presence of a political entity which wishes to inhibit conflict between groups that are geographically distinct. Such an entity is obvious in nations created by European colonialization, where previously unrelated peoples—who traditionally have regarded each other as "foreigners"—are forced to live peaceably with one another—as "brothers"—due to the arbitrary drawing of boundaries by conquerors. In some cases, the various peoples view this as an intrusion into their affairs and try to "carry on business as usual" in spite of it. Others, however, welcome this intervention into their affairs, having long desired peaceful relations while lacking a political mechanism to maintain them.[48]

But such a situation is not unique to colonializing powers. There have been numerous examples of indigenous leaders expanding their authority and creating chiefdoms or monarchies in pre-colonial societies which encompass multiple clans or tribes with a history of hostility toward one another. These leaders were just as intent on developing and maintaining peaceful relations among their various "peoples" as their colonializing counterparts. Local leaders have a power base that is too narrow to achieve such results; so, regional or central authorities take on these broader judicial responsibilities by setting up an administrative hierarchy of chiefs and sub-chiefs who serve as adjudicators, among other responsibilities.[49]

---

[47] See Abrahams, *Political Organization*, p. 164; Buxton, *Chiefs and Strangers*, p. 118; Nadel, *Nuba*, p. 475.

[48] Buxton, *Chiefs and Strangers*, p. 120; Dresch, "Positions of *shaykhs*," pp. 39–46; G. J. Klima, *The Barabaig: East African Cattle-Herders* (New York: Holt, Rinehart and Winston, 1970), pp. 85–87; Marx, *Social Context*, p. 8; Noland, "Dispute Settlement," p. 198; Tosh, *Clan Leaders*, pp. 66–80, 128–79; J. Middleton and D. Tait, "Introduction," *Tribes Without Rulers* (London: Routledge and Kegan Paul, 1958), p. 8; Winans, *Shambala*, p. 115; and Winter, "Aboriginal Political Structure," pp. 159–60.

[49] J. Beattie, *The Nyoro State* (Oxford: Clarendon Press, 1971), p. 130; Eades, *Yoruba Today*, pp. 113–20; A. Kuper, "Kgalagari Lekgota," p. 80;

Another consideration which will take adjudication out of the hands of local leaders is the perceived seriousness of an offense. A paramount chief or state government will often identify certain offenses as crimes which can be adjudicated only by chiefs or state appointees.[50] The justification for identifying an offense as "serious" varies. Sometimes it is the political power associated with adjudication which the central authorities wish to control; in other societies, an offense is considered a threat to the well-being or honor of the society as a whole or of the ruling group. In some societies, especially those with a clear-cut social hierarchization, the seriousness of an offense will vary depending on the relative social standing of the persons involved. For example, one will occasionally find that fathers and older brothers will have the "right" to injure or even kill a dependent member of their immediate family or a servant who has committed an offense against the family, while bodily injury against someone outside

---

Garthwaite, *Khans and Shahs*, pp. 6–8, 34–35, 41; Holy, *Neighbours and Kinsmen*, pp. ix, 116–28; Khuri, *Tribe and State*, pp. 35–36, 47, 65; H. Kuper, *Swazi*, pp. 34–37; Musil, *Manners and Customs*, pp. 426–35; Nadel, *Nuba*, pp. 310–12, 469–70; Read, *Ngoni*, pp. 90–99; Schapera, "Political Institutions," in *Bantu-Speaking Tribes*, pp. 173–95; R. Verdier, "The Ontology of the Judicial Thought of the Kabrè of Northern Togo," in *Law in Culture and Society*, ed. L. Nader (Chicago: Aldine Press, 1969), pp. 143–45; Wagner, "Political Organization," p. 211; and Winans, *Shambala*, pp. 100–104, 123–24.

[50] Abrahams, *Political Organization*, pp. 101, 130–37; I. Cunnison, *The Luapula Peoples of Northern Rhodesia: Custom and History in Tribal Politics* (Manchester: Manchester University, 1959), pp. 92, 181–85; A. Kuper, "Kgalagari Lekgota," p. 90; Nadel, *Nuba*, p. 252; and Schapera, "Law and Justice," p. 208.

The ability of state authorities actually to regulate the adjudication of such cases can be an important indicator of the real strength of the state. See Ahmed, *Social and Economic Change*, p. 44; Bloch, "Decision-Making," pp. 46–54; Eades, *Yoruba Today*, pp. 22, 113–20; Fernea, *Shaykh and Effendi*, pp. 121–23; Musil, *Manners and Customs*, pp. 427–30; Teitelbaum, "Old Age," p. 52; and M. Tymowski, "The Evolution of Primitive Political Organization from Extended Family to Early State," in *Development and Decline: The Development of Sociopolitical Organization*, ed. H. J. M. Claessen, P. van de Velde, and M. E. Smith (South Hadley, MA: Bergin and Garvey, 1985), pp. 184–85.

During the era of Belgian control of the Congo, local chiefs were displaced by European administrators, while local elders retained basically the same (limited) powers they had had prior to the arrival of the Europeans. W. MacGaffey, *Religion and Society in Central Africa: The Bakongo of Lower Zaire* (Chicago: University of Chicago, 1986), p. 17.

the family is strictly forbidden.[51] An offense committed by a "commoner" against a member of a chiefly lineage might be considered more serious than usually is the case, because of the belief that the livelihood of the entire community is maintained by the chiefly lineage.[52]

Similar to this is the perception that some offenses affect the spiritual or sacral integrity of the community. Persons who enjoy the closest contact with the spiritual world naturally must oversee the rectification of such offenses. In some communities, this responsibility still falls to lineage elders or a village headman. More often, it will fall under the "jurisdiction" of a chief or some "ritual specialist" (priest, rainmaker, prophet). The deciding factor will be the community's perception as to what kind of person (political leader, ritual specialist, holder of knowledge) can deal most effectively with the type of offense which has been committed.[53]

Adjudicators

This leads us to consider more directly what principles are operative for explaining who it is that adjudicates. First, it needs to be recognized that disputants typically seek out adjudicators,

[51] The clearest examples of this come from situations of adultery, in which a husband or brother can punish a promiscuous wife or sister without impunity from those around. See L. C. Briggs, *Tribes of the Sahara* (Cambridge, MA: Harvard University Press, 1967), p. 171; M. M. Edel, *The Chiga of Western Uganda* (London: Dawsons of Pall Mall, 1969), p. 10; Moore, "Descent and Legal Position," pp. 391–92; Nadel, *Nuba*, p. 348; Schapera, "Law and Justice," p. 206; and Zeid, "Honour and Shame," p. 254.

[52] See Dresch, "Positions of *shaykhs*," pp. 39–40; and Mitchell, *Yao Village*, p. 54.

[53] For example, among the Mandari, "chiefs" (*mar*) alone deal with religious matters, while lineage elders adjudicate secular matters. J. C. Buxton, "The Mandari of the Southern Sudan," in *Tribes Without Rulers*, ed. J. Middleton and D. Tait (London: Routledge and Kegan Paul, 1958), pp. 67–96.

See also Amanolahi-Baharvand, "Baharvand," pp. 121–23; Bascom, *Yoruba*, p. 40; T. O. Beidelman, "Nuer Priests and Prophets: Charisma, Authority, and Power among the Nuer," in *The Translation of Culture*, ed. T. O. Beidelman (London: Tavistock, 1971), pp. 400–401; D. B. Cruise O'Brien, *Saints and Politicians: Essays in the Organisation of a Senegalese Peasant Society* (Cambridge: Cambridge University, 1975), p. 103; Evans-Pritchard, *Nuer*, p. 6; Fernea, *Shaykh and Effendi*, pp. 95–96; J. Lamphear, "Aspects of Turkana Leadership during the Era of Primary Resistance," *JAfrHist* 17 (1976) 226; and Wagner, "Political Organization," p. 224.

sometimes of their own volition, sometimes at the insistence of family and relatives. The choice usually reflects the socio-political implications of the dispute. For example, the head of a family or local lineage will often mediate disputes between two members of his lineage; the matter does not concern anyone else. If there is greater "social distance" between the disputants, leaders of their respective lineages might oversee its resolution. Or, if the parties involved recognize a common ancestor in their history, then a direct descendant of that ancestor who is a man of respect might be asked to resolve the situation (most often as a mediator or arbitrator).[54] In some cases, certain lineages within the broader society are recognized as "significant" in some way, and respected members of that lineage can be called upon to adjudicate.[55] A fairly common practice among Arab tribesmen is to look to priestly (or cultically significant) lineages to mediate/adjudicate matters, when they are thought to concern some religious aspect of community life.[56] It is also common for disputants to turn to state-

---

[54] However, in general, the more distant the blood-ties, the less likely it is that there will be a sense that resolution is needed. See Abrahams, "Neighbourhood Organization," pp. 177–78; Ahmed, *Social and Economic Change*, pp. 126, 139–40; Buxton, *Chiefs and Strangers*, p. 118; B. Chem-Langhie, "Southern Cameroon House of Chiefs," *IntJAfrHist* 16 (1983) 655; Cole, *Nomads of the Nomads*, pp. 86–87; F. M. Deng, *The Dinka of the Sudan* (New York: Holt, Rinehart and Winston, 1972), p. 111; Eades, *Yoruba Today*, pp. 113–20; Holy, *Neighbours and Kinsmen*, pp. 109, 132; G. I. Jones, "Councils," p. 78; Klima, *Barabaig*, pp. 83–84; A. Kuper, "Kgalagari Lekgota," pp. 84–94; Lewis, *Murle*, pp. 43–44, 72–76; Mair, *African Societies*, pp. 34, 143, 171–77; Moore, "Descent and Lineage Position," pp. 394–95; Nadel, *Nuba*, pp. 254, 458–59; Richards, "Conciliar System," pp. 100–11; Schapera, "Law and Justice," p. 198; Teitelbaum, "Old Age," pp. 42–43, 51; and Tymowski, "Evolution," pp. 189–90.

[55] E.g., shaykhly lineages in some Middle Eastern societies (Dresch, "Positions of *shaykhs*," p. 36; Fernea, *Shaykh and Effendi*, pp. 146–47), and the "dominant" lineages and "leopard-skin chiefs" among the Nuer (E. E. Evans-Pritchard, *Kinship and Marriage Among the Nuer* [Oxford: Clarendon, 1951], pp. 16–23; Beidelman, "Nuer Priests and Prophets," pp. 383–84, 409). See also Abrahams, *Political Organization*, pp. 65, 101; D. S. Jones, "Traditional Authority and State Administration in Botswana," *JModAfrStud* 21,1 (1983) 133–39; Mitchell, *Yao Village*, pp. 55–57; Read, *Ngoni*, pp. 19–21, 88–91; Winans, *Shambala*, pp. 103–104.

[56] See Amanolahi-Baharvand, "Baharvand," pp. 122–23; P. Bourdieu, "The Sentiment of Honour in Kabyle Society," in *Honour and Shame: The Values of Mediterranean Society*, ed. J. G. Peristiany (Chicago: University of Chicago, 1966), p. 201; Gellner, *Saints*, pp. 78, 125–28; R. McC. Netting,

appointed officials as mediators/adjudicators, even in cases which are not explicitly placed under their jurisdiction, and even when those appointments are not technically judicial in nature. However, one must be careful not to assume too much in this. The appeal by disputants to such an official to serve a judicial function is often just that—an appeal. It is done not because it is so mandated by the state, but because the local community sees it as beneficial.[57] The functions of adjudicators, therefore, cannot be viewed in isolation from their general social position. In some situations, agnates are preferred as adjudicators; in others, more "neutral" individuals are preferred.[58]

It is for reasons such as these that one often finds in newly-formed states that traditional leaders are given judicial appointments within the state bureaucracy. To appoint a complete stranger can result in ineffectiveness or local turmoil and discontent. The effect of appointing traditional leaders is that they adjudicate the kinds of matters which they had been adjudicating

---

"Sacred Power and Centralization: Aspects of Political Adaptation in Africa," in *Population Growth: Anthropological Implications*, ed. B. J. Spooner (Cambridge, MA: MIT Press, 1972), pp. 220–33; Peters, "Structural Aspects," p. 281; and A. Tuden, "Leadership and the Decision-Making Process," in *Political Anthropology*, ed. M. J. Swartz et al. (Chicago: Aldine, 1966), pp. 278–82. Cp. n. 53, above.

[57] See Abrahams, *Political Organization*, p. 166; Buxton, *Chiefs and Strangers*, pp. 130–31; Fernea, *Shaykh and Effendi*, pp. 68–69, 121–23, 143, 150–53; G. I. Jones, "Councils," pp. 72–73; Musil, *Manners and Customs*, p. 437; Nadel, *Nuba*, pp. 159–60; Noland, "Dispute Settlement," pp. 195–98; and van Velzen, *Politics of Kinship*, p. 309.

Audrey Richards ("Conciliar System," p. 110) describes the advantage to the Bemba of having outside arbitrators to prevent hostilities between agnates. In fact, she herself was once asked to serve in this capacity, due to her "foreign" status. Cp. A. Kuper, "Kgalagari Lekgota," p. 95. J. G. Peristiany ("Honour and Shame in a Cypriot Highland Village," in *Honour and Shame: The Values of Mediterranean Society*, ed. J. G. Peristiany [Chicago: Chicago University, 1966], p. 178) comments that Cypriot villagers who have traveled extensively are asked to negotiate with extra-village authorities, even if they have no leadership status.

[58] See Ahmed, pp. 26–27, 48–50; L. Bohannan, "Political Aspects," pp. 53–54; Bourdieu, "Sentiment of Honour," p. 237; Cole, *Nomads*, pp. 96–100; Dresch, "Positions of shaykhs," p. 37; Evans-Pritchard, *Nuer*, p. 6; Fernea, *Shaykh and Effendi*, pp. 68–69; A. Kuper, "Kgalagari Lekgota," pp. 95–96; Lindholm, "Kinship Structure," p. 351; Richards, "Conciliar System," pp. 110–12; Tuden, "Leadership," p. 282; van Velzen, *Politics of Kinship*, p. 309; and Winter, "Aboriginal Political Structure," pp. 160–61.

prior to the state's emergence, only now their political status in the society has been altered (sometimes positively, sometimes negatively) by their association with the central authority.[59]

Goals of Adjudication

These expectations placed on traditional adjudicators are more fully comprehended when one perceives how the concept of law in "traditional" societies differs from that in our own Western culture. Ethnographers and legal anthropologists often comment on these differences in explaining processes of adjudication in kinship-based communities. Central to these differences is the assumed goal of adjudication.

Western law is based on formal legislation and the concept of "universal-impersonal application of statutes."[60] It requires a centrally-organized legislative system to delineate crimes and offenses—conceived of according to abstract principles of "right" and "wrong"—and their appropriate punishments. Through that system, the central authority assumes ultimate responsibility for regulating interpersonal relationships, and through a separate

---

[59] See Abélès, "In Search," p. 61; Amanolahi-Baharvand, "Baharvand," pp. 215, 221–23; T. O. Beidelman, "Chiefship in Ukaguru: The Invention of Ethnicity and Tradition in Kaguru Colonial History," *IntJAfrHis* 11 (1978) 244; Fernea, *Shaykh and Effendi*, pp. 136–40; D. H. Johnson, "Tribal Boundaries and Border Wars: Nuer-Dinka Relations in the Sobat and Zaref Valleys, c. 1860–1976," *JAfrHist* 23 (1982) 202; D. S. Jones, "Traditional Authority," pp. 133–34; Lamphear, "Aspects," p. 239; Mair, *African Societies*, pp. 146–48, 154; Musil, *Manners and Customs*, p. 427; Nadel, *Nuba*, pp. 167, 471–72; Richards, "Conciliar System," p. 126.

Sometimes, those individuals' responsibilities are expanded by the state, but the effectiveness of such an expansion will vary from society to society and from town to town for a combination of reasons unique to each. Among the Buganda of Uganda, the power of the traditional king (Kabaka) was enhanced by European colonizers at the expense of the powers of local clan leaders. L. Fallers, *The King's Men: Leadership and Status in Buganda on the Eve of Independence* (London: Oxford University, 1964), pp. 71–72; cp. Tosh, *Clan Leaders*, pp. 128–40; A. Kuper, "Kgalagari Lekgota," p. 80.

In other cases, powers were shifted from traditional "chiefs" to state appointees. For example, traditional Mande chiefs lost much of their power to "commoners" who received state appointments. This did not, however, reduce the traditional powers of local elders (Tymowski, "Evolution," pp. 190–91). Cp. G. I. Jones, "Councils," p. 74; MacGaffey, *Religion and Society*, p. 17; Mitchell, *Yao Village*, p. 38; Teitelbaum, "Old Age," pp. 41–45.

[60] For this phrase, see Newman, *Law and Economic Organization*, p. 12.

system, ultimate control of institutional mechanisms for enforcing that legislation. Ideally, each citizen is seen as "equal in the eyes of the law;" each has "rights," upon which others are not to infringe; and each is culpable for their own commission of wrongs. There are carefully delineated areas of jurisdiction and levels of appeal. The goal of law is to insure, as much as possible, that "right" is upheld and "wrong" is punished equitably.[61]

"Law" is a more flexible concept in most traditional, kinship-based societies.[62] The traditional "jural community" has the same institutional structure as the traditional political community; persons with political power and authority possess parallel judicial power and authority. This might be restricted to a single settlement, but is more likely to be regional. Laws are most often formulated, such as they are, by adjudicators who are also the political authorities. They are "binding" primarily on the basis of the "moral authority" of the person pronouncing them. Disputes of all sorts, of all degrees of significance, are resolved by local and regional adjudicators. The levels between them are often blurred, as disputants may choose to avoid the local adjudicative body and go directly to a regional chief or shaykh with their dispute. Conversely, a regional chief may step into a local dispute and resolve it before the local adjudicators have had an opportunity to deliberate over it.[63]

---

[61] See the essays in Laura Nader, ed., *Law in Culture and Society* (Chicago: Aldine Publ. Co., 1969). Particularly helpful are P. H. Gulliver ("Case Studies of Law in Non-Western Societies: Introduction," pp. 11–23), Sally Falk Moore ("Comparative Studies," pp. 337–47), Max Gluckman ("Concepts in the Comparative Study of Law," pp. 349–73), and Paul Bohannan ("Ethnography and Comparison in Legal Anthropology," pp. 401–18), and the "Bibliography" (pp. 419–37). See also Newman, *Law and Economic Organization*, esp. pp. 1–45, 99–103; A. R. Radcliffe-Brown, "Primitive Law," *Encyclopaedia of the Social Sciences*, Vol. IX (New York: Macmillan Co., 1933), pp. 202–206; and Tait, "Territorial Pattern," p. 187.

[62] Again, there is some debate among sociologists over terminology. The "law" of traditional peoples is most commonly termed "tribal law," "customary law," "primitive law," or "dispute settlement." The fact that matters obviously requiring adjudication (e.g., murder between members of rival families) and seemingly minor disagreements (e.g., over obligations to share farming utensils) are handled in similar ways and by the same persons reflects the difficulty involved in defining "law" in such societies.

[63] See Abrahams, *Political Organization*, pp. 166–67; L. Bohannan, "Political Aspects," pp. 57–58; Dresch, "Positions of *shaykhs*," p. 40; Mitchell,

Situations requiring judgment are conceived of primarily as group conflicts, rather than individual conflicts. While these conflicts technically might involve only two individuals, they are often dealt with as conflicts between two corporate groups (families, lineages, neighborhoods). These groups are seen as sharing a certain relationship, but particular individuals in those groups have acted toward one another in a way which is inconsistent with "acceptable behavior" between persons in such a relationship, thus threatening to undo the relationship between the entire groups. For this reason, one finds that "adjudication" in such societies usually takes on some form of mediation or arbitration. "Litigation... is designed more to reconcile the adversaries than it is to find a right and wrong side. Unless people succeed in this, the conflict is not adequately resolved."[64] "The paramount aim of [legal] proceedings is the restoration of breaches of solidarity. To put it briefly, when one man commits a wrong against another, what concerns the village is not so much the wrong itself as the ill-feelings which it has generated between the parties involved. Thus the principal goal is the restoration of good relations between the men concerned, rather than the administration of justice in some abstract sense."[65] One often

---

Yao Village, pp. 56–57; Richards, "Conciliar System," pp. 110–14; van Velzen, *Politics*, p. 311; and Winans, *Shambala*, p. 104.

The decision over whether to bring a matter before an adjudicative body for resolution is usually left up to the offended party and his/her close relatives in a decentralized society. As a polity becomes more centralized, the more likely it will be that the central powers will assume authority over making that decision.

[64] Deng, *Dinka*, p. 113.

[65] Winter, "Aboriginal Political Structure," pp. 145–46.

Many researchers echo these observations. For some summarizing analyses, see the remarks of Audrey Richards ("Introduction: The Nature of the Problem," pp. 1–12) and A. Kuper ("Introduction," pp. 13–26) in *Councils in Action* (Cambridge: Cambridge University, 1971). For some specific examples, see Abrahams, "Neighbourhood Organization," pp. 178–79; Bascom, *Yoruba*, pp. 39–40; Cunnison, *Baggara Arabs*, pp. 154–55, 179–85; Dennis, *Gbandes*, p. 271; Dyson-Hudson, *Karimojong Politics*, p. 230; Evans-Pritchard, *Nuer*, pp. 162–72; Fernea, *Shaykh and Effendi*, pp. 96–98, 145–47; Holy, *Neighbours and Kinsmen*, pp. 120–28; G. I. Jones, "Councils," pp. 70–74; Klima, *Barabaig*, pp. 83–85; A. Kuper, "Kgalagari Lekgota," pp. 93–97; Mitchell, *Yao Village*, pp. 54–55; Mair, *African Societies*, p. 144; Moore, "Descent and Legal Position," pp. 392–99; Musil, *Manners and Customs*, pp. 426–35; Nadel, *Nuba*, pp. 159–62, 499–500; Noland, "Dispute

reads about "consensus" or "compromise" in judicial contexts in these traditional societies, and rarely about anyone "winning" or "losing" a case. There is generally no appeal system. Instead, "higher courts" exist mostly (a) to resolve conflicts that are left unresolved at the more local level and (b) to resolve disputes between large or geographically dispersed groups.[66] Thus, the goal of "law" is essentially to maintain or reestablish peaceful relations between interacting groups.[67]

This goal is most often achieved through what amounts to negotiations between the leaders of the respective groups. It can also be achieved by an authoritative mandate rendered by a commonly-recognized leader (father, headman, judge, chief, king) or group of leaders (elders, court).[68] Typically, official executors of a decision (police) are absent; so, popular acceptance of the resolution is critical to its enforcement. The one found to be in the wrong complies with the decision because his group insists upon it, and he depends on his group for his own livelihood.[69] Punishments and fines are supposed to reflect traditional standards, necessitating the participation of old men or veteran judges who can declare a "fair" penalty. They appeal to

---

Settlement," pp. 190–202; Peristiany, "Law," pp. 39–49; Read, *Ngoni*, pp. 92–96; Richards, "Conciliar System," pp. 103, 110; Schapera, "Law and Justice," p. 215; Spencer, *Samburu*, pp. 176–77; Tuden, "Leadership," p. 277; van Velzen, *Politics of Kinship*, pp. 308–309; and Zeid, "Honour and Shame," p. 249.

[66] See Abrahams, *Political Organization*, p. 100; Bascom, *Yoruba*, pp. 38–39; Bourdieu, "Sentiment of Honour," pp. 236–37; Buxton, *Chiefs and Strangers*, p. 128; Cole, *Nomads*, pp. 86–87; Holy, *Neighbours and Kinsmen*, pp. 109, 123–29; Khuri, *Tribe and State*, p. 35; H. Kuper, *Swazi*, p. 36; Lewis, *Murle*, p. 76; Read, *Ngoni*, pp. 94–95; Schapera, "Political Institutions," p. 185; Verdier, "Ontology," pp. 143–44; and Winans, *Shambala*, pp. 115–16.

[67] Of course, it is possible that the groups do not care to reconcile. But this will have many socio-political consequences (regarding, for example, inter-marriages, trade, cooperation in war) which must be considered at the group level. Jdgs 21:1–15 provides an example of the potential strength of these sentiments in ancient Israel.

[68] Nadel (*Nuba*, pp. 159–62) describes a shift from one to the other in some Nuba tribes, but the effect of both mechanisms of resolution is essentially the same.

[69] See n. 65, above. Abrahams ("Neighbourhood Organizations," p. 182), like others, talks about the importance given to "reintegrating the offender into his community."

precedents,[70] but only as examples of what the society considers appropriate and fair; they do not render a specific verdict because some precedent or written statute "demands" it.[71] Further, certain misdeeds constitute sacral offenses which will incur the anger of ancestral spirits or divine beings who can bring harm on the entire group(s). As mentioned earlier, those cases require the participation of persons with the closest ties to the spiritual realm (elders, chiefs, priests, rainmakers, *marabouts*, etc.).

Personal Characteristics of Traditional Adjudicators
In this light, one can understand why traditional adjudicators (elders, headmen, chiefs, shaykhs) from a wide variety of locales are found to possess fairly similar characteristics. I have distilled these into four:[72]

---

[70] See Amanolahi-Baharvand, "Baharvand," pp. 139–40; Cunnison, *Baggara Arabs*, p. 158; A. Kuper, "Kgalagari Lekgota," p. 93; H. Kuper, *Swazi*, p. 38; Lewis, *Murle*, pp. 71–79; Richards, "Introduction," pp. 8–9; Schapera, "Law and Justice," pp. 197–98; Verdier, "Ontology," p. 145; and Winans, *Shambala*, p. 130.

"Standards" can fluctuate due to the relative socio-economic situations of the parties involved. I mean by this that punishments and fines are imposed with a certain goal in mind. What is required to achieve that goal depends on what is available to the parties involved. This, in turn, depends on whether the person being punished or fined can look to other members of his group for help.

See also the comments of B. S. Jackson, "Ideas of Law and Legal Administration: A Semiotic Approach," in *The World of Ancient Israel*, ed. R. E. Clements (Cambridge: Cambridge University, 1989), pp. 185–88.

[71] In my opinion, this is the reason why biblical laws are cited so rarely in other biblical texts (compare the situation in Mesopotamia and Hatti). The individual statutes were not conceived of as universal truths in and of themselves. Rather, they were simply exemplary manifestations of a principle of "fairness" which made sense in their cultural setting. For example, are we to assume that a bride-price must never change from fifty shekels (Deut 22:28–29), in spite of fluctuations in the value of the shekel? And would it have to be the same for every bride, regardless of the economic status of her family and the groom's family?

[72] See Ahmed, *Social and Economic Change*, p. 47; Amanolahi-Baharvand, "Baharvand," pp. 133, 223–26; Buxton, *Chiefs and Strangers*, p. 126; Cole, *Nomads of the Nomads*, pp. 96–98; Deng, *Dinka*, pp. 113–14; Dennis, *Gbandes*, pp. 254, 265–66; Evans-Pritchard, *Nuer*, pp. 179–80; Fernea, *Shaykh and Effendi*, pp. 133–36; Garthwaite, *Khans and Shahs*, p. 45; K. Gough, "Nuer Kinship: A Re-Examination," in *The Translation of Culture*, ed.

(1) Adjudicators tend to be **senior members of important families** in their communities. They wield authority firstly in their immediate family or lineage, and consequently in the broader community and society. Persons with knowledge acquired through many years of business transactions, past legal decisions, and community customs are preferred in most disputes[73] and absolutely necessary in the local disputes. Such knowledge often takes the place of written records (for example, regarding the financial details of marriage arrangements), and it directly influences their ability to negotiate or judge in a manner which can be regarded as reasonable and fair by those involved.

(2) Adjudicators tend to be individuals who are **wealthy, but generous**. Their wealth—represented in family size as well as possessions—demonstrates their wisdom and, often, their good standing in the eyes of ancestral spirits or divine beings. It probably reflects the existence of significant economic ties with various portions of the community, ties upon which adjudicators might call in enforcing their decision. Moreover, they are generally known for their generosity, because generosity demonstrates their concern for the welfare of the community as a whole. This spills over into hospitality toward outsiders, a quality which reflects their appreciation of the long-distance ties of the community.

(3) Adjudicators are commonly admired and praised for their **oratorical skills**. Adjudicators most often serve as peacemakers. Peacemaking requires wisdom, to be sure, but also the ability to persuade. Using their extensive knowledge of the community's history and customs, they are expected to render a balanced resolution which demonstrates again that they have the interests of the entire community—not just the individuals—at heart.

T. O. Beidelman (London: Tavistock, 1971), p. 118; Holy, *Neighbours and Kinsmen*, pp. 116–20, 151; Johnson, "Tribal Boundaries," p. 189; H. Kuper, *Swazi*, p. 35; Musil, *Manners and Customs*, pp. 471–72; Schapera, "Political Institutions," pp. 177–79; Teitelbaum, "Old Age," pp. 49–50; Tuden, "Leadership," p. 276; Wagner, "Political Organization," pp. 230–35; and Zeid, "Honour and Shame," p. 250.

[73] Sometimes, disputants prefer an "outsider" who is not influenced by past dealings between them, or who has no personal interest in the case. See nn. 47, 57, 58, above.

(4) Indigenous adjudicators possess **exemplary moral and ethical characteristics** for their society.[74] This is only to be expected. Unlike centrally-appointed judges whose authority derives from the central authority, the authority of indigenous leaders is derived from the respect they naturally command from those around them. This respect is based on their ability to exemplify what is "good" and "right" in their society.[75]

Ancient Near Eastern Judicial Systems

There is much that one might address regarding ancient Near Eastern judicial practices and institutions in connection with the biblical D Code. I will consider in the succeeding chapters various writings which touch directly on one's interpretation of the elders-laws of the D Code. Presently, we are interested in only two questions: What does the evidence from other ancient Near Eastern societies reveal to be "typical" in the way of judicial personnel and structures? and, How do ancient Near Eastern conceptions of law compare with those of traditional, kinship-based cultures, as outlined above? I will deal with each of these broad questions separately, even though they overlap in some ways. I have arranged my survey of the evidence chronologically, separating between law codes and legal/judicial documents.

Judicial Personnel and Structures

The greatest amount of evidence regarding ancient Near Eastern judiciaries comes to us from Mesopotamian and Hittite sources. In addition to law codes, there are numerous legal and administrative documents from these societies, spanning two millennia, which contribute to our basic understanding of judicial practices. That understanding has changed significantly in the past generation, due in large part to greater sophistication in archaeological and ethnological assumptions.

---

[74] While traditional peoples would prefer this of judges imposed on them by a central government, it is not always expected, as they sometimes are looking only for impartiality in such officials. See above, on "neutral" judges.

[75] See Dresch, "Positions of *shaykhs*," p. 41; D. S. Jones, "Traditional Authority," pp. 134, 138; Schapera, "Political Institutions," pp. 187–88; Teitelbaum, "Old Age," pp. 49–54; van Velzen, *Politics*, pp. 309–11.

> The traditional structural approach treated Mesopotamian complex societies as homogeneous, highly centralized entities whose urbanized governing institutions defined and controlled virtually every aspect of economic, political, and social life... [Researchers] tended to view the cuneiform archives of these centralized institutions as complete and representative records of the full range of activities, institutions, and interest groups in Mesopotamian society...
>
> However, although these [cuneiform] documents provide highly detailed information about the administrative workings of temples and palaces, they tell us very little about the overall organization of Mesopotamian society...
>
> The villagers, nomads, independent craft specialists, and other urban commoners... are almost invisible in the cuneiform documents. These latter groups emerge only through archaeological research...[76]

This would suggest that analogies to local adjudication in ancient Israel might not be forthcoming from these written materials. However, this is not the case. The evidence for local practices and institutions is not as extensive as it is for centralized, urban affairs, yet there is enough available to discern some significant details.

Law Codes. Mesopotamian and Hittite law codes are relatively silent regarding who is to adjudicate in a given case. For example, there are approximately eight hundred laws in one of the most recent translations of these codes,[77] yet only about forty (approximately 5%) specify who is to adjudicate. Many of the laws use the passive voice to describe how an offense is to be proved and the guilty party punished. Several laws refer to participants other than the disputants by the impersonal "they."[78] One cannot be certain whether "they" are centrally-appointed functionaries or local persons. This is true across the geographical and temporal

[76] G. Stein, "The Organizational Dynamics of Complexity in Greater Mesopotamia," in *Chiefdoms and Early States in the Near East: The Organizational Dynamics of Complexity*, ed. G. Stein and M. S. Rothman (Monographs in World Archaeology No. 18; Madison, WI: Prehistory Press, 1994), pp. 11–12, 14.

[77] M. T. Roth, *Law Collections from Mesopotamia and Asia Minor* (SBL Writings from the Ancient World Series, 6; Atlanta, GA: Scholars Press, 1995). Abbreviations for law codes are taken from this work.

[78] The D Code is comparable in this regard. Fewer than ten laws there specify the adjudicator(s).

spectra of the codes. Thus, conclusions drawn from these sources are somewhat tendentious.

The most commonly-mentioned adjudicators in the law codes are "judges" (Sum. *dikudde*, Bab./Ass. *dayyanu*) and the king. This is not surprising, considering the fact that the codes are almost certainly generated from palaces. In the Sumerian code of Lipit-Ishtar, "judges" confirm a contract between a craftsman and his apprentice (LL ¶20b), and they can try to restrict a young man from an adulterous relationship (LL ¶30).[79] Old Babylonian law calls for "judges" to decide cases of manslaughter, while more heinous murder cases are heard by the king (LE ¶48). Charges of theft against a centrally-appointed official are to be adjudicated by "the palace" (LE ¶50). Similarly, Hammurabi calls for the fining and removal from office of any "judge" who reverses his own decision (LH ¶5). Parallel claims for ownership to a piece of property are to be examined by "judges" and sworn "before the god" (LH ¶¶9–13). One who accuses falsely is to be flogged "before the judges" (LH ¶127). Some cases involving the legal separation of a person from his/her family (or their incorporation into a new family) are overseen by "judges" (LH ¶168–169, 172, 177; cp. LNB ¶12).

Middle Assyrian law codes reveal similar arrangements in that system. A husband could bring charges against his wife's paramour "before the king or the judges" (MAL A ¶15). Charges against a prostitute are to be brought "to the palace entrance" (MAL A¶40). A destitute soldier's wife is to bring her plea for assistance "before the judges" (MAL A ¶45). Judges are to certify in writing when property has been sold to one outside the family which owned it previously (MAL B ¶6), and judges verify that certain men have refused to cooperate with others in the irrigation of their adjoining fields (MAL B ¶17–18; O ¶5).[80]

---

[79] Admittedly, the "judges" are not functioning in an obviously adjudicative capacity in this law. They are, in fact, giving a "preemptive" ruling, trying to avert a later civil suit, when the man would be held financially responsible for his wife. This reaffirms what we said earlier about the "flexibility" of categories and functions—from a Western point of view—which one often finds in traditional societies.

[80] There are other laws which refer to "judges," but the texts are too badly damaged to ascertain precisely what they do. See MAL C ¶8; E ¶1; L ¶4.

The Hittite laws contain but a single reference to a "magistrate," stating that those rejecting his decision shall be beheaded (HL ¶173a; cp. ¶49?). By comparison, anyone rejecting the king's verdict will have his entire house destroyed (HL ¶173a). Several other matters are to be decided "in the king's court" or "by the king." These primarily involve cases of sorcery (HL ¶¶44b, 111; TelEd ¶50), adultery (HL ¶198), or bestiality (HL ¶¶187, 188, 199, 200a).[81] One important aspect of this not encountered in Mesopotamian laws is the sacral nature of the king's person. While he pronounces judgment on sorcerers and those guilty of bestiality, they are not to appear in his presence. The severity of the punishment for rejecting a royal verdict probably reflects the same conceptual basis.

It seems clear that the "judges" in these various law codes are officials appointed by the central government. The Babylonian king is responsible for reviewing the conduct of judges (LH ¶5). Assyrian judges are supposed to impose judgment on a thief according to standards set by the king (MAL C ¶8). Compliance to the decisions of Hittite "magistrates" and kings is mandated in the same law (HL ¶173a). Also, it is expected that Assyrian judges will have to consult with a town's "mayor and noblemen" (*khazianu rabiute sha ale*) to ascertain current property values in their town, suggesting that the judge is an outsider to the town (MAL A ¶45; cp. B ¶¶6, 17–18; O ¶5).

This raises the issue of the nature of the relationship between centrally-appointed "judges" and local leaders in matters of adjudication, remembering that these law codes were written from the viewpoint of the central authority. The most common situations are those in which "judges" are to look to local "witnesses" (*shibutu*) to provide or verify information (LH ¶¶9–13, z; 122–123; HL ¶71; cp. HL ¶45). Assyrian law requires one to "secure witnesses" regarding a prostitute when pressing charges against her (MAL A ¶40).

This term for "witnesses" is also the term for "elders," which causes some occasional problems for translators (see the alternation between the two in HL ¶XXXV [= ¶¶45 + 71] and

---

[81] I do not understand the significance of HL ¶176a: "If anyone keeps a bull outside a corral, it shall be a case for the king's court."

¶71).[82] But it might also reflect something significant about these witnesses. It is possible that such witnesses were elders in their community. We have already pointed out that community elders in contemporary kinship-based societies are commonly expected to vouch for important business transactions in their community (e.g., marriage agreements and land transactions). It is plausible to conclude that this practice was also true for ancient Mesopotamia, even after written records had become commonplace. On the other hand, LH ¶¶9–13 envisions a situation in which there are "witnesses" for both sides to competing claims to property. If these "witnesses" are "elders" in a typical kinship-based community, one would not expect there to be two groups of elders who have completely separate (and apparently contradictory) knowledge of local business matters. Perhaps this is an urban setting, with distinct wards; or perhaps the parties involved come from different villages; or perhaps these are not community elders at all, but merely family or neighborhood associates of the disputants. Thus, it could be that the term "witnesses" (*shibutu*) is a relic of an earlier stage in the society's development, when the "witnesses" were usually local elders.[83]

Other officials are mentioned more rarely in the laws. Matters involving an absence of evidence (e.g., when property is lost and no invoice exists) are to be brought "before the god" (LH ¶¶120, 126, 131, 240), apparently inferring consultation with a priest. Where one should go to approach "the god" is never specified. The

---

[82] H. Klengel, "Zu den *shibutum* in altbabylonischer Zeit," *Or* n.s. 29 (1960) 358–59.

[83] LH ¶122 calls for witnesses and a written contract to be drawn up, but then either will suffice to verify the agreement (LH ¶123). Why is there a need for both? What role do the witnesses really play? Some records have more than a dozen witnesses (see below). Why so many? Are they confirming the reality of a transaction, or are they serving as guarantors on behalf of the parties involved? What does the existence of competing witnesses (LH ¶¶9–13) indicate about inter-group dynamics in a local community? For some discussion of these questions, see I. J. Gelb, "*SHIBUT KUSHURRA'IM*, 'Witnesses of the Indemnity,'" *JNES* 43 (1984) 263–74.

A more thorough investigation of this question is needed. In contemporary societies, the effect of having elders serve as witnesses is that they inhibit subsequent bickering between the extended families of the parties involved. In other words, should an argument arise later based on how someone has violated a previous agreement, the elders can step in to settle the argument.

"judges" consult with a "city and its governor" (*alum u rabianum*; LH ¶¶23–24)[84] or a town's "mayor and noblemen" (MAL A ¶45) regarding business in their community. But these individuals do not participate in adjudication in these laws. However, when an "outsider" to a family buys that family's field, the "mayor and three noblemen of the city" are to stand opposite various royal officials in certifying the legality of the purchase (MAL B ¶6). The same local leaders apparently carry out the sentence imposed by judges against one who will not cooperate in joint irrigation works (MAL B ¶¶17–18). One cannot conclude from this, however, that local officials only functioned as local representatives of the centrally-appointed judges. These laws are generated by central authorities, and so it is not surprising that they mention only those situations in which central authorities are involved. There could be many situations which are not brought up in these law codes because they would never come before the central authorities.

Other Sources. Our picture comes into better focus when we turn from the law codes to other legal and judicial records from the same regions. Most of these consist of legal records of fines imposed and/or paid, business transactions, and legal agreements and dispute settlements between members of one or two communities. The most striking distinction one finds between these and the law codes in regard to officiants is that judiciary appointees of the central government ("judges") are rarely mentioned, while local leaders ("elders," "mayor") are often mentioned.[85]

Mesopotamian records from the late third and early second millennia show that most local business, including legal matters,

---

[84] On the *rabianum*, see G. Evans, "Ancient Mesopotamian Assemblies—an addendum," *JAOS* 78 (1958) 114, n. 6.

[85] There was some discussion a few years ago regarding local Mesopotamian assemblies based on an episode from the Gilgamesh Epic, but I am skeptical about the usefulness of this example in the present investigation. This episode is an example of a conceptualization of ancient practices which might be based on an accurate recollection of ancient practices, or on current local practices, or on the practices of current royal councils. See comments and notes in Jacobsen, "Primitive Democracy," pp. 159–72; Evans, "Ancient Mesopotamian Assemblies," pp. 1–11; and A. Malamat, "Kingship and Council in Israel and Sumer: A Parallel," *JNES* 22 (1963) 247–53.

was conducted by local elders and/or the town's *khazannu* or *rabianu*. They adjudicated local disputes, served as witnesses to business transactions (esp. those involving land), and acted as representatives for their community directly to the king.[86] Documents of the mid–second millennium from Nuzi[87], Mari[88], Emar[89], and the Hittite capital[90] suggest similar practices in those cities. Town elders sometimes adjudicate disputes by themselves, sometimes in cooperation with local leaders or with government appointees.[91]

These documents also show some of the ambiguity involved in interpreting *shibutu* (or *SHU.GI*) as "elders" or "witnesses." Jankowska's careful study of Nuzi records shows that family and friends typically served as "witnesses" to contracts.[92] Whether these were also senior members (i.e., "elders") of their families is not known. At Emar, there are eighteen documents attesting to

---

[86] Klengel, "Zu den *shibutum*," pp. 357–75; I. M. Diakonoff, "Extended Families in Babylonian Ur," *ZA* 75 (1985) 50–54. The term *mashkim* is used for the local leader in Sumerian and Hittite documents. For the latter, see H. Klengel, "Die Rolle der 'Ältesten" (LU^MESH SHU.GI) im Kleinasien der Hethiterzeit," *ZA* 57 (1965) 231. More generally, see Jacobsen, "Primitive Democracy," pp. 162–65.

[87] N. B. Jankowska, "Life of the Military Élite in Arrapha," in *Studies on the Civilization and Culture of Nuzi and the Hurrians*, ed. M. A. Morrison and D. I. Owen (E. R. Lachemann FS; Winona Lake, IN: Eisenbrauns, 1981), pp. 195–200; idem, "Extended Family Commune and Civil Self-Government in Arrapha in the Fifteenth–Fourteenth Century B.C.," in *Ancient Mesopotamia: Socio-Economic History* (Moscow: Nauka Publishing House, 1969; Schaan: H. R. Wohlwend, 1981), pp. 236–38.

[88] J.-R. Kupper, "La cité et la royaume de Mari: l'organisation urbaine à l'époque amorite," *MARI* 4 (1985) 463–64; V. H. Matthews, *Pastoral Nomadism in the Mari Kingdom (ca. 1830–1760 B.C.)* (ASOR Diss. Series 3; Cambridge, MA: ASOR, 1978), pp. 6, 37, 153–56.

[89] D. Arnaud, *Emar VI: Tome 3, Textes sumériens et accadiens: Texte* (Paris, 1986), ¶¶1–4, 6, 9, 11, 12, 93, 126, 139, 144, 146–148, 150–153, 181, 205, 215, 369; D. E. Fleming, *The Installation of Baal's High Priestess at Emar: A Window on Ancient Syrian Religion* (HSM; Atlanta: Scholars Press, 1992), pp. 103–104.

[90] Klengel, "Die Rolle der 'Ältesten'," pp. 223–36.

[91] It is not certain in every case whether these "appointees" are outsiders imposed on the local population or local citizens designated for special responsibilities by the central government. See, for example, discussion of the Mari official, *sugagu* (Kupper, "La cité," p. 463; Matthews, *Pastoral Nomadism*, pp. 139–46), who is mentioned in several cases there.

[92] Jankowska, "Life of the Military Élite," pp. 199–200.

the sale of land[93] or houses by "Ninurta and the elders of the city."[94] The former is almost certainly represented by a priest. The exact concern of the latter in these matters is not known, but it is likely that they somehow represent the city as a political entity.[95] The recorded witnesses in these documents sometimes include a (royal?) scribe and the *khazannu* ("mayor") of the city. In two other texts, the persons who witness to the making of a will are designated as "elders of the city (of Emar)" (*Emar* VI.93, 181; cp. VI.205, 215). In another, two men in a dispute stand "before Mutri-Ishkur and the great men of the city of Emar," each accompanied by "his witnesses" (*Emar* VI.252; cp. VI.255).

Records from Ugarit reveal similar characteristics in that city-state. There are more texts involving royal personnel; but this is not surprising, considering the strongly centralized political situation. For Ugarit itself, there is at least one reference to "the fathers of Ugarit" (*PRU* IV.17.424C);[96] but it is unclear to me whether these are heads of important lineages or senior royal officials.

In the villages of the countryside, there is some evidence of local governance by town elders and/or appointed officials. One text (*Ug.* V.52) reports negotiations between "the elders of [the town of] Rakba" and the central administration of Ugarit (cp. *Ug.* V.168.28). The names of five men—one of them a royal official (*'akil lim*), three from a single extended family—are listed as those elders. It would not be surprising to find similar groups of leaders in other communities in the region. There are several references to *khazannu*, *sakinu* [=*MASHKIM*], and *rabu* as local officials; however, their authority in relation to the central government and the local elders is not altogether clear from the texts I have read.[97]

---

[93] Arnaud reads *ki-ir-tsi-tu₄*, "cabanon," in some of these texts. In private consultation with Prof. John Huehnergard, he suggested the reading $^{ki}er\text{-}tse\text{-}tu_4$, "field." This seems to make better sense.

[94] *Emar* VI.1–4, 6, 9, 11, 12*, 126, 139, 144, 146–148, 150–153.

[95] The previous status of the land in question is most intriguing. Is it "public" land, or land that has been abandoned for some reason, or land that has been set aside specifically for use by temple personnel?

[96] M. Heltzer, *The Rural Community in Ancient Ugarit* (Wiesbaden: Ludwig Reichert, 1976), p. 79.

[97] Heltzer (*Rural Community*, pp. 80–83) briefly discusses each, concluding that all three are centrally-appointed "officials" and "dependents of the king." I would concur in the case of the *sakinu*, because they were supplied from the

There are several legal documents from Ugarit which mention "elders"/"witnesses" involved in business dealings, as we have seen at other cities. In a survey of texts in *PRU* III, *PRU* VI, and *Ug.* V, I found approximately four dozen texts which list one or more "witnesses" (*shibu*) on a document.[98] More than a third of these also contain an introductory formula stating that the agreement being recorded was concluded "before witnesses" (*ana pani shibuti*).[99] In some cases, the name of a scribe alone is given; in others, as many as ten witnesses are listed. The political and personal status of many of these persons is not known, of course. On the other hand, several documents bear the names of a royal scribe and additional palace officials. For example, several are signed by a scribe named "Samassarru the scribe," who apparently served in the palace of Niqmadu. One document bearing the seal of the king lists "Iliyanu the judge, Yarimmu the scribe, and Samassarru the scribe" as witnesses (*PRU* III: RS 16.156).

Again, the significance of serving as a witness is not clarified for us. Witnesses might simply verify that an agreement was reached or a fine was paid or a piece of land changed hands. Or they could be personally and financially obligating themselves to assist a party which acted contrary to the terms agreed to in a

---

palace storehouses. On the other hand, there are only a couple of references to a *rb qrt*, which might simply designate an important citizen of a village (*PRU* V.8.3 reads, "one great of the village"). There are other usages of the term *rb* which merely identify a "chief" or "leading" member of a group. Perhaps this is not an official title at all. As for *khazannu*, the parallels from Mesopotamia suggest that this term could refer to a village headman. Heltzer cites but one text to demonstrate that a village's *khazannu* was a royal official, but the example is somewhat ambiguous. A Hittite official writes to the king of Ugarit, requesting that the king place the welfare of certain traveling Hittites in the hands of the *khazannu* of a particular village. It is impossible to know the political authority of the *khazannu* without first knowing the nature of the political relationship between Ugarit and that village. He could be a locally-appointed official who represents his village to the central authorities.

[98] From *PRU* III: RS 16.129; 16.114; 8.207; 15.37; 15.180; 16.354; 16.359A; 16.180; 16.263; 16.156; 16.143; 16.250; 15.119; 16.245; 15.138 + 16.393B; 16.285.
     PRU VI.37–40, 43, 50–54.
     Ug. V.4–7, 9, 81, 86–88, 159, 161.
[99] *PRU* III: RS 16.245; *PRU* VI.37, 38, 40, 43, 50–53; *Ug.* V. 5–7, 9, 81, 86, 159, 161. See Heltzer, *Rural Community*, pp. 96–100; and A. Rainey, "Family Relations in Ugarit," *Or* 34 (1965) 10–22.

specific settlement. I mentioned in an earlier footnote that the basic effect of having elders in traditional societies bear witness to a business agreement is that they prevent anyone from having a "legitimate" reason for arguing over the results of that agreement. This should be at least one of the functions of witnesses in these ancient cases. We shall see in the coming chapters that maintaining peace locally is a central goal of much of what elders do; so, it would "fit" to find them aiming toward that goal as legal witnesses. Further, the fact that the term *shibutu* is also used to designate "elders" in some texts sustains the possibility that such witnesses were also "elders" in their community or, in the case of palace personnel, senior members of administrative bodies.

One type of information that would be helpful to the present investigation but which is often missing from these texts is the identity of who heard the disputes settled before these witnesses. Fortunately, that information is provided in several documents from the Neo-Assyrian and Neo-Babylonian empires of the first millennium. These reveal a continuation of the basic patterns and institutions for adjudication in Mesopotamia found previously.

Remko Jas has collected together sixty-two cases from the Neo-Assyrian empire.[100] Virtually all list the names of several witnesses. Many of these are "private citizens," but some are local or royal officials. In one case (No. 14), two sets of witnesses are listed, one set apparently siding with the plaintiff, and one set siding with the defendant. Still, the precise nature of their relationships to the disputants is unknown, nor is any sense of their role beyond verification of the sentence imposed.

Of the sixty-two documents included, twenty-nine mention someone who either imposes or negotiates the settlement to the dispute. This adjudicator[101] is most often a *khazannu* (Nos. 4–6, 9, 14, 19, 27), but might be a priest (Nos. 7, 10, 11, 36), *sartinnu* (Nos. 1, 12, 48), *shangu* (Nos. 13, 31), *sukkallu* (Nos. 18, 35, 44), local "commander" (No. 15), *shakin mati* (No. 16), a pair of these aforementioned officials (Nos. 3, 32, 47), or persons known by name only ("Pasi" in No. 8, "the man from the Inner City" in No. 33, and "Akkullanu" in No. 46). Thieves in one case were told to

---

[100] R. Jas, *Neo-Assyrian Judicial Procedures* (SAAS V; Helsinki: Vammalan Kirjapaino Oy, 1996). The text numbers used here are from this book.

[101] Jas is careful to point out that the actual term *dayyanu* is never used to refer to adjudicators in these documents (*Neo-Assyrian*, p. 4).

have their case heard by "the *sukkallu* and the *sartinnu*" in Nineveh, but insisted instead on having the "bodyguards" who had captured them impose a sentence of their own (No. 32). Absent from these documents is any explicit reference to local elders resolving disputes.[102]

Local elders are frequently mentioned, however, in Neo-Babylonian legal documents. They sometimes hear cases by themselves, but they are often joined by a priest, a local governor, or some other religious or political official(s). These elders, who form a sort of popular assembly (*pukhru*), also designate lands and goods which are to be given to the palace, and occasionally serve as emissaries or even advisors to the king.[103]

Our attention has been focused on judicial and legal structures at the local—and often rural—level, but we cannot forget that those structures are part of a broader judicial system. There is ample evidence in these societies of centrally-organized judiciaries, and these local structures are to varying degrees subject to them. Generally, the closer one moves to the center, the more likely one is to find judicial and legal matters restricted to unresolved disputes (LH ¶9), cases directly involving persons serving the central authority (e.g., LH ¶5; MAL A¶45), and situations arising in the capital (e.g., MAL B¶6).[104] There are laws which call for "judges" to adjudicate matters which seem to be local matters, but further study is required to ascertain whether there might be special circumstances involved which would explain why a centrally-appointed adjudicator might be called on to adjudicate.[105]

---

[102] It is possible that elders resolved those cases for which no adjudicator is mentioned, but that is sheer speculation. However, see the following.

[103] Dandamayev, "Neo-Babylonian Elders," pp. 38–41.

[104] When one is dealing with cases arising in a capital, "local" officials and persons of "local" importance often serve in the state bureaucracy as well. This makes it difficult to determine whether certain officials appear in a particular legal text because of their "official" position or for personal reasons. A more careful study of each document is needed to resolve that question.

[105] For example, LH ¶¶168–169, 172, 177 and LNB ¶12 deal with various questions regarding inheritance and dowry, and these matters are to be adjudicated by "judges," whom we have previously identified as royal appointees. The reason for turning to judges, rather than relying on extended family members and local officials, is unclear. It could be that this is a sign

The extent and nature of the king's personal role in the judicial process is unclear, varying from kingdom to kingdom and even from generation to generation. Certain laws call for matters to be brought before the king, but whether this will actually happen apparently depends on circumstances specific to the king or the case.[106] Centrally-appointed judicial officials (as well as political or military officials who occasionally would serve in a judicial capacity) function as representatives of the king, supposedly rendering decisions that are in the best interest of the king and nation. In parallel fashion, priestly officials assist in disputes involving sacral matters and those concerning temple lands and goods.[107] Such patterns are seen as well in traditional African and Middle Eastern societies.

Based, then, on what one finds at the local level in these contemporary societies, it is not surprising to find that, even in the highly-centralized polities of the ancient Near East, local judicial and legal matters are generally handled by community leaders ("elders") and one or more local officials. The latter might be a local person who has been given an official position, or they might be someone from outside the community brought into it by the central government. In either case, their responsibilities and authority complement rather than displace the judicial and legal

---

that the central government was regulating (or seeking to regulate) land transactions. It could also be that such a case would arise only as a dispute between houses (the husband's family and the wife's family) which could not be resolved locally. Such speculation would have to be tested against the evidence of actual cases.

In contrast to these examples, Jas notes that none of the documents which he surveys refers to "judges" (Neo-Assyrian Judicial Procedures, p. 4). This is so, even though several of the Middle Assyrian laws do call for adjudication by "judges." It could be that some references to "judges" reflect a "top-down" perspective on the part of an author, while other documents reflect a "case-specific" perspective.

[106] "Whether or not the king was always himself an active participant in the administration of the legal system, he was always its guardian, for the application of justice was the highest trust given by the gods to a legitimate king." Roth, Law Collections, pp. 4–5. The example of David (2 Sam 15:1–6) typifies these potentialities. People expect David to hear their complaints, but for personal reasons he does not.

[107] See, e.g., Cyr. 281 and 332, cited in Dandamayev, "Neo-Babylonian Elders," p. 38. Albright ("Judicial Reform," pp. 78–79) mentions how priests in Egypt occasionally served as adjudicators.

responsibilities of the traditional, non-appointed adjudicators. Further, it is not surprising to find that a people's most common term for "elders" also appears in many legal documents with the meaning of "witnesses," because witnessing to past business transactions is a common legal function of elders in contemporary traditional societies. Although it is difficult to know from these ancient documents whether this latter usage of the term reflects a current situation (i.e., that witnesses still are elders), or is a relic from an earlier time, it seems likely that one ultimate purpose of these witnesses is to inhibit further hostilities resulting from the dispute at hand. This is also a common adjudicative goal of elders in traditional societies (see following chapters). With these ideas in mind, we turn our attention to the goal of adjudication in ancient Near Eastern societies.

Goals of Adjudication

There are two conceptual aspects of adjudication evidenced in these various texts which should be highlighted: collective responsibility, and adjudication as a means to reconciliation. I demonstrated earlier how these two conceptions commonly exist in contemporary kinship-based societies. That they are present in the thought of these ancient societies is perhaps noted less often, but they appear to have been just as significant back then as they are now.[108]

Collective Responsibility. I have hinted throughout the preceding survey that serving as a witness might be an indicator of collective responsibility, that "witnesses" function for the good of the entire community by thwarting the possibility of future

---

[108] The original scribes would mention them infrequently because, as ones who hold these concepts, they would feel no need to make them explicit. Nevertheless, "basic to our understanding of the relationship of bureaucracy to those informal, personal interests in any period in the Near East is a comprehension of the nature of the informal groups, the waxing and waning of the strength of kinship organizations; the existence, even in the most urbanized setting, of lineage and other ties; the role of custom in the regulation of very large parts of ancient, medieval and modern life, even in situations where civil law is supposed to carry out the same function. The continuing existence of tribal modes of organization alongside of, but usually subordinated to, state institutions, even though not often made explicit in written records, must be assumed in any period." Gibson, "Introduction," p. 3.

disputes that might be raised on the basis of previous ones.[109] This would be a sign that the individuals in a community thought and acted collectively, and probably along kinship lines (whether real or fictive). Such an interpretation is somewhat speculative; however, it is strengthened by other indicators in the documents reviewed that a sense of collective responsibility, often understood as kinship obligations, was held by members of these ancient societies.

These "ancient family values" are espoused in the Prologue of the Lipit-Ishtar law code, for example, when the king boasts, "I made the father support his children, I made the child support his father. I made the father stand by his children, I made the child stand by his father." (LL, Prol. ii 16–20) Diakonoff notes that "the vendors in the OB period, in at least 30% of the cases [which he surveys], appear in groups, and, although their kinship is never mentioned, there can hardly be doubt that they were in fact kinsmen..."[110] Jankowska argues in a similar fashion regarding debt slavery at Nuzi. Slaves brought in from peripheral regions as a result of military conflict apparently had no legal recourse against their masters; but there are several documents demonstrating how native debtor-bondsmen could be aided by kinsmen.[111] The sense of familial corporateness among the people of Ugarit is obvious and pervasive. "Some records list landowners and other citizens with their wives, children, and even cattle,"[112] reflecting their "oneness"—both legally and conceptually—in the minds of those keeping the records.

A good example of collective responsibility from the first millennium is provided by Jas, in his collection of Neo-Assyrian legal documents. No. 41 of that collection (K289 [ADD 618]) contains the pledge of ten men to help a certain Silim-Ilu pay blood money to the family of a man whom Silim-Ilu had killed. The nature of the death is not known, nor is the nature of the

---

[109] Witnesses could have served as "guarantors" for those placed under some financial obligation by a settlement. In that sense, too, collective responsibility is made evident.
[110] Diakonoff, "Extended Families," p. 47.
[111] Jankowska, "Extended Family," pp. 250–51; cp. Dandamayev, "Neo-Babylonian Elders," p. 38.
[112] Rainey, "Family Relationships," pp. 10–12. One could also add "workmen" (cp. Deut 12:12, 18; etc.); see Heltzer, *Rural Community*, pp. 63–65, 85–89.

relationship between the men making this pledge and Silim-Ilu. The fact that they are willing to pledge this money suggests they share a sense of social obligation to one another.[113] In kinship terms, they consider one another to be "brothers" (due either to blood or adoption, to geographical proximity, or to a common profession). This sense of corporateness is typical in kinship-based communities. Additionally, the text goes on to say who might come to the eleven to demand the money—the dead man's wife, brother, son, or someone else. This, too, is typical of kinship-based communities, where compensation for a killing is paid to the victim's family. We will discuss these ideas more fully in the next chapter. For now, it is enough to see that this situation seems most "at home" in a society whose conceptual basis includes a strong sense of family-oriented collective responsibility.

This sense of corporateness is apparently replicated at the village or regional level, as communities function as a unit in dealings with foreign powers or with their own central government. For example, records from Mari reveal how the Jaminites acted as a unit (through a *sugagu* and elders) in making a treaty.[114] Elders representing one or more communities in a region made treaties with the Hittite kings.[115] This is not to imply that an entire town was composed of a single lineage group. Such is not the case in contemporary kinship-based communities, and it is not to be expected in ancient Near Eastern communities. However, it is likely that a very few kin-groups comprised the bulk of the politically influential groups in a community, and that they thought and acted collectively in legal matters.

Adjudication as Reconciliation. Complementing the preceding evidence that kinship obligation was a core concept in one's political and legal identity is the evidence that the resolution of disputes served to forestall subsequent hostilities between the kin-groups of the disputants. One can only see this by inference in most cases (see above, on witnesses), probably (again) because it "goes without saying" in these societies. And I will be demonstrating this in some detail in regard to certain types of cases in subsequent chapters. However, there is at least one set of examples that I will not examine there that clearly demonstrate

---

[113] Jas, *Neo-Assyrian Judicial Procedures*, pp. 64–65.
[114] Klengel, "Zu den *shibutum*," p. 360.
[115] Klengel, "Die Rolle der 'Ältesten'," pp. 226–28.

this point. These are the Neo-Assyrian documents presented by Jas.

It is stated that the main result of the agreements reached in several of these documents is that they bring reconciliation between disputing families. There are three common formulas, which are used in more than one-third of these documents, which reveal this. Sometimes only one formula is used; sometimes two, or even all three. They are: (1) "There is peace between them" [i.e., the disputants]; (2) "They are mutually quit. One will not argue with the other;" and (3) "Whoever contravenes, [certain named deities, or 'the oath of the king']... will call him to account."[116] Such statements suggest that someone other than the disputants might be thinking about perpetuating the dispute that has just been resolved. Such thoughts would most naturally be held by close relatives of the disputants, because their own honor and economic desires would have been tied up in the dispute. These statements would most logically serve as admonitions and warnings to persons who were not satisfied by the resolution given. This says that any hostilities arising from such dissatisfaction would not be justified; the disputants consider the matter "closed," and so should those near them. Such concerns are common—and the necessity for such statements would be most acute—in kinship-based communities, because neighborhood- or community-wide friction is more likely to follow such disputes in that type of society than in any other.

REEVALUATION OF THE JUDICIAL SYSTEM OF THE D CODE

The preceding examinations show that it is very plausible that the D Code presents a redactionally unified judicial system from a single time period, rather than a conflation of two or more systems from variant eras. In other words, one cannot argue that the existence of a multiplicity of judicial functionaries in Deuteronomy ("elders," "judges [and officers]," and "[levitical] priests") is

---

[116] Jas, *Neo-Assyrian Judicial Procedures*, Nos. 9–13, 18–22, 24–27, 31, 33, 47–48. It is possible that these formulas were so common, that the giving of just one would imply the other two.

evidence of a multiplicity of redactional layers.[117] In fact, such a combination of adjudicators has many analogies in contemporary societies, and it is common in the nations of the ancient Near East. It would be more surprising, in my opinion, if one were not to find a multiplicity of judicial offices. The system depicted in the D Code is fairly typical structurally.[118]

One aspect of this topic which I avoided throughout the preceding survey of ancient Near Eastern judiciaries is the process by which adjudicators are appointed. There are two reasons for this: (1) we have very little information from the ancient Near East on processes for choosing adjudicators, and (2) if contemporary societies are any indication of ancient practices, there would be considerable flexibility in this process in any nation. The Mesopotamian evidence suggests that adjudicators other than city elders are appointed by the central government. However, one can still ask whether such appointees were "locals" nominated by the townspeople and approved by the palace, or "outsiders" chosen by the central authorities. The former would have greater loyalties to the local community while the latter would look more to the palace, but either would have to try to maintain a balance of sorts between the two power foci. There is some evidence from the Assyrians that a "judge" was an outsider in the community in which he judged, while a "mayor" seems to have been a local person of influence who was appointed to his position by the central authorities (see especially MAL A¶45). A similar duality in other nations would not be surprising.[119]

The process of judicial appointment in ancient Israel is not clearly spelled out in the D Code. The command that "you" (sg.) are to "appoint judges and officers" (Deut 16:18) is aggravating in

---

[117] This does not deny that there are redactional layers in the D Code. This simply shows that one cannot use variations in judicial personages as a criterion for isolating those layers.

[118] In some ways, this structure reflects a tripartite political perspective in the society—local ("elders of the city"), regional/national ("judges [and officers]"), and sacral ("[levitical] priests")—and the underlying desire to work for harmony and stability from each of those perspectives.

[119] See, for example, P. Steinkeller, "The Administrative and Economic Organization of the Ur III State: The Core and the Periphery," in *The Organization of Power: Aspects of Bureaucracy in the Ancient Near East*, ed. M. Gibson and R. D. Biggs (SAOC, No. 46; Chicago: Oriental Institute, 1987), pp. 24–27.

its simplicity. Who is "you?" On the one hand, we can easily rule
out the king exclusively (see above), although he might be
involved as leader of the nation. On the other hand, "you" cannot
be taken distributively in this case, as it can in some others (e.g.,
Deut 12:18); every citizen cannot be expected to appoint a judge.
Further, even if one reads this in a common-sense way and has
each tribe or town selecting its own judge, this does not
necessarily mean that the king is left out of the process. This could
simply mean that a town nominates a local person for an
appointment, and the king then confirms and instructs the
appointee.[120] Other texts support the possibility of royal
involvement in judicial appointments (Exod 18:13–27; Deut
1:9–18; and 2 Chr 19:4–11). In each text, the judicial officials
chosen are also traditional leaders in the nation's kinship-based
structure.[121] Those whom Moses chooses are described as "leading
men of your tribes" in Deut 1:15 (cp. Exod 18:21, 25),[122] and
among those appointed by Jehoshaphat in Jerusalem are "heads of
families of Israel" (2 Chr 19:8).[123] The presence of priests among

---

[120] The pattern for choosing a king suggested by Deut 17:14–20 is that
Yahweh chooses the appointee and then the people appoint (ordain?) him.
However, this passage might be a conflation. On this question, see
Rütersworden, *Von der politischen Gemeinschaft*, pp. 58–60.

[121] We must be careful here not to read more into possible parallels
between Israel and Mesopotamian powers in the area of judicial
appointments. Even though we are talking about "judges" in both cases, the
terms used are from different roots. Israel's "judges" (שׁפטים) may be more
akin to Mesopotamian "mayors" (*khazannu*) than "judges" (*dayyanu*).

[122] An important ambiguity exists here, as one cannot be sure whether
Moses makes judicial appointments as a judge, as a prophet or priest, or as a
foreshadowing of kings. On Moses as a king-figure, even in antiquity, see
Silver, "Moses Our Teacher," pp. 123–32; cp. Gerbrandt, *Kingship*, pp. 116–23
on Joshua (and, by extension, Moses) as a model for kings. On the other
hand, it is much easier to see the priestly or prophetic aspects of Moses'
character, and it is not illogical (from the Historian's perspective) to assume
that priestly or prophetic figures could have been responsible for appointing
judges prior to the emergence of the kings (see 1 Sam 8:1–3).
    It seems ironic to me that the Deuteronomistic Historian, who writes from
a basically monarchic perspective, uses the example of a primarily
priestly/prophetic figure (Moses) as his precedent for the making of judicial
appointments; but, on the other hand, the Chronicler, who writes in a king-
less era dominated by priests, uses the example of a king (Jehoshaphat, 2 Chr
19:5–11) as his precedent.

[123] Whether a similar practice was used in the fortified cities (2 Chr 19:5–7)
would probably depend on the social make-up and histories of those cities.

the ranks of judicial officials in the latter (as in Deuteronomy) is also not unexpected, based on the examples of other societies.

But it is not enough to say that it is possible that judicial functionaries in ancient Israel could have had complementary roles. One must also consider the kinds of cases that each type (judges, priests, elders) is said to have adjudicated, to see whether their roles are duplicative or complementary. If there is duplication, then one would tend to conclude that a conflation of independent sources has occurred; if there is complementarity of roles, then there is less reason to assume such a conflation. I will be addressing these questions in regard to city elders in much greater depth in the chapters which follow; so, I will set them aside for the moment. I hope that a very few suggestive comments along this line regarding other passages of the D Code which mention other adjudicators will be sufficient for our purposes here.[124]

The cases which mention other functionaries and not elders vary in terms of the extent and nature of the jurisdiction involved; but they can easily be seen as cases which naturally require the services of someone other than city elders.[125] The cases brought before "the levitical priests and the judge" in Deut 17:8–13 are described as "any case within your towns (lit. 'gates') which is too difficult for you." This presumes that someone else within a town would have heard the case first and found it too difficult to resolve. That could have been local elders. The resolution of the cases considered in Deut 19:15–21 requires an investigation "before the Lord, before the priests and judges." It would make sense to assume that such cases had been heard but left unresolved by local adjudicators, that they too are cases "too difficult for you."[126]

---

[124] I also feel that a lengthy discussion of these passages would be rather redundant in the wake of the studies by Rüterswörden (*Von der politischen Gemeinschaft*) and Levinson (*Deuteronomy*). Their conclusions about a pre-exilic redaction in which Deut 16:18–17:20 basically cohere is consistent with my own findings. My primary revisions to those studies, other than those discussed in this study, would be in the area of the king's involvement in judicial matters.

[125] A similar argument is advanced by Macholz regarding the judicial functions of Israel's kings ("Die Stellung des Königs," pp. 157–81).

[126] See above, on the need for ritual specialists, and Levinson, *Deuteronomy*, p. 129. There are several parallels between Deut 19:15–21 and

This leaves two laws to be considered—Deut 16:18–20 and 25:1–3. Both speak of "judges" hearing cases, but both are ambiguous on one crucial point: whether these judges constitute the very lowest level of adjudication, or are they there, as in Deut 17:8–13, to resolve cases that are "too difficult" for city elders to resolve. We have already shown that the presence of judges in other societies of the ancient Near East does not preclude the existence of additional local adjudicators such as elders. More specifically, the law codes of Mesopotamia contain laws which mention only judges, yet we know from other documents that judges are not the only adjudicators in those places; other appointed officials and elders also adjudicated. So, references to judges in Deut 16:18–20 and 25:1–3 must be seen as ambiguous regarding the existence of other adjudicators; they do not possess a "polemical silence"[127] against other adjudicators. I do not, as yet, see a way—or a need—to overcome this ambiguity.[128]

Acknowledging, then, the ambiguity of a couple of laws, I conclude that the laws of the D Code probably point to a complementarity in the roles of the various judicial officials mentioned. I will show in the coming chapters that cases involving members of a single community typically are resolved by the elders of that community, while cases involving more than one community require the participation of other officials. Similarly, this brief look at passages mentioning judges and priests shows that they hear cases which are "too difficult" for city elders or cases requiring ritual or legal specialists.

Yet another important consideration in evaluating the Deuteronomic judicial system would be the goal of adjudication reflected in these laws. In a law which identifies the judicial officials involved, is the purpose of that law to maintain community harmony and integrity through reconciliation, or does it reflect the authority of the state and its attempts to impose its

---

LH ¶¶9–13. Both involve "witnesses" whose testimony is evaluated by "judges." In the latter, there are witnesses for each of the disputants. Is the same possibly to be assumed for Deut 19:15–21?

[127] Levinson, *Deuteronomy*, pp. 125–26.

[128] For parallel laws, which mention "judges" but no other adjudicators, see LH ¶¶5, 127; MAL B¶17. A couple of additional questions highlight the ambiguity of Deut 25:1–3. First, does the term "dispute" (ריב) cover all legal disputes, or just a certain type? Second, how far does the protasis extend in 25:1—to the end of the first clause, or to the end of the second?

will and control over the people? To make such a determination will require extensive analysis of each law. Time and the nature of the present forum prohibits such analyses here. Still I would make a few tentative proposals regarding this.

The spirit of the laws involving priests and judges is difficult to discern. The laws requiring a plurality of witnesses (Deut 19:15–21) and fixing the number of lashes that could be administered as punishment (Deut 25:1–3) suggest a concern to maintain the dignity of the accused outweighs any concern to maintain the authority of the judge.[129] If it could be shown that the reason for bringing a dispute before a judge in Israel is primarily to humiliate one's legal opponent, then one might argue that these laws serve to mute the effects of that humiliation; but that interpretation remains a mere possibility. The two remaining laws (Deut 16:18–20; 17:8–13) assume that the judicial functions performed are directly monitored by Yahweh, not the state. Such an assumption would go hand-in-hand with a desire for peace between fellow Israelites, because Yahweh represents—in a political sense—that which unites members of all the tribes of Israel. Holding such an assumption in common would further strengthen the sense that city elders and judges and priests exercised complementary functions in Israel's judiciary.

CONCLUSIONS

Reconstructing the contours of social institutions in an ancient society like that of Israel is not easy. Many vital pieces are always missing. The goal here has been to use comparisons with societies thought to be similar to Israel's to help fill in some of the missing pieces regarding Israel's judicial system, as it is described in the D Code. The results suggest an alternative to the more commonly accepted reconstruction. In that reconstruction, community-based judicial institutions which would have originated in the premonarchic period were naturally at odds with and were eventually displaced by state-mandated institutions in the monarchic period, prior to the compilation of the D Code. The

---

[129] Levinson, *Deuteronomy*, pp. 120–21.

elders-laws represent the retention of laws and/or judicial practices from a by-gone era, while the laws calling for the appointment of "judges and officers" and adjudication by "judges" and "priests" represent a Deuteronomic recasting of monarchic institutions.

The present reconstruction suggests complementarity in the functions of these institutions, as elders adjudicate local matters, and judges and priests deal with special and unresolved cases, and with inter-municipal matters. This basic conclusion of complementarity of roles in Israel's judicial system is supported by at least two findings: (1) the existence of dual but complementary judicial institutions in many contemporary kinship-based societies, and (2) the evidence that similar situations existed among other ancient Near Eastern peoples. Such a situation could have had its roots in Israel in the premonarchic period (based on the evidence of contemporary kinship-based societies), and it could have continued to the end of the monarchic period (based on those and ancient Near Eastern examples).

I have also suggested that the goal of reconciliation in the adjudicative process for the sake of community solidarity and integrity is a significant aspect of Israel's judicial conceptualizations, as it is in most kinship-based societies. There is less certainty on this point in the laws mentioning only "judges and officers" and "priests;" so, further investigation is suggested there. I hope to demonstrate its significance in the rest of this study as part of the assumptive matrix of the elders-laws. In the process, it should become clear that reading these laws in the light of these kinship-based institutions and ideas is crucial to a fuller appreciation of the roles and functions of elders in ancient Israel.

CHAPTER 3
HOMICIDE, ASYLUM, AND CITY ELDERS
(DEUT 19:1–13)

Deut 19:1–13 is one of three passages in the Hebrew Bible in which the "elders of the city" participate in cases involving homicide. The second (Deut 21:1–9) is the focus of the next chapter. The third (Joshua 20) is a literary descendant of Deut 19:1–13 and other sources. There is some overlap between Deut 19:1–13 and other passages concerning asylum, but there are several aspects of this subject which are peculiar to Deut 19:1–13. One of those aspects is the mention of the role played by the elders of the community in which the killing took place. Their explicit role here is as representatives of their community to another (one of the asylum-cities), but it is often assumed that an adjudicative role is also implied. Joshua 20 does mention elders, but they are elders of the asylum-city,[1] which is different from the group mentioned in Deut 19:1–13. Elders are not mentioned at all in Exod 21:12–14; Num 35:9–34; or Deut 4:41–43, even though those passages also deal with asylum.

---

[1] The more common designation is "cities of refuge" (עָרֵי מִקְלָט), but it actually appears only in Priestly texts (Num 35:6, 10–15, 25–28, 32; Josh 20:2; 21:13, 21, 27, 32, 38; 1 Chr 6:42, 52); so I am using a slightly different designation here to indicate the distinction. It is obvious, however, that the same institution is meant here as there (cp. "a place/city to which the killer may flee"—Exod 21:13; Num 35:6, 11; Deut 4:42; 19:3; Josh 20:3).

I have organized my examination of Deut 19:1–13 into three sections. First, I lay out the background for the passage by considering the juridical treatment of homicide in contemporary kinship-based societies, the ancient Near East, and narrative texts of the Hebrew Bible. Special attention is given to examples of asylum and to the role played by indigenous leaders (such as elders). Second, I revisit the major source-critical issues of this text, in conjunction with pertinent traditio-historical matters concerning asylum-cities. Only then do I turn to my own interpretation of Deut 19:1–13.

COMPARATIVE EVIDENCE

Homicide in Contemporary Kinship-Based Societies

Numerous ethnographic studies of kinship-based societies include information regarding homicide, because such cases are very helpful in illustrating basic social notions of the peoples being described. There is a lack of uniformity in the ways these various societies deal with homicide, reminding us again that each society is unique. Yet there are many common characteristics, and there are rationales given for practices and ideas which can suggest possible ways of understanding Israelite practices and ideas.

A general synopsis of studies which I have read follows, along with a brief survey of practices regarding homicide in several individual societies. In setting out my findings, I am separating between African and Middle Eastern peoples, because the latter share more in common—geographically and conceptually—with the Israelites. Still, all of these peoples demonstrate some common distinctions in the ways in which kinship-based societies address a situation of homicide. These distinctions are mixed in different ways among different peoples, although some naturally go together.

General Findings among African Peoples

Most kinship-based peoples of Africa recognize a distinction between premeditated murder and accidental killing. Some also

designate certain killings as "justifiable."[2] These distinctions are
evident in the varying severity of punishments meted out against
a killer. There often is flexibility as to punishments. Normally, the
most severe punishment utilized by a society is utilized in
punishing the premeditated murderer, while a lesser punishment
is imposed for accidental manslaughter. Some societies impose a
combination of punishments on the guilty party. Those who are
"wronged" by a homicide (see below) can often call for a lighter
punishment, if they so desire.[3] Punishments vary in some
societies according to the social and geographical distances
between the killer and his victim. In some instances, retaliation is
expected only if the victim is from the same clan group as the
killer; in others, some sort of payment is demanded of near-
relatives, while blood-vengeance is demanded against more
distant kin. Similarly, greater punishment might be exacted from
someone who has killed a neighbor than from someone who has
killed an inhabitant of a distant territory. Typical punishments for
homicide include death, blood-payment, confiscation of property,
the giving of "replacement" persons, banishment, and the
imposition of a curse.[4]

   Three interlocking facets of cases of homicide reveal a lot about
the social dynamics of these societies. These facets are (a) who
deserves to be punished, (b) who is thought to be "wronged" when
someone is killed, and (c) who is expected to exact punishment.
These are tied, of course, to ideas about corporateness (family,
lineage, community).

---

[2] For example, many Bantu tribes believe that killing someone caught in
the act of adultery or practicing witchcraft should not be punished (Schapera,
"Law and Justice," p. 210); the Baganda allow men the right to kill a wife or
slave, without fear of retaliation (Roscoe, *Baganda*, p. 20); the Gbandes allow
persons the right to kill bullies or those who are inordinately angry (Dennis,
Gbandes, p. 281).
[3] Buxton, *Chiefs and Strangers*, pp. 118–26; H. Kuper, *Swazi*, p. 36; Lewis,
Murle, pp. 76–81, 106–107; Nadel, *Nuba*, pp. 148–62, 302–16, 459–76;
Schapera, "Law and Justice," pp. 208–10; E. M. Smith and A. M. Dale, *The
Ila-Speaking Peoples of Northern Rhodesia*, Vol. I (New Hyde Park, NY:
University Books,1968), pp. 415–18.
[4] Buxton, *Chiefs and Strangers*, pp. 118–26; Hammond, *Yatenga*, pp.
144–45; Nadel, *Nuba*, pp. 249–59, 302–307, 314–16; Smith and Dale, *Ila-
Speaking Peoples*, pp. 350–51.

It is naturally thought that the killer himself should be punished, but the sense of collective responsibility inherent in most kinship-based societies often means that another in the killer's kin-group will be the recipient of vengeance instead. This might mean that the victim's kin-group will kill a member of the killer's kin-group. More commonly, this means that members of the killer's family assist him in making a blood-payment to the victim's family. Or it can mean that another member of the killer's kin-group will be handed over to the victim's kin-group for adoption or marriage, as a way of "replacing" the life of the victim.

At one level, these punishments reveal a common principle of equitable compensation (a life for a life). A person holds personal, social, and economic "value" to his/her kin-group (see next paragraph). A killer unfairly deprives the group of that "value," and so they look to him to compensate them for their loss. For example, the Nuba people expect that a person of the killer's kin-group who is most similar to the victim in age and gender is the one upon whom vengeance should be taken.[5] The Murle traditionally called for a person most similar to the victim to be given by the killer's kin to the victim's kin as a "replacement."[6] The Lango essentially accomplish the same goal by demanding the payment of enough cattle for the victim's family to purchase a wife who can bear a child to replace the victim.[7]

Lying behind this principle is the understanding that homicide is a personal offense against the victim and his entire social group (family, lineage, neighborhood). As such, it is not simply a crime which offends the legal sensibilities of the society; it is a moral offense, striking at the integrity (economic, socio-political, and ethical) of the entire community.[8] Because it is a personal offense, members of the victim's family themselves often exact vengeance. This responsibility might fall solely on the shoulders of the closest kin, but it can also be taken up by an entire kin-group. Because it

---

[5] Nadel, *Nuba*, pp. 151–52.

[6] Lewis, *Murle*, pp. 107–108.

[7] Moore, "Descent and Legal Position," p. 392.

[8] Nadel, *Nuba*, p. 502. On this, Peristiany ("Law," p. 43) writes, "[Disputes] are introduced by a private person in defense of sectional interests, ...[who] claims restitution for private damages and not social retribution." I am thinking of the Hebrew term שלום ("peace") when I speak of integrity here. This "peace" means a lack of conflict, but it also entails wholeness.

is a moral offense, the entire community eventually will take action, if the victim's family does not or can not.[9] As a permutation of this, the corporateness of a community is sometimes thought to be embodied in the person of the chief. The killing of any member of the community is understood as an offense against the chief; therefore, he himself determines the appropriate punishment and insures that the community carries it out.[10]

Some peoples also believe that the shedding of blood is a sacral offense, that it violates the sanctity of the natural order. This natural order consists of both the surrounding physical environment and the "local" spiritual world. These peoples believe that, besides any vengeance which family members might obtain, spirits of nature or ancestral spirits (even the spirit of the victim) might also avenge the victim's death (through physical or mental disease, or by natural disaster).[11]

Homicide inevitably has socio-political implications. The death of the victim has economic and social ramifications which affect his entire kin-group. Those ramifications have been caused by an unjustified act of the killer, a member of a parallel kin-group. The well-being of the community is dependent on the cooperative efforts of such kin-groups. Therefore, homicide tears at the social fabric which holds together the two groups, the conditions which brought the two parties into contact with each other in the first place. The greatest dangers to the broader community that arise in situations of homicide, then, are that a feud might develop or that some natural disaster (a curse) will afflict the entire community in which both groups live. The former is particularly acute in societies which hold strong ideas about collective responsibility and expect a corresponding death for a murder. If

---

[9] Dyson-Hudson, *Karimojong Politics*, pp. 220–21; Edel, *Chiga*, p. 12; Mitchell, *Yao Village*, p. 32; Moore, "Descent and Legal Position," pp. 393–95; Peristiany, "Law," p. 44.

[10] Cunnison, *Luapula Peoples*, pp. 182–83; Schapera, "Law and Justice," pp. 208–10; Winans, *Shambala*, pp. 104–10.

[11] Edel, *Chiga*, p. 12; Smith and Dale, *Ila-Speaking Peoples*, pp. 415–18. The Kpelle of Ghana are insistent that an execution is not a show of force. Instead, if someone is found guilty of murder, they are executed by members of their own clan, who explain that the execution is necessary to maintain "the natural order." Teitelbaum, "Old Age," pp. 47–48.

any member of the victim's kin-group can seek vengeance on any member of the killer's kin-group, there is the ever-present danger that the retaliation taken will seem inappropriate. All might agree that the first killing was unjustified and recognize the need to make amends. But the second killing might seem justified to the original victim's group (on the grounds of vengeance) and unjustified to the other (because the second victim was not personally responsible for the first death). The kin of the second victim now feel obligated to avenge that death, and so the feud ensues.[12]

It is in this kind of situation that local elders and chiefs play a critical role. That role is to control the initial exacting of vengeance, in order to diffuse the possibility of consequent hostilities and anger, before they tear the community apart. There are three primary ways in which this is accomplished. First, these leaders sometimes have to provide protection for the killer from angry relatives of the victim, until he can be properly tried and punished. This protection is usually provided at the house of a chief or elder.[13] Second, these leaders then expedite a trial. In this trial, they are expected to determine the guilt of the accused (if that is in doubt) and the exact nature of his crime. But this is in many ways a secondary role. Their primary role is to negotiate a "settlement" that is acceptable to the kin-group of the victim (see following paragraph). Third, if there is a sense that the killing is a sacral offense, the community normally looks to elders or chiefs or "religious specialists" to expiate the offense through a ritual.[14]

The ultimate goal of elders and other community leaders in all of this goes beyond due compensation; they wish to restore the integrity (the "peace") of their community. Their goal is to replace the potential for hostilities between kin-groups with cooperation and "brotherhood," as well as to reaffirm and re-establish the spiritual rightness of the community which existed prior to the

---

[12] Abrahams, "Neighbourhood Organization," pp. 178–79; Klima, *Barabaig*, pp. 85–87; Mitchell, *Yao Village*, pp. 54–55; Roscoe, *Baganda*, pp. 266–67. Cp. Ginat, *Blood Disputes*, pp. 16–18, 40–41.

[13] Lewis, *Murle*, pp. 64–65, 76–81; Nadel, *Nuba*, pp. 257, 305, 314–16; Roscoe, *Baganda*, p. 20; Smith and Dale, *Ila-Speaking Peoples*, pp. 359–60. This last source mentions asylum being taken at a chief's hut, at a temple, or in a sacred grove.

[14] See n. 11, above.

killing. They serve as negotiators between the kin-groups of the killer and the victim and, if necessary, as intermediaries between the community and the spiritual world. They are, above all else, peacemakers.[15]

Specific Examples

S. F. Nadel provides some useful comparisons regarding cases of homicide in his study of ten Nuba tribes.[16] Each tribe has its own practices and beliefs, yet there are numerous ways in which they overlap. Three tribes do not distinguish between premeditated and accidental killing when punishing the offender, but the rest do. The most common punishments traditionally have been blood-vengeance and blood-payment, but four tribes allow exchanges of "similar" persons to take place in certain types of killing. Variations in punishment are based primarily on the "social range" between killer and victim. This "range" falls into three levels: inter-clan, clan, and sub-clan. Resolution is swiftest and the consequences most quickly pass in sub-clan disputes, while hostilities are more prolonged in the wake of inter-clan killings. An imposed state authority now has outlawed blood-vengeance, replacing it strictly with payment of blood-money. Nevertheless, people still feel the threat of vengeance, so a killer and his close relatives will usually flee their home territory to avoid "illegal" retaliation.

This fear of retaliation is still strong, because the people of all these tribes continue to understand killing as an offense by one family against another. The entire family of the victim feels some moral obligation to avenge the death themselves, regardless of what some state power has mandated. Linked to these traditional practices is the persisting notion in all but one tribe that bloodshed incurs some sort of supernatural retaliation. All the tribes holding this belief require sacrifices as a part of the community's response to a killing. Among about half of the tribes, there is no human retaliation to killings between sub-clan

---

[15] Dyson-Hudson, *Karimojong Politics*, pp. 220–21; Edel, *Chiga*, pp. 17, 114–15; Moore, "Descent and Legal Position," pp. 393–95; Peristiany, "Law," p. 43; Smith and Dale, *Ila-Speaking Peoples*, pp. 350–51.

[16] Much of the following summary is distilled from Nadel, *Nuba*, pp. 148–62, 248–59, 302–307, 314–16, 349–51, 459–66, 474–76, 501–507.

members, because the people are confident that leprosy or some other divinely-imposed malady will strike one who is guilty of premeditated murder against a lineage mate.

Community elders act in such a situation with the goal of restoring "the integrity of the whole community."[17] They impose a time of non-contact between the two families involved immediately following a homicide. They oversee the negotiations regarding the nature and magnitude of the punishment of the guilty party. They arrange the sacrificial ceremony to appease the supernatural beings who have been offended by the killing. In short, they make sure that "peace" is restored.

A commonly-cited African example of how kinship-based societies deal with homicide is provided by the Nuer of Sudan. The usual punishment for murder, initially, is the payment of a blood-price in cattle; but, even if this price is paid, the possibility of blood-vengeance remains. The Nuer have retained the notion that the slain person's ghost remains unappeased until a reciprocal life has been taken, either that of the murderer or a member of his family. If it is felt that the ghost of the victim has not been fully appeased by the blood-payment given, hostile relations between the lineages involved can develop into a feud. Whether that results or "peace breaks out" depends on the nature of the kinship-relations between the two parties, and territorial proximity. The closer the kinship-ties, the more likely the parties are to want to avoid conflict. On the other hand, territorial proximity tends to promote conflict. If the parties involved are geographically close, the larger community will become concerned about the outcome. If the parties are relatively close kin, numerous efforts at mediation by elders and the local leopard-skin chief will come into play. A greater effort at mediation translates into a higher blood-price. If two segments are involved which have been at peace with one another, and if they wish to maintain this peace, a higher blood-price (in cattle) will be required. The more distant the ties, the less likely it will be that efforts toward reconciliation will be made. In sum, the Nuer believe that the amount of the blood-price is a

---

[17] Nadel, *Nuba*, p. 502.

reflection of the "price" which the respective segments place on their friendship.[18]

The Mandari people seem to exhibit practices which are opposite to others we have described, yet there are still some basic principles which are the same. For example, the Mandari say that blood-payment does not exist in their society. They claim that, within a single clan, it is impossible for a clan "brother" to compensate adequately the family of one he has killed; so, the only possible response is blood-vengeance. Once vengeance has been taken, hard feelings between the two groups are supposed to be passed. Further, they claim that no compensation is deemed necessary if the killer and victim are from different clans. The result of such a killing is prolonged hostilities between the two clan groups. The reality, though, is that various blood-payments are arranged by chiefs and community elders, based on the desire to restore peace between the competing families or clans. When vengeance actually is taken, it is taken either on the killer himself or on one of his close-kinsmen by one of the victim's close kin. Prolonged feuds are generally rare, because chiefdoms are small and feuds would seriously weaken the groups economically. Moreover, honor is an important component of these interactions, so that those involved in a feud feel constrained to seek vengeance against those who are of comparable rank only.[19]

General Findings among Middle Eastern Peoples

Similar practices and ideas exist among contemporary kinship-based societies of the Middle East. The traditional response to a killing among most Arab tribesmen was for close relatives of the victim to seek vengeance on the killer himself or one of his close relatives. The retaliatory killing then prompted a similar response from the original killer's kin, with this pattern of feuding continuing until a blood-payment was arranged by the elders of the respective groups, in cooperation with a tribal chief or "holy man." Most ethnographers report that this pattern has given way in modern times to blood-payment or exile alone, with blood-vengeance now non-existent. Nevertheless, the threat of blood-

[18] Evans-Pritchard, *Nuer*, pp. 152–64, 220; Beidelman, "Nuer Priests and Prophets," pp. 282–83.
[19] Buxton, *Chiefs and Strangers*, pp. 118–26.

vengeance persists, as killers still must flee because of fear of retaliation by their victims' kinsmen.[20] The amount of the blood-payment varies within each society, dependent again on the killer's intent and the blood-ties and territorial proximity of the parties involved, as it is among African peoples. There is also the custom of seeking out the residence of a tribal chief or "holy man" as a place of temporary asylum from those seeking blood-vengeance. The purpose is to allow time for elders and chiefs to come together to work out an acceptable "resolution" (i.e., an acceptable amount of money or goods) to the dispute, to prevent it from evolving into a feud. Some killers hand themselves over to the state-appointed police for their own protection. In one society, killers are known to seek asylum in the tent of their victim. To provide such protection is an act of great honor.[21]

The notion of "honor" is more pronounced and significant among Middle Eastern peoples than among their African counterparts. The taking of human life is indelibly linked to the relative honor of the families of the perpetrator and the victim.[22] A killing is conceived of as a demonstration on the part of the killer that he can assume the power of life and death over his victim. This suggests that his family is of a higher status than his victim's family. The family of the deceased are expected to obtain retribution in order to "save face" among the other families of the

[20] Briggs, *Tribes*, pp. 122–23, 172–73; Gellner, *Saints*, pp. 125–28; Holy, *Neighbours and Kinsmen*, p. 132. One wonders whether the attitudes of many of these peoples have really changed. It seems that one could argue that central authorities have created a greater urgency to resolve all disputes quickly, rather than allowing the disputing groups to continue on until they tire of the hostilities.

[21] Briggs, *Tribes of the Sahara*, pp. 122–23, 172–73; Cole, *Nomads*, pp. 86–87; Gellner, *Saints of the Atlas*, pp. 125–28; W. R. Smith, *Kinship and Marriage in Early Arabia* (Boston: Beacon, 1885; repr. 1967), pp. 83–84. For the practice of seeking refuge in the killer's tent, see Zeid, "Honour and Shame," pp. 253–54.

[22] In the Hebrew Bible, this general notion is spoken of as one's "name" (שֵׁם). A person's "name" in his community reflects how the community perceives his character or status. Vengeance would be sought "for the sake of [one's] name."

community. Tribesmen feel that a failure to do so "threatens the social equilibrium."[23]

This can be seen most clearly in segmentary lineage societies, where the principle of "complementary opposition" is evident. This principle means that "any opposition between groups (or members thereof) expands automatically to opposition between the largest equivalent lineages of which the contestants are *respectively* members."[24] This does not mean that every member of the respective lineages will become involved in a case of homicide, but it does mean that any can, if they so desire. Culpability for the death and responsibility for the seeking of retribution can thus extend up the lineage chain far beyond one's immediate family. The following description of Egyptian Bedouins provides a clear example of these notions:

> As in all segmentary societies of this type, social and political relationships among the Bedouins depend largely on maintaining a balance between opposed segments and the various kinship groups. A disturbance in this balance usually results in bitter strife and leads to long and bloody feuds. A slight offense inflicted against a lineage or a lineage segment is taken as an unforgivable humiliation requiring immediate retaliation to wipe out the shame, regain honour and restore the same relations as formerly between the groups. This strict defense of honour stands as a guarantee against misconduct and unjustified aggression.[25]

---

[23] Zeid, "Honour and Shame," p. 247. See Bourdieu, "Sentiment of Honour," pp. 202–14; Briggs, *Tribes of the Sahara*, p. 173; Marx, *Social Context*, p. 14.

[24] Sahlins, "Segmentary Lineage," pp. 322–45 [emphasis his]. For further discussion of this principle, see Peters, "Structural Aspects," pp. 263–82; Salzman, "Does Complementary Opposition Exist?" pp. 53–70; idem, "Ideology and Change," pp. 618–37.

Recognition of this concept is particularly important for those who think of homicide as a crime against society in general. In most kinship-based societies, homicide is viewed in terms of families or lineages. This act has disrupted the relationship between them all. It is the responsibility of all those who feel wronged (i.e., the lineage or lineage segment), not society at large, to seek justice. See H. McKeating, "The Development of the Law of Homicide in Ancient Israel," *VT* 25 (1975) 46–47.

[25] Zeid, "Honour and Shame," p. 259. A common Bedouin phrase reflects this feeling. If a murder is committed to avenge a previous murder, the Bedouin describe it as an example of "burial opposite burial," supposedly requiring no compensation (Marx, *Social Context*, p. 11). Cp. J. K. Campbell,

A key component, then, of what is "premeditated" by a killer is the relative strength of his family and their sense of obligation toward their tribal "brothers" vis-à-vis the victim's family. If the one contemplating murder is confident that his family can and will defend him against retaliation from the victim's family, then he will be more likely to proceed. If not, then he will "attack" his opponent in some other way.[26]

Specific Examples

Honor is a significant notion in cases of homicide among the tribes of Kabylia, in Algeria. A killing is viewed as a personal affront by the killer against the honor of the lineage of his victim. The responsibility for vengeance falls successively to the deceased's relatives, according to their genealogical proximity and

---

"Honour and the Devil," in *Honour and Shame: The Values of Mediterranean Society*, ed. J. G. Peristiany (Chicago: University of Chicago, 1966), p. 144. Concerning the Sarakatsani shepherds of northern Greece, he writes, "...the outraged family must answer at once, and with violence, if its reputation is to survive."

The principle at work here pertains in several situations, but homicide is one of two or three offenses which present it in clearest relief. Rape, or sexual misconduct in general, is another. See, e.g., Smith, *Kinship and Marriage*, p. 125; Zeid, "Honour and Shame," pp. 253–56; Bourdieu, "Sentiment of Honour in Kabyle Society," p. 241.

[26] Marx, *Social Context*, p. 13.

An example of these notions in action emerges from the biblical text itself. In Judges 19–21, members of one tribe (Benjamin) rape and murder a concubine of a second tribe (Judah) who is married to a member of a third tribe (Levi) living in the territory of a fourth tribe (Ephraim). The Levite sends out a call for retribution to all the tribes, probably because the involvement of persons from more than one tribe makes this a tribe vs. tribe affair. The text says that all the remaining tribes respond, except for the people of Jabesh-gilead. These tribes, in turn, call upon the entire tribe of Benjamin—not just those closest to the perpetrators—to force the guilty parties to make restitution.

It is likely that only parts of some of the tribes actually became involved (cp. Jdgs 4:4 and 5:14–18). For historical reconstructions of this story, see O. Eissfeldt, "Der geschichtliche Hintergrund der Erzählung von Gibeas Schandtat (Richter 19–21)," *Kleine Schriften* II, ed. R. Sellheim and F. Maass (Tübingen: J. C. B. Mohr, 1953), pp. 64–80; S. Herrmann, *A History of Israel in Old Testament Times* (2nd Edition; Philadelphia: Fortress Press, 1981), p. 122; and Schäfer-Lichtenberger, *Stadt und Eidgenossenschaft*, pp. 269–71.

their relative social status. It is ideally the responsibility of the male next-of-kin. If he is unable or unwilling to fulfill that responsibility, it falls to the next closest male relative, and so on, until someone avenges the wrong. It is understood that the one actually seeking vengeance is a social "equal" to the killer, because it would be considered dishonorable for non-equals to face each other in combat. Defense of both lineages' honor prompts repeated retaliations, leading to an extended feud. This condition continues until elders, local "wise men," and religious specialists (*marabouts* or Sayeds [descendants of Mohammad]) step in to negotiate an end to hostilities through blood-payment. It is essential to this process that the resolution maintain the honor of the disputing groups.[27]

E. L. Peters distinguishes three general categories of homicide among the Bedouin of Cyrenaica. These categories correspond to the lineal distance between the parties involved. If the killer and victim are of the same "tertiary group" (i.e., minimal or minor lineage), actual blood-vengeance is avoided. The killer is exiled instead, leaving him without the security of a kinship-group.[28] A second category entails those of friendly tertiary groups, i.e., the parties are from different minimal lineages, usually within the same clan, but at least on good terms with one another. Such groups are close territorially, too. Murders in this category can only be resolved through the reciprocal exacting of blood-vengeance. A third category of homicide involves parties from separate but near "primary groups" (i.e., clans or maximal lineages of the same tribe). The normal response to a murder in this situation is raiding by the victim's family upon the homes of the perpetrator, to which the raided group responds in kind. The result is a prolonged feud between the lineages, which often leads to a greater distancing between the groups involved.[29]

---

[27] Bourdieu, "Sentiment of Honour," pp. 200–14, 236–37.

[28] Peters, "Some Structural Aspects," p. 264. Marx (*Social Context*, p. 11) reports that the murder of one's close relative in the immigrant Jewish community which he investigates is regarded as proof of one's insanity.

[29] Peters, "Some Structural Aspects," pp. 262–69. Comparable patterns exist among other Middle Eastern tribal groups. C. M. Doughty, in an account of his travels among the Arabs, noted a graded system of blood-vengeance. Some sort of payment for murder was expected, even if the parties involved were in separate tribal groups which were not on friendly terms.

The Baggara Arabs of Sudan evaluate "brotherhood" among kin in terms of the participation of their members in assisting with blood-payments (in the form of money or cattle). A near-kinsman who does not contribute is not really a "brother," while a more distant relative who does give assistance is a "brother." Further, everyone expects the near-relatives and the village leader of a murder victim to seek blood-vengeance against the killer, which will inevitably involve ever-widening circles of kinsmen; therefore, responsibility for the matter is removed from the extended families and placed in the hands of the lineages. Lineage elders and the territorial chief (the omda) step in almost immediately in an attempt to prevent immediate retaliation which would launch a prolonged feud between the two lineages. They isolate the parties from each other, and then they investigate the circumstances which led up to the killing, looking for a way to diffuse the hostilities. Even if they are successful at first, it often takes repeated negotiations, exchanges of gifts, and special sacrifices to put a definite end to the feud.[30]

One can see two strong but competing notions at work here. On the one hand, the notion that vengeance is necessary for restoring a family's honor drives the victim's relatives to retaliate in kind.[31]

The blood-price was considerably higher, however, if the groups were close and on friendly terms. C. M. Doughty, *Arabia Deserta* I (New York: Boni and Liveright, 1936), pp. 402–403, 476.

[30] Cunnison, *Baggara Arabs*, pp. 157–62, 171–86. Cunnison reports one case in which the lineage elders tied those looking to avenge their brother's death to a tree, and then sent them to the police for holding until a peaceful resolution could be arranged. In this particular case, a blood-payment was given, but the anger of the avenging relatives was not assuaged. Two years later, one of the dead man's cousins ambushed a kinsman of the killer, and then was promptly hanged by the state authorities. Further negotiations and a ceremonial reconciliation were needed before the feud was finally brought to a close. Cp. Holy, *Neighbours and Kinsmen*, pp. 136–37.

[31] It might seem odd that Arab tribesmen, who so highly value vengeance as a sign of honor, would accept blood-money for a murder involving kinsmen or close neighbors. Accepting blood-money (rather than exacting blood) seems to be an innovation in the society of relatively recent date, replacing the more traditional system of blood-vengeance and feud. Some attribute the change to the emergence of national governments in the Middle East (see Katakura, *Bedouin Village*, p. 156). Protracted feuds would disrupt the national stability which the supra-tribal governments try to maintain. The practice of paying blood-money—which had formerly been postponed until after several deaths

On the other hand, the society highly values "brotherhood and general peace." The elders and the territorial chief, as representatives of entire communities, are expected to promote this latter notion. They must do so through negotiation, because any resolution must uphold the honor and dignity of all.[32]

Some of the most detailed evidence from the Middle East regarding homicide concerns Arab and Palestinian communities in modern-day Israel. A homicide is dealt with as a dispute between lineages or "co-liable groups." A descent group of related lineages constitutes the core of one of these "co-liable groups" (called hamulas), which also contain many "clients." Due to territorial proximity, cases of murder either involve members of two neighboring "co-liable groups" or two lineages within a single group. Members of the actual descent group or lineage of the victim are obligated by a sense of collective responsibility to seek blood-vengeance, while client-members can participate only by providing blood-money.[33]

Responses to murder vary somewhat between inter-group and inter-lineage offenses. The usual result of the former is a reciprocal killing upon a member of the killer's group and prolonged periods of non-cooperation, with an eventual settlement in the form of a blood-payment worked out by lineage elders and other local leaders. Actual feuds are very rare. Killings involving closely-related lineages more often lead to the exile of the killer and a more sizable blood-payment by one lineage to another. There is sometimes recourse to a temporary (ghura) marriage, in which a female member of the killer's lineage bears a son by a

---

had occurred, or which had been reserved for cases involving distant acquaintances or enemies—is now extended to include cases involving close acquaintances at the beginning of the process.

The price of blood-payments often is extremely high. Doughty (Arabia Deserta II, p. 214) mentions one case which left the murderer's entire fakhd (minimal lineage) financially ruined, while that of the victim suddenly became one of the wealthier in the region. One result of this change, then, has been a rise in the significance of economic ties between parties, sometimes superseding blood-ties. See Peters, "Some Structural Aspects," pp. 279–81; Katakura, Bedouin Village, p. 156.

[32] Cunnison, Baggara Arabs, pp. 184–85.

[33] Ginat, Blood Disputes, pp. 16–19, 21–27.

member of the victim's lineage in order to provide a compensatory life for the one that was taken.[34]

The role played by group elders and local mediators is crucial in developing a resolution to the blood dispute. As in other societies, their concern is with the well-being of the entire community or region. Their goal is to mediate peace between the two groups in such a way that neither feels slighted. Initially, they provide asylum for the killer from those seeking vengeance; then they begin the process of seeking a non-violent end to the hostilities.[35] They are occasionally unsuccessful in their attempts, because of the overriding drive among some disputants to assert their individual or family honor. These mediators appeal primarily to a sense of mutual obligations, but this sense is being eroded as economic reliance on one's lineage and descent group is replaced by "economic and social integration with the wider society." In this, it seems that notions about collective responsibility are shifting from a rural mode to an urban mode. In the latter, the sense of family-oriented obligations becomes limited to one's closest relatives, while obligations previously based on extended kinship ties give way to (weaker) loyalties based on geographic proximity.[36]

This points us to the resolution of homicide as demonstrated among the Baharvand, a sedentary tribal group of western Iran. They too look to lineage leaders, village elders, and Sayeds to negotiate a settlement to the dispute which caused or resulted from a killing. Most blood-disputes are settled with a blood-payment (usually involving concubines); however, if the murder

[34] Ginat, *Blood Disputes*, pp. 40–59.

[35] Ginat, *Blood Disputes*, pp. 31–37, 60–89, 158 n. 8, 161 n. 17.

[36] "Sedentarization [of Bedouins] does not change the distinction between the relationship of co-liable groups to other groups, and between individuals within the co-liable group. A dispute with a different co-liable group will still bring the group as a unit together. But disagreements between members within the group now often result in a more individual approach." Ginat, *Blood Disputes*, p. 138; see also pp. 95–96, 110–11, 125, 137–38, 142–48, 152. Similar evidence is found in societies in other parts of the world under similar conditions. See J. C. Baroja, "Honour and Shame: A Historical Account of Several Conflicts," in *Honour and Shame: The Values of Mediterranean Society*, ed. J. G. Peristiany (Chicago: University of Chicago, 1966), pp. 92–93, 99.

was premeditated, the guilty party is executed. There is no reference to blood-vengeance or feuding here. The economic aspects of such a case parallel what one finds in the societies previously mentioned, but the notion that the honor of the entire community—not just the honor of the victim's lineage or descent group—is impugned by premeditated murder leads the community to deal as a unit with the offender.[37]

By way of summary, it seems clear that the African and Middle Eastern societies surveyed here present a diverse picture with several common features. One of the most important of these is that the shedding of blood is conceived of more as a personal affront than as a moral aberration. One sees this clearly by noticing who retaliates or is compensated for a killing and who "pays" for it. In many cases, it is the lineage of the victim and the lineage of the killer, respectively. Lineage and territorial leaders mediate in these situations to produce a resolution to the overall conflict, which threatens a permanent rift in the community. In some societies, a killing is viewed as an affront to the community as a whole, and representatives of the whole community (e.g., a chief) see to it that proper punishment is meted out. The actual form of the punishment or compensation varies among and within the societies examined. The most common punishments are a reciprocal death or the banishment of the offender, while blood-payment or person exchange often serve as a compensatory substitute. These conventions are augmented in some societies with notions about the sacral aspects of homicide. Members of these societies conceive of the shedding of blood as an affront to certain spiritual beings (ancestral or nature spirits). They anticipate consequences coming upon the killer and perhaps the rest of the community; so, special purification rituals are incorporated into the process of dealing with a homicide.

Community elders play important roles in the process of dealing with cases of homicide. Their primary function is to promote the unity and moral integrity of the overall community. They are concerned that this personal affront not go unanswered, but they are also concerned about reconciling the two groups

---

[37] Amanolahi-Baharvand, "Baharvand," pp. 139–40.

placed at odds by the killing. Their goal is to restore the harmony of the community which had existed prior to the shedding of blood, without compromising its moral ideals. Their task is complicated in societies which consider bloodshed an attack upon a family's essential honor—a notion especially prominent among many Middle Eastern peoples—because their resolution must acknowledge and maintain the honor of both sides in the dispute. In societies which see a significant sacral aspect to homicide, these elders often participate in purification rituals as representatives of their community to the divine realm.[38]

Homicide in Ancient Near Eastern Societies

Most of our evidence from the ancient Near East regarding homicide comes to us through law codes. As seen previously, these span several centuries and a significantly large geographical area. They do not yield a uniform picture, nor is the picture provided by any single law code complete. Each supplies only bits and pieces of a changing whole. In making comparisons among them, I prefer the approach proposed by Raymond Westbrook. He argues that most scholars have made too much of the differences between the various law codes, because they assume that each code intends to be exhaustive in its coverage of a given offense and its punishment(s). His own assumptions about the differences between the law codes are summarized as follows:

> Because these law codes could only have a fraction of their discussion committed to writing, each code contains no more than a few aspects of a given scholarly problem, sometimes overlapping with the aspects preserved in other codes, sometimes not. Moreover, a given system may pursue the discussion in a particular direction, considering variants not discussed elsewhere.
>
> It is by combining the similar and not-so-similar provisions of the various codes that the whole problem and thus the underlying law may be revealed and any peculiarities of the individual systems disclosed. This approach is, to be sure, in some sense an argument from silence, but it is a positive

---

[38] Although I am discussing cases of homicide only, the principles and practices laid out here apply to other types of dispute as well.

argument, that refuses to see contradictions in mere omissions
from sources that are by nature incomplete, when in all other
respects they are complementary.[39]

This approach represents an improvement of some general ideas
held by earlier scholars. Jacobsen, for example, says that "justice
[in ancient Mesopotamia] was normally dispensed by local
assemblies of villagers and townsmen, who judged according to a
body of traditional unwritten common law with which everybody
was familiar."[40] Westbrook modifies this by saying that something
akin to this "body of traditional unwritten common law" even
underlies the law codes. Westbrook also leans toward a
"commentary" method of reading the laws, a method which asserts
the unity of given laws (around a common principle) over the
contradictoriness suggested by historical-critical approaches.[41] I
tend to assume, then, that one should read the laws on homicide
in the various law codes as complementary rather than
contradictory, and that differences between the provisions in the
codes point to "peculiarities" of the society from which each comes.
As we proceed, we will see how this principle applies to biblical
law codes as well.

Mesopotamian and Hittite laws generally call for vengeance or
blood-payment as the just response to a killing. None of the law
codes mentions blood-vengeance as an automatic response by the
victim's kinsmen. Two Assyrian laws allow a member of the
victim's house the option of killing the manslayer or taking blood-

---

[39] Westbrook, "Adultery," p. 548. A small modification I would make to
these statements is in speaking of an "underlying law." This smacks of a prior
literary corpus, when what is really envisioned is a common principle of
justice. See A. Rofé, "The History of the Cities of Refuge in Biblical Law," in
Scripta Hierosolymitana, Vol. 31: Studies in the Bible, 1986, ed. Sara Japhet
(Jerusalem: Magnes Press, 1986), p. 215.

[40] Th. Jacobsen, "An Ancient Mesopotamian Trial for Homicide," *Oriens
Antiquus* 3 (1959) 130.

[41] M. Greenberg, "Some Postulates of Biblical Criminal Law," in *Yehezkel
Kaufmann Jubilee Volume*, ed. M. Haran (Jerusalem: Magnes Press, 1960),
pp. 5–28; reprinted in *A Song of Power and the Power of Song: Essays on the
Book of Deuteronomy*, ed. D. L. Christensen (Winona Lake, IN: Eisenbrauns,
1993), pp. 283–300. Cp. P. Haas, "'Die He Shall Surely Die': The Structure of
Homicide in Biblical Law," *Semeia* 45 (1989) 69–70; R. Westbrook, "A Matter
of Life and Death," *JANES* 25 (1997) 61–70.

payment (MAL A¶10; B¶2), but this power is not self-assumed.[42] Other law codes refer vaguely to the fact that an undefined "they" shall carry out the death sentence against the guilty party (LU ¶1; LL ¶e; LE ¶24; LH ¶229; MAL A¶53).[43] Some laws call for the death of a member of the killer's family who is "most comparable" to the victim (daughter for daughter, son for son, slave for slave; see LE ¶¶23,47A; LH ¶¶210, 230–231). Others prescribe compensation in the form of money (LL ¶¶d, f; LH ¶¶207–209, 211–214, 251–252; MAL A¶51; HL ¶5) or persons (LH ¶219; HL ¶¶1–4, 43, 44a).[44] The amounts of the compensations are usually graded according to the gender and/or social status of the killer and victim, and in consideration of the intent of the killer (premeditated or accidental killing).

There are only a few other cases of homicide from these areas of which I am aware. One is the murder of a palace official of ancient Nippur named Lu-Inanna. The guilt and the necessity of the execution of three male conspirators is automatically acknowledged, but the culpability of the victim's wife is questioned. It seems that she did not actually strike a blow against her late husband, but her obvious complicity in the murder is judged a greater crime than the killing itself, probably because of the depth of the betrayal involved (cp. LH ¶153). The text does not reveal who eventually carries out the sentence of death against these four.[45] In fact, it provides us little information about general Mesopotamian practices regarding homicide, because it deals with a situation that takes place in the palace. Such situations are notorious for being exceptions to common practices.

Allusions to two other cases are made in the Assyrian texts examined by Jas. Both stem from a killer's inability to pay the full

---

[42] One of the edicts of the Hittite King Telepinu gives the victim's heir the right to decide between death and blood-payment as the fate of the killer, but it does not say that the heir will actually exact judgment himself (TelEd ¶49).

[43] MAL A¶52 prescribes a "blow for blow" punishment on one guilty of accidental feticide.

[44] LH ¶218 calls for the amputation of the hand of the physician who causes the death or serious injury of an aristocrat (awilu). HL ¶98 says an arson shall "make compensation" for whatever perishes in a fire he had set; the nature of the compensation is unclear.

[45] Jacobsen, "Ancient Mesopotamian Trial," pp. 130–50.

amount of a blood-payment that had been imposed upon him. In one case (No. 1), the man and his family are arrested and all their property confiscated. In the other (No. 43), the man's father pays the balance of what the man owes.[46] These texts reflect two aspects of homicide cases which are consistent with evidence from the law codes. One is that blood-payment is the accepted mode of punishing one for a killing. (We do not know whether the killings were premeditated or accidental.) The other is that a man's immediate family is held responsible with him for a murder which he has committed. More information is required before one can deduce anything more about Assyrian practices, including what role (if any) community elders played.

In review, this information suggests that the treatment of homicide in ancient Mesopotamia and Hatti probably fell along lines similar to what one finds in contemporary urban kinship-based communities. The punishment for homicide is "stratified" according to the intent of the killer and the social status of the killer and victim. As to intent, premeditated murder warrants a severe response (execution or a corresponding death, blood-payment, or person exchange). This picture is incomplete, however, because of the limited nature of the data base. Underlying assumptions about the goal of adjudication and the roles played by community leaders and judges cannot be discerned.[47]

---

[46] Jas, *Neo-Assyrian Judicial Procedures*, pp. 8–11, 66–67.

[47] Information provided by Demosthenes of ancient Athens supports the idea that the notions concerning homicide which we see in contemporary societies were also held in these ancient societies. Execution was avoided in Athens by the time Demosthenes wrote, but other forms of punishment which we have encountered were used. These he sets forth in great detail in his treatise, "Against Aristocrates." *Demosthenes*, trans. J. A. Vince (LCL; Cambridge, MA: Harvard University, 1935).

First, a convicted murderer could be banished, or, at the least, his movements were severely curtailed. He was forbidden to participate in any community activities or to have access to any privileges of a normal citizen. These privileges included attendance at "the frontier-market, the games, and the Amphictyonic sacrifices." The purpose in these restrictions was to "debar the offender from everything in which the deceased used to participate in his lifetime" ("Against Aristocrates," 38–40). Apparently, the murderer could be killed by near relatives of the deceased, if he transgressed these guidelines.

HOMICIDE IN THE HEBREW BIBLE

The Hebrew Bible is consistent in its portrayal of responses to homicide. The general rule is that a man killed by a fellow Israelite is avenged by one of his close male relatives, called the blood-avenger (גֹּאֵל הַדָּם).[48] One finds exceptions to this rule (see 2 Sam 13:22–29, 37–39), as in any society with this practice, but those do not undermine the reality of the general rule. Deut 19:1–13 assumes this general rule but deals primarily with the most common exception to it: accidental manslaughter. Exceptions are often made in this type of case in kinship-based societies, as we have seen; but the Israelite method for dealing with it is relatively uncommon. Israelite law calls for the setting aside of entire cities, rather than particular homes or holy sites, as places of asylum. We focus here on the Deuteronomist's particular

---

In a case of involuntary manslaughter, the killer was not banished, but he did have to go through a complicated process of reconciliation with the relatives of the deceased before he could resume his normal lifestyle ("Against Aristocrates," 53–60). "And what does the law enjoin? That the man who is convicted of involuntary homicide shall, on certain appointed days, leave the country by a prescribed route, and remain in exile until he is reconciled to one of the relatives of the deceased. Then the law permits him to return, not casually, but in a certain manner; it instructs him to make sacrifice and to purify himself, and gives other directions for his conduct" ("Against Aristocrates," 72). The laws even went further, describing what would happen to such an exiled person if he were accused and acquitted of a second killing. ("Against Aristocrates," 77–78)

Finally, Demosthenes describes what rights the victim's relatives had in apprehending the killer. "If any man die a violent death, his kinsmen may take and hold hostages in respect of such death, until they either submit to trial for bloodguiltiness, or surrender the actual manslayers. This right is limited to three hostages and no more." ("Against Aristocrates," 82) The "hostages" mentioned almost certainly are relatives of the accused (cp. Doughty, *Arabia Deserta* II, pp. 147–48).

[48] See 2 Sam 2:18–28; 3:22–27; 14:4–7. For descriptions of general Israelite practice, see Pedersen, *Israel* I–II, pp. 378–400, 410; de Vaux, *Ancient Israel*, pp. 158–63; Salmon, "Judicial Authority," pp. 164–70; G. von Rad, *Deuteronomy* (OTL; Philadelphia: Westminster, 1966), pp. 127–28; McKeating, "Development," pp. 46–68; Haas, "'Die He Shall Surely Die'," p. 85; Gertz, *Gerichtsorganisation*, p. 139; Bovati, *Re-Establishing Justice*, pp. 57–58. A few laws speak of "justice" rendered against a killer in the passive voice—as in Mesopotamian laws—without identifying the one who is to kill the killer (Gen 9:6; Exod 21:12, 14, 20).

presentation of this institution, but we cannot do so without regard for other presentations in the Hebrew Bible.

Redaction of Deut 19:1–13

Redaction-critical analysis of any passage in the D Code is a complex enterprise. Several overlapping assumptions must be made in order for one to justify his/her conclusions. In the case of Deut 19:1–13, such conclusions must take into account the three other passages which deal with asylum-cities—Num 35:6, 9–34; Deut 4:41–43; and Joshua 20 (cp. Joshua 21 and 1 Chr 6:39–66). These, in conjunction with Deut 19:1–13, reveal two parallel literary traditions regarding the institution of asylum, both probably stemming from Exod 21:12–14. The simplest reconstruction seems to be that Numbers 35 represents a purely Priestly tradition, and Deut 19:1–13 represents a purely Deuteronomic tradition. Deut 4:41–43 derives its information from an early version of the latter, while Joshua 20 is a relatively late text containing mostly Priestly elements, but with some borrowing from Deut 19:1–13 as well. The arguments for this reconstruction are laid out below. The temporal relation between these two traditions in their early stages is unclear, suggesting that there probably are common customary or literary legal sources lying behind both.

An important assumption which touches directly on Deut 19:1–13 concerns the relationship between a Deuteronomic redaction layer—attributed to the "lawgiver"—and one or more deuteronomistic layers—attributed to the "historian(s)"[49] who composed the framework of Deuteronomy and the several books which follow ("the Deuteronomistic History" [DtrH]). There are many phrases which occur in both the D Code and DtrH that are said to be "characteristic" of one or both. One could attribute all of these occurrences to the redactive hand of the historian; or, one

---

[49] I will refer to a single "historian" for most of this discussion. This is not to deny the existence of multiple layers in DtrH—Cross's Dtr1 and Dtr2; or the German DtrG, DtrP, and DtrN—but merely to simplify the task of description.

could argue that they are expressions popularized by the Deuteronomic lawgiver and then adopted by his deuteronomistic successor(s).[50] Both possibilities have merit, and so I will often refer to a phrase as "Deuteronom(ist)ic," meaning it could be either Deuteronomic or deuteronomistic. One must consider these phrases on a case by case basis, but my inclination is to expect them to be Deuteronomic. My understanding of DtrH is that it represents the work of writers who were influenced by the D Code and compiled/composed a history which evaluated the nation of Israel in the light of that law code. It seems more likely that expressions appearing in the D Code—which are crucial to conveying the themes of the D Code—were already present in the version of the D Code available to the deuteronomistic historian, and that he became so imbued with these thematic phrases that he incorporated them—as he found them, or in a modified form—into his narrative. Otherwise, one would have to argue that the historian possessed a law code which did not express the themes he would explicitly use in the history, but that he substantially rewrote the law code so that he could supply himself with an "authoritative source" which utilized those very thematic phrases which he needed. That seems unlikely, because he would first have to convince his audience of the authoritativeness of a law code according to the phraseology with which he had just revised it.[51] For this reason, I am more inclined to think of "Deuteronom(ist)ic" phrases as Deuteronomic than deuteronomistic.

Deut 19:1–13 can be separated phraseologically into two general components: sections which do not contain typical Deuteronom(ist)ic phraseology, and sections which do. Based on this criterion alone, one would conclude that vv 2a, 3aα, 3b–5, 7b,

---

[50] There is also the possibility that an expression originated in pre-deuteronomic circles. For example, one can easily argue that the expression "other gods" is Deuteronom(ist)ic, because it occurs almost exclusively in Deuteronomy–Kings and Jeremiah. However, its presence in the Decalogue seems to be original there; so, one cannot automatically assume that every occurrence of the expression must be attributed to a Deuteronom(ist)ic hand.

[51] In other words, I subscribe to the popular conclusion that the D Code is the "lawbook" discovered in the days of Josiah, and that its themes and expressions guided each of the authors and/or redactors of DtrH.

9b, and 10b–12 are non-Deuteronom(ist)ic,[52] perhaps representing pre-Deuteronomic elements of the text. However, the classification of much of the phraseology in these verses as "non-Deuteronom(ist)ic" can be attributed to the specifics of the situation envisioned. For example, there is no other occasion in the D Code for "setting apart" three cities for a special purpose (vv 2a, 3aα, 9b); so, one would not expect the wording in these verses to occur elsewhere. A reference to these cities as places "to which a killer may flee" (v 3b) occurs in each of the passages touching on asylum (see Num 35:6, 10–15, 25–28, 32; Deut 4:42; Josh 20:2), whether Deuteronomic or Priestly. This suggests that the phrase is used for reasons that are "case-specific" and is not an indicator of the literary preferences of one writer or another. V 7b is a duplication of v 2a, a duplication attributable to the author of v 2a or anyone coming after him. Based on these types of considerations, one cannot use phraseology alone in separating redactional layers in this passage.

Consideration of other aspects of the text seems to clear up this question to some degree. Several early source critics posited an original law consisting only of vv 11–13, primarily because of the reference to elders (see below).[53] This has been revised by more recent studies in two regards. First, the secondary nature of v 13 (as a Deuteronom[ist]ic motive clause) is now generally accepted. Second, it is obvious that vv 11–12 cannot stand on their own grammatically. The regulation begins with וְכִי rather than כִּי, signaling that it is a corollary regulation; and the phrase, "to one of these cities," (v 11b) presumes information found in those preceding verses.

More recent redaction critics argue that an earlier form of this law consisted of two corresponding halves: the first half dealt with those guilty of accidental manslaughter who fled to an asylum-city

---

[52] The assignation of v 6 to a particular layer is problematic. There is a single parallel to the כִּי-clause of v 6a in 14:24. The expression, "judgment of death," in v 6b has parallels in Deut 21:22 and Jer 26:11, 16. The ending of the verse is almost identical to the ending of v 4. These are so infrequent that one could attribute them to a common pre-Deuteronomic source. I have chosen to assign them to a Deuteronomic layer, because nothing of this verse is used in Deut 4:41–43 or Josh 20:1–6 (see below).

[53] R. H. Pfeiffer, *Introduction to the Old Testament* (New York: Harper and Brothers, 1941), p. 238; Rofé, "History of the Cities of Refuge," p. 213.

and were to be allowed to live there (vv 4–6), while the second half dealt with those guilty of premeditated murderer who were to be extradited and executed (vv 11–12).[54] This is plausible topically, but it too does not hold up grammatically. Vv 4–6 assume the existence of data regarding the designation of asylum-cities[55] which one finds only in vv 2–3. Gertz has recently refined this observation. He shows that vv 2b–3a, which contain Deuteronom(ist)ic phrases, are disruptive to the overall flow of thought in these verses; therefore, they can be excised as secondary without destroying the sense of the passage.[56] The clauses that remain (vv 2a and 3b) do provide a sufficient introduction to the regulations of vv 4–6 and 11–12. These findings show that one can reconstruct a plausible law (vv 2a, 3aα, 3b–6) and its corollary (vv 11–12) from the sections which contain little or no evidence of Deuteronom(ist)ic influence.

This is not proof, in and of itself, that these verses constituted the earliest form of this law, but this conclusion can be further refined by the fact that several phrases from Deut 19:2a, 3b–5, 11–12 occur also in Deut 4:41–43 and Josh 20:3–5, while the rest of this passage (including vv 3aα and 6; see n. 33) is not reflected in those two. Those passages are obviously secondary to—and probably derived in part from—this one. Joshua 20 seems to be something of a conflation of materials found in Priestly writings and in Deut 19:2a, 3b–5, 11–12, having elements consistent with

---

[54] Cp. G. Hölscher, "Komposition und Ursprung des Deuteronomiums," *ZAW* 40 (1922) 204–205; J. L'Hour, "Une législation criminelle dans le Deutéronome," *Bib* 44 (1963) 16–17; Rofé, "History of the Cities of Refuge," p. 210; Mayes, *Deuteronomy*, pp. 284–88.

[55] V 4a contains the clause, "who shall flee thither," without indicating where the final destination of the flight would be.

[56] Gertz, *Gerichtsorganisation*, pp. 118–27; cp. H. D. Preuss, *Deuteronomium* (ErFor 164; Darmstadt: Wissenschaftliche Buchgesellschaft, 1982), p. 55.

Gertz also excises v 5a as superfluous. It is so at any level of redaction. There is no hint of it in Deut 4:41–43 or Josh 20:1–6, which might indicate that it was not present in an early layer. On the other hand, none of the phraseology is attributable to other recognized sources, and the use of רע rather than את is consistent with the early layer. I prefer to retain v 5a in this early layer.

both.[57] On the other hand, although Deut 4:41–43 apparently derives from the same source(s) as Joshua 20, it presents an interpretation and application of Deut 19:1–13 which is different from that of Joshua 20. These observations, in conjunction with the fact that vv 2a, 3b–5, 11–12 contain little (if any) Deuteronom(ist)ic phraseology, suggest that these verses represent a "bare-minimum" reconstruction of the earliest layer of this passage, probably pre-Deuteronomic.[58]

We can now move from this earliest level to those which are obviously Deuteronomic. V 7b forms an inclusio with v 2a, repeating again the need for "three cities." Viewed by itself, one could argue that v 7b was part of a pre-Deuteronomic stratum as well. However, v 7a consists of a phrase which is found in a few other passages in the D Code, suggesting that v 7 is part of a Deuteronomic expansion of the law which utilizes clauses already in the earlier layer. The particular phrase used in v 7a—"Therefore, I am commanding you..."—is used in those other passages as part of the Deuteronomist's exhortations to the people to remember how they had been slaves in Egypt until Yahweh "brought them out" or "redeemed them" from that slavery (see Deut 15:11, 15; 24:18, 22; cp. 5:15). These statements are intended to explain how the speaker can feel justified in giving commands to this people. The thought they express—that God's past actions for his people obligate them to submit to his will—is a key component of Deuteronomic theology.

This thought is linked in this redactional layer to at least two other important Deuteronomic ideas: the divine gift of the land,

---

[57] It is possible that Joshua 20 and the Priestly materials stem from a common independent source. It has often been argued that the names of the six "cities of refuge" preserve an authentic list of such cities. But if this is the case, that list must be from the period of the United Monarchy. On the provenance of these lists, see below.

Some argue for the priority of Josh 20:4–5 over Deut 19:1–13 (see M. Noth, *Numbers*, trans. J. D. Martin [OTL; London: SCM, 1968], pp. 253–54). This is based primarily on the view that all P materials are later than all D materials.

[58] An intriguing stylistic phenomenon emerges from this reconstruction. Two main sections emerge in this layer—vv 4–5 and 11–12. These present opposing scenarios. The first ends with the phrase, "and he shall live;" the second ends with the phrase, "and he shall die."

with its continuing agricultural blessings, and the centralization of worship. The motif of the land as divine gift is mentioned in each of the first three verses in this passage, indicating the importance of this motif to the passage (see also vv 8–10, 13b). Commands to provide for the poor and for one's slaves elsewhere in the D Code are predicated on the reminder that Yahweh has blessed—and will continue to bless—those who live in the land which he has given them (15:4, 7, 10, 14). Similar ideas undergird the laws for providing for "the alien, the orphan, and the widow" (24:17–22). This implies that the phrases regarding the land as divine gift (vv 1, 2b, 3a) are Deuteronomic,[59] as is the divine promise, "and it will go well with you" (v 13b; cp. 5:16, 29, 33; 6:3, 18; 12:25, 28; 22:7).

At least two passages connect these thoughts to the Deuteronomic centralization motif. Deut 16:5–6 stresses the importance of worshipping Yahweh at the place that he will choose in the land given to the Israelites. Similarly, those who "possess" and "dwell" in the land which Yahweh has given to them (19:1) are to bring their firstfruits "to the place which the Lord your God will choose" (26:1–2). The emphasis in this passage on the land as gift (19:1, 2b–3a; cp. vv 8–10, 13b) suggests that the Deuteronomic lawgiver sees a connection between centralization—which is the most significant component of the Deuteronomic legislation—and these asylum-cities.[60] The

---

[59] The historicizing introductory formula ("der historisierenden Gebotseinleitung") in v 1 does appear often in deuteronomistic texts (Deut 2:21; Josh 19:47; 21:43). However, like Rüterswörden, I would argue that those texts arose in a Deuteronomic *Vorlage* (17:14; 19:1; cp. 12:29; 26:1; see Rüterswörden, *Von der politischen Gemeinschaft*, pp. 53–58). For the view that all examples of this formula are deuteronomistic, see N. Lohfink, "Kerygmata des Deuteronomistischen Geschichtswerks," in *Die Botschaft und die Boten. Festschrift für H. W. Wolff*, ed. J. Jeremias and L. Perlitt (Neukirchen-Vluyn: Neukirchener Verlag, 1981), pp. 87–100; Gertz, *Gerichtsorganisation*, pp. 30–31, 118–27.

[60] J. Wellhausen, *Prolegomena zur Geschichte Israels* (6th ed.; Berlin: Walter de Gruyter, 1927), p. 156; Pedersen, *Israel* I–II, p. 396; Hölscher, "Komposition," pp. 204–205; Pfeiffer, *Introduction*, p. 235; M. Greenberg, "The Biblical Concept of Asylum," *JBL* 78 (1959) 131–32; de Vaux, *Ancient Israel*, p. 162; von Rad, *Deuteronomy*, pp. 128–29; Weinfeld, *Deuteronomy and the Deuteronomic School*, pp. 236–37; G. Seitz, *Redaktionsgeschichtliche Studien zum Deuteronomium* (Stuttgart: W. Kohlhammer, 1971), pp. 111–13,

interpretive significance of this connection will be discussed shortly. These findings strongly suggest that at least Deut 19:1–7, 11–13 were present in the Deuteronomic redaction of this law.[61] What of the remaining section, vv 8–10? Several critics regard these verses as supplementary to the Deuteronomic layer, representing a later expansion of the law.[62] The key to this conclusion is the sense of the expansion formula which begins this section ("If the Lord your God enlarges your border," v 8a; cp. 12:20; Exod 34:24). Many link this directly to the military expansion of Judah during the reign of Josiah, therefore attributing vv 8–10 to a pre-exilic deuteronomistic redactor.[63] The remaining phrases in these verses, however, have numerous parallels in Deuteronomic sections of the book; there are so many, in fact, that one could argue that they too might be Deuteronomic.[64] Even if that is not the case, it seems most

---

230; Boecker, *Law*, p. 184; Preuss, *Deuteronomium*, p. 91; Rofé, "History of the Cities of Refuge," pp. 207–21. Some deny any connection between the asylum-cities and cult centralization; see Salmon, "Judicial Authority," pp. 155–64; Mayes, *Deuteronomy*, p. 284. For additional bibliography, see Gertz, *Gerichtsorganisation*, pp. 130–31 n. 55.

This does not eliminate the possibility, in my mind, that asylum-cities emerged prior to cult centralization. I merely contend that the land ideology associated with centralization also influences D's prescriptions on asylum. See Salmon, "Judicial Authority," pp. 155–64; J. Milgrom, "Sancta Contagion or Altar/City Asylum," in *Congress Volume, Vienna 1980*, ed. J. A. Emerton (SVT 32; Leiden: E. J. Brill, 1981), pp. 302–303.

[61] For virtually identical conclusions, see Seitz, *Redaktionsgeschichtliche Studien*), pp. 111–13, 224–30, 303–11; Mayes, *Deuteronomy*, pp. 284–88.

[62] De Vaux, *Ancient Israel*, pp. 161–62; Mayes, *Deuteronomy*, pp. 284, 287; Gertz, *Gerichtsorganisation*, pp. 120–21. L'Hour ("Une législation criminelle," pp. 16–17) places v 10 in the earlier layer, but vv 8–9 in a secondary layer; Preuss (*Deuteronomium*, p. 55) reserves only vv 8b–9a (+ 13) for this final layer.

[63] For the most recent survey, see Levinson, *Deuteronomy*, pp. 36–43. Levinson's own conclusion tends to place the expansion formula at an earlier stage in the D Code's development than most would accept. Cp. von Rad, *Deuteronomy*, p. 93; Seitz, *Redaktionsgeschichtliche*, p. 311; Preuss, *Deuteronomium*, p. 191; Rofé, "History of the Cities of Refuge," pp. 214–21. Gertz (*Gerichtsorganisation*, p. 121) says this is a post-Josianic literary fiction.

[64] Those who believe that the historicizing introductory formula in v 1 is deuteronomistic (see n. 10) could also argue that vv 1, 2b–3a, 7–10, 13 are all

implausible to assign vv 8–10 to an exilic redaction, if one believes that the main redaction was pre-exilic. It makes little sense to think that an exilic writer would take up a pre-exilic law that can apply only while Israel is in possession of her own land and, at a time when Israel is landless, pen an addendum that is based entirely on the possible expansion of Israel's borders. Based on these considerations, it is more reasonable to conclude that Deut 19:1–13 reached its present form prior to the Exile.

Traditio-Historical Considerations

Before proceeding to a discussion of the interpretation of this passage, we should consider how other passages which mention asylum-cities might influence one's reading of the regulations given here. There are five related passages: Exod 21:12–14; Numbers 35; Deut 4:41–43; Joshua 20–21; 1 Chr 6:39–66 (54–81, EV).

Many commentators rightly describe Exod 21:12–14 as the foundation upon which the asylum-laws build.[65] That passage sets forth the general principle that execution is the only divinely-ordained response to an act of murder, allowing an exception for

---

from a common deuteronomistic layer. I am disinclined to do so, however, because that type of interpretation would tend to remove several key phrases from those related to centralization.

A stylistic consideration supports the inclusion of vv 8–10 in a Deuteronomic layer. V 10 ends with a warning about "innocent blood" being shed and the consequence that "bloodshed will be upon you." V 13b balances this with the inducement that "you will purge the innocent blood from Israel, and it will be well with you." (Cp. n. 59, above, and Gertz, *Gerichtsorganisation*, p. 123)

[65] S. R. Driver, *A Critical and Exegetical Commentary on Deuteronomy* (ICC; New York: Charles Scribner's Sons, 1895), pp. viii–ix; de Vaux, *Ancient Israel*, p. 160; O. Eissfeldt, *The Old Testament, An Introduction*; 3rd Edition, trans. P. R. Ackroyd (New York: Harper & Row, 1965), p. 220; E. Sellin and G. Fohrer, *Introduction to the Old Testament*, trans. D. E. Green (Nashville: Abingdon, 1968), pp. 170, 173; A. Weiser, *The Old Testament: Its Formation and Development*; 4th Edition, trans. D. M. Barton (New York: Association Press, 1968), p. 131; Milgrom, "Sancta Contagion," pp. 299–302.

cases of accidental killing.[66] There is no explanation given here of how to handle this exception; rather, there is a vague mention of "a place" which God will set aside "to which the killer may flee" (v 13). Most commentators equate this "place" with the shrine associated with the altar mentioned in v 14 (cp. 1 Kgs 1:50–53; 2:28–34).

This basic outline is then expanded and concretized in other passages discussing asylum (Num 35:9–34; Deut 4:41–43; 19:1–13; Joshua 20). A couple reiterate the principle that execution alone is a just punishment for murder (Num 35:31–32; Deut 19:13), but the primary purpose of all of them is to explain how the exception for accidental killings is institutionalized through the designation of entire asylum-cities.[67] Still, a common assumption has been that the designation of entire cities is a development that arose subsequent to the writing of Exod 21:12–14.

Moshe Greenberg questions this assumption on the consideration that a shrine could not adequately provide for the long-term needs of such persons.[68] It does seem awkward to refer

---

[66] The law is very brief, yet the sense is obvious. The general principle is given first (v 12), the exception for cases of accidents follows (v 13), and then the general principle is reiterated for all other killings (v 14; see also vv 20–21, which reveal that differences based on social status are found in Israel, as they were in other ancient Near Eastern societies). The accidental-premeditated sequence (vv 13–14) matches that of the foundation layer of Deut 19:1–13. Numbers 35 moves from accidental (vv 9–15) to premeditated (vv 16–21) back to accidental (vv 22–28). Deut 4:41–43 and Josh 20:1–6 mention only accidental manslaughter.

[67] Greenberg, "Biblical Concept of Asylum," pp. 131–32; W. F. Albright, "The List of Levitic Cities," in *Louis Ginzberg Jubilee Volume*, ed. S. Lieberman, *et al*. (New York: American Academy for Jewish Research, 1946), pp. 51–52; M. Weber, *Ancient Judaism* (trans. H. H. Gerth and D. Martindale; Glencoe, IL: Free Press, 1952), pp. 172–74. The original occasion for the institution of asylum-cities is unknown. See D. Benjamin, *Deuteronomy and City Life* (Lanham, MD: University Press of America, 1983), p. 151. He believes that some of the asylum-cities fulfilled this function even before they were "retribalized" under Israelite control, and that they brought this function with them when they entered into the Israelite league. Cp. M. Haran, "Studies in the Account of the Levitical Cities. I. Preliminary Considerations," *JBL* 80 (1961) 51–52. Rofé contends that blood-payment was practiced in Israel until it was prohibited in the Priestly law code ("History of the Cities of Refuge," pp. 205–206, 235).

[68] Greenberg, "Biblical Concept of Asylum," pp. 126–30; see von Rad, *Deuteronomy*, pp. 128–29; Milgrom, "Sancta Contagion," pp. 299–302; Mayes,

to an "altar" as a "place," and most actually do interpret "place" as
the building or city in which the altar resided. But perhaps even
that is reading this passage too narrowly. One wonders how
necessary it would have been to tell people that they could go to
an altar when seeking mercy. Moreover, it seems strange that God
would refer so vaguely ("a place") to something which he specifies
in the very next sentence. I would suggest that it is because "my
altar" is not intended as the specifier for "a place." The word order
in Exod 21:14b puts the phrase, "from my altar," at the beginning
of the apodosis, emphasizing it. The sense of the entire verse
seems to be, "If a man attacks his neighbor to kill him by
treachery, even from my altar shall you take him for execution."
This reiteration (v 14) of the general principle with which the law
begins (v 12) is worded to imply that someone might attempt to
avoid his deserved punishment by appealing to Yahweh personally
at his altar (because of its inherent sanctity and, perhaps, because
of its closer proximity). But this merely acknowledges that an
altar was a natural alternative to any "place" designated for
asylum; it does not necessarily imply that an altar is the only
option available. In any case, Exod 21:12–14 does not provide most
of the details regarding asylum which one finds in the other
asylum-laws; the only item mentioned is that God himself
recognizes an accidental killing as the exception to the general
rule, allowing for asylum in the place of blood-vengeance.[69]

Deuteronomy, p. 285. For earlier discussion of this issue, see A. C. Welch, *The
Code of Deuteronomy: A New Theory of Its Origin* (New York: George H.
Doran, 1924), pp. 133–44; W. C. Graham, "The Modern Controversy about
Deuteronomy," *JRel* 7 (1927) 410–11.

[69] See Salmon, "Judicial Authority," pp. 161–64. Rofé suggests a similar
interpretation of the exchange between "place" and "altar" ("History of the
Cities of Refuge," pp. 214–19). He deduces from this that Jerusalem was
always a city of refuge, and that the initially three and then six cities of
refuge were added once all other sanctuaries were forbidden in the wake of
D's centralization program. He is correct to an extent. It makes sense to say
that the concern expressed in 19:6 ("because the distance is too great") is in
respect to the distance a killer might be from Jerusalem. I do not concur with
his conclusion that Jerusalem therefore served as a city of refuge throughout
Israel's history. One could always go to the altar/Temple in Jerusalem and
request asylum; but this does not make the entire city a place of refuge. For
example, when Benaiah takes Joab from the altar, he does not have to take

The remaining asylum-passages reflect the tradition that there were (eventually) six cities to which an accidental killer might flee; however, Deut 19:1–13 represents something of a transition text in the development of this tradition. Two of these passages (Joshua 21; 1 Chr 6:39–66) give the names of some of the six cities within lists of the names of forty-eight Levitical cities (cp. Num 35:1–8). Deut 4:41–43 names three of the cities and Joshua 20 names all six, each without reference to the Levitical cities.[70] These lists do not greatly influence one's understanding of Deut 19:1–13, except that they tend to support the general historicity of the tradition regarding six cities (see below).

Deut 4:41–43 names the three transjordanian asylum-cities and says that they were already constituted as such in the days of Moses.[71] This contradicts the clear implication of Deut 19:1–13, which speaks of three cities to be designated for asylum after the conquest of the land, plus three more should the territory be expanded. Some have argued that this is due to the fact that that writer did not have 19:1, 2b–3a, 6–10, 13 in his possession (see preceding discussion). Those verses are clearly Deuteronom(ist)ic,

---

him out of the city in order to kill him. The cities provide a place, apart from a sanctuary (or "sanctuaries"?), to which a killer could "flee... and ...live."

[70] Redaction critics recognize an original separation between the cities of refuge and the Levitical cities in Numbers 35 and Joshua 20–21. In the case of Numbers 35, the earliest layer consists of vv 1–5, 7–8. Because of the "inherently" priestly character of the cities of refuge, instructions about them were added in vv 9–15. V 6 was also inserted at this time to tie the two sections together. Either simultaneously or shortly thereafter, vv 16–34 were added, providing many details regarding the definitions of accidental and premeditated murder (Noth, *Numbers*, pp. 253–54; A. G. Auld, "Cities of Refuge in Israelite Tradition," *JSOT* 10 [1978] 27).

The combining of the two lists is paralleled in the redaction of Joshua 20–21. The record of the tribal allotments ends in Josh 19:51. The list of Levitical cities in Joshua 21 should logically have come immediately after this, for it serves as an "allotment" for the "tribe" of Levi. Instead, chapter 20 and the cities of refuge appear at this juncture. See Albright, "List of Levitic Cities," pp. 49–50; R. Boling, *Joshua* (AB; NY: Doubleday, 1982), pp. 58–59, 66–67; Auld, "Cities of Refuge," pp. 33–38; idem, "The 'Levitical Cities': Texts and History," *ZAW* 91 (1979) 194–200; Rofé, "History of the Cities of Refuge," pp. 232–36.

[71] Num 35:13–15 presents the same 3 + 3 scheme, but it does not name the cities, nor does it attribute Moses with personally designating the three transjordanian cities.

and they assume that all the asylum-cities are in territories yet to be occupied by the Israelites.[72] Thus, the apparent contradiction created by Deut 4:41–43 is attributed to the use of a (pre-) Deuteronomic version of Deut 19:1–13, in conjunction with other information about the location of the six cities of refuge.

This argument is not conclusive in and of itself, though. V 2a, which should be included as part of the earliest literary layer in the passage, also speaks of these as places yet to be designated as asylum-cities ("Three cities you *shall* set apart for yourself"). Therefore, one cannot attribute the contradiction created by 4:41–43 simply to an early form of 19:1–13. Rather, the problem is more likely to lie in the lists of the cities of refuge preserved in Josh 20:7–9 (cp. Joshua 21 and 1 Chr 6:39–66). Those lists place three of the six cities east of the Jordan River. Those cities were thus situated in territory conquered by Moses, according to the historical traditions. It might make sense to a writer—in a misguided attempt to harmonize his information—to assume that those cities had already been constituted for asylum by Moses himself.[73]

This raises the question of the provenance of the list of names of cities of refuge, a question which has stirred considerable debate. Three views prevail, usually in tandem with theories regarding the development of Levitical cities. One view, championed by Wellhausen and modified only slightly by scholars such as Alt and Noth, is that the cities of refuge are to be associated with Josiah's reform.[74] W. F. Albright and B. Mazar[75]

---

[72] Like some early and medieval Jewish writers, Milgrom ("Sancta Contagion," pp. 304–305) concludes that 19:1–13 envisions a total of nine asylum-cities (cp. Weinfeld, *Deuteronomy and the Deuteronomic School*, p. 237 n. 3; Rofé, "History of the Cities of Refuge," p. 222). The six mentioned here would all be west of the Jordan River, and the reader is supposed to realize that the three transjordanian cities of 4:41–43 had been previously constituted for this purpose. However, there is no textual corroboration for such an interpretation.

[73] I would question the wisdom of trying to place the author of Deut 4:41–43 within any deuteronomistic camp. Besides this unnecessary attempt at harmonization, these verses are obviously intrusive to their general context. The passage appears to be a late (post-deuteronomistic) marginal insertion. Cp. Preuss, *Deuteronomium*, p. 91.

[74] Wellhausen, *Prolegomena*, pp. 153–58; A. Alt, "Die Heimat des Deuteronomiums," *Kleine Schriften zur Geschichte des Volkes Israel* II

stand as the major proponents of a second view, which places the origin of these lists in or near the reign of Solomon. A small handful push this date into the pre-monarchic period.[76] A third view considers the lists to be idealizations created during the Exile.

The position of Albright and Mazar seems to be the most plausible. Some of the cities of refuge are not well-known. In fact, two of them (Bezer and Golan) appear in the Hebrew Bible only in these lists. No traditions have been preserved to explain why these sites, rather than others in the same general vicinities, would have been so designated. This indirectly supports the authenticity of the list of cities of refuge. Further, some of the cities, like Bezer, do not appear to have been under Israelite control any later than the time of Solomon, while some important religious sites are missing from the list, most noticeably Jerusalem and Bethel. Taken together, these facts suggest that a writer living in Josiah's time or later would have no reason to choose these cities as cities of refuge, as this would seem to go even beyond the expectations of an "ideal" or "utopian" programme. This implies that the lists are based in history, to some extent. If the lists are historically based at all, they must date no later than the days of the Davidic Monarchy.[77] This does not mean, however, that the passages which contain these lists in their present form (Joshua 20–21; 1 Chr 6:39–66) are that ancient. Rather, it merely suggests that their composers are faithfully transmitting authentic lists from that earlier time.

(Munich: C. E. Beck, 1953), p. 274; idem, "Die Ursprünge des israelitischen Rechts," *Kleine Schriften* I, pp. 294–97, 306–15; Noth, *Numbers*, pp. 253–55; see M. David, "Die Bestimmung über die Asylstädte," *OTS* 9 [1951] 30–48; N. M. Nicolsky, "Das Asylrecht in Israel," *ZAW* 7 (1930) 158–64; and de Vaux, *Ancient Israel*, p. 162.

[75] Albright, "List of Levitic Cities," pp. 49–59; B. Mazar, "The Cities of the Priests and the Levites," *SVT* 7 (1960) 193–205; see Milgrom, "Sancta Contagion," pp. 299–300.

[76] Attributed to Y. Kaufmann, *Commentary on Joshua* (Jerusalem, 1959), p. 262; see Rofé, "History of Cities of Refuge," pp. 207–10 for this and further bibliography on all three views.

[77] F. M. Cross, "Reuben, First-Born of Jacob," *ZAWSup* 100 (1988) 47–48 (see also the reading in 4QSam[a]); Haran, "Studies," pp. 45–53, 156–65; J. A. Dearman, "The Levitical Cities of Reuben and Moabite Toponymy," *BASOR* 276 (1989) 55–66.

Numbers 35 and Deut 19:1–13 differ from those passages in that they give the number of cities (six) but not their names. Those who argue that the lists are exilic idealizations sometimes use this datum for support, explaining the absence of the names here as evidence that the exact location of the cities had not previously been determined.[78] Seitz provides a reasonable but opposing interpretation of this evidence. He proposes that the Deuteronomic lawgiver (and the composer of Numbers 35?) is aware of an ancient list of the names of the cities, but he omits the names of those cities from this law because he knows that some of those cities are no longer in Israelite hands.[79] His concern is to see that asylum is available for accidental killers, but not to predicate the perpetuation/revival of that institution on an outdated list of cities.

The preceding source-critical analysis of Deut 19:1–13 suggests some further nuancing to this reconstruction. The earliest layer of this law mentions only three asylum-cities. Not only does the law not name these cities, it is likely that it is not even concerned with developing a well-planned geographical distribution, as one finds in later redactions.[80] This makes the stipulation that there be three cities (and three more later) all the more intriguing. I have accepted the position that the lists of six asylum-cities found elsewhere preserve a tenth-century situation, but I am also implying in my source-critical analysis that a law composed between the times of the Covenant Code and the D Code calls for only three asylum-cities. I conclude from this that the political situation in the intervening years deprived Israel of some of those cities and reduced the extent of Israelite territory such that only three were deemed necessary. The extending of those borders again at a later time necessitated additional asylum-cities (vv 8–10). We are left with no explanation for instituting asylum-

---

[78] David, "Die Bestimmung," pp. 30–48; de Vaux, *Ancient Israel*, p. 162.

[79] Seitz, *Redaktionsgeschichtliche Studien*, pp. 225–26.

[80] This depends on whether one includes vv 3aα and 6 in the earliest layer. I have chosen to exclude them (see above), but this is primarily an argument from silence (i.e., nothing in these verses shows up in Deut 4:41–43 or Josh 20:1–6). It should be noted that v 3aα and v 6 go together topically. They are both concerned with making sure that the asylum-cities are distributed so that they are of the greatest benefit to the fugitive. If these verses are included in the earliest layer, then it changes this particular conclusion.

cities in multiples of three in this law (maybe it just happened that way?), while the explanation given in Deut 4:41–43 is obviously an idealizing retrojection.[81]

Two other issues derived from comparisons between Deut 19:1–13, on the one hand, and Num 35:9–34 and Josh 20:1–6, on the other, touch directly on our understanding of the Deuteronomic law. These issues are: (a) the mention of the high priest in the other laws, and (b) the location of the "trial" of the accused killer. They cannot be entirely separated from one another, and so I will discuss them together.

Num 35:9–34 and Josh 20:1–6 order the accidental manslayer to reside in the city of refuge until the death of the high priest (of the city of refuge? of the entire nation?).[82] No such reference is made in Deut 19:1–13. The latter could be due to a simple omission or to the non-existence of the office of high priest at the time of the law's composition. I see no way of resolving this question based on the evidence that we have.

There are a couple of matters of perspective which might need to be considered, though, by those examining this question from the viewpoint of the Priestly redaction. First, the D Code has very little to say at all about cultic matters or cultic personnel, even though centralization of the cult is a major concern. It would not be surprising to find that the lawgiver simply did not feel it necessary to mention in this law the role to be played by a high priest. Second, this law (and the others we will be examining) tends to look at these matters primarily in terms of how they concern the local town.[83]

The possibility that this latter point is significant is brought out by considering the location of the killer's trial. At first glance, the venue prescribed in Deut 19:11–12 seems to contradict that of the

---

[81] Mayes attributes this to monarchic bureaucracy (*Deuteronomy*, p. 285). This might be the best assumption about how a group of cities could receive a special designation simultaneously, but it still does not explain the reason for multiples of three.

[82] The latter option (that the high priest is priest at the central sanctuary for the entire nation) is commonly assumed (see Gertz, *Gerichtsorganisation*, p. 149). On the former, see Weinfeld, *Deuteronomy and the Deuteronomic School*, pp. 236–37 n. 6.

[83] See L'Hour, "Une législation criminelle," pp. 26–27; Pedersen, *Israel* I–II, pp. 33–38.

other laws. This law refers to the elders of the killer's city alone taking any sort of action. Num 35:22–25 and Josh 20:6 call for the manslayer to be brought from the city of refuge to "the congregation" to be judged. The obvious meaning of this is that the entire nation must be brought in to observe every murder trial.[84] Such a scenario seems unnecessary and unrealistic in any period of Israel's history,[85] but it is consistent with P's tendency to hyperbolize an action by any part of the nation as an action performed by the entire sacral community ("the congregation;" see Lev 4:13; 24:14–16). The D Code more realistically conveys the sense that an action by a local community can be carried out on behalf of or for the sake of the entire nation.[86]

Other problems are made evident by Josh 20:4–6 regarding the location of the trial. In its present form, two trials appear to be commanded. First, the manslayer pleads his case before the elders of the city of refuge to which he has fled (20:4). Second, he is to remain there "until there is a trial before the congregation, until the death of the one who is high priest at the time" (20:6a). This

---

[84] It is theoretically possible that "congregation" could refer to the assembly of one town (cp. Korah's "congregation" in Num 16:5, 6, 11, 16, 40; 26:9–10; 27:3), and so it is possible to read Numbers 35 and say that the original intent of the law was to have the killer returned to his hometown for trial. But a survey of the use of עדה throughout Numbers and other P materials leaves no doubt that the entire nation is intended in the present text.

[85] See Noth, *Numbers*, p. 255; J. Sturdy, *Numbers* (CBC; Cambridge: Cambridge University Press, 1976), pp. 241–42.

Irregular gatherings of the entire nation seem absurd, from a geographical perspective, unless the nation is very restricted territorially. But in that case, there would seem to be little possibility of—and no reason for—cities of refuge. These considerations suggest to me that the asylum-law in Numbers 35, in its present form, is a later, idealized redaction.

[86] For example, the exaction of blood-vengeance on a premeditated murderer is ordained by a single city; yet, by so doing, "you shall purge the guilt of innocent blood from Israel" (19:13; cp. 21:18; 22:21, 22, 24). Similarly, the elders of one city perform a sacrifice that expiates the entire nation (21:8).

The Deuteronomic lawgiver seems to have taken several "municipal" laws and rewritten them for a national audience. However, his purpose is not to say that some local matters must be dealt with nationally. This is what is done in P. D, on the other hand, simply shows that local matters often have national implications; but D does not call for adjudication by the entire nation. Instead, most cases are still to be tried locally, but with the rest of the nation "watching in."

might seem like a dual conflation. Not only are there two trials, but there are two results to the first trial—either the killer goes to (a second?) trial before the congregation, or he remains in the city until the high priest's death. A trial "before the congregation" seems unnecessary, if a trial has already been conducted at the city of refuge; so, the most economical way to remove the conflict is to say that the reference to the second trial ("before the congregation") represents a conflation of sources. But the parallel in Num 35:22–25 contains both the trial before the congregation and references to a high priest; so, if one is excised on the basis of conflation, both should be.

But Josh 20:1–6 is not self-contradictory.[87] Josh 20:4 probably does not refer to a full trial in which the elders of the city of refuge are thought to render a final verdict. Only the fugitive speaks "his words;" there is no word from the blood avenger. Rather than a trial, this is a formal petition for asylum by the fugitive. The elders of the city of refuge, acting in their capacity as representatives of their city to outsiders,[88] take him in temporarily because it is their social obligation to do so in the face of the "hot anger" of the blood avenger. Only after a trial under "cooler" conditions before the congregation has proved the killer's claim is his permanent residence in the city of refuge established.

---

[87] These verses do indicate a conflation of sources, though. The Priestly expression בִּשְׁגָגָה is duplicated in v 3 by the Deuteronomic expression בִּבְלִי דַעַת (see v 5). The Priestly phrase "cities of refuge" (v 2) seems purposefully avoided in vv 4–5, while the phrase "elders of that city" (v 4) appears elsewhere only in Deut 19:12; 21:3–6, 19–20; 25:7–9. The affirmation of the accidental nature of the deed (לֹא שֹׂנֵא הוּא לוֹ מִתְּמוֹל שִׁלְשׁוֹם; v 6) is Deuteronomic in style (see Deut 4:42; 19:4). Also, the manslayer's victim in v 5 is "his neighbor" (רֵעֵהוּ; cp. Deut 19:4–5, 11), not just "any person" (נֶפֶשׁ; cp. v 3; Num 35:11, 16).

These impressions receive textual confirmation from the LXX. All evidence of Deuteronomic redaction (בִּבְלִי דַעַת in v 3, and all of vv 4–5) is absent from LXX[B] and several minuscules. An explanation of this would involve a much broader examination of the textual traditions of the Book of Joshua, but it would appear that a Priestly text has been expanded due to influence from Deuteronomic materials. See Auld, "Cities of Refuge," pp. 26–40; Rofé, "History of the Cities of Refuge," pp. 231–32.

[88] Gertz argues that Josh 20:4 shows a later idealization because it places adjudication in the hands of city elders (*Gerichtsorganisation*, pp. 151–56). The present line of argument undermines that interpretation.

This still leaves a striking contrast between Deut 19:1–13 and the Priestly laws in Num 35:9–34 and Josh 20:1–6. The Deuteronomic law implies that the case is ultimately heard by the elders of the city in which the killing took place; the Priestly laws call for a trial "before the congregation," apparently meaning before the entire nation gathered as a sacral community. The latter passages probably are more concerned with conveying the ultimate religious implications of such a case, bringing out the fact that killing encroaches on the sacredness of the entire nation. Deut 19:1–13 does not ignore that fact, but it deals with it in a more "realistic" way. The Deuteronomic lawgiver brings out the inherent sacredness of the land by repeatedly reminding his audience that the land is a gift from Yahweh (19:1, 2b–3a, 8–10, 13), but he calls upon the community immediately involved—not the entire nation—to provide expiation for its pollution (cp. Deut 13:7–19; 21:8–9).

Thus, Deut 19:1–13 stands as a Deuteronomic expansion of a law intended to clarify Exod 21:12–14.[89] Certain details of other asylum-laws are simply omitted. Most important to the present investigation is the omission of the fugitive's petition before the elders of the city of refuge (Josh 20:4). Such a hearing is not contradicted by the prescriptions of Deut 19:1–13, and it probably is assumed by the Deuteronomic lawgiver to be a "natural" component of this situation.[90] Only two substantive differences are evident. One is that the Deuteronomic law implies a change in the identification of the cities to which a manslayer may flee. The number and/or location of the cities of refuge do not appear to have been Deuteronomic creations. In fact, the list of locations preserved in the Hebrew Bible probably originated early on in the Israel's history. Deut 19:1–13 demonstrates, however, that the implementation of the principles of earlier laws on asylum was not tied to the specific cities listed previously.[91] The other substantive

---

[89] One might make some similar comments about Numbers 35 as a Priestly redaction of the law. Determining its date of composition requires an independent study. It does not appear to have had any influence on Deut 19:1–13.

[90] This is but one example of the complementarity of the law codes of the Hebrew Bible, parallel to what one finds in other ancient Near Eastern societies.

[91] See Benjamin, *Deuteronomy and City Life*, p. 151.

difference is in the location of the main "trial" of the killer. Priestly law places cases of murder under the immediate jurisdiction of "the congregation," apparently meaning the entire nation as sacral community. The specifically Deuteronom(ist)ic sections of the law in Deuteronomy (19:1, 2b–3a, 6–10, 13) highlight the notion of Israel as sacred land by emphasizing Israel's indebtedness to Yahweh for possession of it. But the Deuteronomic view is that each local community is primarily responsible for maintaining the sacral purity of its own territory. Other laws in the D Code suggest that the nation takes collective action only after a local community has failed to carry out its own obligations in this regard (Deut 13:13–19).

Preliminary Conclusions

In conclusion, one sees that Deut 19:1–13 is one of several passages touching on the Israelite practice of asylum. The basic principles are laid out in Exod 21:12–14. One guilty of killing a fellow Israelite should expect death for his deed (vv 12, 14); the only exception made is for a killing that can be proven to have been accidental (v 13). The subsequent laws of asylum (Num 35:9–34; Deut 19:1–13; Josh 20:1–6; cp. Deut 4:41–43) set the parameters (literally and figuratively) within which the killer in such an exceptional case must live in order to avoid death at the hand of a blood-avenger. The tradition of setting aside six cities apparently has its roots in the tenth century, as evidenced by the names of cities of refuge embedded in Joshua 20–21 and 1 Chr 6:39–66. This ancient tradition is perpetuated or revived in the laws of Numbers 35 and Deut 19:1–13.[92] The locations of the cities are not given here, however, probably because those have changed due to the vicissitudes of history.

Two or three redactional layers can be discerned in Deut 19:1–13. The earliest (Deut 19:2a, 3aα, 3b–6, 11–12) merely elaborates on how the basic ideas set forth in Exod 21:12–14 were realized in the nation's history through the designation of asylum-cities. The Deuteronomic lawgiver placed these ideas within the

---

[92] McKeating, "Development," p. 54.

setting of the land as a gift from Yahweh (Deut 19:1, 2b–3a, 6–7, 13), a setting which implies the notion of the sacredness of the land. This setting is a significant component of the Deuteronomist's centralization ideology, but it also served as a foundation which would support the institution of asylum-cities and allows "expanded" application of the institution in tandem with any territorial expansion which the nation might enjoy (19:8–10). Such an institution, placed within this religio-political thought-world, would seem most at home in the days of the monarchy. Later texts idealize the geographic distribution of these cities and the historical beginnings of this institution by attributing its implementation directly to Moses and Joshua, and by explaining its expanded application (the 3 + 3 scheme for the establishment of asylum-cities) through the nation's territorial expansion under their specific leadership (Deut 4:41–43; Joshua 20; cp. Num 35:13–15).

A careful comparison of the various passages indicates that they are not exhaustive in their intent, that procedural matters contained in each are not necessarily mutually exclusive of those in other passages. Up to a point, the different traditions appear to be in agreement, complementing one another in the information they provide. When a killing occurred, the killer expected retaliation at the hands of the blood-avenger, a member of the victim's family. The killer could attempt to escape by fleeing to an altar (Exod 21:14) or to one of the asylum-cities (Num 35:6, 10–11; Deut 4:41–43; 19:3–6; Josh 20:2–3). If he went to an asylum-city, he had to make a request of the elders of that city for "official" asylum (Josh 20:4–6), which they probably were obligated to grant. It is not until this point that an actual trial would commence. And this is where the literary traditions diverge. In the Priestly tradition, the killer goes from the city of refuge to "the congregation," before whom he and his accuser (the blood avenger) stand and have their case judged. He then is either executed by the blood-avenger (in cases of premeditated murder) or returned to the city of refuge (in cases of accidental killing), remaining there until a high priest dies (Num 35:9–34). In the Deuteronomic tradition, the killer remains in the asylum-city while the elders of his hometown try his case. If he is found guilty of accidental manslaughter, he remains in the asylum-city; if he is found guilty of premeditated murder, he is remanded to the blood avenger for execution (Deut 19:4–5, 11–12). Any attempt to reconcile these two traditions seems futile. A partial explanation for their differences lies in their respective perspectives on Israel as sacral society. The Priestly tradition seems to view the entire nation of Israel as immediately responsible for encroachments against the sacredness of any of its parts. The Deuteronomic tradition also emphasizes the religious unity of Israel and the common obligation to maintain its sacral purity; but it places the responsibility for correcting sacral infractions on the local community. Only if the local community fails to act does the broader nation interpose itself.

The Deuteronomic Asylum-Law

These findings must now be interpreted in the light of the evidence presented earlier regarding the handling of homicide in contemporary kinship-based societies and ancient Near Eastern societies. I will address two interrelated issues. One is the issue of how the main purpose or goal of the original law (Deut 19:2a, 3b–5, 11–12) would have been augmented or modified by subsequent literary revisions. The second question concerns the particular role(s) played by city elders in cases of homicide. This role should be interpreted in the light of what we have seen regarding similar societies past and present.

Goal of the Pre-Deuteronomic Law (19:2a, 3b–5, 11–12)

Three cities you shall set aside for yourself..., so that any killer may flee there.

And this is the case of the killer who shall flee there and live: Who[ever] strikes his friend unknowingly, though he held no hatred toward him previously—[for example, one] who comes with his friend into the forest to chop wood and his hand stretches out with the axe to cut the tree and the iron slips from the wood and it finds his friend and he dies—that one shall flee to one of these cities and he shall live.

But if a man hates his friend and ambushes him and rises against him and wounds him mortally so that he dies, and he flees to one of these cities, then the elders of his city shall send

and they shall take him from there and they shall give him into
the hand of the blood-avenger and he shall die.

The law falls into three parts. The brief introduction
establishes flight to an asylum-city as the "general rule" for
anyone who kills a fellow Israelite. Then, the two main parts of
the law give the two outcomes possible: asylum for an unspecified
length of time ("he shall flee there and live") for accidental
manslaughter, and death at the hand of the blood-avenger for
premeditated murder. We can deduce that the elders of the city in
which the killing took place are the ones primarily responsible for
the adjudicative aspects of this process, even though most of the
information on their role is omitted from this law.

The introduction of this law (19:2a, 3b) points to a shift in focus
from the earlier law of Exod 21:12–14. The focus of that earlier
law is on the principle that a murderer is deserving of death. This
principle is so important that the sacredness of the altar itself is
not violated by the execution of a murderer. The law acknowledges
accidental manslaughter as a divinely-recognized exception, but
its main concern is to affirm the notion of commensurate
retaliation.[93] The focus of this asylum-law shifts the attention
toward the welfare of the whole community and the need to limit
the effects of a wrong once it has been committed. It affirms that
"any/every killer may flee" (19:3b) to an asylum-city. It gives no
indication that anyone is turned away at the asylum-city, whether
the killing was accidental or premeditated. The call for three
asylum-cities implies the desire for adequate accessibility,
accessibility that shows the greatest concern for the fate of the
killer immediately after he has killed. The asylum-cities naturally
serve to provide an automatic "cooling-off period" when relations
are understandably "hot."

These observations suggest the appropriateness of several
assumptions. These need to be clarified as we look from the
introduction ahead into the main parts of the law. First, one can
assume that the principle that a murderer is deserving of death
(Exod 21:12–14) is still maintained; otherwise, the killer would
not fear for his life. But from whom does he flee? It is most logical

---

[93] Bovati uses the phrase "proportionate retribution" (*Re-Establishing Justice*, p. 59 n. 76).

to assume that he flees from one of the victim's male relatives. There is ample evidence from other biblical materials for this assumption, even though it is not stated in the earlier law or in the introduction of this one.[94] It is confirmed later in the law, however, by the reference to the blood-avenger (v 12; see below). A third assumption deduced from the main sections of the law which follow (vv 4–5, 11–12) is that the elders of the city in which the killing took place are the ones primarily responsible for hearing the case and rendering a verdict.

No mention is made of the actual process of adjudication, but the most logical conclusion is that the elders of the city in which the killing took place take the lead in performing this function. Most commentators have accepted this point,[95] but the recent counter-proposal by Gertz prompts me to argue it anew. Gertz's position is based on the conclusion that this law is in the same redaction layer (Deuteronomic) as the command for the appointment of "judges and officers" (Deut 16:18). He further assumes that judges and city elders would serve duplicative adjudicative roles, and he points out that this law specifically states only one function of the city elders, that of representatives for their community to others. So, he concludes that professional judges render a verdict in these cases, and then the elders commission a message on their behalf to the asylum-city.[96] I would contend that there is no precedent or parallel for such a procedure in such societies, either ancient or contemporary. Gertz's reconstruction essentially places the city elders in the role of "errand boys" for the judge, an arrangement which would be below the dignity of any group of local elders. Had a judge rendered the decision, then he would have sent his own messengers ("officers"?) with the request for the killer's extradition. Furthermore, as I have shown above, there is ample evidence that appointed judges and traditional local elders can work in complementary fashion, without duplicating their judicial functions; so, Gertz's assumption in that regard is unwarranted. In short, it is more logical to assume that the city elders render

[94] See above, on גאל הדם.

[95] Salmon, "Judicial Authority," p. 404; Mayes, *Deuteronomy*, p. 288.

[96] Gertz, *Gerichtsorganisation*, pp. 137–40, 151–56; see also Bovati, *Re-Establishing Justice*, p. 58.

the decision in the case, the result of which they then communicate to the leaders of the asylum-city.

But this issue cannot be completely answered in this way; an additional consideration must be included. It is helpful to recognize that the identification of the killer is assumed. There is no uncertainty about who killed whom. The killer flees to the city of refuge because he has killed his "friend." A blood-avenger chases him and him alone, because he knows who the culprit is. The killer does not deny that he has killed someone; in fact, he openly admits it. The fact that he has killed must be known by the citizens of the asylum-city, if he is to expect them to provide him with protection from the blood-avenger. Thus, the matters for discussion in a "trial" would not include the determination of the guilty party; instead, the adjudicators would be concerned with the motive of the killing (was it premeditated or accidental) and the form of punishment that such a killing warrants. The latter is determined by custom and reaffirmed by this law. But the former is precisely what Deuteronomic law says is to be addressed by judges and priests (Deut 17:8–9). They are to decide "between one kind of bloodshed and another." They do not do this in all cases, only in cases which are "difficult."[97] The most logical conclusion is that city elders normally determine the exact nature of a killing, but that they can hand it over to other judicial functionaries (judges and priests) in difficult cases. Such an arrangement is well-represented in analogous societies (see above).

The law addresses cases of accidental manslaughter first. Comparative data show that kinship-based societies usually employ a less severe form of punishment in such cases, and this part of the law shows that the same is true for ancient Israel. The form of punishment employed is exile. Weinfeld concludes that there is no punishment for accidental manslaughter, because it says here that the one guilty of accidental manslaughter "shall live" (19:4–5).[98] This interpretation is untenable. The notion was

---

[97] Levinson, *Deuteronomy*, p. 128.

[98] "The asylum is not the place in which he [the killer] serves his punishment, but the place which protects him from the vengeance of the blood-redeemer... he is to remain there until the rage of the avenger subsides." Weinfeld, *Deuteronomy and the Deuteronomic School*, p. 237; cp. Rofé, "History of Cities of Refuge," pp. 230–32.

always strong in Israel that the shedding of blood is a serious infraction, but the intent of the heart is also considered. The punishment—or better, the consequence—in this case is banishment from one's home.[99] This is recognized most clearly in the fact that the law twice identifies an asylum-city as a place to which someone might "flee... and live" (vv 4, 5). The two actions—"flee" and "live"—are complementary to each other. There is no mention of returning to one's home to live. One lives at the place to which one has fled. The fact that the killing was not done in anger removes the need for retaliation, but the killing has deprived some family of one of its members. In a sense, forcing the killer to live away from his family "equalizes" things with the victim's family. The absence of the killer from his home and family would have created a significant financial burden upon his family, which apparently was viewed as sufficient punishment for the crime committed. His family is deprived of the services and benefits that might be provided by one of its members, just as he deprived the victim's family of the benefit of one of its members.[100]

The duration of this banishment is not stated in this law. Contemporary analogies suggest that this would be determined by community leaders, in consultation with the victim's family. The leaders' concern is two-fold. They are concerned that proper honor and consideration be given to the victim's family, that the death of one of their members not be trivialized. But the leaders are also concerned about the welfare of the community as a whole. The strength of each part of the community—even the strength of the victim's family—is tied to the strength of the whole. The weakening of the killer's family can have adverse effects on the rest of the community, including the victim's family. So, after some time has passed, community leaders might call for an end to the killer's banishment.

The Israelite example that comes closest to being a case of actual banishment is provided in the stories of Absalom. He flees to his mother's home in Moab after killing Amnon, until David calls for his return (2 Sam 13:37–14:33; cp. Moses' flight to Midian, Exodus 2:11–15). David partially represents both of the

---

[99] See Greenberg, "Biblical Concept of Asylum," pp. 128–31. Also, see the quote from Demosthenes, n. 47, above.

[100] Pedersen, *Israel* I–II, pp. 378–80.

opposing groups in this story. He is anguished for a while as the father of the victim, expected perhaps to plot his revenge (see 2 Sam 13:31, 37–39). The killer banishes himself before the victim's family takes any retaliatory action;[101] but then Joab points out to David the negative effects caused by the killer's continued absence, and so he assumes the role of community leader for the palace in allowing the killer to return. This suggests that, in other cases, the duration of the banishment was determined by the leaders of the community (thinking of David as the head of the palace "community") and by the victim's family (thinking of David as the head of Amnon's family). This law's omission of any guidelines for this aspect of the case allows for flexibility, leaving the decision (and responsibility) ultimately in the hands of the local community.[102]

The city elders take center stage in the final section of this law (19:11–12). They send word to the asylum-city to have the killer extradited to their community, and then they hand the killer over to the blood-avenger (v 12). Their actions indicate that they are acting on behalf of their community as a whole. They represent their community to another community when they send for the killer. The question which must be addressed, then, is why this requires the services of persons who represent the entire community.

One significant aspect of this law which is too easily minimized is that only one city is really involved. The use of the term רֵעַ ("neighbor"/ "friend") suggests that the killer and his victim were acquaintances prior to the killing.[103] Likewise, the premeditated nature of the killing determined in this case (vv 11–12) would naturally infer a previous acquaintance between killer and

---

[101] The exact form of punishment expected is not clear. It could be that banishment is the appropriate punishment, because the killing might have been considered "justified," given the circumstances.

[102] It is different, of course, in the Priestly regulations, where the duration of the banishment is tied to the life of the high priest. This places ultimate control in the hands of the entire nation.

[103] In fact, the use of the term in some contexts reveals that one's relative could also be his "friend" (2 Sam 13:3; see also 1 Sam 30:26; 2 Sam 15:37; 16:16–17; 1 Kgs 4:5; 1 Chr 27:33; Ps 35:14; Jer 9:3).

victim.[104] But those in the asylum-city are not involved—in fact, cannot be involved—in the process of determining the killer's motive. The goal of an "investigation" is to determine the motive for the killing, if any. This requires detailed knowledge of relations between the parties involved (by the elders themselves or reliable witnesses who know the two well) for some time prior to the killing. Those who adjudicate have to be able to determine whether there was "enmity" (שׂנא) between the two prior to the incident. This is best determined by local persons (the elders—and local judges and priests, if needed). This confirms again that the "hearing" mentioned in Josh 20:4 can only be an official petition for asylum, but not a "trial."

We must now move beyond the fact that local leaders "try" the case of murder to a sense of the goal of that adjudication. The comparative material surveyed earlier strongly suggests that the Israelites understood a homicide as a personal affront against the victim's family and their honor, and vengeance is the accepted method by which the family can restore its honor. The victim's family would want to seek vengeance first from the manslayer himself. There are two risks to the broader community likely in this, though, and each is treated in this law. If the manslayer is caught and killed, but his own lineage mates feel that his death is unnecessary or unjustified, then they will feel obligated to avenge his death, and a feud could easily erupt. This is the motivation for the first main section of the law (vv 4–5). If the killer cannot be apprehended, the blood-avenger might strike out against one of the killer's kin, again causing his lineage mates to feel obligated to

---

[104] See Deut 22:25–26, where the rape of a woman in an open field is compared to a man murdering his "neighbor." The text implies that the rapist had taken stock of the situation prior to the act. He had tried to insure that no one would be around to stop him or bear witness to the crime, in the same way that a man who kills his neighbor would plot and wait for the most opportune moment to strike.

Of course, this need not exclude other possible scenarios; this law simply envisions the most common one. If the victim's family lived in a different city than the killer's family, the victim's family probably would have engaged the services of the elders of their city to approach the elders of the other city with their complaint. There are several examples of this. See Evans-Pritchard, *Nuer*, p. 163; Peristiany, "Law," p. 46; Bourdieu, "Sentiment of Honour," pp. 201–202.

avenge the second killing, thereby starting a feud. This is the
motivation for the second main section (vv 11–12).[105]
    The city elders (and the judges and priests, on some occasions)
play a crucial role in sorting out this kind of situation, because
they represent the community as a whole. Their concern is to do
what is best for the entire community, what will lead to "healing"
between two significant segments of the community. Asylum for
any killer provides the elders of a city with a "cooling-off period,"
during which they can meet with the two segments and negotiate
a resolution to the societal rift caused by the killing. If the killing
was an accident, the granting of asylum provides the elders with
the time they need to convince the victim's family of that fact,
before they commit an unwarranted killing which will escalate
into a full-fledged feud. If the killing was premeditated, this
"cooling-off period" allows the elders the time they need to
demonstrate that fact to the killer's family, and to convince them
of the "rightness" of the killer's own death.
    The significance of handing the killer over to the blood-avenger
should not be minimized either. The ancient principle of personal
blood-vengeance is affirmed by the elders in this law, as they
insure that the premeditated murderer is remanded to a member
of the victim's family.[106] This move is best explained as a

---

[105] See Pedersen, *Israel* I–II, pp. 388–95, 410. Rofé assumes that the law
restricts an avenger to taking his revenge on the killer only, that even prior
to the law's composition custom had so restricted the institution ("History of
the Cities of Refuge," p. 206).
    [106] Phillips has argued that the הדם גאל was a public official, not a
member of the victim's family. Further, he contends that this person acted as
an agent on behalf of the elders of the killer's city, going to the city of refuge
to retrieve the killer and return him to his home for punishment (*Ancient
Israel's Criminal Law*, pp. 103–106; cp. Mayes, *Deuteronomy*, p. 287).
    Phillips's premise that הדם גאל designates a special גאל is correct;
however, he need not look outside the family for this person. The usual גאל
was the *paterfamilias* (or whatever close relative was best able to help
financially; see Lev 25:47–55), the one who was to "redeem" someone who was
in financial straits. The הדם גאל need not have financial prowess, but
military ability, i.e., the one best able to avenge his dead relative with
strength and courage.
    One must also be careful not to read too much into the role of the גאל הדם
from Joshua 20. The killer in that case is not guilty of premeditated murder.
The גאל הדם there must have come to the city of refuge on his own behalf,
without the support of the elders of his city. On the other hand, in Deut

manifestation of a concern for recognizing the honor and dignity of the victim's family, for affirming the society's traditional attitude toward premeditated murder, and for maintaining peace in the community. The blood-avenger restores his family's honor by this deed, as he implicitly refutes any power that the killer implicitly claimed over the victim's family by his act. More important, this execution reaffirms that this community holds to the notion that "Whoever sheds the blood of a man, by man shall that man's blood be shed" (Gen 9:6). A failure on the part of the elders to see that the murderer be punished would leave a permanent stain on their community and a permanent rift in the community. To allow that punishment to fall on someone other than the killer himself would also lead to prolonged hostilities between two families in the community, splitting it permanently. For all these reasons, the elders act as representatives for their community and send to the asylum-city to have the killer returned.[107]

The intent of the original law, then, is to establish some procedural parameters by which Israelites can be guided in their quest for an honorable resolution to a killing, because only an honorable resolution can prevent long-term hostilities and restore the integrity of the community as a whole. The participation of the elders in the case shows that the effects of such a crime are not limited to individuals, but rather extend out into the community, amongst the relatives and neighbors of the parties involved. The killer has fled to an asylum-city so that the victim's family can no longer reach him. If they turn and avenge themselves on another member of the killer's family or lineage, that lineage would feel obligated to avenge the second death, because they would deem such an action unjustified. Things could quickly escalate into a protracted feud, involving major segments of the city's population. The elders are sympathetic to the feelings of the victim's family, because vengeance is an honorable thing in this society. To take

---

19:11–12, the manslayer is guilty of premeditated murder, the elders have so judged the case, and the elders of the city of refuge hand the guilty man over for extradition.

[107] The elders of the asylum-city comply with this request for some of the same reasons. They too want to support the society's adherence to the notion that murder deserves the severest reaction. And they do not wish to harbor someone who so defiles his community.

no action would mean humiliation for the victim's family and running the risk of having things escalate into a feud; so, the city elders step in on the side of honor and community solidarity.

Deuteronom(ist)ic Expansions (19:1, 2b–3a, 6–10, 13)

The remaining parts of this law represent one or two redactions (see the source-critical analysis, above). In either case, they are consistent and unified in the essential ideas which they contribute to the law; so, I will discuss all these verses together.

The most prominent concept which these verses add concerns divine land grant. The Deuteronom(ist)ic writers speak of the land as the "land which the Lord your God is giving you" (v 1a); "your land, which the Lord your God is giving you to possess" (v 2b); "your land, which the Lord your God is causing you to inherit" (v 3a); "the land which he promised to give to your ancestors" (v 8b); "your land, which the Lord your God is giving you as an inheritance" (v 10a). This emphasis on the land as divine gift implies the inherently sacral aspect of the land. Whether this sacral aspect was understood when the earlier layer of this law was penned cannot be ascertained, but it certainly is emphasized by the redactor(s). This sacredness would be compromised by "the shedding of innocent blood," in the minds of the ancient Israelites. That would result in the removal of divine blessing from the land, meaning famine and death for its inhabitants.[108]

Verses 10 and 13 give the clearest evidence of this notion, applying it to each of the outcomes envisioned by the law. In the case of accidental manslaughter, failure to provide adequate asylum-cities could result in unmerited death ("shedding of innocent blood") at the hands of a blood-avenger, "and bloodguilt will be upon you" (v 10). The blame does not rest solely on the one taking vengeance; the entire nation ultimately is at fault. It has failed to provide adequate opportunity for the killer to reach an asylum-city, and it has failed to give the city elders an opportunity to negotiate a resolution to the present hostilities. The land, which provides nourishment for all the people, has been polluted as a

---

[108] M. Weinfeld, "On 'Demythologization and Secularization' in Deuteronomy," *IEJ* 23 (1973) 230–32; McKeating, "Development," pp. 57–59; Mayes, *Deuteronomy*, p. 287; Bovati, *Re-Establishing Justice*, p. 380. Cp. Deut 21:1–9; 28:15–24.

result of their collective negligence.[109] In contrast to this, "it will go well" (agriculturally) with the Israelites once a murder has been properly avenged. The blood-avenger actually executes vengeance on the murderer, but the entire nation—through his act—"purge[s] the guilt of innocent blood from Israel" (v 13). This notion is linked, in turn, to Deuteronomic cult centralization. On one level, centralization reminds the reader of the fact that the land is Yahweh's. On a more practical level, centralization increases the importance of each asylum-city. The interpretation of Exod 21:12–14 given earlier allows for the possibility that any Yahwistic sanctuary could serve as a temporary place of asylum, paralleling the function of an asylum-city prior to the rendering of a verdict in an actual "trial." Cult centralization removes all the local sanctuaries form the scene, depriving a killer of several possible asyla. It is not so surprising, then, that we find the Deuteronomist emphasizing that the asylum-cities need to be evenly distributed in the land (v 3a).[110] He also explicitly states the danger in the potential for vengeance, pointing to the great distance to an asylum-city as something which would give the blood-avenger an advantage which is not to be desired (v 6). Then, he repeats the opening line of the original law, but now he attributes the need for three asylum-cities to the potential danger of vengeance faced by the killer (v 7). The implication is that a failure to provide adequate asylum will jeopardize the people's well-being.

The seriousness of this danger—and the consequent extent to which it places the entire nation in jeopardy—explains the subsequent expansion of asylum-cities called for in vv 8–9. It might seem overly optimistic to assume that the nation's territory will expand so quickly that it will immediately need three more asylum-cities, instead of one or two. This might be something of an idealization, aiming at a restoration of the territorial extent enjoyed under David and Solomon. It could also signal a sense that it is better to have too many than to have too few. The main concern is that there be enough asylum-cities to prevent

---

[109] Greenberg, "Biblical Concept of Asylum," p. 125; L'Hour, "Une législation criminelle," pp. 26–27; Haas, "'Die You Shall Surely Die'," p. 78; Bovati, *Re-Establishing Justice*, pp. 382–85.

[110] Pedersen, *Israel* I–II, pp. 396–97; Mayes, *Deuteronomy*, pp. 285–86.

unwarranted retaliation killings, because such killings compromise the sacredness of the land.

Finally, we must recognize that these newer layers do not alter the sense of the earlier layer upon which they build. The ultimate goal is still the unity and integrity of the local community; that is what is threatened if this law is not followed, and that is what the elders are trying to maintain by their actions. These later layers provide a theologically-based rationale that complements that goal, without undermining or minimizing the interpersonal motivations. They also give a national perspective to the law. The local community and its leaders still do the work of resolving the dispute that has arisen between two of their families, but now the entire nation is expected to insure that they do not lose sight of that goal of integrity and unity.[111]

In sum, the Deuteronom(ist)ic expansions in this law augment the earlier layer, but they do not really modify it. These expansions provide a clear theologically-based rationale for the asylum-law. No explicit rationale is expressed in that earlier layer, but it is logical to deduce that concern for family honor and the integrity and unity of the local community are the primary motivations for negotiating a resolution. This is still the case in the present form of the law.[112] The elders still operate to resolve differences between two families before a full-fledged feud erupts. The difference now is that the sacral aspects of this case are made explicit and of greater significance. Failure to adhere to the principles of this law will result in agricultural calamity brought on by the "shedding of innocent blood." Because such a calamity is likely to have adverse effects on more than one community, warnings about possible implications and appeals for prevention

---

[111] In a sense, the idea of community is being expanded to a national scale. The concern for unity and integrity is manifested in the measures which the city elders take to restore and maintain peace between two families, because the community needs all of its families working together in order to succeed. The Deuteronom(ist)ic redaction(s) of this law elevate this principle to a national level. Instead of families, town are involved. Just as the integrity of each family benefits (or damages) the whole community, so the integrity of one city threatens the integrity of the entire nation.

[112] Cp. these conclusions to the remarks of M. Weinfeld, "The Origin of Humanism in Deuteronomy," *JBL* 80 (1961) 242–43.

are stated on a national scale. An "uncooperative" community should face the disapproval of the rest of the nation.

CONCLUSIONS

Comparative evidence from the ancient Near East and contemporary kinship-based societies provides a necessary backdrop to our understanding of Israelite practices and ideas regarding homicide and its consequences. The evidence surveyed here suggests that the ancient Israelites were more "rural" than "urban" in their conceptualization, that obligations to one's family/lineage and its honor were paramount. This is realized in cases of homicide through the "necessity" of blood-vengeance, exacted by a close male relative of the victim. Most of these societies allow for exceptions to this basic principle, based on the intent of the killer, and they stipulate lesser forms of retaliation for such killings. Once again, Israelite practice parallels this. Israel is unusual, however, because it allows exceptions in but one type of case: accidental manslaughter. The "lesser" punishment in such a case is banishment from one's home community.

Deut 19:1–13 is one of five passages dealing with this subject. The earliest layer of this law (vv 2a, 3b–5, 11–12) is an elaboration of the earliest biblical law on the subject (Exod 21:12–14). This early layer, composed in the monarchic period, calls for the designation of three asylum-cities. These serve as places in which any killer can seek refuge. This allows his fellow-townspeople the time to sort through the circumstances of the killing and determine whether it was accidental (vv 4–5) or premeditated (vv 11–12). This determination is crucial, because a homicide pits the families/lineages of the killer and his victim against one another, when they need to be cooperating with one another in order for their community to prosper. The elders of the city take the lead in making this determination, although they can turn to judges and priests in unresolved cases. Their task (which is not elaborated upon in the text but revealed through comparative analysis) is to establish the exact nature of the killing and convince the relatives of those involved that the traditional responses to such a crime are warranted and sufficient. Their goal is to restore the peace to the community while maintaining the deserved honor of everyone involved.

Subsequent pre-exilic Deuteronom(ist)ic redaction(s) of this law augment it by emphasizing the sacral aspect of such a case. The land has been given to Israel by Yahweh. It is defiled by the "shedding of innocent blood," the blood of a victim of premeditated murder or the blood of one upon whom vengeance is exacted undeservedly. The implicit threat (which the swift actions of the elders avert) is that Yahweh will curse the land, if innocent blood is allowed to be shed. The greater concern at the time the final redaction is made is that a blood-avenger will have an unfair advantage over one guilty of accidental manslaughter. It is tempting to correlate such a concern to a time of territorial expansion (e.g., the reign of Josiah). To offset it, the law in its final form calls for the possible designation of three additional cities as asylum-cities (vv 8–10).

CHAPTER 4
ELDERS AND THE PURITY OF THE LAND
(DEUT 21:1–9)

The law presented in Deut 21:1–9 deals with some special circumstances in a homicide which would not have been covered by the asylum-law.[1] The latter assumes that the identities of the victim and killer are known; this law assumes that neither is known. The preceding chapter describes much of the conceptual foundation for understanding Israelite notions regarding homicide and blood-vengeance. Because the identities of the victim and his killer are not known here, notions about blood-vengeance play a diminished role. This law, then, primarily enriches our understanding of other aspects of the conceptual world concerning homicide: the effects of a homicide on the sacredness of the land, and how that is manifested in agricultural productivity.[2] These aspects are themselves part of a broader field of assumptions about the symbiosis between human beings and their natural environs, assumptions commonly held by members of traditional agricultural societies. These aspects are only occasionally

---

[1] Several critics conclude that Deut 21:1–9 originally came immediately after Deut 19:1–13. See J. A. Bewer, *The Literature of the Old Testament*, 3rd edition (New York/London: Columbia University Press, 1922/1962; pp. 129–30; A. Rofé, "The Arrangement of the Laws in Deuteronomy," *EphThL* 64 (1988) 271. The resolution of that issue is not crucial to the present investigation.

[2] See von Rad, *Deuteronomy*, p. 135.

mentioned in modern ethnographies or in ancient documents, but this does not diminish their significance. Particularly pertinent to the present investigation are inferences of a conceptual link between the fertility of the land and the sacral powers of local elders.

COMPARATIVE EVIDENCE

Contemporary Kinship-Based Societies

The clearest examples of these notions among African peoples are expressed by the Nuba of eastern Africa. They put together two separate notions to infer a third. The first two are that the land is sacred and that certain offenses (adultery, rape, murder) are more serious than others. Consequently, "most sinister of all" are those instances in which the gravity of those offenses is aggravated by "committing these secular crimes blasphemously on cultivated land. All these acts constitute a desecration of the land, and endanger its fertility."[3]

The link between the (im)morality of human activity and the natural world manifests itself in other ways as well. Among the Murle of southern Africa, "if a man was found dead in the bush and his kin suspected foul play, some of his bones were put into the nearest permanent water, in the hope that his killer or a close relative would drink of that water and die."[4] The operative notion is that death passes from a human corpse to its natural environs. Similar beliefs about the relationship between criminal or sacral offenses and the (in)fertility of the land serve to hold together naturally autonomous Yatenga communities of West Africa, inhibiting any inclinations individuals might have to stir up strife.[5]

---

[3] Nadel, *Nuba*, p. 149. The Nuba generally recognize the unpleasant necessity of occasional quarrels and fights; however, one tribe considers such actions to be sinful, if they take place on cultivated land (p. 459).

[4] Lewis, *Murle*, p. 107.

[5] Hammond, *Yatenga*, p. 143.

A couple of studies tie these notions directly to the authority of a community's elders. The authority of an elder among the Konkomba people is based on the belief that an elder is a "Guardian of the land." To oppose or offend an elder is to risk one's agriculturally-based livelihood.[6] Similarly, the pastoralist Karimojong of Uganda are entirely dependent on the land to supply food for their herds. As a result, they recognize as elders those who are best able to "control the environment by intercession with the deity."[7]

The only Middle Eastern parallels of which I am aware come from the Islamic *qasamah* laws. These consider the possibility that a corpse whose killer is unknown might be discovered almost anywhere. The laws require that various oaths be taken by those nearby, denying any knowledge of the killing or its circumstances. If these measures are not taken, then consequences associated with wrongful death or improper handling of corpses become operative.[8]

Ancient Near Eastern Societies

There are only a few analogous examples found in ancient Near Eastern materials. The most obvious come from Ugaritic treaties which mandate that the nearest town is held liable if a foreigner is killed in its vicinity. If the killer is known, the town (which should have been protecting its visitors) makes a financial compensation to the victim's home country. If the killer is not known, "the citizens in whose land the offense was perpetrated will proceed to the land of the victim and there swear an oath affirming their ignorance of the murderers."[9] Zevit cites as analogous the curse by Dan'el on the three towns nearest to where the corpse of Aqhat

---

[6] Tait, "Territorial Pattern," p. 188.

[7] Dyson-Hudson, *Karimojong Politics*, p. 211.

[8] W. R. Smith, *Kinship and Marriage*, p. 64; S. Dempster, "The Deuteronomic Formula KI YIMMATSE' in the Light of Biblical and Ancient Near Eastern Law: An Evaluation of David Daube's Theory," *RB* 91 (1984) 207 n. 60.

[9] Dempster, "Deuteronomic Formula," p. 205; cp. A. Jirku, "Drei Fälle von Haftpflicht im altorientalischen Palästina-Syrien und Deuteronomium cap. 21," *ZAW* 79 (1967) 359–60.

lay.[10] There is one reference in the Hittite laws of the New Hittite period to the liability of a landowner or a village in the case of an unsolved killing (HL ¶IV). Corresponding to this was the belief that certain serious offenses negatively affected the reputation of the offender's entire city.[11] It is easy to see how that idea would lead to the notion that his entire city should be held liable for his misdeeds. Similar ideas in cases of robbery are mentioned in the story of Wen-Amun,[12] and in the Code of Hammurabi (LH ¶23–24).

One can also find analogies to the ritual performed by the elders in Deut 21:3–8. Babylonian documents reveal that ancient Near Eastern peoples were careful to bury someone properly, because they believed that the "spirit" (*etimmu*) of a dead person would "haunt" those responsible, if the burial were improper. This would manifest itself in the form of physical or mental diseases or financial ruin.[13] More obvious connections are exhibited in certain Hittite and Mesopotamian rituals through which persons tried to transfer diseases from people to animals or distant places (cp. 1 Sam 6:2–12).[14]

As a whole, these various studies reflect the widespread belief among contemporary kinship-based societies and ancient Near Eastern societies that the unrequited shedding of blood yields physical, mental, or environmental distress in the region of the killing. The people of the region usually resort to ritualistic measures to avert or remove these negative consequences. In some cases, local elders officiate over these rituals. We can turn our

---

[10] Z. Zevit, "The *'egla* Ritual of Deuteronomy 21:1–9," *JBL* 95 (1976) 389.

[11] "By committing such an act he has brought impurity upon his fellow townsmen and made them liable to divine wrath. Thus the townsfolk must protect themselves by eradicating the cause of divine wrath, i. e., either by executing the offender(s) or removing them permanently from the town." H. A. Hoffner, Jr., "Incest, Sodomy and Bestiality in the Ancient Near East," in *Orient and Occident* (FS Cyrus Gordon; AOAT 22; Neukirchen-Vluyn: Neukirchener Verlag, 1973), p. 85.

[12] See Jirku, "Drei Fälle," p. 359.

[13] S. H. Hooke, "The Theory and Practice of Substitution," *VT* 2 (1952) 10–11; M. Bayliss, "The Cult of Dead Kin in Assyria and Babylonia," *Iraq* 35 (1973) 116–21. See n. 11 in Chapter 3.

[14] D. P. Wright, "Deuteronomy 21:1–9 as a Rite of Elimination," *CBQ* 49 (1987) 400–403.

attention now to Deut 21:1–9, using these findings as a backdrop to our interpretation.

REDACTION-CRITICAL MATTERS

There is general agreement about the redactional history of most of Deut 21:1–9. The majority attribute vv 1aαγb, 2 (omitting "your judges"), 3–4, 6–7, 8b to a pre-Deuteronomic layer, the remaining sections to Deuteronom(ist)ic redaction.[15] Vv 1aβ, 8a, and 9 consist of typical Deuteronom(ist)ic phraseology, confirming the validity of these conclusions for those sections.[16] V 5 seems out of place in this context, and most of it seems to be derived from the law on the central judiciary (17:8–13) and one part of the prescriptions concerning the Levites (18:5, 7).[17]

A few phrases that are commonly identified as Deuteronom(ist)ic additions warrant reconsideration. These include the reference to "judges" in v 2, the mention of "priests, sons of Levi" in v 5, and the beginning of the elders' petition in v 8.

Many redaction critics—particularly those of the first half of this century—point to the references to elders (vv 2, 3, 6) as one

---

[15] Seitz, *Redaktionsgeschichtliche Studien*, pp. 115–16; P. Dion, "The Greek Version of Deut 21:1–9 and Its Variants: a Record of Early Exegesis," in *De Septuaginta: Studies in Honour of John William Wevers on His 65th Birthday*, ed. A. Pietersma and C. Cox (Mississauga, Ont: Benben Publ., 1984), pp. 152–58; Wright, "Deuteronomy 21:1–9," p. 392; Preuss, *Deuteronomium*, pp. 56, 141; Buchholz, *Ältesten Israels*, pp. 69–72; Gertz, *Gerichtsorganisation Israels*, pp. 158–72.

[16] V 1aβ is identical to 19:2b (see Chapter 2; cp. Deut 3:18; 9:6; 15:4; 25:19). The אשר-clause of v 8a contains the lesser Deuteronomic theme of Yahweh "redeeming" Israel from Egypt (cp. 7:8; 9:26; 13:6; 15:15; 24:18; Jer 26:15; Jon 1:14). There are two Deuteronom(ist)ic motive clauses in v 9 (for v 9a, see 4:3; 19:10, 13; for v 9b, see 6:18; 12:25, 28; 13:19; 17:2).

[17] The designation "priests, sons of Levi" occurs elsewhere only in 31:9 (see below). The notice that the Levites are to "serve... the Lord" is found in 10:8; 17:12, 15; 18:5, 7. The stipulation that they render a judgment in every ריב and נגע echoes their judicial role laid out in 17:8, 10 (cp. 19:15). See von Rad, *Deuteronomy*, p. 136; Zevit, "The *'egla* Ritual," p. 382; Mayes, *Deuteronomy*, p. 299; cp. Macholz, "Geschichte der Justizorganisation," pp. 333–38.

piece of evidence for the existence of a pre-Deuteronomic layer, believing that the elders were displaced by appointed judges as part of the Deuteronomic centralization program (see 16:18–20). The reference to "your judges" in v 2 is explained by most of these critics as the Deuteronomic lawgiver's allusion to this displacement.[18] This is a very tenuous proposal. If the lawgiver felt free to insert "judges" in v 2 for the purpose of indicating the displacement of "elders," one would expect him to do the same in vv 3 and 6. And if he really is intending to indicate a displacement, it seems odd that he would feel free to add the new but reticent to remove the old. For these reasons, I am less inclined to assume that the reference to "judges" in v 2 is a secondary insertion.[19]

A better interpretation presents itself when one considers contemporary and ancient analogs. The complementarity of the roles of local elders and appointed officials (see Chapter 1) is most obvious in inter-village matters. The natural "jurisdiction" of elders is limited to a single community. When a situation involves more than one community, it is common for the elders of the respective communities to turn to indigenous chiefs or royal appointees (i.e., someone with broader influence and authority) to mediate between the two groups.[20] It is natural to assume that

[18] Hölscher, "Komposition," p. 209; Albright, "Judicial Reform," p. 77; von Rad, *Deuteronomy*, p. 136; Phillips, *Ancient Israel's Criminal Law*, p. 22; Seitz, *Redaktionsgeschichtliche Studien*, pp. 115–16; Zevit, "The *'egla* Ritual," p. 382; Mayes, *Deuteronomy*, p. 298; Preuss, *Deuteronomium*, p. 136; G. Braulik, "Zur Abfolge der Gesetze in Deuteronomium 16,18–21,23. Weitere Beobachtungen" *Bib* 69 (1988) 89; Buchholz, *Ältesten Israels*, pp. 69–72; Gertz, *Gerichtsorganisation Israels*, pp. 161–65; cp. Reviv, "Traditions," pp. 566–75; Wright, "Deuteronomy 21:1–9," pp. 388–89.

[19] Some also consider the pronominal suffixes ("*your* elders and *your* judges") to be secondary, explaining them as consequences of 16:18–20 and pointing out that they disrupt the impersonal casuistic style of the rest of the law (see Dion, "Greek Version," p. 152). On the other hand, there must be some sort of qualifier here, because "the elders (and the judges)" would be too ambiguous. The belief that it was originally "the elders (of Israel)" (see preceding note) transforms this into a national affair, which it is not (even in its final form). The use of "your" allows for some flexibility, as it can refer to the entire nation or just a part of it.

[20] For example, the Pakistani government allows the Pathan tribesmen of Pakistan to settle most of their own disputes, with political agents getting involved only if the dispute is between tribes (Ahmed, *Social and Economic*

functionaries like judges would be involved from Israel's earliest days in a multi-municipal situation such as this one. Furthermore, it would not be surprising for their task to be complete once a determination had been made as to which city was responsible. That would explain the absence of any subsequent references to these judges in this law.

The mention of "priests, the sons of Levi" in v 5 should be examined more methodically as well. The lengthy justification given for involving them (וכל־נגע ... כי) does not fit the situation at hand,[21] as it refers to their cultic ("bless" and "serve") and adjudicative functions. Those are mentioned in other Deuteronomic passages (18:5–7 and 17:8–10, respectively), but they do not fit their function here;[22] so, the justification clause seems to be derived from those other passages, without much thought for the present context. The priests do not perform any ritual function here either, as some have mentioned previously.[23]

These observations make the inclusion of any reference to the "priests, the sons of Levi" all the more puzzling. I would suggest,

---

Change, p. 44). Nuer tribesmen enlist the services of a leopard-skin chief if a dispute is unresolved; and, if the dispute is between members of separate villages (usually implying different lineage segments), then the leopard-skin chief serves as mediator between the elders of the respective villages (Evans-Pritchard, *Nuer*, p. 163). L. Holy describes how the Berti people look to city elders and/or a regional *omda* to settle disputes between villages (*Neighbours and Kinsmen*, pp. 132–37). More generally, Arab tribesmen customarily turn to a well-respected shaykh or emir to hear difficult cases. If he is respected by members of several tribes, community elders will bring their inter-tribal disputes before him in order to avoid a feud (Katakura, *Bedouin Village*, pp. 28, 61, 70, 155; Cole, *Nomads of the Nomads*, pp. 86–87).

For additional examples, see A. Kuper, "Kgalagari Lekgota," pp. 89, 96; Lamphear, "Turkana Leadership," pp. 226–27; Moore, "Descent and Legal Position," pp. 394–95; and van Velzen, *Politics of Kinship*, pp. 310–11.

[21] This section is omitted from LXX manuscript d; see Dion, "Greek Version," p. 155.

[22] The rest of the passage does not mention the participation of the priests in any ritual. Also, they would be unable to make any determination about the type of homicide here (accidental or premeditated) as prescribed in 17:8–10, because the circumstances leading up to the killing are completely unknown.

[23] Driver, *Deuteronomy*, pp. 242–43; Hölscher, "Komposition," p. 208 n. 1; G. Minette de Tillesse, "Sections 'tu' et sections 'vous' dans le Deutéronome," *VT* 12 (1962) 81; Seitz, *Redaktionsgeschichtliche Studien*, p. 116.

then, that the reference to the priests arises in the earliest layer of this law. This is implied by v 7. The elders of the city closest to the discovered body make a formal pronouncement (cp. 25:9) about their lack of any knowledge regarding the killing. Such an announcement must be made before witnesses. Normally, the elders of a city would serve as witnesses (see Chapter 1); but this situation requires that other persons serve that function. This might have been fulfilled by the judges, mentioned in v 2. But the fact that the text unexpectedly refers to a group other than the judges (viz., priests) suggests that they actually filled that role. Thus, it would seem that the initial reference to priests in v 5 reflects an early reading. The priests "draw near" to observe the hand-washing ritual and hear the oath of the elders.[24] They do not supervise the ceremony,[25] but they serve instead as non-partisan witnesses to it at a later date. The rationale given in the text does not fit the present situation, confirming the general conclusion that it constitutes a later (perhaps non-deuteronomistic) expansion.

These conclusions lead us to reconsider v 8. Some critics retain v 8b as part of the original law while excising v 8a.[26] The latter makes sense in the case of the אשר-clause, since that clause consists of a Deuteronom(ist)ic expression (cp. 7:8; 15:15; 24:18). Further, the expression "innocent blood" in the next clause (in contrast to "this/the blood" in vv 7 and 8b) occurs elsewhere only in Deuteronom(ist)ic passages (19:10, 13; 21:9). V 8b is very unusual, containing a unique form of the verb כפר (נכפר). It is less likely that a Deuteronom(ist)ic redactor would use such an unusual form, so I would concur in retaining it as part of the pre-Deuteronomic law. But it is awkward to retain v 8b by itself immediately after v 7. V 7 consists of an oath of innocence. But the

---

[24] The connotation of the root נגש to describe the action of the priests (v 5) is determined by the context. Persons can "draw near" to speak (Gen 44:18; Deut 20:2; 25:1; Josh 21:1; 1 Sam 9:18) or to hear what is being said (Gen 27:22; 45:4; Josh 3:9). The subsequent declaration of the oath by the elders indicates that the priests "drew near" to hear. Again, this is contrary to the rationale stated in v 5 itself.

[25] So Driver, *Deuteronomy*, p. 243; J. A. Thompson, *Deuteronomy* (Downers Grove, IL: Inter-Varsity, 1974), p. 227.

[26] Wright, "Deut 21:1–9," p. 392; Buchholz, *Ältesten Israels*, pp. 69–71; Gertz, *Gerichtsorganisation Israels*, pp. 160–61.

people here cannot be concerned simply about their reputation and their legal responsibilities; they are concerned about the agricultural productivity of their land as well. The ultimate purpose in this ceremony is to avert or remove any sort of curse which might result from the presence of a corpse in a cultivated field. One would assume that a petition for this purpose would be included. V 8b reports the (implicit) acceptance of that petition by the deity. The necessary transition from oath to acceptance of a petition is the statement of the petition itself, which is given here in v 8a. I would retain, then, the single non-Deuteronom(ist)ic phrase of v 8a: כפר לעמך ישראל יהוה.[27]

INTERPRETATION OF THE PRE-DEUTERONOMIC LAW
(21:aαγb, 2–5aα, 6–8aαb)

The preceding source-critical considerations yield the following reconstruction for the earliest formulation of this law:

> If a body is found on the ground, ...lying in the field—it not being known who struck him—then your elders and your judges shall go out, and they shall measure to the cities which surround the body. And as for the city nearest the body, the elders of that city shall take a heifer which has not been brought into subjection, which does not pull with a yoke. And the elders of that city shall bring out the heifer to a perennial wadi, which has not been worked [i.e., cultivated] and has not been sown, and they shall break the neck of the heifer there in the wadi. Then the priests, the sons of Levi shall draw near, ...and the elders of that city—those who were nearest to the body—shall wash their hands over the heifer whose neck was broken in the wadi. And

---

[27] One should include "O Lord" at the end of the clause; otherwise the petition has no addressee.

Another consideration is germane to this discussion. The more common expression for the exodus from Egypt is that the Lord "brought you out" (see 1:27; 4:20, 37; 5:6, 15; 6:12, 21, 23; 8:14; 9:12, 26, 28; 13:6, 11; 16:1; 26:8). The use of the less common "redeem" makes more sense when one realizes that פדה and כפר sometimes occur as a word pair (see Exod 21:30; Ps 49:8). It is logical to conclude that the presence of כפר in an earlier version of the law prompted the use of פדה by the redactor. There is also a possible connection between the breaking of an animal's neck and פדה (see Exod 13:13; 34:20).

they shall answer and say, "Our hands did not shed this blood, and our eyes did not see [the killing]. Pardon your people Israel, ...O Lord." ...And the blood shall be pardoned on their behalf.

There are two widely-discussed questions that arise from this early law. One, concerning the references made to "judges" and "priests," was discussed in the preceding section. The other question concerns the nature of the ceremony performed by the elders. An excellent survey of past views is provided by David Wright.[28] His survey of approximately thirty previous examinations of this question shows that there are five ways to understand this ceremony: as a non-priestly sacrifice; as a symbolic execution of the killer; as the symbolic punishment of the elders, if they are lying; as the placement of guilt onto the animal, according to the pattern of the scapegoat; or as the "reenactment" of the murder, to "eliminate" the curse (caused by bloodshed) from the cultivated land by placing it on uncultivated land.[29]

The sacrificial interpretation is weak, because there are no other examples of sacrifices being carried out in this manner (see below). The next two interpretations, taken without elaboration, provide no plausible rationale for conducting the ceremony in an uncultivable valley. The comparison to the scapegoat is not completely adequate, because this ceremony implies that the water—not the animal—carries away the guilt.[30] This leaves the final interpretation: the ceremony is a "reenactment" of the murder to "eliminate" bloodguilt from the land.

---

[28] "Deuteronomy 21:1–9," pp. 388–89.

[29] This is the interpretation which Wright accepts; cp. R. Patai, "The 'Egla 'Arufa or the Expiation of the Polluted Ground," *JewQR* 30 (1939) 68.

"In the case of the unsolved murder, it is true that expiation is sought for the people and not the land (21:8), but the ceremonial of the broken-necked heifer is incomprehensible without the assumption that blood does contaminate the land on which it is spilt and that this ritual transfers the contamination to untillable land." J. Milgrom, "The Alleged 'Demythologization and Secularization' in Deuteronomy," *IEJ* 23 (1973) 157; cp. Weinfeld, "On Demythologization," pp. 230–33.

[30] For more lengthy criticisms, see Wright, "Deuteronomy 21:1–9," pp. 390–94.

Biblical parallels suggest that breaking an animal's neck actually desecrates it.[31] Exod 13:13 (cp. 34:20) is an exception clause in a law about consecrating the firstborn of one's livestock to Yahweh. It allows for one to keep a firstborn donkey, provided a sheep is sacrificed in its place. However, if the terms for the exception are not followed, then the donkey's neck is broken. The religious implications of this act are not revealed here. We can simply conclude that an animal which had been kept from Yahweh is now useless to its owner. The implications drawn from Isa 66:3 are more obvious. The author there indicates that breaking a dog's neck is comparable to committing murder, offering pig's blood, or mimicking idolatrous rituals. The performance of those other three acts defiles the one who performs them. This implies that the one who breaks a dog's neck defiles himself in that act.

The exact understanding of the breaking of the heifer's neck in Deut 21:4 is unclear, but these observations provide a plausible interpretation. The breaking of an animal's neck seems to yield the same defilement as the killing of a man.[32] This implies that the elders' action is as "serious" an offense as the killing of the man whose body has been discovered. Apparently, the ceremonial performance of an act which is comparable to the malicious performance of a prior act is thought to transfer the effects of that first act to the location of the second, so that the guilt of the first act can be removed in the hand-washing ritual in the second. This is admittedly speculative, but such a notion is suggested by similar ritual acts performed by Israel's neighbors (see above).[33]

---

[31] This might be attributable to the simple fact that the blood is not drained from the body. If this is true, then Patai and Wright go too far when they claim that the elders are disavowing the shedding of the heifer's blood. Patai, "The 'Egla 'Arufa," p. 67; Wright, "Deuteronomy 21:1–9," p. 394.

[32] The word for "killing" in Isa 66:3 is מכה. This is the same root that is used in Deut 19:4 in referring to accidental manslaughter. If these two authors have the same understanding of this term, it would imply that the defilement incurred here comes simply from the shedding of blood and is not based on the intent of the perpetrator.

[33] One of the intriguing questions raised by this law is about how this non-cultic—and presumably non-Yahwistic—ceremony would be preserved in this most Yahwistic of documents. Such a ceremony seems to run contrary to the strong warnings elsewhere in the book against tolerating non-Yahwistic

Leaving that question only partially resolved, let us turn to the primary focus of this study: the role which the elders play; in particular, the reasons for their participation in this case and for their statements in vv 7–8. The former touches on their social role; the latter, their sacral role.

The situation considered in this law involves segments of Israel's population which are more divergent than those involved in the cases in Deut 19:1–13. The text states that the identity of the killer is unknown (v 1) and implies that the identity of the victim is unknown as well. No blood-avenger steps forward seeking a reciprocal death, so the victim's home is probably at some distance from the scene of the crime. Likewise, no one flees to a city of refuge in fear for his own life, and there are no clues as to the circumstances of the killing. This is in direct contrast to the circumstances assumed in the asylum-law. In fact, the entire process by which a city is deemed to be "involved" here has an air of detachment about it, which betrays the local inhabitants' unfamiliarity with the victim. Early Jewish interpreters said that the elders' disclaimer in vv 7–8 reflects a resident-visitor relationship between the elders and the victim. The phrase "our eyes did not see" was taken to mean they did not see this sojourner in need of a place to stay and yet fail to provide shelter for him.[34]

The simple recognition of the inter-municipal nature of the case in Deut 21:1–9 allows a more objective assessment of what is said to transpire. A murder has been discovered, but the murderer is unknown, even to the members of the victim's lineage. If they ever learned of the killing but were still ignorant of who might have done it, ancient Near Eastern examples indicate that they would naturally hold as liable those living closest to the scene of the crime. The measurement taken in v 2 identifies who is to be held liable. The elders of that city then serve to represent their city in the proceedings that follow.

It is important to recognize that only the elders serve in this representative role, even in the final redaction of this law. As

practices. Perhaps the fact that it is preserved indicates that it is Yahwistic in origin.

[34] This view is found in the Mishna; see Patai, "The 'Egla 'Arufa," p. 67, who argues against the Mishnaic interpretation.

elders, they would most likely be leading members of important lineages in the community. They speak not only for their community, but as representatives of the lineages within their community vis-à-vis lineages in other communities. The giving of the oath (21:7) is in part a declaration to other lineage groups that theirs did not participate in this crime. This would prevent the possibility of a feud erupting later between the local lineages and those of the victim's hometown.

In this light, the references to the participation of additional functionaries in this passage make good sense. These are persons whose influence would have superseded and cut across lineages. The judges prevent one lineage from inappropriately placing liability on another, and the priests stand as potential witnesses to the oath given by the elders who are liable. Their participation facilitates the prevention of an inter-clan or inter-tribal feud in the future.[35]

The social aspect of the representational role played by the elders is eclipsed in this law by the sacral aspect. The care that is taken in choosing the heifer to be killed and the untillability of the ravine in which the ceremony takes place clearly exemplify the kind of precision one finds usually in the context of a religious ritual. The elders are representing the members of their community before Yahweh. The entire community is held liable, not only by the victim's family, but by Yahweh. The entire community faces the possibility of divinely-ordained agricultural ruin. For these reasons the elders wash their hands on behalf of their entire community; they pronounce an oath of innocence on behalf of their entire community.[36] They embody the lineages of which they are a part, along with the clients and neighbors with whom they have overlapping social and economic ties, and they stand as a community before Yahweh.

---

[35] It is impossible to decide when in Israel's history these particular functionaries would have first assumed these duties, because the dilemma which they resolve could have arisen at any time. Therefore, the date of this law's origin cannot be ascertained by consideration of who participates in this sacrificial ceremony.

[36] The "elders of the congregation" serve in a similar representative capacity in Lev 4:13–21. The difference is that the "community" represented in Leviticus 4 is the entire nation. See Zevit, "The ʿegla Ritual," p. 385.

In the background is the notion that there is a direct link between the moral and religious integrity of the elders themselves (as representatives of their community) and the agricultural productivity of the land they inhabit. The example of integrity which the elders have set—which has led to their recognition as elders—prompts their community to look to them as their representatives to the deity who oversees the productivity of the land. The people rely on their integrity (to be "worthy" to perform this ceremony), and they in turn rely on the people's integrity (to make the ceremony acceptable). Both are considered crucial if the community is to expect continued blessings from Yahweh.[37]

The gravity of the oath and the urgency of the petition (vv 7–8) now stand out boldly. The elders, speaking as representatives for an entire community of people, are fearful for the financial and physical well-being of their immediate families and all the families in the area. The rest of the community depends on the abilities of the elders to appease Yahweh and preserve or regain his blessings. To that end, the elders symbolically wash their hands of any contamination that would result from the shedding of blood, thereby transferring its adverse consequences to an "already-cursed" area; they solemnly deny any participation in this killing, but further imply their community's complete disapproval of such a deed at any time; and they appeal (either implicitly or explicitly) to Yahweh for pardon from any guilt that might be associated with the killing. The final clause indicates that they can expect to have been successful.

---

[37] Israelite communities (like virtually all communities in the ancient Near East) saw a direct link between the agricultural productivity of their land and their own righteousness, even though this is not made explicit in this passage. Other passages do make the connection explicit; see Gen 4:9–12; Num 35:33–34; Deut 21:22–23; 24:1–4; 28:15–18, 38–40; 29:19–23; 2 Sam 21:10–14; Hos 2:4–15.

The connection between the land and righteousness in Deuteronomy is stated primarily in terms of possession, not productivity. The people are exhorted to obey the law so that they might live in the land a long time. Statements about agricultural productivity are encapsulated in the phrase "that it may go well with you" (Deut 4:40; 5:16, 29, 33; 6:3, 18; 12:25, 28; 19:13; 22:7), which is sometimes expanded with clauses regarding taking or extending possession of the land. Agricultural productivity is mentioned most often in the Deuteronom(ist)ic framework of the book (Deut 28:3–5, 11–12, 15–18, 20–24, 38–42; 29:19–23; 30:9–10).

DEUTERONOM(IST)IC EXPANSIONS
(21:1aβ, 5aβb, 8aβ, 9)

The primary difference one sees in this law with the addition of Deuteronom(ist)ic sections is its explicitly nationalistic viewpoint. These sections also supplement the ideas regarding the desecratory nature of this killing that were already apparent. The same emphases were made in the Deuteronom(ist)ic sections of Deut 19:1–13. The situation addressed in this law was originally a strictly local concern. Only the cities near the field in which the body was found had anything to worry about. And once they had identified the nearest city, it alone felt that it was at risk of agricultural ruin, because only its elders had to be concerned to declare its innocence and seek the mercy of Yahweh. The Deuteronom(ist)ic redaction transforms this local matter into a national concern, but one still dealt with locally.

The sacral perspective of this law is reinforced in several ways in this redaction of the law. The land-gift clause in v 1 reminds the people that the land—of which the field is a part—ultimately belongs to Yahweh. This highlights the notion that the shedding of blood on it is an offense against Yahweh himself. The repetition of the expression "innocent blood" (vv 8, 9) points toward the ultimately sacral implications of the crime, as do the exhortations to "purge" this desecratory thing and to "do what is upright in the eyes of the Lord" (v 9).

Unlike Deut 19:1–13, this sacral undergirding was already present in the old law which is redacted here. This might explain why this law was incorporated into the D Code. The sacral ingredient of Israelite laws is important to the Deuteronomists, who bring it out in their redaction. But this ingredient is not an innovation; rather, its emphasis in redactional layers represents a shifting or sharpening of the focus of the laws as a whole.[38]

---

[38] One need not interpret these two passages together according to a strict evolution of thought. It is true that the sacral aspect is silent in the asylum-law until one includes the Deuteronom(ist)ic sections. But the conceptual link between agricultural productivity and human righteousness probably was a basic presupposition of all peoples of the ancient Near East (see von Rad, *Deuteronomy*, pp. 135–36). Agricultural productivity was commonly understood as a sign of a deity's positive (or negative) judgment of a people's lifestyle. The fact that this conceptual aspect is not made explicit in the

The other important piece of that refocusing in this law is in the broadening of the concern of the law to a national level. Unexpectedly, it is the entire nation that is in need of pardon (v 8); the desecrating blood must be purged from the midst of the entire nation (v 9). These national concerns are clearly expressed by the redactor, yet he preserves the notion that only one city is ultimately to be held responsible. It is the elders of but one city who petition Yahweh for the sake of the nation. It is the appropriate actions of one city's elders which purge the guilt from the nation.

The feeling of incongruity which this creates is left unresolved. This reveals something, again, about the point of view of the Deuteronom(ist)ic redactor(s). Even though worship and the cult are to be centralized, he does not require that a situation like this one—which involves "cultic" notions and procedures—must be dealt with at the national level. But that does not mean that this is strictly a "local matter," either. What he is advocating is a continuation of previously-utilized local practices which are compatible with his theological and religio-political views, but he wants those practices to be performed with one eye to the rest of the nation. If there is a tendency to minimize an infraction or to hesitate or be irresolute about an appropriate reaction because of local considerations, then the supplementary clauses remind the persons involved of their broader obligations. They are part of a larger body, all of which was "redeemed" by Yahweh (v 8). They are thus accountable to the entire nation, if they neglect their traditionally-recognized responsibilities before Yahweh.[39]

---

asylum-law until the later stages of its redaction (19:10; cp. 21:22–23) does not necessarily reveal a conceptual innovation. It is more likely that the redactor simply wanted to make that notion explicit as he brought out the idea of the land as divine gift. It is possible that he chose to include a pre-existing law which already made this notion explicit (the early layer of 21:1–9) for the very reason that it promotes that idea.

[39] This dilemma would be resolved in the Priestly materials by transferring the elders' responsibilities to "the congregation" and national cultic personnel. The final redaction of v 5 points in that direction by implying that this situation falls under the umbrella of the responsibilities of the central priests laid out in 17:8–13. The fact that this situation does not fall under those categories, coupled with the observation that what is mentioned here does not even correspond with the nationalizing sections in this passage which are obviously Deuteronom(ist)ic in origin and perspective,

CONCLUSIONS

In both Deut 19:1–13 and 21:1–9, the city elders are concerned with the social and sacral welfare of their entire community. The social is seen in their desire to maintain peace between rival segments of their community (Deut 19:1–13) and between their city and others (Deut 21:1–9). The sacral aspect includes issues of divine blessing and moral honor. In the asylum-law, this honor is preserved or restored by insuring that blood-vengeance is exacted properly. In this law, honor is simply assumed and reaffirmed through a solemn oath. The activities of other officials in the situations already investigated do not alter this in any way; in fact, the perspective of the laws seems to be that those other persons provide local functions which merely supplement those fulfilled by the elders.

The law presented in Deut 21:1–9 is in many ways supplementary to the asylum-law of Deut 19:1–13. It appears that the "original" (pre-Deuteronomic) law has been altered only slightly by Deuteronom(ist)ic and other redactions. The primary differences between the circumstances of this law and those of the asylum-law are (1) that this killing automatically is inter-municipal in scope and (2) that the identities of the killer and victim are unknown. Because of the latter difference, the potential for a feud is diminished, or better, it is postponed. Still, the reality of that potential plays a significant role in spurring the participants to the actions they do take. The overall diminution of the danger of a feud causes the sacral concerns that inhere to any killing to come to the fore. The result is that the prescribed ceremony is directed primarily toward Yahweh. The ceremony is more explicitly described than any other in the D Code, displaying its ultimately religious basis. The oath and petition included in it are directed toward Yahweh. The ceremony and its associated statements only secondarily touch on the social interaction between lineages which is so much a concern in most homicides.

The roles played by the elders, judges, and priests reflect these differences as well. The judges and priests are involved at

---

shows how a non-Deuteronom(ist)ic redactor can utilize Deuteronomic material (cp. 4:41–43).

different stages in the progression of the case, but strictly for its social aspects. The judges probably serve as mediators between the societally equal groups of elders who represent the various cities. The priests do not serve as cultic or judicial figures, but as witnesses, to contribute to the diffusion of any feud which might erupt in the future. The elders serve primarily in a representative capacity, as there is no judicial decision that can be made. But their representative role reveals some important aspects of their place in Israelite society. Not only do they represent their city in "negotiations" with other cities, they also represent their city before the deity (Yahweh). The moral reputation of themselves and of their entire city must be defended. This is a matter of honor, as in the asylum-law, but it is also a matter of livelihood. Divine blessings (including agricultural productivity) are thought to be dependent on Yahweh's acceptance of the citizens of the community as a whole, and the elders embody that community.

Deuteronom(ist)ic redaction of this law brings forward ideas which reinforce the sacral aspects of the earlier law. There is a repeated reminder of the belief that the land is Yahweh's, so the people there must protect its sanctity. This law also provides another example of how the Deuteronom(ist)ic redactor takes something which is a "local" matter and makes it a national concern.

CHAPTER 5
ELDERS, PARENTS, AND THE REBELLIOUS SON
(DEUT 21:18–21)

Deut 21:18–21 is one of several passages commonly mentioned in discussions of the evolution of judicial authority in ancient Israel.[1] There is perceived to be a shift in authority here from the *paterfamilias* (to borrow a term from Roman society) to the community and/or the state. It is my belief that certain aspects of this change in judicial authority have been inappropriately exaggerated in most previous studies. In particular, I would question the conclusion that this law seeks to restrict "the exercise of authority at the household level."[2] Comparative evidence advises caution in assuming the absolute authority of parents over their children in "traditional" societies, and the biblical evidence of such authority is not as conclusive as many have argued.[3] In the case of Deut 21:18–21, the comparative evidence will allow us to

---

[1] Salmon ("Judicial Authority," pp. 24–41) provides a good example. His investigation of this development includes Genesis 16, 31, 38; Num 5:11–31; Deut 21:18–21; 22:13–21; 24:10–11; Jdgs 6:30–32; 1 Sam 2:22–25; 8:1–15; 2 Sam 14:7. Other passages often cited from Deuteronomy are Deut 19:1–13; 21:1–9, 15–17.

[2] Joseph Blenkinsopp, "Deuteronomy and the Politics of Post-Mortem Existence," *VT* 45 (1995) 4; cp. Salmon, "Judicial Authority," pp. 428–45; Whitelam, *Just King*, p. 42; L. Stulman, "Sex and Familial Crimes in the D Code: A Witness to Mores in Transition," *JSOT* 53 (1992) 58.

[3] Since most of the latter involves cases of adultery or rape, I have chosen to postpone my examination of it to Chapter 6.

remove some unnecessary assumptions based on those previous studies and consider the intent of this law afresh. I will set the stage for this investigation, then, by looking at some examples of how members of contemporary kinship-based societies, ancient Near Eastern societies, and even Roman society have conceptualized the rights, authority, and obligations of persons whose immediate family members are guilty of persistent wrongdoing. Then we will turn our attention once again to the redactional history and present interpretation of this law. Special consideration will be given, of course, to the role played by the city elders.

COMPARATIVE EVIDENCE

Comparative evidence from kinship-based societies helps in the interpretation of two particular aspects of the law in Deut 21:18–21. One aspect involves the rights, authority, and social obligations which particular family members (especially fathers) have. These are theirs naturally in kinship-based societies, not by mandate of any "higher" authority. The other aspect concerns the way in which entire communities deal with the habitual wrongdoer in their midst. As in Deut 21:18–21, the immediate family and the broader community often coordinate their efforts in this kind of situation.

Contemporary Kinship-Based Societies

Contemporary societies provide numerous examples of a family's right to impose and execute punishments of all sorts on one of its members for criminal or immoral behavior, without recourse to judicial authorities. The extent of that right varies, and it is not held solely by fathers/husbands. For example, there are scattered examples of the killing of family members who are openly criticized by the broader community. B. A. Lewis records the following story from the Murle of East Africa:

> In 1940 a young man... was hanged by his elder brother and mother for being a confirmed thief. He had been imprisoned in

1939... for stealing goods from a merchant's shop... This did
not cure him, however, and he continued to steal; his relatives
were being threatened frequently by people claiming
compensation for his thefts. Eventually his mother and brother
could stand it no longer, and about six months after his release
from prison, hanged him from a tree.[4]

S. F. Nadel reports an incident in which a woman among the
Otoro tribe is buried alive by her sister for being "an incorrigible
thief." In another case, neighbors are pressuring a young man to
kill his sister for being a thief. Eventually, he appeases them by
selling her as a slave.[5] Max Gluckman shows another way in
which the community and immediate family can interact in this
kind of situation. He reports that community elders sometimes
declare someone to be an habitual wrongdoer and order his
execution; however, to avoid the possibility of a feud, they require
that a member of the wrongdoer's own family execute him.[6]

There are other examples that involve less severe punishments.
J. G. Peristiany describes how, among the Kipsigis pastoralists of
Kenya, people shun the entire family of an habitual wrongdoer
until he is expelled from the family. Then, the elders of his
community impose a collective curse on him.[7] The Ila peoples of
Rhodesia choose from a variety of punishments for habitual
troublemakers. Thieves, arsonists, and those prone to promiscuity
can expect mutilation; one against whom fines are repeatedly
imposed will eventually find himself cut off from his family; and
one who shows disrespect to community leaders could face
banishment. Village elders rarely resort to this, however, because
banishment means the community loses one of its workers.[8] M.
Edel mentions that a young criminal among the Chiga people
faces a sort of double indemnity for his actions. He first endures the
judgment and punishment of the community, but then he has to
face his father. His father has free rein to deal with his shameful

---

[4] Lewis, *Murle*, p. 77.

[5] Nadel, *Nuba*, p. 150.

[6] M. Gluckman, *Politics, Law and Ritual in Tribal Society* (Chicago:
Aldine Publ. Co., 1965), pp. 116–17.

[7] Peristiany, "Law," p. 44. Actually, the collective curse is a lesser
punishment imposed by British rule.   Prior to the British presence, the
wrongdoer was killed by the community.

[8] Smith and Dale, *Ila-Speaking Peoples*, pp. 352, 358.

son as he sees fit, even to the point of invoking a "death-bed curse" on him, which forces him from the protection of the community.[9]

Middle Eastern societies provide similar examples. Both mothers and fathers among some Saharan tribes are permitted to beat their children with impunity, until those children reach adulthood.[10] Moroccan tribesmen resort to banishment (which they term "good fratricide") if they believe that the person's evil actions will bring hardship on the broader group.[11] Among the Berti, one who continually behaves contrary to the will of the community (being quick-tempered, lazy, quarrelsome, etc.) "exposes himself to the danger of a whole series of sanctions on the part of his neighbours." These "sanctions" gradually force the man into compliance, or they force him to leave the area and rely on the help of strangers. The latter dooms him to poverty.[12]

The basic principles underlying these actions on the part of family members are family honor and collective responsibility. Collective responsibility pulls in two directions. Individuals are obligated to assist their immediate family members, sometimes in matters which place them at odds with the rest of their community. The obligation to side with a family member who is guilty of wrongdoing, either by paying part of a fine or moving with him away from the community, is but one common example of this principle.[13] But there are also obligations to one's community. These obligations are often linked to the principle of honor. Family members must choose whether to side with the wrongdoer and suffer some level of shame and ostracization, or side with the community and try to reestablish the family's honor among their neighbors. Taking action against one's own relative, then, is usually for the purpose of preserving or restoring the family's honor in the face of the humiliation brought on by the wrongdoer's shameful actions. These observations point, in turn, to the fact that such action is usually taken in response to social pressure (whether assumed or actually seen and heard) from the broader community.

---

[9] Edel, *Chiga*, pp. 113, 122.
[10] Briggs, *Tribes*, p. 171.
[11] Gellner, *Saints*, pp. 46–47.
[12] Holy, *Neighbours and Kinsmen*, pp. 128–29.
[13] See Schapera, "Law and Justice," p. 219.

Roman Law

The special influence which Roman analogies have had on modern interpretations of the biblical materials related to this issue prompt me to break from my typical pattern and discuss briefly the evidence from ancient Rome. Several commentators draw comparisons between the traditional authority of Israelite fathers and the authority of the *paterfamilias* of ancient Roman society. Some assume that the Roman *paterfamilias* represents an early step in the evolution of judicial authority in most traditional societies, including ancient Israel.[14] It seems, however, that the authority of the *paterfamilias* has sometimes been slightly exaggerated. Traditionally, a *paterfamilias* had, among other powers, power of life and death over his wife, offspring, and slaves. This is a generalization, though. A father who exercised such authority arbitrarily could be punished by the "censors;" and over time, various restrictions were placed on this authority (particularly under the emperors). Also, Roman writers themselves (Gaius, Dionysius) commented that they did not know of parallels to the traditional powers of the *paterfamilias* in any other society, except perhaps among certain Galatians (Gauls?).[15] Thus, the Roman example is not necessarily uniform, and it shows paternal authority to be controlled somewhat by other authorities. This should make one cautious about using the model of the Roman *paterfamilias* to justify assumptions about the absolute authority of Israelite fathers.

---

[14] E. C. Clark (*History of Roman Private Law. Part III: Regal Period* [Cambridge: University Press, 1919], p. 51 n. 14) mentions a "controversy between Locke and Filmer as to the alleged *patria potestas* among the Hebrews." I have not been able to ascertain the nature of that debate.

[15] W. W. Buckland, *A Text-Book of Roman Law from Augustus to Justinian* (Cambridge: Cambridge University Press, 1921), pp. 103–13, 131–34; J. Declareuil, *Rome the Law-Giver* (Westport, CT: Greenwood Press, 1927/1970), pp. 95–98; R. Taubenschlag, *The Law of Greco-Roman Egypt in the Light of the Papyri (332 B.C.–640 A.D.)* (New York: Herald Square Press, 1944), pp. 38, 97–115; H. F. Jolowicz, *Roman Foundations of Modern Law* (Westport, CT: Greenwood Press, 1957/1978), pp. 181–203; A. Watson, *The Law of the Ancient Romans* (Dallas: SMU Press, 1970), pp. 10–11, 21–22, 37–39.

Ancient Near Eastern Societies

Evidence from the ancient Near East suggests that familial authority was usually circumscribed by the community. Babylonian law mandates, "If a child should strike his father, they shall cut off his hand" (LH ¶195). This shows the perceived severity of the offense, but it also demonstrates that the community ("they")—not the father—metes out the punishment. The remaining evidence comes from cases of disinheritance. For example, one Sumerian law deprives an adopted son of any inheritance if he denounces his parents (SLEx ¶4).[16] Babylonian law calls for the mutilation of the adopted son in similar instances (LH ¶¶192–193). A pair of laws reveal that "judges" supervise a father's right to disinherit a son who is guilty of "grave offenses" (LH ¶168–169). The assumption in all of these cases is that judicial authorities regulate these family disputes.

Ugaritic documents suggest that similar practices existed there. One contract (RS 16.129) records a father's disinheritance of his son (for reasons not mentioned), while another (RS 8.145) threatens disinheritance against sons who show disrespect (*uqallil*) to their widowed mother.[17] The simple fact that both examples appear in contracts demonstrates that this process is controlled by legal functionaries.

Viewed together, these examples expose the struggle that exists in these societies between the family and the community. In African and Middle Eastern societies, the honor and reputation of the family has priority, as seen in the right of the family to "deal with" its own dishonorable members. This they do usually by removing the unwanted kinsman from the group, either by killing him or banishing him. But the community can also act like a "family" toward an individual family, threatening reprisals on the entire family which is slow to punish the wrongdoer in its midst. The ancient Near Eastern examples show the community in direct control of disputes between parents and children.

---

[16] Surprisingly, the following law provides for the opposite possibility as well—if the parents wrongfully disown the adopted child, they forfeit their estate.

[17] Rainey, "Family Relationships," pp. 13–14.

One must be careful, however, not to infer too much from these differences. The expulsion (disinheritance) of the wrongdoer in contemporary societies is always a response to the disfavor of the community. It is likely that the capricious expulsion of a son by his father would prompt community intervention in the opposite direction. Ultimately, the authority of the family is "circumscribed" by the community. The ancient Near Eastern evidence must be interpreted in similar ways. The documents we possess are official documents, representing only those cases which come before an appointed official of some sort. Whether these constitute a denial of the rights of a father/husband to mete out his own justice is not addressed. Evidence from parallel cases must be considered before one reaches a final decision (see Chapter 6).

Underlying all these examples, I see a concern for preserving the honor of the community as a whole, as well as the honor of its individual members. It cannot be denied that community pressures (either formal or informal) effectively restrict the powers of individuals, but they do not do so at the expense of the personal reputations of those individuals. In fact, what these laws and customs do is to provide ways for an entire community and its individual members to preserve their honor in shameful situations.

REDACTION-CRITICAL MATTERS

There is general agreement among redaction critics that Deut 21:18–21aα preserves, for the most part, a pre-Deuteronomic law, while the second and third clauses of v 21 consist of Deuteronom(ist)ic supplements.[18] Significant verbal parallels to

---

[18] V 21aβ is another instance of the Deuteronomic purge-formula (cp. 13:6; 17:7, 12; 19:13, 19; 22:22, 24; 24:7). V 21b ("hear and fear") is a less common motive clause (cp. 13:12; 17:13; 19:20).

See C. Carmichael, *The Laws of Deuteronomy* (Ithaca: Cornell University Press, 1974), pp. 44–45, 140; A. Phillips, *Deuteronomy* (CBC; Cambridge: Cambridge University, 1973), p. 143; idem, "Another Look at Adultery," *JSOT* 20 (1981) 8; Mayes, *Deuteronomy*, pp. 304–305; E. Bellefontaine, "Deuteronomy 21:18–21: Reviewing the Case of the Rebellious Son," *JSOT* 13 (1979) 13; P. R. Callaway, "Deut 21:18–21: Proverbial Wisdom and Law," *JBL* 103 (1984) 344; E. Otto, "Der Dekalog als Brennspiegel

the former appear primarily in pre-Deuteronomic sections of other laws (see especially 22:13–21; 25:5–10;[19] also see on 13:7–12, below). Brief consideration of the structure of these laws confirms this impression, because some of the laws in which one finds the verbal parallels also follow the same structural pattern as 21:18–21.[20] This suggests that these laws stem from a common legal source or tradition which the Deuteronomist has incorporated into his work.

There is also general agreement that v 20b ("he is a glutton and a drunkard") is secondary. There are three reasons for this conclusion: (1) it moves the accusation by the parents beyond the narrator's description of the son's behavior (v 18); (2) the behavior described here is of a different sort than that mentioned previously; and (3) there is a parallel to this expression in Prov 23:21 (although the order is reversed).[21] I hesitatingly concur with this conclusion. The description of the son as "a glutton and a drunkard" is not intended as a specifier. In other words, it does not define the only way that one is to interpret the general description of the son given

---

israelitischer Rechtsgeschichte," in *Alttestamentlicher Glaube und Biblische Theologie* (FS H. D. Preuss); ed. J. Hausmann and H.-J. Zobel (Stuttgart, 1992), p. 63; Gertz, *Die Gerichtsorganisation Israels*, pp. 180–82.

[19] See, e.g., L. M. Epstein, *Sex Laws and Customs in Judaism* (New York: Ktav, 1948), p. 165; A. Rofé, "Family and Sex Laws in Deuteronomy and the Book of the Covenant," *Henoch* 9 (1987) 143–44.

In addition to adjudication by the elders, critics cite as evidence of pre-Deuteronomic composition the use of יסר (cp. 4:36; 8:5; 11:2; 22:18), reference to adjudication at "the gate" (cp. 16:18; 22:15; 25:7), and "bringing out" the son (cp. 22:21, 24; the usage in 17:5 is a Deuteronom[ist]ic appropriation of this expression). More controversial is the use of רגם instead of סקל (cp. 13:10; 22:21) in v 21. See Hölscher, "Komposition," p. 216; Eissfeldt, *Old Testament*, p. 224; Seitz, *Redaktionsgeschichtliche Studien*, p. 118; Phillips, *Deuteronomy*, pp. 142–43; Mayes, *Deuteronomy*, pp. 304–305; G. J. Wenham and J. G. McConville, "Some Drafting Techniques in Some Deuteronomic Laws," *VT* 30 (1980) 252 n. 9.

[20] Buchholz, *Die Ältesten Israels*, pp. 61–63; Gertz, *Die Gerichtsorganisation Israels*, p. 176; cp. Seitz, *Redaktionsgeschichtliche Studien*, pp. 118–19; Wenham and McConville, "Some Drafting Techniques," p. 252 n. 9.

[21] Hölscher, "Komposition," p. 209; Seitz, *Redaktionsgeschichtliche Studien*, p. 118; D. Marcus, "Juvenile Delinquency in the Bible and the Ancient Near East," *JANES* 13 (1981) 48–50; Preuss, *Deuteronomium*, p. 56; Otto, "Der Dekalog," p. 63; Gertz, *Die Gerichtsorganisation Israels*, pp. 181–82. Bellefontaine ("Deuteronomy 21:18–21," pp. 20–23) attributes this to a second law lying behind the present Deuteronomic law.

in vv 18 and 20 ("stubborn and rebellious"). Instead, it provides but one example of how "stubborn and rebellious" might be manifested in a son's life. In this regard, it is parallel to the example of accidental manslaughter placed in the asylum-law (Deut 19:5a). It is being too restrictive of the author, however, to assume that the only possible inspiration for the phrase "a glutton and a drunkard" is Prov 23:21. Besides the possibility that the latter is derived from this law, one must also admit that these are common vices which could have been a part of everyday parlance at any time. Therefore, while the first two arguments cited above do suggest that v 20b is secondary, the considerations just mentioned show that it could have been added at any stage in the law's development, even prior to its adoption by the Deuteronomic lawgiver.

TRADITIO-HISTORICAL CONSIDERATIONS

Many commentators struggle with the rationale given for the son's execution in this law. He is "stubborn and rebellious." This seems a bit vague, and the reaction to it a bit harsh. For this reason, scholars look to other laws involving parent-child disputes to clarify this law, placing Deut 21:18–21 within a particular tradition of parent-child laws. Most would agree with the description of Deut 21:18–21 as "an extension of the fifth commandment" ("Honor your father and your mother"—Exod 20:12; Deut 5:16). The parents are accusing their son of dishonoring them.[22] But a more direct line of development is often drawn between Deut 21:18–21 and the negative counterpart of that commandment, found in Exod 21:15, 17 ("The one who strikes [מכה]/curses [מקלל] his father or his mother shall surely be put to death"). Parallels to the latter in biblical (Lev 20:9; Deut 27:16) and extra-biblical texts (Ugaritic text RS 8.145; see n. 18, above) point to the importance of this notion among Israelites and their neighbors. This information is then used to clarify the meaning of the Deuteronomic law. If one understands that the

---

[22] The quote is from Phillips, *Deuteronomy*, p. 142; cp. Otto, "Der Dekalog," p. 63; Thompson, *Deuteronomy*, p. 230.

accused has assaulted or cursed one of his parents, the offense
seems more verifiable and the reaction more understandable.[23]
  Bellefontaine   argues   cogently   against   this   latter
interpretation.[24] The son is not accused of an isolated offense of
striking or cursing his parents. He has done something for which
they have "disciplined" (יסרו) him, and yet he has continued to do
it; he does not "listen to" (שמע) them.[25] This suggests that this law
is more closely related to the commandment (Exod 20:12; Deut
5:16) than to the laws of the Covenant Code (Exod 21:15, 17; cp.
Lev 20:9; Deut 27:16). The son is guilty of "persistent disobedience"
toward his parents, not an isolated act. It seems best, then, to say
that Deut 21:18–21 represents a tradition of applying the
commandment, a tradition which is parallel to the one represented
in Exod 21:15, 17; but both traditions stem directly from the
Decalogue.

  There are numerous verbal and conceptual links between this
law in its present form and Deut 13:7–12 (see below). This suggests
some sort of literary connection between the two passages. The
easiest reconstruction gives priority to this law. There is

---

[23] Driver, *Deuteronomy*, pp. iv–vii, 247; G. R. Berry, "The Code Found in
the Temple," *JBL* 39 (1920) 45; Carmichael, *Laws*, p. 138 (but also see the
much-needed critique by B. M. Levinson, "Calum M. Carmichael's
Approach to the Laws of Deuteronomy," *HTR* 83 [1990] 227–57); Seitz,
Redaktionsgeschichtliche Studien, p. 117; Thompson, *Deuteronomy*, pp.
230–31; Phillips, *Deuteronomy*, p. 142; Marcus, "Juvenile Delinquency," pp.
46–49; Preuss, *Deuteronomium*, pp. 104–05; Callaway, "Deut 21:18–21," pp.
342–44; Otto, "Der Dekalog," p. 63. For several of these scholars, this is an
example of the D Code building on the Covenant Code or the Holiness Code.
  One writer takes this in a different direction, arguing that Deut
21:18–21 limits those who "curse" their parents to persons who are gluttons
and drunkards. J. Fleishman, "Offences against Parents Punishable by
Death: Towards a Socio-Legal Interpretation of Ex. 21:15, 17," *The Jewish
Law Annual* 10 (1992) 36.
[24] Bellefontaine, "Deuteronomy 21:18–21," pp. 17–20.
[25] The description of the offense is purposefully left vague, to allow the
elders to use their own discretion in judging it, but it must be something
which the community would recognize as egregious (on v 20b, see below).
Bellefontaine points to LH ¶192 as the closest parallel (cp. ¶193). That law
concerns an adopted son who repudiates his parents, saying, "You are not
my father," or "You are not my mother." It stipulates that the son's tongue
shall be cut out. LH ¶¶168–169 present a better parallel to this law, in my
mind. They regulate the disinheritance of the son who has committed a
"grave offense." Again, the ambiguity of the description allows the "judges"
to use their own discretion.

Deuteronom(ist)ic phraseology throughout 13:7–12, but only in the hortatory conclusion of 21:18–21. Also, several have commented on the use of the non-Deuteronomic term, רגם, in reference to stoning in 21:21a.[26] These clues lend support to the conclusion that Deut 21:18–21aα is pre-Deuteronomic, in contrast to Deut 13:7–12, which is Deuteronom(ist)ic. It appears, then, that the lawgiver is taking the sentiment of the earlier law and applying it specifically to the problem of religious apostasy.

Another aspect of redaction concerns the placement of this law within the D Code. We have already noted certain links between Deut 21:18–21 and the elders-laws in 22:13–21 and 25:5–10 (see n. 19, above). The work of scholars such as G. Seitz, G. Braulik, and A. Rofé exposes other literary and verbal links between this law and those that surround it in Deuteronomy 21.[27] Particularly intriguing here is the observation that the ordering of 21:15–21 matches the arrangement of LH ¶¶167–168.[28] This raises the possibility that there was a long-standing legal tradition of sequencing these laws together.

One might wish to consider possible thematic reasons for this sequencing. Reading this law in conjunction with the one that precedes it (Deut 21:15–17, concerning the distribution of inheritance), one might conclude that a concern of this law is to prevent the improper exclusion of a son from his inheritance by accusing him of "rebelliousness." In that vein, some have suggested that this law supports the requirement that the testimony of two witnesses—in this case, both parents—must be given in cases of capital punishment (Deut 17:6; 19:15–21).[29] This

---

[26] Mayes, *Deuteronomy*, p. 304; Callaway, "Deut 21:18–21," p. 343; Gertz, *Die Gerichtsorganisation*, pp. 190–91.

The fact that this term usually appears in Priestly materials leads Gertz to argue that this is an exilic text. However, none of the rest of the law is Priestly, and the term does appear in 1 Kgs 12:18 (probably preserving the reading of a pre-deuteronomistic source). It seems more prudent simply to say that the term is non-Deuteronomic and admit the possibility that Priestly writers of the Exile could appropriate a term known previously. (And is it even appropriate to assume that all Priestly materials are exilic?)

[27] Seitz, *Redaktionsgeschichtliche Studien*, p. 117; Braulik, "Zur Abfolge," p. 90; idem, *Deuteronomium II, 16,18–34,12* (Würzburg: Echter Verlag, 1992), pp. 156–59; Rofé, "Arrangement," p. 272.

[28] Seitz, *Redaktionsgeschichtliche Studien*, p. 117.

[29] Thompson, *Deuteronomy*, pp. 230–31; Bellefontaine, "Deuteronomy 21:18–21," p. 30 n. 37.

would imply that the law intends to thwart the abuse of traditional patriarchal authority by preventing a father from acting alone and denying the son of a disliked wife his proper inheritance. Since this law mentions the testimony of both father and mother, and since such a mother would probably be acting contrary to her own long-term well-being with such an accusation, this law would actually give the wife a way of thwarting her husband's schemes against her and her son. On the other hand, such a line of interpretation ignores the way in which this law is stated. First of all, this law does not call for disinheritance; it calls for the execution of the son. Moreover, there is no suggestion that the man might be acting against his wife's best interests. The protasis (v 18) clearly states that the son is rebellious, that he is disobedient toward both father *and* mother, that *both* parents have "disciplined" him. Had the author wished to address a situation of multiple wives and strife between their respective children, he could have easily done so. But there is no mention of more than one wife in this law, nor even of more than one son. So, while this law might complement the preceding law in some cases, that would seem to be a peripheral purpose.[30] The reason for its placement here seems to be based primarily on verbal links.

INTERPRETATION OF THE PRE-DEUTERONOMIC LAW
(21:18–20a, 21aα)

Keith Whitelam succinctly states what many consider to be the primary significance of this law.

> Deut. xxi 18–21 points to a situation where the *paterfamilias* no longer held responsibility for the pronouncement of the death penalty. The fact that the jurisdiction appears to have rested with the elders of the town (זקני העיר) suggests that

---

[30] To argue that complementarity accounts for the present arrangement of certain laws is certainly legitimate; but even if complementarity is deemed probable, that still does not necessarily explain the original or primary intent of the two laws. This pair of laws shares a common cast of characters—a husband, a wife, and a son. Perhaps that commonality alone is sufficient to explain their proximity to one another.

urbanization, possibly under the monarchy, contributed to the decline of the authority of the *paterfamilias*.[31]

The conclusion is that this law, composed prior to any Deuteronomic reform,[32] intends to deprive a father and mother of their right to execute their son, because the author of the law believes that undermines the authority of the community-at-large. This naturally infers a couple of additional conclusions. First, it is typical to associate this community authority with an increase in the authority of the central administration. Second, this interpretation infers that parents who execute their own son without bringing him before the city elders would themselves be subject to prosecution.[33]

These conclusions need to be thought through again; they are not necessarily supported by the evidence. This calls into question the assumption that a basic intent or result of the law is the restriction of the authority of Israelite fathers.

In examining the assumption that this law marks a transition from parental right to community and state authority, one must look beyond the possible change alone to logical rationales for it. One logical rationale would be political. State authorities realize that controlling power over life and death gives one political leverage in a local community. Locals who have previously utilized capital punishment as a social control mechanism can be deprived of that weapon by the state. Conversely, state authorities can declare which actions are capital offenses and which are not in light of what will benefit them the most, thereby indirectly bringing about other changes in the local communities. Another rationale for taking over control of capital punishment is a humanitarian desire to prevent a wrongful death. Again, there are several examples of state governments doing this in an attempt to bring to an end practices which are deemed "barbaric" by the international community.

---

[31] Whitelam, *Just King*, p. 42.

[32] Phillips, *Deuteronomy*, pp. 142–43; Mayes, *Deuteronomy*, p. 304.

[33] L. Stulman, "Encroachment in Deuteronomy: An Analysis of the Social World of the D Code," *JBL* 109 (1990) 624; D. Patrick, *Old Testament Law* (Atlanta: John Knox, 1985), p. 133; Driver, *Deuteronomy*, p. 248; von Rad, *Deuteronomy*, p. 138; Thompson, *Deuteronomy*, pp. 230–31; Marcus, "Juvenile Delinquency," p. 46; Blenkinsopp, "Deuteronomy and the Politics," pp. 1–5.

The law of Deut 21:18–21 does not seem to support either of these rationales. Control over capital punishment is not being given to state authorities; that control stays in the hands of the elders of the city. They represent local authority, not state authority.[34] It does not really make sense to say that city elders are concerned to give themselves power formerly reserved for the *paterfamilias*. Each elder is a father. The most one could conclude, in terms of holding authority, is that authority once reserved for individual "fathers" now rests in the hands of a collective of "fathers." But there is nothing in this law to suggest that that collective has its authority in the matter compromised by the central (state) authority. And one cannot cite humanitarian concerns as a strong rationale in this case, since the accused is still to be executed.

The most that can be said is that this law might force Israelite fathers to shift their perspective from what one family would like for itself to what is best for the entire community. This, however, is a foundational aspect of community life in kinship-based societies, an aspect which typically is central for elders and promoted strongly by them. Individuals are elevated to the status of elder *because* they make decisions based on placing the well-being of the community above the personal desires of any single family.

These considerations raise the possibility that this law does not intend to produce any change to social controls over life and death. The brief survey of societies given above reveals that many kinship-based societies do not give fathers absolute authority of life and death over their children. Some do, but one cannot conclude from this that all must. That authority sometimes rests in the hands of the entire community (represented by their elders), because the accused is of value to the community (perhaps as a worker or a warrior), not just to his own family. The evidence of other societies shows that one cannot automatically assume that Israelite fathers once possessed absolute authority of life and death over their children. It is just as likely that that authority had always rested ultimately in the hands of the whole community (i.e., the elders). And even if it did reside with individual fathers at one

---

[34] Stulman's assumption ("Sex and Familial Crimes," pp. 53–62) that the elders represent the state government is without basis.

time, its transfer to the hands of the entire community could have taken place prior to national political centralization.[35]

To evaluate whether this law intends to redefine parental rights and authority, I would suggest that we consider this law from the standpoint of how the law might be broken. Then we can turn to the question of what role the elders—the authorities in this case—would probably play. The inference made by many recent studies seems to be that this law would be broken if the parents (either one or both) were to execute their son without bringing him formally before the city elders for trial. From this perspective, the law intends primarily to restrict the rights of parents to kill their rebellious children. The assumption is that they had that right previously (as do members of some of the societies discussed above); but to exercise such a right now would be considered presumptuous, as the law places the authority to kill solely in the hands of the community.

On the other hand, the focus of concern in Deut 21:18–21 does not seem to be with parents who would act presumptuously. In other cases of killing in Deuteronomy, the concern is that the killing will be unjustified and escalate into a feud. This law is about a son who is "stubborn and rebellious." The narrator twice mentions that the son does not "hear" the voice of his parents (v 18); the parents repeat this in their accusation before the elders (v 20). It is highly unlikely that, had the parents killed the "stubborn and rebellious son" on their own, the community would have interpreted it as an unjustified killing requiring community retaliation. The law makes it clear that the son is not "innocent," for he has dishonored his parents by not "listening to" them (see Exod 21:17; 1 Sam 2:25)[36]; killing the son removes "evil" from the community (and from Israel).[37] It is more logical to assume that the author of the law, as well as the later redactor(s) of the D Code,

---

[35] I cannot think of any biblical examples of this sort of patriarchal authority. On the other hand, there are two stories of the early monarchic period of "popular opinion" overturning the "commands" of royal fathers (1 Sam 14:45; 2 Sam 14:12–21).

[36] On this passage, see Fleishman, "Offences Against Parents," pp. 19–23.

[37] The fact that this clause (v 21aβ) is part of a Deuteronomic redaction does not undercut this statement. The redactor is merely stating in national terms what is obvious from the earlier law about the nature of the son's offense.

would expect the local community to condone the killing of a rebellious son by his parents. If the elders were to reprimand a father who has acted to eliminate a son who is a threat to the community's integrity, they would be saying that they are more concerned with their own authority than with the well-being of their community.

The other way in which this law might be broken would be for the parents to harbor a rebellious son from the wrath of the community. The law does not set out to prevent the death of a son; it insures it. There is no mention of the son having an opportunity to respond to the charges brought by his parents; there is no question of his guilt. So, there does not seem to be a concern that a son who is innocent might be going to his death wrongfully. Instead, the concern of the law seems to be that the parents might be reluctant to execute their son.[38]

That parents might be reluctant to execute their son is quite understandable. The physical and economic well-being of both might be at stake. The father is accusing one who is supposed to perpetuate his name (cp. Deut 25:6–7; Ruth 4:5, 10; 2 Sam 14:4–11), and the mother is accusing one who is probably expected to care for her in her old age (see 2 Kings 4). This law assumes, however, that concern for the integrity of the broader community must override any one family's aspirations and desires. In this light, this law is analogous to Deut 13:7–12, where the religious integrity of the community supersedes any autonomy which an individual might claim (see below).

The survey of comparable kinship-based societies above suggests that an execution for the kind of offense implied by this law is most likely to come only after considerable gossip and ill-

---

[38] It is widely noted that the rabbis interpreted the call for execution as hyperbole. See, for example, Rofé, "Family and Sex Laws," p. 144. H. McKeating points to the book of Proverbs for the possibility that lesser punishments could have been implemented ("Sanctions Against Adultery in Ancient Israelite Society, with Some Reflections on Methodology in the Study of Old Testament Ethics," *JSOT* 11 [1979] 67).

Salmon ("Judicial Authority," pp. 34–35) argues that the subjectivity involved in judging the son's offenses might have made it difficult for one so biased as a father to see that his son was guilty of criminal activity; so, the community must assume the role of judge in such cases. To the contrary, the father pronounces the charges against the son, rather than speaking in the son's defense. If the father were too biased to acknowledge his son's crime, then he could not in good conscience accuse his son of wrongdoing.

feeling toward the offender (and his family!) have been circulating in the community.[39] Some might suggest that the situation envisioned in this law is a private, family matter and not of concern to the public—not even known publicly—thereby negating comparisons with those other societies. Bellefontaine has shown, however, that accusing the son of being "stubborn and rebellious" indicates that the problem is both chronic and public,[40] as it is in those other societies. Similarly, it makes the most sense to assume that the involvement of "the men of the city" in the execution reflects the fact that this is seen as an offense against the entire community in some way.[41]

Offenses both social and religious might be implied by the description of the son. From a social perspective, two concerns logically show themselves. The first (and most obvious) is that the son does not "honor" his parents. This tears at the essential fabric of the community, which derives some of its strength from its traditionalism. Members of the society understood their identity within a multi-generational framework. Those living were perpetuating the "names" of their ancestors, and they were expecting their descendants to do the same for them. Economic security and political standing were based on such notions.[42] The son is disrupting this traditional framework by being "stubborn and rebellious" toward his parents. This, in turn, betrays a lack of concern for the well-being of the group. His behavior could influence others of his generation to pursue an equally disruptive course. Persons with such a disposition pose a threat to the future life of the community, whose prosperity probably depended on mutual aid. In this light, the charges which the parents make are most likely a response to considerable pressure from the community, as one finds in those other societies. They represent—among other things—the family's reaffirmation of its commitment to the community.

---

[39] See nn. 4–13, above; Bellefontaine, "Deuteronomy 21:18–21," p. 22.

[40] Bellefontaine, "Deuteronomy 21:18–21," pp. 17–19; cp. C. Pressler, *The View of Women Found in the Deuteronomic Family Laws* (BZAW 216; New York/Berlin: Walter de Gruyter, 1993), p. 18; Phillips, *Deuteronomy*, p. 142.

[41] One might contrast this to Deut 19:13, where the murderer is handed over to the blood avenger.

[42] Brichto, "Kin, Cult, Land and Afterlife," pp. 1–54; Blenkinsopp, "Deuteronomy and the Politics," pp. 1–3.

There is also a religious perspective to be considered. The commandment to honor one's parents is a part of Israel's foundational religious tenets. The "stubborn and rebellious" son is blatantly contemptuous toward that commandment. This betrays a contempt for Yahweh himself. Such a person threatens to bring divine wrath down on the entire community. To avert that, the community must see to it that that person is removed from their midst.[43]

The role played by the city elders, then, is to uphold the moral integrity of the community. They do not adjudicate in this case. There is no evidence to be weighed and verified. If Israelite communities were at all like contemporary ones, they know the guilt of the son. The elders represent the community and probably have been among those pressuring the parents to "do something" about their son. But they do not circumvent the parents to punish the son. They honor the parents (even though the son does not) by waiting for them to hand over the rebellious son to the community. The only alternative available to the parents is to leave the community with their child. By allowing them to hand him over, the elders signal the community's continuing acceptance of the rest of the family.

This exemplifies a basic struggle one faces in kinship-based societies. That struggle is to maintain a balance between competition and cooperation in one's interactions with others. Brothers compete against one another, but they also cooperate with one another in competing with more distant relatives. Families in the same community compete with one another, but they also cooperate with one another in competing with other communities.

In summary, this pre-Deuteronomic law (Deut 21:18–20a, 21aα) does not really address the question of the authority of

---

[43] Many of my conclusions have been anticipated by Carolyn Pressler in her own brief discussion of this passage. She, too, sees the parents fulfilling a community responsibility in bringing accusations against their son; and she sees the son's offense as an offense against the community and against Yahweh. The prescription for stoning by the community does not indicate the limited nature of the parents' authority, but the breadth and gravity of the offense. Pressler, *View of Women*, pp. 17–20.

For similar conclusions regarding Deut 21:15–17 and 24:1–4, see Pressler, *View of Women*, pp. 15–16, 60–62; and Rofé, "Family and Sex Laws," p. 153.

parents over their (obviously grown) children. It is not even necessary to assume that the absolute power over life and death had ever been held by Israelite parents prior to the writing of this law. The law's concern is not to define or restrict the authority or rights of parents. Its primary intent is to affirm the sentiment (which seems to have already been present) that everyone—even parents—must place the interests of the entire community above their own personal aspirations and desires. Comparative materials suggest that the son's improper behavior is known in the community, and that the community has been urging the family to discipline him. The situation is now considered more serious, because the son has refused to "listen to" his parents' corrections. He is challenging some of the conceptual framework on which the society has been built, and he is demeaning the place of his parents in that society and its history. If the man and his wife do nothing more to their son in the face of the community's criticism, they would also be suggesting that they condone the kind of behavior in which their son is engaging. This would put the entire family at risk in terms of its ability to co-exist with the other families in the community. Mutual economic and social responsibilities would not be met. And from a religious standpoint, the problem must have been visible and serious enough that the neighbors were worried about it incurring the wrath of God. For the sake of the community and their own identity, the parents hand their son over to the community for judgment and retribution. The elders "accept" the son on behalf of the community, and then they insure that the community metes out punishment in order to preserve/restore its moral integrity.

DEUTERONOM(IST)IC EXPANSIONS
(21:20b, 21aβb)[44]

The Deuteronomic lawgiver inherited a law which placed ultimate authority over the life of a "son" in the hands of his

---

[44] I will not be commenting on v 20b. It merely provides one example of how a son might demonstrate that he is "stubborn and rebellious." There is nothing to associate the clause with any particular redaction (see earlier comments).

community. It is perhaps significant that the redactor leaves that authority there; he does not transfer it from the community to the state bureaucracy. Thus, the redacted law perpetuates the status quo at the local level. The well-being of the community still supersedes the wishes of an individual family. The rights of the parents are still circumscribed because of their social obligations to the broader community. The Deuteronomic formulation of this law continues to withhold from them the right to harbor a "rebellious" son, because that would allow him to persist in behavior which is detrimental to the community.

What the supplementary Deuteronomic clauses of v 21aβb do is expand the reader's point of view on this matter from the local community to the entire nation. The effect is to broaden the local community's understanding of its visibility and accountability. The local community should recognize that it is not autonomous, that what goes on within its walls does influence the rest of the nation. In a sense, it is a reflection of an evolution in Israel's identity. The notions that were traditionally held regarding family/lineage and community (some of which underlie this law) are expanded by the Deuteronomic redactor to the level of the nation. Ideas regarding mutual aid and accountability which previously had kept lineages and communities together are now applied to inter-municipal and national relations.

The clearest evidence of this comes from the final clause, "And all Israel will hear and fear." The redactor here picks up an important thread from the earlier law and weaves it together with one of his own. The thread he picks up is the threefold reference to the son's refusal to "hear" his parents. In the original law, this point is used to justify the harsh punishment imputed to the son. Now the redactor uses the son's fate as a warning to the rest of the nation, exhorting them to "hear" the law. This carries a couple of potential applications. One is its distributive application in Israelite communities. It shows that dishonoring one's parents should not be tolerated in any Israelite community.[45] The other application is national. The Deuteronomic redaction of this law implies that, if the nation does not "listen to" the correction of its "parent" (Yahweh), it will face the same fate as this inattentive son.

---

[45] Rofé, "Family and Sex Laws," p. 145.

This same duality is inherent in the penultimate clause, "you shall purge the evil from your midst" (cp. 13:6; 17:7; 19:19; 22:24; 24:7). This duality arises from the ambiguity in the use of "you" in this clause. "You" can refer to the entirety of Israel (the variant in 17:12 and 22:22 reads, "you shall remove the evil from Israel"), but it often takes on a distributive sense (see 12:12, 18; 14:26; 16:11, 14; 22:1–2; passim). In a sense, both are understood together. Each community is responsible for maintaining its integrity as God's people; each community is responsible for upholding these laws. But each community is part of a larger whole, part of the nation of Israel.[46] Just as a community "polices" the individual families within it, so the nation pays attention to what each community does. If an entire community fails to "listen to" Yahweh, the rest of the nation is obligated to "purge the evil" from its midst.

The expansion of the conceptual point of view exhibited in these redactional layers parallels the progression of thought in Deut 13:7–12 (see above). That passage speaks of apostasy as a family/local community matter, prescribing the harshest response to a close relative who encourages the worship of other gods. The readers are warned, among other things, not to "listen to" (שָׁמַע) such a person; they are to show him "no pity" (cp. Deut 7:16; 13:9; 19:13, 21; 25:12),[47] but to "stone (סָקַל) him with stones and he shall die" (cp. 21:21a). The perspective then expands to the national level, speaking of how Yahweh delivered "you" (both the individual family and the nation) out of Egypt. It closes with the exhortation that "all Israel shall hear and fear" (cp. 21:21b), and never again shall "this evil" be done "in your midst" (cp. 21:21aβ). The subsequent verses (13:13–19) further this expanded perspective, essentially calling on the nation to deal with an apostate city in the same way that a family or community is to deal with an apostate individual in its midst.

---

[46] "It is probably misleading to ask whether it is people speaking in the name of the state or local groups who are responsible for such laws because that suggests that the two are in complete opposition or constitute entirely separate worlds. Their opposition notwithstanding, they are parts of a single system; the actions of neither can be understood without the other." Y. A. Cohen, "Ends and Means in Political Control: State Organization and the Punishment of Adultery, Incest, and Violation of Celibacy," *AmAnthro* 71 (1969) 668.

[47] See Rofé, "Family and Sex Laws," p. 145.

These observations show how this passage (more than those already examined) brings out an important aspect of Deuteronomic thinking. The lawgiver is taking traditional ideas which have been operative at the community level and reinterpreting them for his audience at the national level. This does not mean that community institutions are now to be displaced by national ones. Rather, the Deuteronomist brings out how local functions must be exercised with the entire nation (not just the local community) in mind.

This might be an innovation in thinking, or it might simply be a shift in emphasis. It would depend on the strength of inter-regional ties over the centuries. The strengthening of these ties would naturally go hand in hand with the centralization of the Israelite cult; so, one could argue that this is an innovation to be associated with the Deuteronomic reform. On the other hand, the promotion of a national perspective would also be in the best interests of any monarchy. It is just as logical to assume, then, that communities had long considered such situations from a national perspective, and the redactor is simply emphasizing this in conjunction with cult centralization.

CONCLUSIONS

Deut 21:18–21 consists of a pre-Deuteronomic law (vv 18–20a, 21aα), supplemented by an example of the sort of offense being considered (v 20b) and Deuteronom(ist)ic exhortations (v 21aβb). The early law deals with a problem found in many kinship-based societies: the perpetual wrongdoer. This law looks to the immediate family of the wrongdoer to mete out punishment. Although the punishment is severe (stoning), the notion behind it is a common one. That notion is that community members must put the well-being of the overall community above their personal aspirations. The son here is guilty of dishonoring his parents, of putting himself above them and the community. This threatens the family's identity in the community and the community's overall integrity, and it raises the possibility of divine retribution. The parents hand their son over to the city elders to prevent all these things. In so doing, they reaffirm their own commitment to the welfare of the community.

The Deuteronom(ist)ic supplements take this community spirit and expand it to encompass the entire nation. The redactor does not shift traditional authority at all; he merely places a traditional community function within a national framework. This standardizes the community function, making it applicable to all Israelite communities (to which it probably applied previously). It also makes the community accountable to other Israelite communities to maintain its integrity. Just as individual families had been accountable to their broader communities, the redactor shows that individual communities are accountable to the nation. The same notion underlies the prescriptions in Deut 13:7–19 regarding foreign worship practices. It is possible that adopting a national perspective is a "new" notion, but it is also possible that this simply brings forward an old one.

CHAPTER 6
ACCUSING A BRIDE OF UNCHASTITY
(DEUT 22:13–21)

The two-part law recorded in Deut 22:13–21 (the bride accused of non-virginity) has much in common with the law in Deut 21:18–21, discussed in the preceding chapter. Both cases involve parents accusing their child before the elders of the city; both call for the stoning of the guilty child; they share a common motive clause (the purge formula) and a common literary structure.[1] They also lead modern interpreters to the same conclusions regarding the subject of parental authority in ancient Israel. This law, perhaps even more than the law of the rebellious son, is used to show how the D Code restricts the traditional authority of an Israelite male over his wife and children. In this particular situation, these restrictions are explained as a direct result of the rise of monarchic/state authority. As in the previous chapter, we will re-examine these conclusions in the light of analogies from ancient and contemporary societies. It will also be necessary to consider the intent of this law in conjunction with those which

---

[1] Seitz, *Redaktionsgeschichtliche Studien*, p. 119; Wenham and McConville, "Drafting Techniques," p. 252 n. 9; Benjamin, *Deuteronomy and City Life*, p. 228; Rofé, "Family and Sex Laws," pp. 143–44, 151; C. Locher, *Die Ehre einer Frau in Israel: Exegetische und rechtsvergleichende Studien zu Deuteronomium 22,13–21* (OBO 70; Göttingen: Vandenhoeck & Ruprecht, 1986), pp. 60–64; Buchholz, *Die Ältesten Israels*, pp. 62–63; Gertz, *Die Gerichtsorganisation*, p. 211.

follow it (22:22–29), since they deal with similar concerns (adultery, rape, seduction). All of these provide insights into views on sexuality in the D Code, views which inform one's interpretation of this particular law.

COMPARATIVE EVIDENCE

Contemporary Kinship-Based Societies

Contemporary African societies display some variety in their traditional beliefs and practices regarding marriage and sexual conduct, but this variety falls within a relatively narrow spectrum. A couple of the most common characteristics are especially pertinent to the present investigation. One is that marriages are usually viewed as financial arrangements between the males of two families. The exchange of marriage gifts between the groom and the bride's father (or brothers) is necessary to the recognition of a marriage as "official" or legitimate.[2] Likewise, the legal proceedings that take place at the dissolution of a marriage typically are carried out between the males of the respective families.[3] As we have seen in other inter-familial financial matters, the local elders in these traditional societies naturally oversee these arrangements. They commonly serve as witnesses to the exchange of gifts, and they oversee the appropriate return of such gifts if the marriage eventually dissolves (in cases of death or divorce).

Another relatively common characteristic of kinship-based societies is their understanding of sexual offenses. A sexual offense is conceived of (1) as a personal offense against the male who "controls" the sexual rights of the female involved, and, in some societies, (2) as a sacral offense. The former seems to be primary, based on the mode and the nature of punishments in such cases. In most of these societies, the husband (or

---

[2] Nadel, *Nuba*, pp. 119–24, 225–26, 433–34; Schapera, "Law and Justice," pp. 202–203; Verdier, "Ontology," p. 144; Winans, *Shambala*, p. 107.

[3] Deng, *Dinka*, p. 113; Nadel, *Nuba*, pp. 123, 225–26, 434; Verdier, "Ontology," p. 144.

father/brothers) of the female is afforded the right to seek vengeance ("self-help") against the person(s) by whom he feels wronged (the other man, the female, or both). Even when there are "official" responses that have been established (i.e., by legal mandate), the offended male often is not punished when he seeks vengeance on his own.[4] The punishments employed by the offended male vary somewhat, both within one society and between societies. They range from simple divorce to fines to banishment to physical beating or mutilation to death.[5] In some societies, the community can determine the punishment, either instead of the male's response or in addition to it. Even in cases where the community or central authority claims control over such cases, great latitude is allowed to a husband who discovers his wife with another man *in flagrante delicto*.[6] Also, besides whatever immediate physical punishments are imposed by the offended male and/or the legal authorities, the guilty person(s) will probably have to face the prolonged effects of public and divine disapproval.[7]

The roles played by elders and other traditional leaders in these cases are similar to the roles they play in cases of homicide. Factors such as lineage and territorial distance, economic interdependence, and personal honor—which are significant in determining the type and severity of the reaction to homicides—are of similar significance here. Elders again are concerned primarily with maintaining the reputation of the overall community (toward outsiders and toward the divine world) and with preserving peace and harmony between disputing families. This entails reviewing and/or imposing punishments, as well as the "sorting out" of financial obligations. They will try to

---

[4] See Nadel, *Nuba*, pp. 248–49, 302, 348, 460; Schapera, "Law and Justice," p. 204; van Velzen, *Politics*, p. 308.

[5] Some cases precipitate a combination of these punishments. See Dennis, *Gbandes*, pp. 87, 277–78; Hammond, *Yatenga*, p. 146; Nadel, *Nuba*, pp. 248–49, 348, 460; Read, *Ngoni*, p. 96; Roscoe, *Baganda*, p. 261; Schapera, "Law and Justice," pp. 205–11; Winans, *Shambala*, p. 108.

[6] See Nadel, *Nuba*, p. 506; Schapera, "Law and Justice," pp. 200, 206; Winans, *Shambala*, p. 108.

[7] See Hammond, *Yatenga*, p. 146; Roscoe, *Baganda*, p. 262.

ensure that, whoever responds to an act of sexual misconduct, the response will be "reasonable" in the eyes of the community.[8]

Similar aspects of marriage and the response to sexual misconduct stand out in the traditional practices of contemporary Middle Eastern societies. One aspect, again, is the financial nature of marriages. As in African societies, marriage is conceived of as a business agreement between the men of two families. The exchange of gifts, which take place primarily between the groom and the bride's father, establish the marriage; divorce demands the return of the marriage gifts by the one initiating the divorce. Further, the most common cause for divorce is friction between the families of the couple, not between the couple themselves.[9]

The ideational aspect of these issues that is most important is the common concept of honor. Middle Eastern peoples look upon the preservation of a woman's sexual propriety as a man's "most sacred trust." Some consider rape to be a more heinous offense than homicide, and they reserve the right to full vengeance against rapists and adulterers, and against promiscuous females of their own family. Still, they sometimes resort to less drastic measures under certain circumstances. For example, the parents of an unmarried girl who is having sex with an unmarried boy might insist that the couple marry; or they might move away from their home region in shame, rather than kill their daughter.[10]

Joseph Ginat provides a detailed analysis of traditional ways of dealing with sexual misconduct in his study of Bedouin in modern-day Israel.[11] He devotes an entire chapter to cases of girls guilty of fornication. The majority are killed by their father or brothers, typically by being cast into a well. He emphasizes that in each killing, no action is taken by the girl's family until there has been much gossip and even public accusation against the family. When it reaches that level, however, her male kinsmen are made to feel morally obligated to punish her.

---

[8] Moore, "Descent and Legal Position," p. 395; Nadel, *Nuba*, p. 348; Roscoe, *Baganda*, p. 262; van Velzen, *Politics*, p. 308.

[9] Cole, *Nomads*, p. 75.

[10] Smith, *Kinship and Marriage*, p. 125; Zeid, "Honour and Shame," pp. 253–56.

[11] Ginat, *Blood Disputes*, pp. 90–151.

Accusation is always based in the violation of the norm that a girl or single woman who has "sinned" must be punished by death unless she marries her partner... If the offending girl is to be punished according to the norms, it is always the obligation of her natal family to punish her. Although the killer himself might be inclined to instigate some lesser form of sanction, in order to preserve family honor he has no other alternative but to kill. In effect, he is pushed to kill by the person who made the public accusation.[12]

In spite of this sentiment, less extreme punishments are often imposed on unmarried girls; but they are still administered in most cases by her family. If the family deals with the matter before community gossip becomes significant, and if it can be done in a way that does not increase the shame of the family, the girl will be married off (either to her partner, or to some other man of lower status) or forced into some menial occupation (away from her hometown).[13] Also, state authorities will often try to intervene and mediate a resolution before extreme measures are felt to be "warranted."[14]

This is not to imply that only the females are held responsible for cases of sexual misconduct. A man who is known to have several illicit sexual affairs can be banished from his community. One case of adultery mentioned by Ginat resulted in divorce and then the murder of the paramour. Another affair, involving a Druze woman and a Muslim man, resulted only in divorce. It also sparked prolonged hostilities between the religious segments of the community, as the Christian kin of the woman's husband felt

---

[12] Ginat, *Blood Disputes*, p. 115.

Ginat refers to similar attitudes regarding adultery that have been reported in other studies from the Middle East. He quotes from one such researcher who states, "If she [an adulteress] is killed [by her male relatives] the group not only reasserts its position but also rises in prestige scale. If she is not killed they suffer loss of prestige." *Ibid.*, p. 116, from A. Cohen, *Two Dimensional Man: An Essay on the Anthropology of Power and Symbolism in Complex Society* (London: Routledge and Kegan Paul, 1974), p. 116. See also Zeid, "Honour and Shame," pp. 253–54; and, Bourdieu, "Sentiment of Honour," pp. 239–40.

[13] "One general feature stands out—whenever there is a possibility of hiding shame (through marriage with the person responsible, for example), the woman is not punished." Ginat, *Blood Disputes*, p. 114.

[14] For specific cases, see Ginat, *Blood Disputes*, pp. 135–51.

obligated to retaliate against the Muslim man's kin. In another case, a man reported to his father that his step-sister was having an affair with his brother-in-law. After several months of growing public cognizance of the affair and no response from the father, the man and his brother killed the couple and then fled. No punitive action followed.[15]

All of these responses are carried out under the oversight of community elders. For example, banishing a promiscuous person from the group requires the approval of the group. It is the immediate family which actually "performs" the banishment, but they do so for the sake of the entire community. The person being banished contributes something to the whole community, and so the decision for banishment must be weighed according to its effect on the whole.[16] Similarly, the consideration which ultimately pushes a male to kill his "sinful" female is the negative effect of her actions on the community, an effect verbalized by the community in the form of gossip. The community is embodied most forcefully in both cases by the elders, who impose or withhold sanctions regarding "collective responsibility" between the accused and the rest of the community.[17]

In summary, a perusal of recent studies of kinship-based societies of Africa and the Middle East reveals that there are a couple of common ideas held regarding marriage and sexual misconduct (which threatens marriages). One is that marriage is viewed as a financial arrangement concluded between the males of two families. A key component of that arrangement is the implicit acknowledgment of who oversees the sexual activity of the woman. Consequently, sexual misconduct—whether occurring before or during a marriage—is regarded as a personal offense against the males who oversee the woman's sexual activity. This usually gives them the right to avenge personally the violation of that sexuality. The mode of punishment varies from society to society, and it even varies within a given society, if the people believe that circumstances warrant it. Community moral standards and religious ideas place additional obligations on those involved. How

---

[15] Ginat, *Blood Disputes*, pp. 93–95, 122–23, 131.

[16] This is analogous to the story of Saul and Jonathan in 1 Samuel 14, where the will of the army superseded Saul's call for Jonathan's execution.

[17] Ginat, *Blood Disputes*, pp. 90–91, 94–96, 104–10.

a man responds to the sexual misconduct of those under his leadership affects his standing in the community. Community members can use gossip, accusation, and ostracization to coerce close family members to punish those guilty of inappropriate liaisons. Not to do so would result in the dishonoring of an entire family and the community in which they live. Local elders take the lead in promoting their community's overall moral reputation and harmony between the families involved in such cases. They believe "that the unity of the group comes first and that this unity should have the highest priority in determining the actions and speech of any individual" in the group.[18] They ensure that action taken against those guilty of sexual misconduct is warranted and proportionate to the offense.

Ancient Near Eastern Societies

There are numerous cuneiform laws and related documents which testify to notions concerning marriage and sexual misconduct (adultery, rape, seduction, and accusations of such activities). These are similar in many ways to the notions just described among contemporary African and Middle Eastern peoples. Complicating any investigation, though, is the absence of absolute clarity and consistency. For example, references to execution in these cases are often worded in an impersonal, ambiguous way ("X shall be killed," or "they shall kill X"). Others specify that a particular individual (i.e., the husband or father of the female) may serve as judge and executioner. A comparison of all the laws and records dealing with extra-marital sexual activity suggests great complexity and flexibility in a given system. Also, there often are significant differences between what is prescribed in the law codes and what is described in the contemporaneous written records. One must consider the variations and flexibility thus demonstrated when evaluating ancient Near Eastern parallels to Deut 22:13–21.

The extant Sumerian laws contain directives regarding seduction, rape, divorce, and accusations of sexual misconduct, but

---

[18] Ginat, *Blood Disputes*, p. 109.

none deals directly with adultery. Only the woman is culpable in a case of seduction (LU ¶7). The laws concerning rape make distinctions on the basis of the female's marital status and social standing. A man who rapes a betrothed woman is to be executed (LU ¶6), while the rape of a slave elicits the payment of a fine (LU ¶8). The "deflowering" of an unbetrothed girl can result in a marriage, although the offense must be proved (SLEx ¶¶7'–8').[19] Laws concerning divorce call for the husband to provide monetary compensation (to his wife? to her family?), hinting at the importance of the financial aspect of marriages, an aspect made clearer in later codes and contracts (LU ¶¶9–11; cp. LU ¶15; LL ¶29; SLHF ¶iv 12–14). Further, unproved accusations of promiscuity against a young woman (which would diminish her "value" to her parents) yield a fine (LU ¶14; LL ¶33).[20] There is at least one record of a charge of adultery against a wife which is preserved in a Sumerian "literary legal decision" from the Old Babylonian period. It lists a divorce payment, mutilation, and public humiliation among the punishments imposed on the guilty woman, but the document says nothing about what measures (if any) were to be taken against her paramour.[21]

A survey of Old Babylonian laws on marriage reveals just how significant the financial aspects of a marriage were in that society. The laws treat a marriage as a financial agreement between the groom (who gives a brideprice, *terkhatum*) and the bride's father (who provides a dowry, *nudunnu*).[22] A marriage is not recognized without the exchange of the marriage gifts (LE ¶¶27–28; LH ¶128).[23] The termination of a betrothal leads to the return of the

<hr/>

[19] See J. J. Finkelstein, "Sex Offenses in Sumerian Laws," *JAOS* 86 (1966) 357–67.
[20] See Finkelstein, "Sex Offenses," pp. 367–70; cp. Locher, *Die Ehre einer Frau*, pp. 324–38.
[21] S. Greengus, "A Textbook Case of Adultery in Ancient Mesopotamia," *HUCA* 40–41 (1969/1970) 33–44; cp. Locher, *Die Ehre einer Frau*, pp. 93–110.
[22] For a discussion of Nuzi documents (and a more general discussion) concerning dowry and brideprice, see K. Grosz, "Dowry and Brideprice in Nuzi," in *Studies on the Civilization and Culture of Nuzi and the Hurrians* (E. R. Lacheman Festschrift), ed. M. A. Morrison and D. I. Owen (Winona Lake, IN: Eisenbrauns, 1981), pp. 161–82.
[23] Cp. Winans, *Shambala*, p. 107. He reports the imposition of a fine in addition to the bride-price if a couple elopes.

(pre-) marriage gift by the offending party, sometimes with a fine attached (LE ¶25; LH ¶¶159–161), while the amicable dissolution of a marriage or early death of a bride or groom necessitates the return of at least a portion of such gifts (LE ¶¶17–18, 59; LH ¶¶137–140, 148–149, 162).[24]

Some of the laws on marriage and sexual misconduct suggest an underlying assumption, the recognition of which is important to their interpretation: the financial well-being and moral reputation of males is preeminent in these matters. Conversely, a woman is financially dependent on the males around her—her father, her husband, or her sons—and her actions are assessed primarily in terms of how they effect the moral reputation of the male(s) upon whom she is financially dependent. For example, there are laws which call for the drowning of the wife of a prisoner-of-war for entering another man's house in her husband's absence, unless it is a financial necessity. Those laws give that soldier legal claim over his wife and children upon his return, but they deny the same to a deserter (LE ¶29; LH ¶¶133–136). By viewing these possibilities together, we see that, while allowances are made for the well-being of the wife, the greater concern is with the soldier's financial stability and social standing. The act of restoring his family to him upon his return gives recognition to the nobleness of his incarceration while fighting for his people. The deserter, on the other hand, has shamed himself and his people, and so he is punished with personal financial ruin; but his wife is not affected. As another example, when a wife is guilty of disrespectful behavior, she is either divorced or enslaved, or drowned in a river; but if the husband is the guilty party, he merely restores her dowry to her and sends her back to her father (LH ¶¶141–143).

Such disparity makes sense when we see the laws as concerned ultimately with males, and the woman as dependent upon them. If the woman is innocent of misconduct, she can return to her father

---

[24] See E. M. Good, "Capital Punishment and Its Alternatives in Ancient Near Eastern Law," *Stanford Law Review* 19 (1967) 956–59, for a general discussion of these laws, and p. 956 n. 42 for references on the financial aspects in particular. For other written records dealing with marriage matters, see S. Greengus, "The Old Babylonian Marriage Contract," *JAOS* 89 (1969) 505–32.

and expect to be provided for by him, and she is still viewed as "marriageable" by her community. Her personal reputation is intact, and her father's "name" is not defamed in any way if he takes her in; but her husband is expected to be able to provide for himself, while bearing the shame for his own behavior. On the other hand, if the woman is guilty of misconduct, her shame would be viewed as a reflection on her male protector. Her father would not take her back because of the shame of having a misbehaving daughter and the bleak prospects of finding another husband for her, in addition to the financial burden she would bring upon him. She has nowhere to go. Moreover, the husband's damaged honor is restored in the eyes of the community by the punishment of the one who has dishonored him. This is of financial significance to him, because his own ability to provide for himself depends largely on the willingness of others to do business with him. They would be reluctant to do business with one who has a tarnished personal reputation. So, a primary concern in these laws is how the males involved are affected financially and in terms of their own reputation and honor.[25] The females are certainly more vulnerable, but the laws address that inherent vulnerability by noting certain responsibilities which the males must fulfill. Failure to do so would be dishonorable.

The Old Babylonian laws dealing with cases of rape, adultery, and the accusation of adultery are clarified by a recognition of these concepts. As in the Sumerian laws, rape is treated according to the status of the woman. The rape of a betrothed woman is punishable by death (LE ¶26; LH ¶130), while compensation for the rape of a slave woman is monetary (LE ¶31). The payment in the latter case almost certainly goes to the master of the slave, because he is considered to be the one ultimately wronged here. Adultery is punishable by death, although lesser punishments seem to have been allowed. LE ¶28 mentions only the execution of the unfaithful wife, but the law's silence regarding the paramour

---

[25] Another example of this sort of "double standard" is the fact that a wife could be publicly humiliated for declaring her desire for a divorce, while there are no references to the punishment of a husband for the same offense. See Greengus, "Textbook Case," pp. 43–44; J. Huehnergard, "Biblical Notes on Some New Akkadian Texts from Emar (Syria)," *CBQ* 47 (1985) 428–34; Locher, *Die Ehre einer Frau*, pp. 270–314; Westbrook, "Adultery," pp. 559–60.

does not necessarily mean he goes unpunished. The context suggests that the law is concerned only with specifying that a betrothed woman—whose parents have finalized the marriage with the groom financially—is to be viewed by the law as the groom's wife, even prior to the sexual consummation of the marriage. Whatever laws applied in cases of adultery applied here as well. LH ¶129 calls for the death of both the man and the woman, but allows for the wronged husband to assess a lighter sentence.[26] This is the typical ancient Near Eastern response. It is not, however, an indication of the partial retention of patriarchal authority. For that to be the case, one would have to say that the husband enjoyed authority over his wife *and* her paramour. Such is not the case. Rather, the main section of the law shows that the husband retains the right (not the authority) to avenge his honor in the face of a personal affront.[27] The exception clause then protects the honor of the male paramour. There is the danger that the husband will spare his wife but avenge himself on her paramour; but that would suggest that the man alone is to blame. Westbrook has shown that such a scenario could have been used to entrap one's social enemy.[28] This law prevents that by requiring that the (accused) lovers receive equal punishment.

Two other laws deal explicitly with accusations of sexual misconduct (LH ¶¶131–132; cp. ¶127). In the first, the husband brings the charges against his wife; in the second, another man brings the charges. No physical evidence is produced; rather, the wife must appeal to a deity to prove her innocence. This involves submission to the "River Ordeal" in the second case. This is done, however, not to clear the woman's name, but "for her husband." It is his reputation which is of greatest concern; it is his name which must be cleared (cp. MAL ¶¶17–18).[29]

---

[26] In LH ¶¶129–132, the sequence proceeds from mutual blame to blaming the male only to blaming the female only.
[27] Westbrook ("Adultery," pp. 557, 564–65) says that this offense transcends a violation of one's honor.
[28] Westbrook, "Adultery," pp. 554–55. One weakness in Westbrook's suggestion here is that an accusation of rape would better serve such a plot. I would not say, then, that the threat of entrapment is the only impetus for this law, but it is a plausible concern.
[29] Locher, *Die Ehre einer Frau*, pp. 339–72.

Hittite laws on marriage and related matters are similar to the Old Babylonian laws. Several deal with the financial aspects of the early dissolution of a marriage (HL ¶¶27–30), in terms comparable to those in LE and LH. Distinctions are made in cases of marriage between a free person and a slave (HL ¶31). There are also analogous prescriptions regarding rape and adultery (HL ¶¶197–198). One new "wrinkle" relates the location of a sexual offense to culpability. An incident in the countryside is blamed entirely on the man, while an incident in the woman's house is blamed on her (cp. Deut 22:23–27). As before, a husband has the right to kill both lovers, if he catches them in flagrante delicto, or he can leave that decision up to the king.[30]

The Middle Assyrian laws treat questions regarding marriage and violations of it more extensively than any other ancient Near Eastern law code. Several laws concern financial matters in terms similar to those discussed previously, thereby suggesting similar assumptions about the contractual nature of marriage.[31] We can lay those aside, then, and focus on the laws dealing with sexual misconduct.

There are eleven paragraphs (MAL A¶¶9, 12–18, 22–24) dealing with eighteen possible situations of sexual assault, rape, adultery, seduction, accusation of promiscuity, and complicity in infidelity (six paragraphs consist of a primary situation and one or two possible variations). In ten of the eighteen situations (¶¶14a, 14b, 15b, 16a, 22a, 22b, 23a, 23b, 24a, 24c), the husband of the woman involved ultimately decides the fate of his wife; and in five of the cases (¶¶14a, 15b, 16b, 22b, 23a), the fate of the paramour matches that imposed by the husband on his wife. There are several references to an ambiguous group ("they") which prosecutes and/or punishes the guilty party, sometimes in cooperation with the husband (¶¶9, 12, 13, 14a, 15, 16b, 18, 22b,

---

[30] Good, "Capital Punishment," pp. 956–58; Westbrook, "Adultery," pp. 551–56, 571.

[31] Several laws in sequence consider what is to be done with properties following a death (MAL A¶¶25–35; cp. LE ¶¶17–18, 25, 59; LH ¶¶137–140, 148–149, 159–162), in the case of an extended absence (MAL A¶¶36, 45; cp. LH ¶¶133–135), or in a divorce settlement (MAL A¶¶37–38).

23, 24a).[32] Similarly, there are two paragraphs (MAL A¶¶55–56) dealing with three situations involving sex between a man and an unmarried girl. The first paragraph deals with rape, with the slightly different outcomes (¶55a,b) dependent on the marital status of the male perpetrator.[33] The second paragraph (¶56) deals with a case of mutual consent between the girl and the man. In both laws, the father ultimately determines the punishment for his daughter, while the punishment against the man is predetermined.[34]

There are two issues which are crucial to one's interpretation of these laws which also influence one's interpretation of the laws in Deuteronomy: (1) the identification of "they" in several of these laws; and (2) the significance of having the husband/father determine the punishment in many cases.

It is easy to assume that "they" refers to the community-at-large or a city tribunal of some sort. This assumption underlies a recent diachronic interpretation of some of these laws (¶¶12–16) by E. Otto. He reconstructs from this group of laws a redaction of "public laws" into a collection of older "private laws." The offended husband metes out justice in the older collection, but that authority is passed over to the municipal judicial authorities ("they") in the later redaction.[35] But this assumption is made too

---

[32] MAL A¶17 does not mention anyone executing the sentence, but simply says that the plaintiffs will make an agreement and "undergo the divine River Ordeal."

[33] The father automatically gives his daughter "into the protection of the household of the fornicator," if the man is married. If he is not married, then the father can decide whether to make the man marry his daughter or give her to someone else. In either case, the father receives monetary "compensation." Based on the typically financial nature of these marriages, it is logical to assume that the major consideration in the father's decision about whether the girl will marry the perpetrator is the financial well-being of the man.

[34] On a related subject, there is at least one paragraph (¶59; also ¶¶57–58?) delimiting what corporal punishments a man could inflict on his wife. For discussion of several of these laws, see Locher, *Die Ehre einer Frau*, pp. 128–55, 353–72.

[35] E. Otto, "Die Einschränkung des Privatstrafrechts durch öffentliches Strafrecht in der Redaktion der Paragraphen 1–24, 50–59 des Mittelassyrischen Kodex der Tafel A (KAV 1)," *Biblische Welten. Festschrift für Martin Metzger zu seinem 65. Geburtstag*, pp. 131–66; ed. W. Zwickel (OBO 123; Göttingen: Vandenhoeck and Ruprecht, 1993); idem, "Das

hastily. It is just as logical to assume that "they" could refer to the
offended husband's/father's house. The use of "they" in ¶56
provides the best evidence for this possibility. In the preceding
law, part of the punishment on a man who has raped an
unbetrothed virgin is that his wife will be taken in by the girl's
father and he will "hand her over to be raped." It is most likely
that the ones allowed to rape the wife would be members of the
girl's house, not the entire community. The subsequent law
(¶56)—where the sexual relations were consensual and not
forced—stipulates that "they shall have no claim to his wife."
"They" are almost certainly the males of the girl's house, not all
the males of the city. The same assumption about "they" in ¶15
makes the most sense there. If an adulterous couple are caught *in*
flagrante delicto, "they shall kill both of them; there is no liability
for him (i.e., the husband)." There should be no reason to hold the
husband liable for the deaths of the couple, if "they" are a
community body that has executed the sentence; but if the
husband and his family have killed the couple, then the
community could easily hold the husband liable (cp. LH ¶129).
The same assumption makes the most sense in the preceding
clause, "they shall prove the charges against him and find him
guilty." It is most likely that "they" are the husband and his
family, who apparently are justifying to a city tribunal their
punishment of the paramour. This interpretation makes the best
sense of the other laws on sexual misconduct as well.[36] In this

---

Eherecht im Mittelassyrischen Kodex und im Deuteronomium. Tradition und
Redaktion in den §§12–16 der Tafel A des Mittelassyrischen Kodex und in
Dtn 22, 22–29," in *Festschrift for K. Bergerhof*, pp. 259–81 (ed. M. Dietrich
and O. Loretz; AOAT 232; Kevelaer: Butzon & Bercker; Neukirchen-Vluyn:
Neukirchener Verlag, 1993); idem, "Aspects of Legal," pp. 160–96 (esp. pp.
163–68).

[36] See also ¶14, where the husband "shall prove the charges against his
wife." Likewise, ¶25 stipulates that a widow's brothers-in-law are allowed to
reclaim their family's property from the widow. In this process, "they" (i.e.,
the brothers-in-law) provide proof of ownership and take their rightful
possessions.

This proposal is not to imply that "they" means "family members" in
every law of the code. The use of "they" or the passive voice probably assumes
that the readers of the law know the traditional means of adjudication, and
the laws would simply be perpetuating those traditions.

light, Otto's delineation between adjudication by the husband and adjudication by the community disappears.[37] The resolution of that issue helps to clarify the issue of the husband's/father's role as the one who determines the fate of the couple. As J. J. Finkelstein and others have noted, adultery in ancient Mesopotamia was "at bottom a civil invasion of a husband's domain, and it was left to him to take as serious or as lenient a view of the matter as he chose..."[38] The same principle can be extended beyond adultery to other sexual crimes. The husband (or father) has been injured personally—his honor has been impugned—and he has the right to seek retribution for his injuries. The main question to be answered in each case is, Who has injured him: the other man, the "injured" man's wife or daughter, or both? Related to that is the belief that, among a man's responsibilities, a primary one is the "protection" of the sexuality of the women in his house.[39] If the community perceives that the husband/father has not responsibly fulfilled his duty to "protect" his wife's/daughter's sexuality, then his reputation as an honorable man is in jeopardy. These laws show how the community allows him (apparently with the help of his family) the opportunity to "redeem" himself by being the one to punish the

---

[37] Moreover, it seems that Otto's demarcation between these laws and the ones that follow is somewhat arbitrary. Following the law concerning a woman's seduction of one man, there are two laws concerning a promiscuous woman (the seduction of several men; ¶¶17–18) and two laws concerning a promiscuous man (¶¶19–20). Then, following a law about injury to a fetus—which is another type of injury inflicted by a man on another man through the second man's wife—there are laws about possible sexual misconduct when a married man and a married woman travel together (¶22), about a woman bringing a married woman into her house for the purpose of prostitution (¶23), and about a married woman who is "seized" after moving into another house (¶24).

[38] Finkelstein, "Sex Offenses," p. 372. Cp. Good, "Capital Punishment," p. 976; M. Roth, "'She Will Die by the Iron Dagger': Adultery and Neo-Babylonian Marriage," *JESHO* 31 (1988) 186 n. 1; Pressler, *View of Women*, pp. 25–29, 41–43.

[39] See above, on common sentiments regarding female sexuality in contemporary Middle Eastern societies. The fact that a retaliatory death is allowed in these Mesopotamian laws indicates that the same was probably true in antiquity.

wrongdoer, whether that be the other man or the wife/daughter or both.[40]

In brief, it is most likely that the Middle Assyrian laws intend to perpetuate the right of a man, with the help of family members, to avenge himself upon anyone under his care who defames his honor through illicit sexual activity. As in earlier law codes, this is the exercise of a right, not authority. The primary concern of the judicial establishment is that the revenge be justified. Unjustified retaliation could jeopardize the stability of the community, as in cases of homicide. Conversely, a failure to punish the wrongdoer(s) could jeopardize the moral and religious fabric of the community.

The primary laws (MAL A¶¶12–18, 22–24) proceed according to two general criteria: locality and culpability. MAL A¶12 concerns a rape "along the main thoroughfare." The woman resists, and the man is solely to blame. The next three laws (¶¶13–15) consider situations of "mutual culpability," the first (¶13) occurring at the paramour's house, the second (¶14) at a "neutral site" ("in an inn or in the main thoroughfare"), and the third (¶15) (apparently) in the woman's house. Within these general parameters, variant situations are considered: whether the man knows that the woman he meets at "an inn" is married (¶14b),[41] and allowing a case to be adjudicated locally or before magistrates (¶15b). MAL A¶16 involves seduction by the woman at an unspecified location, but most likely at her own house.[42] The variant considers what to do if the supposed seductee turns out to be the aggressor (¶16b). Attention is focused on the possible laxity of the husband in MAL

---

[40] The same principle of interpretation can be applied to a couple of other laws where the male head of the family determines the fate of a perpetrator (MAL A¶¶3, 10). As for women preserving their reputations, one might consider the case of an Assyrian woman of the court who is responsible for the punishment of any servant-girl under her (MAPD ¶18). In this case, the reputation of the slave's mistress is at stake.

[41] It is unclear whether the exception of ¶14b (the man's knowledge of the woman's marital status) applies only to ¶14a, or to ¶13 as well. The fact that no such exception clause is given in ¶15 further supports the conclusion that the liaison was discovered by the husband in his own house.

[42] The location of ¶15 in the woman's house is based primarily on the fact that her husband catches them. The same conclusion for ¶16 is based on the apparent punishment of the wife, even though the man forces himself upon her. This suggests some culpability on her part. The most logical explanation for such culpability is that she allowed the man access to her house.

A¶¶17–18, and then on other men and women who might facilitate sexual liaisons in MAL A¶¶22–24. These considerations, read in conjunction with the notion that concerns for the honor of the husband/father are preeminent, help us to understand the actions that are prescribed. In MAL A¶12, the other man is entirely at fault because (a) he confronts the woman at a place where she should be safe and (b) there are witnesses to the fact that he forced himself upon the woman. The killing of the man avenges the affront to the husband of the one raped. MAL A¶¶13–14 situate the woman and her lover away from her house (away from the protection of her husband), but there is no mention of the man using force.[43] If this were understood primarily as a moral affront against the community, then the law would end here. But there is the further possibility that the paramour was unaware of the woman's marital status, removing any culpability from him. The act is the same, but the response has changed. Now the woman alone is culpable, and the husband determines her punishment. Why? Because, in either scenario, it is ultimately an offense against him, first and foremost. Her actions are interpreted as a sign that, at the least, her husband is ineffective at controlling those under his care. His wife is flaunting her freedom from his control. This is an affront to his masculine honor, and so he punishes her to restore that honor.[44]

The next law (¶15) places additional shame on the man, if we are correct in assuming that the couple are caught in the woman's house.[45] Not only is the man not able to control his wife, but he is

---

[43] There is good evidence to suggest that the places mentioned in ¶14 are "the typical haunts of a prostitute." See Westbrook, "Adultery," p. 550.

[44] Nothing is said of what would happen if the husband did nothing to punish his wife and/or her paramour. Probably nothing would be done, unless the wife's behavior became "common." That would be an offense against the honor of the city, and a "rumor campaign" against the woman would probably result. This potentiality lies behind ¶¶17–18.

[45] Unfortunately, the circumstances under which a wife is caught in adultery are not delineated in LH ¶129, making it impossible to draw detailed comparisons. The claim that the adultery of MAL A¶15 takes place in the woman's house might seem illogical at first, because the husband still must "prove the charges" against the couple. However, some of the evidence from the ancient world suggests that it could have been difficult at times for a

also someone who is unable to prevent the use of his house for illicit sexual activity. The option of bringing the case before the king or his judges only applies when the husband tries to retaliate against the man alone. As in other law codes, the intent is to prevent a husband from laying blame solely on another house, thus incurring more community stigma on them than is merited. There must be some acknowledgment of the wife's role, a fact which brings some shame on her husband and his house. To save his own honor, the husband must retaliate; and he does so by punishing his wife. The same concern underlies MAL A¶16, as the wife must bear at least as much blame as the other man.

The response of the broader community is not explicitly mentioned until MAL A¶17. This law and the one that follows demonstrate the nature of community response. Here, a woman is accused of being promiscuous. Not only is she guilty of sexual misconduct, but the repetition of the act suggests that her husband is "derelict in his duty" to preserve her sexuality. In some sense, he would also be to blame. It is at this point that the community's collective honor would be impugned. One of its male citizens is permissive in regards to his wife's sexual activity. The response is not, however, the seizing and execution of the woman. Rather, a gossip-campaign begins, to which the husband—not the wife—must respond, because he is the one held ultimately responsible.

Additional examples of the principle of male responsibility are provided by MAL A¶¶22–24. In MAL A¶22, a man is fined simply for placing a married woman in a vulnerable situation (i.e., on a journey, away from her protecting male relatives). The owner of the house is not mentioned in MAL A¶23, when the wife goes to another house as a guest of the woman of the house. This silence might be meaningless, but a comparison with MAL A¶24 suggests that the husband is unaware of the other woman's presence in his house, a condition which would explain why his wife is punished but he is not. In MAL A¶24, a penalty is assessed against a man who brings a married woman to live in his house, making a distinction in guilt based on whether he was aware that she was

husband to prove such charges. See Roth, "'She Will Die,'" pp. 192–97; cp. Schapera, "Law and Justice," p. 206; Winans, *Shambala*, p. 108.

married or not. However, the penalty is much higher if he was aware.

The nature of the information on marriage and sexual misconduct from Neo-Babylonian society is of a slightly different sort. The extant materials from the law codes concern only the financial aspects of a marriage, and they reveal no significant differences from earlier codes (LNB ¶¶8–15). There are, however, ten marriage contracts from this society which contain an "adultery clause." These call for the death of the wife, if she is caught in adultery. No reference is made to who would actually kill her, and it is unclear whether such a killing would come after judicial deliberations or could be an immediate response on the part of the husband, though the evidence seems to give greater support for the latter. Nothing is said about the possibility of lesser punishments, nor is there any reference to possible actions against the wife's lover.[46] The most that can be said, then, is that the Neo-Babylonian evidence shows that adultery was thought of as an offense against a husband, an offense punishable by death.

Summary

Ancient Near Eastern laws and legal documents assume common ideas regarding the ultimate responsibility of males toward their economic dependents and the associated honor accorded to those who fulfill that responsibility. An important aspect of that responsibility is the control ("protection") of female sexuality. Therefore, the laws afford those males the right to retaliate personally against anyone who impugns their personal honor through sexual misconduct. It cannot be denied that certain laws effectively restrict the powers of those males (e.g., requiring equal punishments in cases of mutual culpability), but they do not do so at the expense of their personal reputations. In fact, what these laws do is provide ways for individuals (usually men) to "save face" in potentially shameful situations. The severity of the response to sexual misconduct is left up to the one most directly

---

[46] Roth, "'She Will Die,'" pp. 186–206.

offended, but all of the societies considered accept the killing of the offender(s) as a justifiable option.

REDACTION-CRITICAL MATTERS

There is little evidence of Deuteronom(ist)ic redaction in Deut 22:13–21. The introductory clause (v 13a) has parallels in 24:1, 5, but this is due to the common circumstance of marriage. A similar explanation (the circumstance of execution) most easily accounts for the parallels between 22:21a and other references in the D Code to "stoning" (13:11a; 17:5; 21:21a; 22:24).[47] Some scholars have argued that the entire corollary case (vv 20–21) was penned by the Deuteronomic lawgiver.[48] This is based on thematic grounds, rather than linguistic or stylistic ones; so, I will hold off discussion of that issue until we consider the intent of the law. The only clause which clearly derives from a Deuteronom(ist)ic hand is the purge-formula in v 21b (cp. 13:6; 17:7, 12; 19:13, 19; 22:22, 24; 24:6).[49]

---

[47] A case can be made for placing 21:21a and 22:21a in a common pre-Deuteronomic source (see n. 1, above), a source which could have influenced the wording in 13:11 and 17:5. For a fuller discussion of redaction-critical matters, see Locher, *Die Ehre einer Frau*, pp. 33–116.

Several commentators cite the mention of "elders" as adjudicators as evidence of a pre-Deuteronomic layer. See Hölscher, "Komposition," p. 216; Phillips, *Deuteronomy*, p. 143; idem, "Another Look at Adultery," p. 8; Mayes, *Deuteronomy*, p. 310; Preuss, *Deuteronomium*, p. 136; Benjamin, *Deuteronomy and City Life*, p. 233.

[48] Phillips, *Deuteronomy*, p. 148; idem, "Another Look at Adultery," p. 10; Rofé, "Family and Sex Laws," pp. 135–43. For those retaining vv 20–21a as pre-Deuteronomic, see Mayes, *Deuteronomy*, p. 309; Preuss, *Deuteronomium*, pp. 56–57; cp. Locher, *Die Ehre einer Frau*, pp. 60–64, 107–16; Gertz, *Die Gerichtsorganisation*, pp. 210–14.

[49] But see R. Sonsino, *Motive Clauses in Hebrew Law: Biblical Forms and Near Eastern Parallels* (SBLDS 45; Chico, CA: Scholars Press, 1980), p. 115; Locher, *Die Ehre einer Frau*, pp. 60–64.

OTHER BIBLICAL REFERENCES TO SEXUAL MISCONDUCT

There are passages throughout the Hebrew Bible regarding sexual misconduct. These can be divided into three groups: evidence from other legal materials, evidence from narrative sources, and evidence from prophetic and wisdom writings. Each group has had its own type of influence on scholarly interpretations of this law. The unusual circumstances assumed in this law, together with a general consistency in the prescribed punishment of sexual misconduct, make it rather difficult to evaluate the role played by this law in the overall development of biblical teachings on the subject of adultery.

Evidence from Legal Materials

The law in Deut 22:13–21 addresses a highly unlikely situation, and it is probably for that reason that there are no direct parallels to it in the biblical (or ancient Near Eastern) law codes. Still, there are enough similarities to other laws on sexual misconduct in the biblical law codes to recognize that this law is consistent with the others in its assumptions and prescriptions.

Other Law Codes

The foundational notion for this law is, of course, the general prohibition against adultery in the Decalogue (Exod 20:14; Deut 5:18). This suggests that any case of adultery is understood to have a sacral aspect to it, and other laws specifically reflect that notion (see Lev 18:6; Num 5:11–31, esp. v 21). We can deduce from several biblical references that adultery is understood as sexual relations between a man and a married woman; therefore, it is also understood as an offense against the woman's husband.[50]

---

[50] Many have argued that some of laws (including Deut 22:13–21) reflect a shift in the conception of an offense from the realm of "private law" to that of "public law," from "civil law" to "criminal law," or from "family law" to "sacral law." I am not convinced that making such absolute differentiations is always possible, much less helpful. This question points to the more basic issue of the use of Western legal categories to describe non-Western legal phenomena. For some discussion of this issue, see M. Buss, "The Distinction between Civil and Criminal Law in Ancient Israel," *Proceedings of the Sixth World Congress*

(Similarly, sexual misconduct involving an unmarried woman would be understood as an offense against the woman's father, brother, or other male guardian.) Deut 22:13–21 is one of several laws which clarify that the sexual rights of an Israelite man over his wife begin with their betrothal. This is typical, as evidenced by the number of ancient Near Eastern laws which specify that marital rights and obligations are enforced during the time between the giving of the initial marriage gifts and the wedding of the couple (see above; cp. Lev 19:20–22; Deut 22:23–27). Thus, the groom's accusation against his bride in Deut 22:13–21 is an accusation of adultery.

Laws in the biblical codes expand on and supplement the basic adultery law in various ways. Several clarify or prescribe punishments for adultery (Lev 18:20; 20:10; cp. Deut 27:20); some deal with related situations, such as rape (Exod 22:15–16), homosexuality (Lev 18:22; 20:13), bestiality (Lev 18:23; 20:15–16; cp. Deut 27:21), incest (Lev 20:11–12, 14, 20–21; cp. Deut 27:22–23), or suspicion of adultery (Num 5:11–31).[51] There is an entire series of regulations regarding "uncovering the nakedness" of various kin (Lev 18:6–19; 20:11, 17–21).

The biblical laws are fairly consistent regarding the punishment for sexual offenses. The usual punishment in cases involving a married woman is death, which is prescribed in cases of rape (on the man), bestiality, and adultery (on both parties). No alternative punishments are mentioned, nor is there any reference to who would carry out the sentence (such as the woman's husband, as mentioned in cuneiform law). Adultery involving a slave woman is punishable by a sacred fine, paid in the form of a sacrifice (Lev 19:20–22). Adultery which cannot be proved with physical evidence (or, apparently, the testimony of witnesses) is punished by God himself (Num 5:11–31). The penalty for "uncovering the nakedness" is outcasting (Lev 18:24–30; 20:18).[52]

---

on *Jewish Studies*, 1973, Vol. I (Jerusalem: Jerusalem Academic Press, 1977), pp. 51–62; Gluckman, "Concepts," pp. 349–73; Gulliver, "Case Studies," pp. 11–23; and Radcliffe-Brown, "Primitive Law," pp. 212–19.

[51] On this final passage, see T. Frymer-Kensky, "The Strange Case of the Suspected Sotah (Numbers v 11–31)," *VT* 34 (1984) 11–26.

[52] This punishment is conceived of on two levels. It is most likely that the primary sense is that the guilty parties would be banished from their families ("cut off from among their people"—Lev 18:29). The derived sense applies this

Sexual relations between a man and an unbetrothed virgin—whether forced or consensual—were to result in their marriage and/or the payment of the brideprice to the virgin's father (Exod 22:16–17; see below on Deut 22:28–29). This final case points to the fact that marriages in Israel, as elsewhere, were conceived of as business arrangements between the groom and the bride's father.

The consistency in the treatment of similar sexual offenses in all of the biblical law codes precludes most speculation about how Deut 22:13–21 might fit on a continuum of the development of Israelite sex laws. The law which is closest to this one is the Sotah law of Num 5:11–31. It also concerns a man accusing his wife of infidelity; but the woman's punishment (if she is guilty) is not execution, but physical malady, barrenness, and shame. This difference does not necessarily indicate a temporal change or conceptual shift (to "sacral law"), though. In the Sotah law, the man makes an accusation for which he cannot be expected to produce any physical evidence; he is simply suspicious. Yahweh alone can determine the woman's guilt; so, he alone proves her guilt (through the prescribed rituals), and he alone punishes her. On the other hand, the verdict in Deut 22:13–21 depends on the ability of the accused's parents to produce evidence. A difference in the nature of the evidence—not a difference in the social milieu—accounts for the difference between the punishments in the two cases.

The Deuteronomic Code

Deut 22:13–21 is the first in a series of four laws dealing with adultery (22:13–19+20–21; 22:22) and rape (22:23–24+25–27; 22:28–29).[53] Since the law of vv 13–21 is without parallel in the

---

sentence nationally, warning that the land might "vomit you out," if these types of activities are allowed in the nation (Lev 18:24–28).

[53] Some would treat these as six separate laws (see Pressler, *View of Women*, p. 21). I prefer to speak of items introduced with *we'im* (here, 22:20–21 and 22:25–27) as subordinated variants rather than separate laws. Even though they perhaps existed at one time as independent laws, they are now often truncated and dependent on the main law preceding them for much of their content and context. For another view, see Rofé, "Family and Sex Laws," pp. 135–43. But also see Wenham and McConville, "Drafting Techniques," pp. 248–52.

extant cuneiform law codes,[54] and since it in particular among these has attracted attention as an example of the restriction of paternal authority, it deserves to be treated apart from the others. Still, we cannot ignore those other laws when interpreting this one, because they deal with a common subject. These laws must be interpreted together in comparison with other law codes, as Westbrook has argued.[55] So, I will briefly discuss those other laws as part of the immediate backdrop to the law in 22:13–21.

The law concerning adultery in Deut 22:22 is obviously much briefer than its Mesopotamian counterparts. The former speaks only generally about adultery and mentions but one punishment, while there are six paragraphs in the Assyrian laws (MAL A¶¶13–16, 22–23) and four in Hammurabi's laws (LH ¶¶129–132) on various possible scenarios in which adultery might occur (see above). There is some variation in possible punishments in each scenario (cp. LU ¶¶6–8).

What are we to make of this difference between Deut 22:22 and other laws on adultery? The brevity of the biblical law might suggest that the lawgiver here wishes to collapse all possible manifestations of adultery into one basic infraction, that adultery under any circumstances is a sacral offense, demanding the most severe punishment—execution. On the other hand, this is not the only law concerning adultery in the D Code. The laws on either side also deal with cases of adultery. If 22:22 is intended to deal with all cases of adultery, the others would be redundant or contradictory to it. A closer examination shows that this is not the case. The protasis of the law in v 22 states that the couple has been found *in flagrante delicto*.[56] The preceding law (22:20–21) assumes the post facto discovery of the adultery (the groom finds signs on the wedding night of his bride's prior sexual activity), while the succeeding law (22:23–27) does not speak of how the offense is discovered. In this light, the seemingly broad law in Deut 22:22 emerges as a rather narrow law with limited direct applicability.

---

[54] There is a parallel from Qumran. See Rofé, "Family and Sex Laws," pp. 157–58, and the references there.

[55] See the preceding chapter, and Westbrook, "Adultery," p. 548.

[56] On cases of discovery *in flagrante delicto*, see Roth, "'She Will Die,'" pp. 192–97.

There are two other considerations to be raised at this point. First, there is a striking parallel between Deut 22:22 and specific cuneiform laws (LH ¶129; MAL A¶15a). In LH ¶129, the identity of those who discover the couple is not given, as is the case in Deut 22:22; but in MAL A¶15a, the woman's husband discovers the couple. In the Mesopotamian cases (LH ¶129; MAL A¶15a), it is first stated that both the paramour and the wife are to be killed. Then, another possible outcome is given—namely, that the husband can opt for a lesser punishment against his wife, with the crown insuring that the sentence upon her paramour be proportionate. Second, in both of those cuneiform codes, other outcomes are prescribed when the couple is not discovered "in the act" (LH ¶¶131–132; MAL A¶¶17–18, 22). The laws in Deut 22:20–21 and 22:23–27 suggest that the offenses mentioned there become known some time after they have been committed. Again, the logical conclusion is that the law in Deut 22:22 prescribes execution as the appropriate (or preferred?) response in cases of discovery *in flagrante delicto*; but this does not exclude a different outcome, if the offense comes to light in a different way. Such differences are, again, suggested by comparisons with cuneiform law codes and non-legal materials in the Bible.[57]

It is likely that Deut 22:22 (and other laws concerning sexual misconduct) intends to establish what punitive response is preferable ("they should die"), but not necessarily what is obligatory ("they must die").[58] The former possibility is supported also by the parallels in cuneiform laws and by references to adultery in non-legal writings of the Hebrew Bible (see below).[59] Others have read the prescription as obligatory, thereby severely limiting the husband's authority.[60] The preceding chapter's discussion of punishment given in the case of the rebellious son could apply here as well. It seems that a central concern of that law is to instill the law's recipients with the idea that the well-

---

[57] Cp. McKeating, "Sanctions," pp. 57–59, 65–68; Westbrook, "Adultery," pp. 542–79; R. Knierim, "The Problem of Ancient Israel's Prescriptive Legal Traditions," *Semeia* 45 (1989) 7–23.

[58] See Buss, "Distinction," pp. 55–56; cp. Westbrook, "Adultery," p. 544.

[59] See Westbrook ("Adultery," pp. 545–46) for references. Also Buss, "Distinction," p. 56; McKeating, "Sanctions," pp. 59–63, 67–70.

[60] See Phillips, "Another Look at Adultery," pp. 3–4, 17; Frymer-Kensky, "Law and Philosophy," p. 94.

being and integrity of the community supersede the interests of the individual and his immediate family. Perhaps the same principle is assumed here. Perhaps these laws are saying to the people of Israel that, although there are historical and cultural precedents which allow a variety of responses, the best response—for the sake of the family and the broader community—is the execution of the offending wife and her lover. In fact, it is possible that this law intends to allow the offended husband the right to kill the couple. It does not specify who should carry out the judgment. The law could be read to suggest that anyone who executes judgment here—even the husband—would be doing something that is for the good of the community.

How one resolves this question lies at the heart of the issue of the relationship between the D Code and the development of patriarchal authority in ancient Israel. The assumption that this law intends to make execution obligatory in every case of adultery—in contrast to the options mentioned in cuneiform law—leads inevitably to the conclusion that this law seeks to supersede the authority of the Israelite male. This is admittedly an argument from silence, but the result is parallel to the laws on homicide, where cuneiform laws allow for the monetary compensation which biblical law forbids. On the other hand, Deut 22:22 could be understood to include an affirmation of a man's right to kill someone who has offended his name, even without interpreting it as a legal obligation.

The same uncertainties which arise from v 22 carry over into the dual law in vv 23–27. Again, there are parallels in the cuneiform laws (LU ¶¶6–8; LE ¶26; LH ¶130; HL ¶¶197–198; MAL A¶55–56), which often make distinctions based on whether both parties are culpable, or only one.[61] Again, the biblical cases mention fewer options than are mentioned in those other sources. And again, we are left to argue from silence about what these prescriptions infer about the authority of an Israelite father or husband, with the same questions left unanswered.

There are a couple of major differences between these biblical laws (Deut 22:22–27) and the cuneiform laws. One is that the

---

[61] For some discussion of these cuneiform laws, see Finkelstein, "Sex Offenses," pp. 356–57.

former make no mention of other possible responses, while the cuneiform laws do give such options; but this leaves us only with ambiguity based on silence. The other is that the biblical laws stipulate that the offending parties be executed at the city gate (Deut 22:24). This might seem to exclude or minimize the role the father or groom play in the process, indicating an intent to limit their authority; but not necessarily.

I would suggest that we consider this case in the same way that we considered Deut 21:18–21. Would an offended male be a lawbreaker if he took vengeance on the couple himself, without bringing them out to the gate for execution? If one intent of the law is to restrict their authority, then one would have to conclude that they would have to be charged with some crime, if they take vengeance themselves. This appears unlikely. Instead, it seems that the intent of the law is to say that sexual misconduct is an offense against one's community, an offense deserving of death. If this is the primary intent, then execution by the offended male—even though not carried out in the city gate—would be viewed as an appropriate and sufficient response.[62] The other possibility is that the offended male would not seek vengeance against the offender. The logical explanation for reticence on the part of the offended would be fear, due to his weakness vis-à-vis the perpetrator and his family. Thus, the law could be a deterrent against those who might feel that they could commit this crime without fear of retaliation. The ultimate intent, though, is the same: By killing the offender, community harmony and stability is maintained.

At first glance, the final law in this series (22:28–29) seems to be less ambiguous about its intent to limit patriarchal authority, but closer examination frustrates us again on this point. In this final case (the rape of the unbetrothed maiden), there are not only parallels in the cuneiform laws (LE ¶31; MAL A¶55; and a case

---

[62] The only risk involved in such a scenario is that the (now) dead man's family might dispute the legitimacy of the charge of rape which prompted the killing. The law might intend to prevent such a development; but if it does so intend, then the concern is for the harmony and stability of the local community. And that could be achieved by the city elders whether the offended male himself took vengeance or the "men of the city" executed judgment.

from Nippur),[63] but also a parallel law in the Covenant Code (Exod 22:15–16). The cuneiform laws and the Covenant Code leave a father/owner with the option of deciding whether his daughter/slave-girl will marry her attacker or be saved for some other man, while the law in the D Code states only that the man will marry the girl. Many have argued that this difference indicates that the D law is stripping the father of any real say in the matter, effectively negating his authority.[64] Westbrook's cautionary remarks should be considered here again, though. The position just mentioned rests on the assumption that the D Code intends to be exhaustive, that it is to be read without any consideration of other laws. It could be, however, that we are expected to read this law in the light of Exod 22:15–16. Perhaps this law of the D Code only intends to clarify two points in the prior law of the C Code. In that law, the amount of the fine imposed on the rapist is not absolutely fixed ("he shall give the marriage present for her"); the D law clarifies what that amount will be. Similarly, the final clause denies the man the right ever to divorce his "newly-acquired" bride. The reason for this is almost certainly economic, as we have argued earlier in treating the parallel Assyrian case (see n. 11, above, on MAL A¶55).[65] Thus, it would appear that this is not necessarily an example of a law being sacralized;[66] it could reflect a desire to specify a couple of purely economic aspects of a case in the context of its broader legal tradition. If the father gives his daughter to the man, the man can never give her up. But the father's option to give his daughter to

---

[63] This is 3N–T403+T340, discussed in Finkelstein, "Sex Offenses," p. 359; cp. Locher, *Die Ehre einer Frau*, pp. 93–106.

[64] E.g., Frymer-Kensky, "Law and Philosophy," pp. 93–94; N. Steinberg, "The Deuteronomic Law Code and the Politics of State Centralization," in *The Bible and the Politics of Exegesis. Essays in Honor of Norman K. Gottwald on His Sixty-Fifth Birthday*, ed. David Jobling, P. L. Day, G. T. Sheppard (Cleveland: Pilgrim Press, 1991), p. 165.

[65] Cp. Pressler, *View of Women*, p. 41; Stulman, "Sex and Familial Crimes," p. 61; Carmichael, *Laws of Deuteronomy*, p. 169; Weinfeld, *Deuteronomy*, p. 285). The same stipulation (for the same concern) is given in Deut 22:19.

[66] According to Weinfeld, this law moves the case from the "civil-financial" realm into the "social-moral." M. Weinfeld, *Deuteronomy 1–11* (AB; New York: Doubleday, 1991), pp. 20–21; idem, *Deuteronomy and the Deuteronomic School*, p. 285.

another man—who would retain the right to divorce her later—might still stand, even though it is not explicitly mentioned here. If this is correct, conclusions regarding a shift in an Israelite father's authority are shown to be unwarranted.

Evidence from Narrative Sources

Deut 22:13–21 has been compared with the stories of Dinah (Genesis 34)[67] and Judah and Tamar (Genesis 38). There are two primary conclusions usually drawn from these comparisons. One is that sexual misconduct justifiably yields a punishment of death on any guilty party, although circumstances might allow for a lesser response. This is essentially consistent with the laws in Deut 22:13–29 and elsewhere in the Bible. The other conclusion is that the stories in Genesis reflect an early stage (probably pre-monarchic) in the evolution of Israelite judicial practices, a stage when males enjoyed absolute authority over the females in their families. Consequently, they were directly responsible for protecting the sexuality of their females, as well as avenging its violation.[68] In contrast to those examples, Deut 22:13–21 prescribes that a father and a mother are to bring a case concerning sexual misconduct in their family to the city elders for judgment. It is often claimed that the law intends to limit parents to this course of action in such a case, implicitly precluding the possibility that they could mete out their own justice against their daughter. Based on the differences between the stories and this

---

[67] The correlation here is primarily mentioned in the use of the term נבלה to describe a sexual offense (Gen 34:7; Deut 22:21). Driver, *Deuteronomy*, p. 256; von Rad, *Deuteronomy*, p. 142; A. Phillips, "NEBALAH—a Term for Serious Disorderly and Unruly Conduct," *VT* 25 (1975) 237–42; Mayes, *Deuteronomy*, p. 311; Buchholz, *Die Ältesten Israels*, pp. 66–67; Braulik, *Deuteronomium II*, pp. 165–67.

[68] The stories of Bathsheba (2 Samuel 11) and Amnon and Tamar (2 Samuel 13) might be mentioned as further evidence of the same "traditional values" in the early monarchy; however, the fact that these stories involve the royal family mitigates against their use as examples of what was "normative" for early Israel. The many unique circumstances of the story of Jephthah's daughter (Jdgs 11:29–40) also prevent one from making generalizations about Israelite society based on it.

law, researchers reconstruct a broad transformation in authority, moving from a center in the *paterfamilias* to a center in the state, the latter being mediated through the elders of the city. This transformation is explained as a natural development brought on by urbanization and the emergence of the monarchy.[69]

This evidence is not as easy to interpret as some have assumed; the reasons for the actions taken in the Genesis narratives are more complex than is often realized. It is overly simplistic to say that the men in those stories are exercising certain privileges accorded to their gender at the time. More careful consideration of their details reveals that there is far less difference between assumptions about authority in the Pentateuchal stories and in the laws in the D Code than is usually surmised.

For example, interpreters say that the story of Shechem and Dinah (Genesis 34) illustrates how a family (represented particularly by Levi and Simeon) would traditionally have been free to respond on its own when it felt its honor had been compromised. Dinah's sexuality has been violated, and her brothers move on their own to exact their revenge. One cannot overlook the fact, however, that there is no state authority—nor even a municipal authority—through whom they must go to voice their grievances and resolve the dispute brought on by the rape. No authority even questions their actions. Biblical law (Deut 22:28–29) and cuneiform law (MAL A¶¶55–56)—which reflect legal practices under a monarchic system—suggest that, in a state system, Dinah's family would expect Shechem to pay a special brideprice and then marry Dinah. As a matter of fact, Hamor attempts to make such an arrangement with Jacob (Gen 34:8–12), suggesting that the "state-mandated" response might have derived from pre-state custom.

This arrangement is nullified, however, when Jacob's sons avenge the defilement of their sister. This response should not be generalized into proof of the juridical independence of pre-monarchic Israelite families, though. Another important factor explains this response: the nature of the social relationship

---

[69] Salmon, "Judicial Authority," pp. 30–32; Wilson, "Israel's Judicial System," p. 233; Steinberg, "Deuteronomic Law Code," pp. 165–69; Stulman, "Sex and Familial Crimes," pp. 53, 57–59; Gertz, *Die Gerichtsorganisation*, p. 217.

between Jacob's family and the people of Shechem. At the time of
the rape, the two groups were not inter-marrying (Gen 34:13–17);
they were separate "peoples." Had they been inter-marrying, it is
logical to assume that the sons of Jacob would not have reacted as
they did. They would have felt more pressure as members of an
"endogamous" group to resolve the situation in a more peaceful
way. But Jacob's family and the people of Shechem viewed one
another as separate "nations" or "peoples," as "enemies" and
"foreigners." They did not think of themselves as a unified
community under a common judicial authority. There was no
higher authority to whom the two groups could turn to mediate a
resolution, and Jacob's sons apparently felt no need at this stage
in their relationship to do so. Therefore, they responded as any
"nation" would toward a "foreign" group that had violated its
sanctity, by "taking matters into their own hands."[70]

This, then, is not a story about interactions between two
Israelite families. For that reason, one cannot infer from it what
rights or authority pre-monarchic Israelite families would have
possessed in responding to the rape of one of its female members.
The nature of any response depended to some degree on the social
relationships between the families involved. If they considered
themselves to be part of a common social group, it is likely that
they would not have felt compelled to respond as Jacob's sons did,
and they would have opted for a peaceful response instead. To do
otherwise would have provoked a consequent response from the
broader group of which the two families were members.[71]

The story of Judah and Tamar (Genesis 38) seems to provide
stronger evidence of the judicial autonomy of a man over his
family in early Israel, because Judah orders the "unchaste" Tamar
to be burned when her illegitimate pregnancy is discovered (Gen

---

[70] Cp. Frymer-Kensky, "Law and Philosophy," p. 95; Moore, "Descent and
Legal Position," p. 395.

[71] One could look again to Judges 19–21. Why does the Levite not respond
on his own, or simply with his own family, to the rape and murder of his
concubine? I would suggest it is because the parties involved recognize their
common "membership" in the entity known as Israel. The incident is viewed
instead as a violation by one tribe (Benjamin) against members of two other
tribes (the Levite man and the Judahite concubine). The inter-tribal aspect to
the incident prompts a response from the entire nation.

38:24).[72] A few items again suggest caution against a quick interpretation of the story. First, Judah had sent Tamar back to her father's house (38:11). Even though there is no mention of her father being there, there would certainly have been some male figure(s) there under whose care (it is assumed) Tamar would live. Surprisingly, no such person is ever mentioned in the story, even when Tamar is seized to be taken away for execution. No blame is put on her house for what she does. This suggests that the story is somewhat incomplete. Second, when Tamar's prostitution is mentioned, it is Judah—not someone from the house of Tamar's father—who reacts with indignation. Has her family not heard? Or is it not their responsibility? Third—and most importantly—one has to consider the nature of Judah's call for execution. To most, the fact it is expressed as a command suggests that she is still under his authority.[73] But what kind of "protection" was he giving her if he had sent her out of his house? If he does not provide for her protection, how can he claim authority over her behavior? Furthermore, Judah calls upon some unidentified persons (of his household? of her household? of the community?) to bring her out for execution. The ambiguity as to who brings Tamar out is analogous to the ambiguity one finds in many cuneiform and biblical laws which call for capital punishment (e.g., LH ¶129; MAL A¶¶13,15; Deut 22:22–25). Are we to conclude that Judah is ordering them to execute her, that he wields authority over the unidentified persons who seize Tamar?

---

[72] "Although only a few cases are recorded in the Bible, we know that the paterfamilias enjoyed absolute authority over his extended family (bet-'ab), and that women, children and slaves were viewed as personal property of the head of the household (e.g., Gen. 31 and 38)." Stulman, "Sex and Familial Crimes," p. 57; cp. Salmon, "Judicial Authority," p. 25; Boecker, Law, pp. 29–30; Bovati, Re-Establishing Justice, p. 71.

It is not helpful to enter into a discussion of the chronology between Genesis 38 and the laws in Deuteronomy. The literary priority of D would not preclude the possibility that Genesis 38 might be orally prior to the D Code, or that it might still reflect conditions which actually existed prior to the composition of the D Code. Moreover, previous discussions have assumed the priority of the social norms assumed in Genesis 38, and my intent here is to evaluate the assumptions held in those discussions.

[73] Phillips, Ancient Israel's Criminal Law, p. 117; Rofé, "Family and Sex Laws," p. 145. See Stulman, "Sex and Familial Crimes," p. 57 n. 2 for additional references.

Perhaps Judah is merely voicing his opinion in the matter, an opinion which requires community acquiescence for its execution.[74] His statement could be a strong request rather than a command. So, rather than interpreting Judah's statement as a unilateral sentence invoked by a *paterfamilias*, it seems just as appropriate to understand it as an appeal for justice by one who feels that he personally has been wronged.[75]

Evidence from Prophetic and Wisdom Writings

Henry McKeating has sufficiently demonstrated the importance of considering prophetic and wisdom evidence in assessing the Israelite attitude toward adultery. The sages speak of the damage to a man's reputation, when he commits adultery. They likewise mention the anger of the woman's husband and the certainty that he will exact some sort of revenge. In neither case do they say anything about execution as a punishment (see Prov 6:27–35; 7:4–27; 9:13–18; Eccl 7:26). Similarly, Hosea is typical of Israelite prophets when he calls for the public humiliation of his adulterous wife, but not her execution (Hos 2:4–15; cp. Jer 3:6–10; 13:20–27; Ezek 16:15–52; 23:1–49). These passages show that, at least in some periods of Israel's history, the Israelites shared with their

---

[74] "Methodologically, the assumption that declaratory language is by definition adjudicatory is not necessary, traditional as the assumption has been. In fact, we have reason to think it is wrong." Knierim, "Problem," p. 11. Cp. McKeating, "Sanctions," p. 58.

[75] For similar interpretations of this story, see Westbrook, "Adultery," pp. 546, 572; Pressler, *View of Women*, pp. 31–35.

It seems that Judah might be responding to the news of Tamar's pregnancy for purely personal reasons, and not out of a desire to preserve the family's good name. She is supposed to be "saving herself" for his third son, and now she has not. The narrator tells us that the third son is now of age, so it is clearly Judah's fault for not bringing the two together. He apparently had been blaming her for the deaths of his two sons and his consequent lack of grandchildren. She, by her pregnancy, is showing that that is not her fault. Moreover, by having Judah be the offender in the story, his culpability in causing the situation is highlighted.

neighbors the opinion that punishments less than death were sufficient responses to adultery.[76] These observations raise several possibilities for the interpretation of Deut 22:20–21 and the two subsequent laws (vv 22–24), which call for the execution of adulterers. At least three interpretations present themselves. (1) Deut 22:20–24 reflect an early Israelite attitude toward adultery. This attitude moderated during the monarchy—perhaps even because of pressure from the monarchy—as reflected in the prophetic and wisdom materials. Yet, the old attitude was preserved in the D Code.[77] (2) The Deuteronomic laws reflect an innovation in Israelite thinking, but not necessarily its practice. The other materials are more consistent with general ancient Near Eastern culture, out of which ancient Israel first emerged. Deuteronomic law tried to enhance the significance of adultery by transforming it from a personal offense to a sacral one, making a more severe punishment necessary. It is likely, however, that "such harsh measures could not be applied and were eventually interpreted out of existence."[78] (3) All the biblical evidence must be taken together, as it reflects attitudes always held, albeit in tension with one another. Israelite society always held that adultery was an offense serious enough to

---

[76] McKeating, "Sanctions Against Adultery," pp. 57–63. Cp. Phillips, "Another Look at Adultery," pp. 3–25; Westbrook, "Adultery," pp. 577–80.

[77] This would be the logical consequence of adopting the view of someone like Kornfeld, who contrasts Israel's use of capital punishment in cases of adultery to the flexibility one finds in other ancient Near Eastern law codes. W. Kornfeld, "L'adultère dans l'orient antique," *RB* 57 (1950) 92–109; cp. Greenberg, "Some Postulates," pp. 11–13.

[78] Rofé, "Family and Sex Laws," p. 142; see also pp. 146–49. Cp. McKeating, "Sanctions Against Adultery," pp. 64–65. Phillips believes execution actually preempted other punishments because of the laws on adultery in D and H ("Another Look at Adultery," pp. 3–17).
    This line of reasoning yields another traditio-historical dilemma: the historical setting for the composition of the Pentateuchal stories. For example, one might wish to argue that Genesis 38 is contemporary with the D Code, because both call for the death of an adulterer. Rofé provides a dubious route of escape from this dilemma by positing a tension in early Israel between the theoretical understanding of adultery as a sacral offense and the "legal practice" of allowing the injured party to determine the punishment. Rofé, "Family and Sex Laws," p. 148.

warrant death, yet lesser punishments were commonly deemed to be sufficient.[79]

The biggest hurdle to overcome in the first two interpretations is the correlation of the Deuteronomic attitude to that of Jeremiah and Ezekiel, because the vast majority of redaction critics would see Deuteronomy as a close contemporary with those prophetic works. The problem with giving the Deuteronomic prescriptions historical priority over Jeremiah and Ezekiel is that one is then compelled to adopt a pre-Hoseanic date for them, because the attitude of those prophets flows directly from Hosea.[80] This makes a late exilic or even post-exilic date for the D Code more attractive; but then one runs into other problems. Such a late date would require one to adopt an early exilic or even pre-exilic date for the writing of Proverbs and Ecclesiastes, which most today would reject. One would also have to consider the justification for such an attitudinal shift in the sixth century. The return from Babylonian Exile would have been interpreted as proof of the prophetic teachings about Yahweh's willingness to accept his unfaithful wife back into his house. It probably would have been difficult to justify the adoption of a new attitude that was harsher than Yahweh's. Further, one must consider the historical reality of post-exilic Judaism, from which we have no examples of capital punishment in cases of adultery.[81]

These considerations make the third interpretation listed above the most attractive. The preceding considerations reveal how

---

[79] Westbrook, "Adultery," pp. 549–77.

[80] One cannot say that execution is only espoused in the pre-Deuteronomic layers of the D Code. The Deuteronom(ist)ic purge-formula (22:21b, 24b) reinforces this attitude.

[81] The examples of Susanna and the pseudo-Johannine story of the woman caught in adultery do not really fit the laws, because only the woman is threatened in each story (cp. Deut 22:22). The attitude attributed to Jesus is that divorce is the appropriate response for adultery (Matt 19:3–9; cp. 5:27–30), and this attitude seems to have been typical for early Judaism. Finally, the case which most closely approximates that of Deut 22:13–21 is the birth of Jesus. Joseph's betrothed bride is pregnant, which he would naturally understand as "obvious" proof that she has not been faithful to him. He does not call for her execution, though. Instead, "her husband Joseph, being a just man and unwilling to put her to shame, resolved to divorce her quietly." (Matt 1:19)

frustrating it is to read the legal materials[82] as prior or posterior developments to the prophetic and wisdom writings. It is much easier if we do not assume that they are mutually exclusive of one another, but rather are to be held in tension with one another. Besides eliminating the need to ignore all other evidence regarding the literary development of the Hebrew Bible, this interpretation allows ancient Israelites to hold competing notions regarding adultery in tension, just like their neighbors did (see above, on ancient Near Eastern evidence). The laws reflect the seriousness of adultery, while other writings demonstrate the flexibility with which those laws are actualized. But the laws do not simply intend to indicate that adultery is a "serious" offense. Rather, they show what type of response is justified in a case of adultery. Whether the persons involved in a situation of sexual misconduct would actually use the prescribed punishment would be determined according to the particulars of the case.

INTERPRETATION OF THE PRE-DEUTERONOMIC LAW (22:13–21a)

The primary case (vv 13–19) sets forth two circumstances which lead to responses by the city elders. First, a man accuses his bride of not being a virgin when their marriage is consummated (vv 13–14). Whether these are formal accusations or informal gossip in unclear.[83] Second, the bride's parents counter with their own accusations against the groom before the city elders, accusations which they support with physical evidence of their daughter's virginity (vv 15–17). The evidence proves the parents' case, and the elders punish the groom by flogging him, imposing a fine

---

[82] We must keep in mind that the perspective of the D Code on adultery is not different from that of the other law codes. One would have to lump together the adultery laws of all the codes in such an attempt to develop a consistent chronological reconstruction.

[83] Bovati discerns a particularly forensic connotation to "bring out" (v 14) in several other laws (Re-Establishing Justice, p. 372 n. 79). There is a possible parallel to this in the use of "seize" in cuneiform laws (see LH ¶129–132; MAL A¶15; Boecker, Law, pp. 22–23).

(which is double the original brideprice) to be paid to the bride's father, and forbidding him ever to divorce the girl (vv 18–19).

The corollary law (vv 20–21a) reverses the first circumstance, saying that the groom's accusation is true. This is proved by a reversal of the second circumstance—the inability of the parents to produce contrary evidence (v 20). This results in the stoning of the bride by the men of the city at the entryway to her father's house (v 21a).

A dominant view of the previous generation of scholars is that this law intends to shift the perception of adultery from a private offense (against the husband) to a sacral offense (against God). This takes the legal authority to deal with adultery out of the hands of the husband, and places it in the hands of the community (i.e., the city elders). McKeating and Phillips argue this point at length, concluding that this law represents a significant shift from the usual ancient Near Eastern view. Whether this shift in perception resulted in a change in practice is a separate matter, as McKeating has shown through his examination of non-legal materials (see above).[84]

This explanation has been modified recently by scholars who appeal to sociological considerations as providing a better explanation of the intent of the law. Naomi Steinberg advances the view that this law provides a way for the state to assume ultimate control over sexual unions. This control is exercised through the city elders, whose power base has shifted from lineage groups to the central authority. This law (read, "the state") intends to promote the stability of the nuclear family over the lineage. Previous sociological studies have shown that such a strategy inevitably strengthens the powers of the central state as well; so, it would fit nicely into a program of centralization.[85] Similar assumptions are made by Louis Stulman in his recent treatment of this law.

---

[84] McKeating, "Sanctions against Adultery," pp. 57–72; Phillips, "Another Look at Adultery," pp. 3–19; cp. Wilson, "Israel's Judicial System," p. 233.

[85] Steinberg, "Deuteronomic Law Code," pp. 165–69; cp. Blenkinsopp, "Deuteronomy," pp. 3–5. For sociological backgrounds, see Cohen, "Ends and Means," pp. 665–66. Eissfeldt, on the other hand, finds no evidence of centralization in this law (*Old Testament*, p. 224).

> In Deut. 22.13–21, D removes the case from the exclusive domain of the male head of the household [the groom] and family law and places it instead under the jurisdiction of the larger community. Now under the judicial authority of the city elders, the accused girl (נערה) has recourse to the courts and the power of the paterfamilias is limited. The power of life and death no longer resides in the husband, but rather in the community through the mediation of municipal judges.[86]

He assumes that the city elders—these "municipal judges"—exercise centrally-based authority, referring to them as "regional tribunals under state authority." He develops these ideas further in arguing that such a shift increases the status of women, because it affords them the right to appeal to the central authority through these city elders.[87] This supplementary conclusion regarding women is challenged by Carolyn Pressler. She finds no evidence that this law enhances a woman's status, because the charges made against her also impugn her father.[88] I would echo Pressler's observations, thereby calling for a reexamination of the assumption here that "D removes the case from the exclusive domain of the male head of the household and family law."

The case in Deut 22:13–21a involves countering charges. The progression of the proceedings and the punishments meted out for each offense reflect the multi-familial nature of the case. In the main case (22:13–19), the father brings formal charges of slander

---

[86] Stulman, "Sex and Familial Crimes," p. 58; cp. his "Encroachment in Deuteronomy," p. 622.

[87] Stulman, "Sex and Familial Crimes," pp. 55–63. This contrasts somewhat with Weinfeld's contention that the D Code enhances the status of women for "humanitarian" reasons (*Deuteronomy*, pp. 282–97).

Naomi Steinberg oversimplifies matters when she says, "All family issues are controlled [in the Deuteronomic legislation] to suit the sociopolitical aims of the form of government that replaced the old kinship-based social system." ("Deuteronomic Law Code," p. 169) A better appreciation for the complexity of the issues involved is reflected in the remarks of Knierim ("Problem," pp. 7–23), as he discusses the relationship between law-giving and adjudication. A centralized perspective (as is assumed by the Deuteronomic redactor) does not require the use of centralized institutions for its realization.

[88] Pressler, *View of Women*, pp. 22–35. Pressler is discussing the laws in vv 22–27, but her comment on this point naturally implies vv 13–21 as well.

against the husband in response to the husband's own accusation.[89] The fact that the father—rather than the bride—responds to the husband's initial charge shows that the matter involves the bride's family, not just herself. The husband is not merely accusing his wife of adultery; he is also accusing another male of "selling damaged goods" (to borrow Phillips's characterization).[90] The accusation by the groom includes an accusation against the bride's father. This would have always required that the case come eventually before some sort of community authority, because it would call for the reversal of an earlier agreement (the marriage) made between two men, an agreement which had required legal ratification before witnesses.[91] Therefore, this is a case of "public law" by its very nature. It never could have been resolved unilaterally by an Israelite husband; it always required the participation of community judicial functionaries. The original agreement required legal ratification; any attempt to undo that agreement (the husband's accusation) would prompt public legal action, and the prescribed "amendment" to that agreement (the imposition of a fine for attempted breach of contract) does as well.

For similar reasons, one cannot say that the antithesis in vv 20–21a reflects a restriction of the authority of a male head of household. The husband could not unilaterally execute his bride, because the adultery of which she is guilty occurred while the woman was still under the care of her father, before she became the responsibility of her husband. The reputation of the father, not the husband, is impugned here, although the husband might bring

---

[89] A. Phillips, *Deuteronomy*, p. 149; Pressler, *View of Women*, p. 24. A Sumerian parallel to this case appears in the Laws of Lipit-Ishtar (LL¶33). On that law, see Finkelstein, "Sex Offenses," pp. 355, 367.

There has been some disagreement over the meaning of עלילת דברים (vv 14, 17). Either the groom is guilty of spreading "wanton words" about his bride, or he is accusing his bride of "wanton deeds." In either case, if the accusation is unfounded, the husband is guilty of slander. See Driver, *Deuteronomy*, pp. 254–55; Mayes, *Deuteronomy*, p. 310; Pressler, *View of Women*, p. 23.

[90] A. Phillips, *Deuteronomy*, p. 149; idem, "Another Look at Adultery," pp. 6–7.

[91] On the inherently legal nature of all marriages, see Greengus, "Old Babylonian Marriage Contract," pp. 505–32.

shame upon himself if he did nothing to show his disapproval of his bride's behavior.[92] On the other hand, because the woman has now been passed from her father to her husband, her father no longer has a unilateral right to punish her either.[93] The father failed to preserve the sexual purity of his daughter while she was under his roof, and so he is guilty of that. But now he has added to that offense the second wrong of trying to deceive (defraud?) another man by giving him a deflowered girl, all the while declaring that she is a virgin. Now he is the one guilty of a breach of contract ratified before witnesses. Therefore, when his daughter is executed as an adulteress, the stoning takes place in front of his house instead of the city gate (cp. 22:24). This indicates that he too bears some blame (and shame?) for her misconduct.[94] He should

---

[92] It is possible that the wording of the husband's accusation would serve to distance the husband from any sexual misconduct on his own part. The narrator says that the husband "took" his wife "and went in to her" (וּבָא אֵלֶיהָ). In his accusation, the husband alters the description of his own actions, saying, "I drew near to her" (וָאֶקְרַב אֵלֶיהָ). Perhaps he wanted people to think that he discovered her non-virginity before he actually had intercourse with her (cp. Gen 20:4; but see Lev 18:6, 14, 19; 20:16; Isa 8:3).

[93] Frymer-Kensky explains well how the sin of the woman here "upsets the hierarchical arrangements of the cosmos," thereby threatening the well-being of the entire community. ("Law and Philosophy: The Case of Sex in the Bible," Semeia 45 [1989] 92–93; cp. Pressler, View of Women, pp. 41–43) The arguments being advanced here merely add another dimension to our understanding of the case. As Frymer-Kensky says, "the father has the full determination of his daughter's sexuality" (p. 92) until she is wedded. This also implies that he bears full responsibility if his daughter is not circumspect about her sexuality. All of this is complicated, then, when the husband (with his own reputation and responsibilities) is drawn into the situation at the time of the wedding.

[94] Cp. Buss, "Distinction between Civil and Criminal Law," p. 57. Pressler (View of Women, p. 29) points out that both the woman and her father are wronged by the husband's accusations in vv 13–19. By the same token, then, both are guilty of wrong if the husband's accusations are true. Phillips contends that the husband is trying to get back the money that he had given as a bride-price ("Another Look at Adultery," p. 6). However, vv 20–21 make no mention that reimbursement is part of the punishment against the woman's father. His only punishment is the shame.

For another interpretation, see Finkelstein, "Sex Offenses," p. 367; idem, "On Some Recent Studies in Cuneiform Law," JAOS 90 (1970) 244 (citing J. Klíma, "La patria potestas dans les nouveaux fragments législatifs sumériens," Symbolae Iuridicae et Historicae Martino David Dedicatae, ed. J.

have taken greater precautions to prevent his daughter from doing such a thing, and he should have accused and/or punished her for her "folly" before she went to her husband.[95] But because he "allowed" it to get to the point of involving another man—another family—the matter has gone beyond his jurisdiction and must be handled by the community authorities.[96]

Moreover, it is presumptuous for scholars even to assume that the emergence of the conception of adultery as a public offense would be the result of external (i.e., state) forces entirely. Sociologists warn against such an assumption.

> Finally, does the definition of adultery as a capital offense... originate with the central rulers, or is it initiated in the local community? Unfortunately, there are no data regarding this; the lack highlights our ignorance about the crucial transitional period from stateless to state levels of integration. In any case, what is clear is that regardless of the [adultery] law's provenience it is always administered at the village level of organization when only commoners are involved in the action.[97]

Once again, it is inappropriate to characterize the intent of such a law as a move to restrict the authority of a male head of household. This case *naturally* comes before the city elders because it entails a dispute between two families. Such a case could not be adjudicated by one husband or father alone, because

---

A. Ankum, R. Feenstra, and W. F. Leemans; Vol. II, Iura Orientis Antiqui [Leiden: E. J. Brill, 1968], pp. 1–8).

[95] Frymer-Kensky suggests that the bride's parents could have easily fabricated the evidence for her virginity. ("Law and Philosophy," p. 93) Since we are not certain as to the nature of the evidence being given, her suggestion must be accepted with caution. But if she is correct, it could shed additional light on this secondary regulation. If the parents could easily fabricate their evidence, but the father does not do so (v 20), then it would imply that he knew that his daughter was not a virgin and still gave her to her husband with the understanding that she was. This would magnify his guilt (cp. Phillips, "Another Look at Adultery," pp. 9–10).

There has been significant discussion of the nature of the evidence produced by the parents (the בתולים). See G. J. Wenham, "*B*e*tulah*, a Girl of Marriageable Age," *VT* 22 (1972) 326–48; Mayes, *Deuteronomy*, p. 310; Phillips, "Another Look at Adultery," p. 7; Pressler, *View of Women*, pp. 25–27.

[96] An analogous principle underlies Deut 19:1–13. See Chapter 3.

[97] Cohen, "Ends and Means," p. 668.

it involves persons outside their individual jurisdictions. It is a matter for the community to adjudicate, and it is resolved in such a way that the welfare and integrity of the larger community is seen to be paramount. A failure to resolve this situation would result in continuing disharmony between two families, a situation which could threaten the cohesion and economic well-being of the entire community.

The punishments are intended to forestall any future hostilities. The father will do nothing more against an offending son-in-law, because his daughter is a permanent member of the latter's house (her husband can never divorce her). The husband will do nothing more against an offending father-in-law, because he has already been humiliated before the community. The death of his daughter has deprived the father of any economic benefit he might have hoped to derive from the marriage. Also, placing the execution before his door shows that he is the only male in the town held liable for the offense.[98]

DEUTERONOM(IST)IC EXPANSION
(22:21b)

The purge-formula (v 21b), again, is a Deuteronom(ist)ic supplement. Its effect is to shift the scope of concern from the individual community to the entire nation, as we have seen in previous laws. Such a shift would not necessitate any change in procedures. The case would still be tried at the local level, and the city elders would still exact the same punishments as before and still for the sake of their own community's well-being and integrity. Thus, it appears that the Deuteronom(ist)ic redactor has taken a law which reflects concerns of the local community and

---

[98] No reference is ever made to the bride's former lover. We can deduce that this is consistent with the succeeding laws, based on the principle that the woman is culpable if she does not cry out for help (cp. v 24). In the present situation, the woman did not cry for help or report the incident to anyone. She would have been seen as complicit, at the least; and it is even possible that she would have been judged guilty of seduction (cp. LU ¶7; MAL A¶16). Thus she and she alone is guilty of committing "folly" in Israel.

supplements those with concerns for the well-being and/or reputation of the whole nation.

In this light we also see the shortcomings of the view that there was a time, reflected in the early stages of this law, when the Israelites conceived of adultery strictly as an affront against a man, with no thought of sacral implications. The thought that a family matter carries community-wide implications—or that a community matter carries nation-wide implications—is based on the notion that the deity will somehow hold the broader group accountable for the offensive actions of a sub-group within it. There are inherent sacral implications in such notions. One cannot infer the absence or insignificance of those sacral implications just because they are not explicitly mentioned.[99]

But this is not the end of the matter. "Israel" appears twice earlier in this law, and it is in a subordinated causal clause in both instances ("for he brought out an evil name against a virgin of Israel," v 19; "for she committed folly in Israel", v 21).[100] One might choose to attribute both causal clauses—or just "Israel"—to the redactor in both cases. It is also reasonable to retain both as pre-Deuteronomic elements of the law. No parallels exist for either in the rest of the D Code. Furthermore, these two references to "Israel" seem to use the term more as a designation of ethnicity, while the term in the purge-formula clearly points to a political entity. If nothing else, this suggests that the transition from a conception of these situations as local matters to the belief that they have "national" implications is not as marked as one might assume. Moreover, these references point to the idea that Israelites associated their identity with their moral standing. It is most likely that that self-concept derived in part from their understanding of the character and moral expectations of their

---

[99] The examples of men offering a woman in place of male visitors (Gen 19:8; Jdgs 19:24–25) might infer that sexual assault is an affront against the host alone; but one could also infer that sexual assault against a woman is seen as a lesser offense (against the host and against God) than sexual assault against another man. Other stories clearly indicate the desacratory nature of a sexual offense (Gen 20:3–6; 2 Sam 11:26).

[100] On the purge-formula as a Deuteronomic characteristic, see above. For some, the use of נבלה indicates that the offense is considered a public or sacral matter. See Thompson (*Deuteronomy*, pp. 235–36) and Mayes (*Deuteronomy*, p. 311) for references.

deity—i.e., that there was an inherently sacral aspect to their concept of adultery as an offense.

CONCLUSIONS

The present investigation highlights three common aspects of marriages in contemporary kinship-based and ancient Near Eastern societies which are related to the case presented in Deut 22:13–21. Each of these reaffirms the widely-recognized assumption that the authority and reputation of males are often the primary concerns in cases of adultery and other sexual misconduct. First, marriages are usually seen as financial arrangements between the groom and the bride's male guardian(s). Second, a husband's exclusive rights to his wife's sexuality begin with the initial exchange of pre-nuptial gifts. Any infringement on those rights is considered adultery. Third, adultery and other sexual misconduct are seen as personal offenses against the male guardian (husband, father, brother) of the woman involved, and often as sacral offenses. Complicating the matter in this situation is the fact that protection of the woman's sexuality is being transferred from her father to her husband, and that transfer takes place over many months (from the time the initial gifts are exchanged until the wedding). The law is sensitive to the desire to preserve the honor of everyone involved.

The Israelite laws place greater significance on the sacral/religious aspects of these cases than their ancient Near Eastern counterparts; but one must be careful with this observation. The biblical texts are set in a religious context (for example, the speeches of Moses which comprise the Book of Deuteronomy serve collectively as a model for later religious gatherings; see Deut 27:1–8; Josh 8:30–35; 24:1–27). Even if that were not the case, one cannot assume that the sacral considerations given in these laws exhaust the conceptual framework within which they are to be read. One must also read these laws as part of a stream of legal materials pertaining to this issue. They emphasize a particular perspective within a broad tradition, but they do not intend to displace all preceding laws.[101]

But this conclusion also points to the more fundamental difficulty that is involved in assuming that ancient Israelites (and ancient Near Eastern peoples in general) made precise distinctions between "family law" and "sacral law"—or between "private law" and "public law"—the way that modern Western peoples do. For some modern interpreters, this law shows that certain crimes are no longer thought of as offenses against the family alone, that they are *now* understood as offenses against God and the community; consequently, only the community has the right to administer "justice" in such a case. I would first question the assumption that adultery was ever thought of as an offense against the family but not against God.[102] Further, I would suggest that the Deuteronom(ist)ic additions which serve to broaden one's view of who is affected by offenses merely imply that whoever is responsible for determining what would be "just" in a given case—whether "private" or "public," "civil" or "criminal"—is also supposed to consider the implications for the broader national community in making that decision.

Another significant conclusion reached here which is at odds with much recent study of this passage is that this law does not reflect or promote a shift in the judicial authority of an Israelite

---

[101] Another possibly significant factor that could contribute to differences between Israel's legal tradition and that of Mesopotamia is the relative size and population densities in the respective cultures. On this latter point, see the quote by Whitelam in Chapter 5, concerning Deut 21:18–21. He attributes a perceived proscription of patriarchal power to urbanization in Israel. On the other hand, there is more said in the laws of the much more urbanized societies of Mesopotamia about the personal discretion of fathers and husbands in these cases than is said in Israelite laws on the same subject.

[102] Cp. Westbrook, "Adultery," pp. 549–69; Pressler, *View of Women*, pp. 17–18, 107–108 n. 42. See also n. 50, above.

Rofé provides a good summary of the discussion over whether adultery in the cuneiform laws is treated as a criminal offense or a civil offense ("Family and Sex Laws," pp. 146–49). I am not convinced, however, that making such distinctions is helpful. In my analysis of those laws (see above), I conclude that the person responsible for the female offender might adjudicate on his (or her) own, but that their decision is made nevertheless with the feelings of the broader community in mind.

man.[103] Deut 22:13–21 does reflect the fact that there were limitations to the authority of an Israelite head of household. These limitations were not as extensive as many previous scholars have claimed, though, and the explanations for them need to be completely reevaluated. In the first place, it seems quite likely that limitations on the authority of the Israelite father were present in the pre-Deuteronomic layers of the laws of the D Code. The limitations that are there, therefore, are not restrictions placed on fathers as part of a Deuteronomic centralization program. Rather, they are limitations arising naturally within local communities. They are based on the fact that the case inherently concerns more than one family and involves the possible alteration of a publicly-mediated agreement. By its very nature it requires the legal administration of a person(s) with broader authority than a single male. It is for this reason the case is heard by the elders of the city.

This points us to the role played by the elders in this law. As we have discovered in other laws, the elders here reflect a natural concern for the welfare of the community as a whole. Their presence is an indication that this matter has implications in the broader community. Two families had previously negotiated an agreement (probably in the presence of some or all of the elders overseeing the present case) which strengthened the relationship between their members in a profound way. A marriage affects other social ties in the community, particularly those involving the extended families of the bride and groom. The accusations made in this case endanger the relationship between the immediate families of the bride and groom in a way that could have repercussions among many other families. The potential for a neighborhood- or community-wide rift is very real. For these reasons, the elders of the community are involved in trying to resolve the situation in a way that will yield the broadest stability. The resolutions prescribed would have the effect of precluding any warrant for additional hostile actions between the families involved, thus promoting stability in the broader community. This

---

[103] The conclusions reached by Pressler on other laws seem to substantiate my own conclusions regarding this law. See, for example, her conclusions on Deut 21:15–17 and 24:1–4 (*View of Women*, pp. 15–16, 60–62). Also, on 21:15–17, cp. Rofé, "Family and Sex Laws," p. 153.

highlights, once again, that a primary goal pursued by city elders is to maintain peace in their community. Their responsibilities for administering inter-familial economic affairs and for maintaining the community's integrity guide them in a significant way as they pursue that goal.

These aspects of the law probably existed in its earliest layers. Contrary to the positions taken in the recent studies of Steinberg and Stulman, I find nothing in this law that suggests an attempt by a central administration to shift the focus from the welfare of the community to the welfare of the nuclear family. If anything, the opposite is true. The limitations on the husband's authority assumed in this law seem to reflect the principle that a concern for one's community should supersede the personal interests of an individual man and his nuclear family. Such a principle could have arisen somewhat naturally as a consequence of groups of families living together in the same community. The examples cited from present-day societies support this interpretation.

Further, if I have correctly delineated the Deuteronom(ist)ic elements in the laws considered, then the innovation of the D Code in this regard is really nothing more than the expansion of this principle from the local community to the entire nation. In other words, the law implies that the moral corruption of a single family (evidenced in the promiscuity of the bride) threatens the integrity of the entire community; therefore, the men of the community mete out the punishment against her before her father's house. The Deuteronom(ist)ic redactors expand this principle by implying that a community which would not punish such an offense would be threatening the moral integrity of the entire nation; therefore, the traditional punishment of this "sacral offense" is reaffirmed because it "purge[s] the evil from your [Israel's] midst" (v 21b).

CHAPTER 7
THE LEVIRATE LAW
(DEUT 25:5–10)

One of the more intriguing practices of ancient Israel was levirate marriage, denoted by the Hebrew root יבם ("to perform the duty of a husband's brother," RSV). The term is used in only two passages: in the story of Tamar and Judah's family (Genesis 38), and in this levirate law (Deut 25:5–10). A significant amount of energy has been spent discussing whether the marriage of Ruth and Boaz is also a marriage in levirate (Ruth 4:1–17). I shall address this question briefly, primarily from the vantage point of comparative ethnological evidence. The same background information will help provide a better perspective from which to interpret the Deuteronomic law and the role played by the elders in it.

DEFINITION OF LEVIRATE MARRIAGE

Taken in its most literal sense, "levirate marriage" designates the marriage of a widow to her brother-in-law (from the Latin, "levir"). One would be hard-pressed, however, to find a society in which *only* an actual brother-in-law would be allowed or expected to marry a widow in levirate. There might be several reasons for a widow to look to some male other than a brother-in-law to take the place of her late husband. The most obvious—but certainly not only—reason would be that her husband might not have any brothers. In any case, a widow often turns to some other close relative of her late husband who will carry out those levirate responsibilities, even though he is not literally a levir. In other words, while it might be considered ideal that a brother-in-law assume the dead man's responsibilities toward the widow, there seem to be no legal distinctions between instances in which an actual brother-in-law assumes those responsibilities and instances in which they fall to some other close male relative (see the survey of ethnographies below).

More germane to the discussion among social anthropologists regarding the classification of a marriage as "levirate" has been the issue of descent lines. The "true" levirate marriage is defined as one in which children born to a widow and her levir are reckoned as offspring of her first husband, regardless of their genitor. If the children of a union between a widow and her first husband's kinsman are reckoned as offspring of their biological father, it has been considered more accurate to refer to this second union as "widow-inheritance," that is, a man's widow has been "inherited" by his brother (or some other kinsman). Unfortunately, many ethnographers have been imprecise in their use of these terms, designating marriages as "levirate" which actually fall into the category of "widow inheritance."[1]

Moreover, one cannot presume what second-marriage customs will be followed in a given society. There are examples of children born in a widow's second marriage claiming to have two fathers (their "pater" and their genitor). Some peoples make no distinction between the social roles of "brother" and "step-brother" (or "half-brother" or "clan brother"), thus blurring the lines of distinction

[1] For discussions on the definition of levirate marriage and related practices in African societies, see Evans-Pritchard, *Kinship and Marriage*, pp. 38, 109–16; A. R. Radcliffe-Brown, "Introduction," in *African Systems of Kinship and Marriage*, ed. A. R. Radcliffe-Brown and Daryll Forde (London: Oxford University Press, 1950), p. 64; Max Gluckman, "Kinship and Marriage Among the Lozi of Northern Rhodesia and the Zulu of Natal," in *African Systems of Kinship and Marriage*, ed. A. R. Radcliffe-Brown and D. Forde (London: Oxford University Press, 1950), p. 183; R. G. Abrahams, "Some Aspects of Levirate," in *The Character of Kinship*, pp. 163–74, ed. Jack Goody (Cambridge: Cambridge University Press, 1973).

along which Westerners tend to categorize social relationships. There are societies in which a dead man's kinsman (not his brother) sires children in the dead man's name through his widow; there are others in which his brother marries his widow, and yet the brother's children by the widow are considered his own offspring and not the offspring of the dead man; and in some cases, the levir himself takes on the name of his dead brother for descent purposes.[2]

Because of these considerations, I have found it impractical to investigate "levirate marriage" in its narrowest sense (that is, strictly as a marriage between a widow and her brother-in-law for the purpose of bearing children for her first husband) in isolation from other similar practices. Instead, the survey which follows takes into consideration any marriage involving a widow.

There are two areas of concern addressed by levirate marriage and similar practices, one economic and one social. The economic concerns are the more concrete and, therefore, more easily recognized. These include the on-going financial support and physical protection for the widow (and her children), modifications to financial agreements between the families of the widow and the dead man (bridewealth, dowry), and management of the dead man's property in inheritance. All the societies with levirate marriage use the custom for these reasons. The primary social concern has to do with lines of descent, viz. the "place" of the widow's children within the extended family and the perpetuation of the dead man's "name" in his line.

These two concerns are not easily separated.[3] Some societies have other mechanisms for addressing them, so that the function of levirate marriage might be more limited in its scope or overlap

---

[2] Similarly, there are examples of sororate marriage (in which a widower marries an unmarried sister-in-law or some other female relative to "replace" the dead woman) and "ghost-marriage" (in which a man takes a wife "in the name of" a man who has died). See Evans-Pritchard, *Kinship*, pp. 109–12; Edel, *Chiga*, pp. 77–78; Cunnison, *Luapula*, pp. 93–95.

[3] Pedersen (*Israel* I–II, pp. 509–10) comments on the inseparability of such needs in the Hebrew mind. "The duties of the members of the family, the conception of its property and the position of the wife—all this can only be understood as links of an organic structure that must be taken as a whole..." It would not be surprising, then, to find levirate marriage in Israel addressing several of these needs.

238 THE ELDERS OF THE CITY

with other institutions, in some cases.[4] Additionally, levirate marriage is viewed as an obligation in some societies, but it is nothing more than a preference in others. These and other variations will be noted in the survey which follows.

COMPARATIVE EVIDENCE[5]

Contemporary Kinship-Based Societies

Levirate marriage is looked upon more as an attractive option than an obligation by many of the African and Middle Eastern peoples among whom it is practiced. It seems that any close male relative may take in the widow, though preference is usually given to the dead man's brothers. The sense of obligation hinges primarily on the need to keep the dead man's property within the control of his family and to perpetuate his name in his lineage. Ironically, the societies which feel the obligation for a widow to marry in levirate most acutely are often those with the strictest rules concerning incest.[6]

A survey of several societies quickly reveals the sorts of variations possible in levirate marriages. J. J. Burckhardt's

---

[4] Adoption and surrogacy (by handmaids) are two of the better known institutions among the Semites for purposes similar to levirate marriage. See M. Burrows, "The Ancient Oriental Background of Hebrew Levirate Marriage," *BASOR* 77 (1940) 3, 5. In African societies, it is difficult to distinguish levirate marriage, widow-inheritance, and adelphic polyandry. See Abrahams, "Some Aspects of Levirate," pp. 163–74.

[5] Several previous commentators have mentioned how common levirate marriage is in kinship-based societies. Those surveyed here are simply those to which I had easy access. See R. Gordis, "Love, Marriage, and Business in the Book of Ruth: A Chapter in Hebrew Customary Law," in *A Light Unto My Path*, ed. H. N. Bream, et al., p. 248; Driver, *Deuteronomy*, pp. 282–83; T. and D. Thompson, "Some Legal Problems in the Book of Ruth," *VT* 18 (1968) 95. For typical ancient Near Eastern examples, see Burrows, "Ancient Oriental Background," pp. 2–14; de Vaux, *Ancient Israel*, p. 124. A fuller list is given by D. Manor, "A Brief History of Levirate Marriage as It Relates to the Bible," *ResQ* 27 (1984) 130–31.

[6] See Evans-Pritchard, *Kinship*, p. 38.

comments on levirate marriage among the Bedouin gives a good example of Middle Eastern practices.

> If a young man leaves a widow, his brother generally offers to marry her; custom does not oblige him or her to make this match, nor can he prevent her from marrying another man. It seldom happens, however, that she refuses; for by such an union the family property is kept together.[7]

One finds similar sentiments among contemporary African peoples. First, one finds some variation regarding a widow's sense of obligation to marry in levirate. Independent of the widow's obligation to remarry within her husband's lineage group is the question of which male relative she will choose (and most do have a choice). She can usually choose from among the dead man's brothers, half-brothers, father, uncles, cousins, and sons by another wife. Often a man younger than the deceased is preferred, because he can be expected to provide for the widow longer than an older man could. For example, among the Teda of North Africa, it is normal for couples to become engaged at a young age and to remain engaged for several years before they are married. If the groom-to-be dies, "[he] is customarily replaced by a younger brother or some other close relative of his." Levirate marriage for East African Nyima widows is "desirable, but no pressure is exercised" upon them to marry only within the dead man's clan. Preferably, the second husband will be younger than her first husband. The same is true of the Berti, Swazi, Tswana, and Luapula peoples. Among the Luapula, the families of the dead man and his widow meet together several months after the man's death to negotiate for a suitable "successor" husband from among her first husband's close relatives. On the other hand, the ultimate decision about whether a widow will marry in levirate or outside her husband's group is left up to the widow in the Koalib and Moro tribes.

There are other differences among the customs of these peoples. The Koalib forbid levirate marriage with a blood-brother, but allow it with half-brothers and clansmen. Only one of the dead

---

[7] J. J. Burckhardt, *Notes on the Bedouins and Wahabys* (1830), p. 64; quoted by H. H. Rowley, "The Marriage of Ruth," in *The Servant of the Lord and Other Essays* (London: Lutterworth, 1952), p. 178.

man's widows may remarry in levirate; the rest are expected to marry outside their husband's group. The neighboring Moro tribesmen prefer marriage between widows and their late husband's full-brothers, giving the eldest the option of marrying as many of the dead man's widows as he wishes. The Mesakin "allow" a widow to marry her brother-in-law, but only if she has children who are all less than ten years of age. Older widows return to their own families, while childless widows must marry into a different clan. Tallensi widows may marry their brother-in-law, if they wish to strengthen their husband's lineage. Because a Chiga wife is considered to be under the care of her husband's family, one of his brothers or near relatives is expected to marry her upon her husband's death. If she wishes to marry outside his family, she must acquire a formal divorce. For Nuer men, "It is permissible, indeed to some extent obligatory, to take the places of the husbands in leviratic marriage." The levir is usually the dead man's younger brother; but if he has no younger brother, she can choose his sister's son or a (younger) cousin. If he had been an old man with a young wife, his widow might go to one of his sons of a different wife. Levirate marriage is "expected" for Heiban widows, while it is "nearly compulsory" among those of the Otoro tribe, and it is the only marriage option open to widows of Dilling tribesmen. The Heiban regard marriage between a widow and her late husband's blood-brothers as incest, but his eldest half-brother has the right to marry as many of the dead man's widows as he wishes. The Otoro give preference to full-brothers, but they permit a man to marry only one widow; however, they expect every brother-in-law to marry one of the dead man's widows. Otoro widows have some say in which brother-in-law they are willing to marry (if any), and they are expected to wait at least a year after their husband's death before entering into any second marriage.[8]

[8] Briggs, Tribes, p. 173; Nadel, Nuba, pp. 119–21, 225, 289–90, 352, 376–77, 404, 434; Cunnison, Luapula, pp. 93–94, 98–99; Evans-Pritchard, Kinship, pp. 38, 57, 112–15; H. Kuper, "Kinship Among the Swazi," in African Systems of Kinship and Marriage, ed. A. R. Radcliffe-Brown and D. Forde (London: Oxford University Press, 1950), p. 97; I. Schapera, "Kinship and Marriage among the Tswana," in African Systems of Kinship and Marriage, ed. A. R. Radcliffe-Brown and D. Forde (London: Oxford University Press, 1950), p. 153; Mair, African Societies, p. 59; Edel, Chiga, p. 77; Holy, Neighbours and Kinsmen, p. 139.

In each of these societies, exceptions to these general rules can be identified.

Another question that must be addressed by a widow's second marriage is the placement of the children within descent lines. In some cases, the children of these special marriages belong to their biological father's group (so the Heiban, Otoro, Nyima, and Tullishi); but there are variations. The children of Mesakin widows are usually adopted by their mother's brother(s). Children born to a Moro and Koalib widow who remains unmarried are considered offspring of her first husband; but the children of those who do remarry belong to their second husband's lineage. This is taken a step further by the Dilling, who allow second marriages only with near-kinsmen. Children of a second marriage are reckoned as offspring of their genitor; however, widows can remain unmarried and bear children outside of marriage with non-kinsmen, and those children are considered the offspring of her first husband. Among the Zulu, the children born to a widow—whether she marries a levir or someone outside the family group—are all considered offspring of her first husband. The Nuer determine descent lines in terms of payment of bridewealth (see below). The Lozi have completely different customs, requiring a second marriage and bridewealth payment when a widow marries, even if she marries a member of her first husband's immediate family. Additional variations arise depending on the number and ages of the children born in the first marriage, and whether the family lives alongside the man's family or near the woman's family.[9]

Further considerations are made regarding the bride-price paid in the first marriage and whether there is a need for another in the second. Normally, payment of a bride-price by a widow's second husband is not required in cases of levirate marriage, but it is required if the widow marries someone outside her first husband's group.[10] This is because the marriage is seen as part of a financial arrangement between two extended families, and there is no reason to reestablish the arrangement between the same

[9] Nadel, *Nuba*, pp. 119–21, 225, 289–90, 352, 376–77, 404, 434; Evans-Pritchard, *Kinship*, pp. 98, 112–15; Gluckman, "Kinship," pp. 183–88; Holy, *Neighbours and Kinsmen*, p. 139; Dyson-Hudson, *Karimojong Politics*, p. 206.
[10] Nadel, *Nuba*, pp. 225, 289–90, 404, 434.

families. For example, a Nuer man takes the cattle for the bridewealth from a herd owned collectively with his brothers. Any offspring sired by him or one of his brothers through his wife are considered part of the same line, because she came into the family of both through the same bridewealth payment. No second marriage to unite the levir and the widow is deemed necessary, and she is considered still to be the wife of her first husband. The Zulu understand such cases similarly. In some societies, it is clear that there is greater concern for providing an economic foundation for the dead man's sons than there is for the well-being of the widow. The people of the Tullishi tribe emphasize that a widow holds her husband's property "in trust," until her sons are old enough to work the land themselves. She can remarry or turn to adult males of her own extended family for her own economic support, if necessary; but her sons must have property (inherited from her husband's family) with which to establish their own financial stability. Other situations allow the dead man's property simply to revert to his family, who are to pass it on to his offspring at the proper time.[11]

A less tangible concern—but one that often is related and just as significant—is the perpetuation of a man's "name" through his offspring. The Tallensi encourage widows to marry their brother-in-law for the expressed purpose of strengthening the lineage of the first husband and carrying on his memory in the group. The Gbande people of Liberia commonly utilize levirate and sororate marriages specifically to preserve a man's name, saying, "One who has many children, his name will never die." A Luapula levir can divorce his brother's widow only after he has publicly declared that he has assumed from her the responsibility of perpetuating the dead man's name in his lineage.[12]

---

[11] Evans-Pritchard, *Kinship*, pp. 98, 114; Nadel, *Nuba*, p. 352.

[12] Mair, *African Societies*, p. 59; Dennis, *Gbandes*, pp. 88–90; Cunnison, *Luapula*, pp. 96–98.

Cunnison (p. 98) writes: "Perhaps the situation may be better understood by considering individuals not as persons but as holders of names, positions or offices. Each man has a name. On his death, the name subsists as an attribute or possession of the lineage. After a while the lineage finds a member to succeed to the name. This member is then the embodiment of two positions, and holds two names, his own and the one he inherits. Of these the inherited overrides the original name and position, because it is either of a

It is particularly in regard to inheritance and the perpetuation of a "name" that local elders tend to become interested and involved in cases of widow-marriage, just as they are with primary marriages. The strength of local lineages is at risk when the death of one of its members occurs. Having a brother or near-relative of the deceased assume his social and economic responsibilities results in a relatively smooth continuation of the status quo, thereby minimizing the negative effects on the lineage caused by the death. Moreover, the simple fact that they serve as witnesses to property transactions necessitates their involvement in situations which have the potential of altering significantly the economic balance of power in the community.[13]

These examples give some indication of the concerns that arise in connection with marriages of widows and the variety of ways that might emerge to respond to them in kinship-based societies. These should help us understand better the limited written evidence from ancient Near Eastern law which we possess. That, in turn, will provide us with a better frame of reference for interpreting the biblical law on levirate marriage.

Ancient Near Eastern Societies

The extant cuneiform laws suggest that marriages between a widow and one of her husband's close relatives might have been a widely-accepted (but not obligatory) practice in the ancient Near East. What is less certain is whether these marriages actually fit the definition of levirate marriage used by sociologists. The few direct references to these marriages which exist in the law codes are subsumed within broader contexts, such as inheritance, providing for widows, or incest. Fundamental to many of these laws are ideas regarding the responsibilities of males toward the female members of their families. Every woman is under the "protection" of a particular male. A father is responsible for his daughter for his entire life, although his primacy is supplanted by

---

senior generation, or else is senior in the same generation... Children, in these terms, are children of a position rather than of an individual. For men are mortal; a name can be inherited from generation to generation."

[13] See Cunnison, *Luapula*, p. 96; Holy, *Neighbours and Kinsmen*, p. 126.

her husband once she is married.[14] On the death of her father, his responsibilities pass to his sons (see LL ¶23; LH ¶¶166, 184; MAL A¶48), and from them to their sons. Similarly, once the primary responsibility for a woman has been passed from her father to her husband, it is then "inherited" by his closest male relatives (see HL ¶193; MAL A¶46). Many extenuating circumstances can influence who actually assumes that responsibility.[15] Some laws describe situations in which a widow is allowed to marry any man of her choosing; others assume she will marry her husband's close relative (see below). This indicates that levirate marriage, if it was practiced, was merely one of several options available to a widow for dealing with the consequences of the death of her husband.

A couple of Hittite laws (HL ¶¶192–193) show that levirate and sororate marriages (or something akin to them) were allowed in Hittite society, but they are very vague as to the exact nature of these practices.[16] This vagueness exists because the laws are concerned primarily with distinguishing incestuous and non-incestuous relationships (HL ¶¶188–200 deal with permitted and unpermitted sexual relations), and because of some uncertainties regarding the readings and interpretation of the laws. HL ¶192 reads: "If a man's wife dies, [he may take her] sister [as his wife.] It is not an offense." The following law says a man's brother "shall take his widow as wife." In his absence, this obligation/option falls to the deceased's father, then his uncle. Several clarifications would help us interpret these two laws more precisely. The restored reading in the first points to the inherent ambiguity in the translation. The laws either prescribe that a secondary union "shall" ("must"?) take place, or they might simply allow it ("may"). The fact that the first law concludes with the explanation, "It is

---

[14] The respective levels of responsibility vary, however, depending on whether the couple lives in the house of the bride's father or in the groom's house (see LE ¶17–18).

[15] For example, MAL A¶45 calls for the city to provide for a woman whose husband is away because he is fighting on behalf of the city. In some cases, a woman would return to live with her own father (LH ¶142).

[16] For literature and a brief discussion of these laws, see Donald A. Leggett, *The Levirate and Goel Institutions in the Old Testament, with Special Attention to the Book of Ruth* (Cherry Hill, NJ: Mack Publishing Co., 1974), pp. 21–24.

not an offense," suggests that the latter is more likely.[17] Moreover, HL ¶195 begins, "If a man sleeps with his brother's wife, while his brother is alive, it is an unpermitted sexual pairing." The intent of the preceding laws seems to be to indicate by way of contrast that, if persons were to enter into a sororate or levirate relationship, they would not be guilty of incest.

We cannot be absolutely certain, however, that these should be considered levirate and sororate marriages. There is no indication of how these unions affected inheritances and descent lines; so, it could be that what is assumed here is really widow inheritance, rather than true levirate marriage.[18] On the other hand, it is not absolutely clear whether these secondary unions were even considered "marriages." The translation reads that the brother shall "take" the widow, but this apparently is not the same phraseology used to denote marriage (see HL ¶31, "takes her as his wife"). Perhaps, as in some African societies, the widow is still considered the wife of her first husband, and the levir is merely his surrogate. That would indicate that this is a true levirate arrangement.

Several laws within various Mesopotamian law codes address questions which arise naturally in all cultures (for example, the marriage of a widow to a second husband), but also many which are peculiar to cultures in which polygamy and unions involving slaves are common. Many of the laws exist because all marriages in those societies involved the exchange of significant gifts and the adoption of financial obligations between the families of the bride and groom. The most significant of these financial obligations in the laws are dowry (given by the bride's father to the bride and inherited by her children) and bridewealth (given by the groom to his father-in-law). If a marriage dissolves or ends, or if either spouse is involved in a second marriage, these and other financial obligations are affected. Further considerations arise if there are children at the time that a marriage situation is altered, and the outcomes will vary depending on the ages of those children. In this

---

[17] Some later versions of HL ¶193 also add this clause, indicating that those copyists so understood that law. See Roth, *Law Collections*, p. 240 n. 63.

[18] HL ¶171 deals with a woman's control over her son's inheritance. Another version of ¶192 gives a widow control of her husband's inheritance (Roth, *Law Collections*, p. 240 n. 62).

broad context, levirate marriage stands as but one of many possible options.

Approximately one dozen of Lipit-Ishtar's laws deal with marriage and inheritance (LL ¶¶21–32), only a few from the laws of Eshnunna (LE ¶¶17–18, 29–30). Three of the former (LL ¶¶25–27) address questions of inheritance when more than one wife/partner is involved, but none entertains a situation in which the husband dies. LE ¶¶17–18 stipulate what is to be done with marriage gifts in the case of the death of either spouse; but no mention is made of how these changes would affect the children. The right of a returning prisoner-of-war to his wife is affirmed by LE ¶29, even if she has married and had children by someone else during his absence. However, the fate of any children born in his absence is not mentioned. Such details are spelled out in laws of later periods (see below). Also, no mention is made in either law code of the possibility (or prohibition) of marriage to a kinsman of the first husband.

A long series within Hammurabi's laws deals generally with making sure that wives and children have adequate provisions and are treated fairly in inheritance matters, particularly in the absence of their husband/father (see most of LH ¶¶133–184). One stipulates that, if a man is absent due to a war and his wife marries another, any children born "shall inherit from their [biological] father" (LH ¶135). A husband can give property to his wife which she eventually passes on to her children; but transference to an outsider is strictly prohibited (LH ¶150; cp. ¶177). Certain pieces of property can be given to a woman by her father as part of her dowry. They are to be held by her and/or taken care of by her husband, but they ultimately belong only to the children she bears (LH ¶¶162, 167, 171). A widow who is not supported financially by her children is free to marry "a husband of her choice," but her dowry is still divided equally among all the children she bears (LH ¶¶172–174, 177). Similar solutions to similar situations are prescribed in laws of the Neo-Babylonian period (see LNB ¶¶8–15). There is no reference in either code to marriage in levirate.[19]

---

[19] Leggett, *Levirate and Goel*, pp. 10–12.

There is also no clear-cut evidence of levirate marriage in the extant documents from Nuzi or Ugarit. See Leggett, *Levirate and Goel*, pp. 24–26.

There are also several Middle Assyrian laws dealing with similar sorts of situations (see MAL A¶25–46; B¶1–5; O¶1–3). For example, the wife of a man gone on a lengthy journey is expected to wait five years before marrying another man, while a soldier's wife need wait only two (MAL A¶¶36, 45). Any children born within those time-frames belong to the first husband, while those born afterward belong to their respective genitors. Similarly, if a man dies while his wife is pregnant, the child that she bears will inherit from that man and not from any future husband she might have (MAL A¶28). A few laws anticipate that a widow might return to live with her own father, but "she is indeed a widow" only if her father-in-law is also dead and she has no sons (MAL A¶33).

A difference in these laws, however, is that a few of them specifically mention marriages which at first glance appear to be levirate or sororate in nature. One involves a father whose married son has died and whose second son is only engaged. The father can request that the widowed daughter-in-law be cared for by his second son's father-in-law; or, failing that, he can give his daughter-in-law in marriage to his second son (MAL A¶30). Similarly, a man whose wife/bride has died has the option of marrying one of her sisters, if he so desires (MAL A¶31). It is clear that a marriage under these circumstances is strictly optional, the ultimate decision being left in the hands of the male heads-of-household (see below on MAL A¶46). It is likely that the decision in each case would depend on the importance of the persistence of the financial/social ties which, in reality, are just being created between the two families involved. It is not certain, though, that these marriages meet the strict definition of "levirate." Nothing is said about whether the offspring of such unions would be considered heirs of the deceased, which one would expect in a true levirate marriage, or if they would inherit from their genitor. It

---

There are two wills from Emar which reveal that a man could make his wife the heir to his property, if there were no male heirs (Huehnergard, "Biblical Notes," pp. 429–33). It is not certain whether this was the exception or the rule.

might be more appropriate to categorize this as widow inheritance.[20]

Another law calls for special allowances to be made for a bride subsequent to her public anointing by her future father-in-law (MAL A¶43).[21] Two related outcomes are envisioned. In the first, if the engaged son dies before the wedding, his father may choose another son to replace him.[22] The second scenario supplements the preceding one by assuming that the man's father has died as well. The groom in this scenario obviously has another wife and children already, because his "replacement" is one of his own sons. Should none be available, the marriage agreement is voided and the bride's father returns certain pre-marriage gifts. Logically, the woman would then be free to marry any man she wished. MAL A¶46 deals with similar circumstances, but after there have been several years of marriage. Here, the widow is to be supported either by her own sons or by the sons of a primary wife. In the latter case, one of those sons has the option of marrying the secondary widow as a part of providing for her (MAL ¶46). These are the sorts of unions that can be made in levirate marriages; but again, nothing is said about the relationship between the deceased and subsequent offspring. It is possible that these too are examples of widow inheritance rather than levirate marriage.[23]

There obviously are some parallels between these ancient Near Eastern laws and the customs found in contemporary kinship-based societies of Africa and the Middle East, as summarized above. For example, the option of having a widowed second wife marry a son of the primary wife appears in these laws and is among the customs of several African peoples. Similarly, one finds in these laws and in many contemporary societies a brother or sister being offered as a "replacement" spouse when an engaged person dies. There are also, however, some significant differences. Two seem most significant. The first is that the

---

[20] For a lengthier discussion of previous treatments, see Leggett, *Levirate and Goel*, pp. 12–21.

[21] The significance of this action eludes me.

[22] This is yet another proof that marriages were viewed primarily as business deals between the men of two families. In this case, the father of the groom is standing behind his family's part of the agreement to provide a husband for the daughter of the other man involved in the "transaction."

[23] See Leggett, *Levirate and Goel*, pp. 16–17.

right/responsibility to serve as a "replacement" is restricted to a narrower pool in ancient Near Eastern society than in most African societies. The Assyrian laws mention a brother or sister as a "replacement" only in cases where the deceased was engaged and the "replacement" is not yet married. No other possibility is mentioned. The only other occasion for marrying a close relative is when a secondary widow marries a son of the primary widow (MAL A¶46). The possibility that the dead man's (already married?) brother or cousin might play a role is not entertained here either. The Hittite laws reveal a slightly wider pool of candidates. There, the responsibility for the woman passes from the husband to his brother, then to his father, and finally to his uncle.

Taken together, these point to a second significant difference between the ancient and contemporary societies examined thus far. Several have noted that the cuneiform laws are oriented more toward the living than the dead.[24] The cuneiform laws are more concerned with the financial well-being of the dead man's surviving women and children, while contemporary African and Middle Eastern customs often betray a greater concern for the standing of the (dead) male and his lineage. There is nothing said in the cuneiform laws about preserving the name of the dead man or making sure he has offspring. A man has a moral obligation to provide for his wife(s) and children, but he is not obligated to help his more extended family. Once a man is married and has children, his familial obligations are restricted primarily to his own household.[25] This entails his own nuclear family, plus any responsibilities he might inherit from his father for women and children that had been under his (the father's) care. But his married brothers are considered financially and socially independent of him in most respects. This is not to say that persons in the ancient Near East are unconcerned with their family's "name." Conversely, it would be wrong to infer that contemporary peoples ignore the needs of widows and their

---

[24] See Leggett, *Levirate and Goel*, pp. 19–21; E. W. Davies, "Inheritance Rights and Hebrew Levirate Marriage," *VT* 31 (1981) 140.

[25] In fact, even his familial obligations are superseded to some degree by his obligation to the city-state, as a man who deserts his city is deprived of his family upon his return home (LH ¶136).

children. Rather, it is a matter of emphasis. The cuneiform laws focus on aspects of these situations which concern the (living) women and children; the customs and ideas expressed in present-day societies (and ancient Israel) tend to highlight the concerns of the (dead) men.

One can only speculate about the reasons for this difference. Two related explanations seem most obvious. One is that there might be a significant difference in the importance of a lineage group. The present-day societies surveyed here represent life in small, rural communities. These communities rely heavily on mutual aid between families and family-groups for their livelihood. Military service usually is voluntary, prompted by a sense of obligation by blood or marriage ties to others involved in the conflict. The ancient societies in which the law codes arise rely on a centralized government to unify people's efforts and to sustain peace and prosperity. There are larger concentrations of peoples of diverse lineage backgrounds. The perpetuation of a lineage for several future generations is less of a concern to the solidarity of a family than other things (such as a murder) might be. One naturally considers other factors (the financial welfare of the widow) to be of greater importance. If some other means to accomplish this seems just as reasonable, there will be less impetus for a recourse to the almost-incestuous levirate marriage.[26]

REDACTION-CRITICAL MATTERS[27]

There are no phrases in Deut 25:5–10 which one would label "Deuteronom(ist)ic." The only significant link to other laws in Deuteronomy is the reference to elders, who are approached at the

---

[26] A few societies emphasize consideration for the motivation for sexual relations between a widow and levir. If the motivation is physical rather than for duty, the relationship can be deemed incestuous. See T. and D. Thompson, "Some Legal Problems," p. 95.

[27] There are no significant textual variants in this passage, although one might omit "his brother" from v 6 with the LXX. The meaning is not changed, whether this is retained or removed.

gate (cp. 16:18; 17:5; 22:15; Ruth 4:1). This, together with certain stylistic considerations, has led some source critics to posit the existence of a pre-Deuteronomic collection of elders-laws.[28] I agree that these laws have a pre-Deuteronomic origin, but to speak of an isolated collection of "elders-laws" is somewhat speculative. These laws could have been part of a larger collection at the pre-Deuteronomic level. Whatever the configuration of that pre-Deuteronomic collection, there is nothing in the levirate law's present form to suggest editing at the time of its inclusion into the D code.[29] Therefore, we should conclude that the law in its pre-Deuteronomic form also served the Deuteronomist's purposes. I shall return to implications of this conclusion a bit later.

TRADITIO-HISTORICAL CONSIDERATIONS

Three passages in the Hebrew Bible touch directly on the subject of levirate marriage—Genesis 38; Deut 25:5–10; and Ruth 4.[30] Other passages are often brought into the discussion to affirm or clarify certain aspects of the Israelite practice of levirate marriage (e.g., Num 27:1–11; 36:1–12; Ruth 1:6–18; 2 Sam 14:4–11), but they do not significantly influence traditio-historical discussions. Two laws in Leviticus forbidding sexual relations between a man and his brother's wife (Lev 18:16; 20:21) were very important in the early Jewish discussions of levirate marriage.[31]

---

[28] This proposal goes back at least to Hölscher, "Komposition," p. 216; cp. Pfeiffer, *Introduction*, p. 234.

[29] Burrows, "Levirate Marriage," pp. 24–26; Eissfeldt, *Old Testament*, p. 224; Preuss, *Deuteronomium*, pp. 58, 136. An alternative proposal posits a strictly oral source/custom preceding the Deuteronomic edition. So Driver, *Deuteronomy*, p. lvi.

[30] The root בָּם ("husband's brother;" fem., "brother's wife") actually occurs only in Gen 38:8; Deut 25:5–10; and Ruth 1:15. This final instance denotes the relationship between Ruth and Orpah, so that it really means "brother-in-law's wife." Perhaps similar relationships could be so denoted as well (e.g., "sister's husband," "husband's sister," "wife's brother").

[31] An entire tractate of the Mishnah (*Yebamoth*, the first tractate in *Seder Nashim*) is devoted to this subject. For discussion of the tractate and its rabbinic interpretations, see S. Belkin, "Levirate and Agnate Marriage in Rabbinic and Cognate Literature," *JewQR* 60 (1970) 288–329.

The view that those laws are absolute effectively eliminated the possibility of levirate marriage for many of those early Jewish interpreters and for their Jewish and Christian descendants over the centuries. It seems likely, however, that the incest laws considered such a union to be illicit only while the brother/husband was still alive (cp. Lev 18:18, and Hittite laws, above).[32]

There are two or three competing proposals regarding a possible evolution in the institution of levirate marriage in Israel, based on developments supposedly reflected in the three main passages mentioned.[33] Virtually all agree that the story of Judah and Tamar in Genesis 38 represents early traditions, reflecting practices of a pre-state society.[34] The principal debate, then, concerns the sequencing of Deut 25:5–10 and Ruth 4. Its resolution depends mostly on one's view of the date of the Book of Ruth. The primary argument based on the recorded levirate customs concerns who may serve as a levir. The levir is the deceased's father in the Judah-Tamar story, a "kinsman" in the Boaz-Ruth story, and a brother in the Deuteronomic law. Those who attribute an early monarchic date to Ruth see a perpetuation of pre-state conventions there, because the levir is still drawn from a wider pool than in the levirate law, which apparently intends to restrict levirate obligations and rights to brothers only.[35] Others insist that Ruth is a late document (exilic or post-

---

[32] See E. Neufeld, *Ancient Hebrew Marriage Laws, with Special References to General Semitic Laws and Customs* (London: Longmans, Green and Company, 1944), p. 43; Thompson, *Deuteronomy*, p. 251.

[33] For more detailed discussion, see Leggett, *Levirate and Goel*, pp. 143–63, 271–91. See also E. F. Campbell, Jr., *Ruth* (AB; Garden City: Doubleday, 1975), pp. 23–28.

[34] The only exception to this of which I am aware is J. A. Bewer, "The Ge'ullah in the Book of Ruth," *AJSL* 19 (1903) 143–44. He gives priority to Ruth simply because someone more distantly related than the deceased's father serves as Ruth's levir.

[35] M. Burrows, "The Marriage of Ruth and Boaz," *JBL* 59 (1940) 453–54; Rowley, "Marriage of Ruth," pp. 179–81; C. M. Carmichael, "A Ceremonial Crux: Removing a Man's Sandal as a Female Gesture of Contempt," *JBL* 96 (1977) 332–36; Neufeld, *Ancient Hebrew Marriage Laws*, pp. 34–36; H.-F. Richter, "Zum Levirat im Buch Ruth," *ZAW* 95 (1983) 125–26. Some see rabbinic law going the next step in that it virtually eliminates the possibility of anyone serving as a levir.

exilic), so it represents a re-expansion of the pool of who could serve as a levir.[36] A third group despairs of resolving the issue of the date of Ruth, and they also tend to argue that the marriage of Ruth and Boaz is something other than a levirate marriage. For these interpreters, there are only two passages concerning levirate marriage, and Deut 25:5–10 is the later of the two.[37]

I am skeptical of such reconstructions. The reasons for my skepticism will become clear as I proceed. Basically, I believe that the narrative examples of levirate marriage (Genesis 38 and Ruth 4) and particularly the levirate law (Deut 25:5–10) have been read too narrowly. The former usually do not provide explanations for why certain things regarding the levirate are done; yet, they are read as "normative" for their time.[38] More troublesome is the way in which the levirate law is virtually always read as if it intends to provide a comprehensive definition of levirate marriage in Israel. I will show why I think such an assumption is unwarranted.

What follows, then, is a brief treatment of Genesis 38 and Ruth 4 which, in comparison with the materials already surveyed, will help to expand our understanding of the Israelite background from which we should interpret the levirate law. This will be followed by a more detailed analysis of the levirate law itself, in which I will highlight the role played by the city elders.

Genesis 38

The story of Judah's family and Tamar (Genesis 38) provides the most explicit example of levirate marriage in the Hebrew Bible (see preceding chapter for additional comments). Many commentators argue that it reflects a pre-Deuteronomic stage in the custom's development. They do so for a simple reason: the levirate law mentions only a brother-in-law as a possible levir,

---

[36] J. Morgenstern, "The Book of the Covenant," *HUCA* 7 (1930) 180–83; Phillips, *Deuteronomy*, pp. 168–69; Davies, "Inheritance Rights," pp. 264–67.

[37] Belkin, "Levirate and Agnate Marriage," pp. 284–88; Gordis, "Love, Marriage, and Business," pp. 243–52, 259 n. 7; Leggett, *Levirate and Goel*, pp. 162–63; Sonsino, *Motive Clauses*, p. 20; D. R. G. Beattie, "The Book of Ruth as Evidence for Israelite Legal Practice," *VT* 24 (1974) 251–67.

[38] See M. Burrows, "Levirate Marriage in Israel," *JBL* 59 (1940) 23; Beattie, "Book of Ruth," pp. 260–61.

while this story has the widow's father-in-law ultimately fulfilling that function. The understanding is that the Deuteronomic law intends to restrict previous practice, such as that portrayed in Genesis 38; therefore, Deut 25:5–10 reflects a stage in levirate marriage that is later than that reflected in the Judah-Tamar story.[39] I shall say more about that shortly. First, we need to see precisely what is the evidence provided by this story. The pertinent information comes primarily from Gen 38:6–11:

> Judah took a wife for Er his firstborn, and her name was Tamar. But Er, Judah's firstborn, was wicked in the sight of the Lord; and the Lord slew him. Then Judah said to Onan, "Go in to your brother's wife, and perform the duty of a brother-in-law to her, and raise up offspring for your brother." But Onan knew that the offspring would not be his; so when he went in to his brother's wife he spilled the semen on the ground, lest he should give offspring to his brother. And what he did was displeasing in the sight of the Lord, and he slew him also. Then Judah said to Tamar his daughter-in-law, "Remain a widow in your father's house, till Shelah my son grows up"—for he feared that he would die, like his brothers. So Tamar went and dwelt in her father's house.

A few subsequent statements also figure into one's interpretation of the levirate aspects of the story. The writer explains Tamar's decision to seduce Judah in verse 14b by saying, "for she saw that Shelah was grown up, and she had not been given to him in marriage." When Judah is notified that she is pregnant "by harlotry" (לזנונים), he demands/commands that she be burned (v 24). She then produces the tokens he had left with her, and, "Judah acknowledged [the tokens] and said, 'She is more righteous than I, inasmuch as I did not give her to my son Shelah.' And he did not lie with her again" (v 26). Further, there are three genealogical texts which include Judah and his immediate descendants (Gen 46:12; Num 26:19–22; 1 Chr 2:3–6). All three refer to the twins born to Tamar as Judah's "sons," who shared a common status with Er, Onan, and Shelah in the lineage. This information raises a series of interpretive uncertainties, none of which can be resolved with absolute confidence. These will be

---

[39] Neufeld, *Ancient Hebrew Marriage Laws*, pp. 34–43. Arguing against this conclusion is Beattie, "Book of Ruth," pp. 260–61.

addressed first in regard to the possible motivations for the actions of Judah, Tamar, and Onan, then in regard to the ultimate outcome of those actions.

First, there is no indication that levirate marriage is mandated by law in this story,[40] nor does Tamar's father insist on it; so, Judah's motivations for using this custom might be personal. That he is able to do so is a reflection of his patriarchal authority; it is his right, but not an externally-bound obligation.[41] Analogous situations in other societies indicate that he probably could have gone to Tamar's father to "undo" the marriage, prompting a return of wedding gifts by both families. His reason for choosing levirate marriage instead is not divulged, but there probably were economic considerations (e.g., the amount of Tamar's dowry) which made it more attractive. It is also logical to assume that his precarious status as a "sojourner" made it harder for him to arrange marriages for his sons which would build the strength of his lineage. In any case, the fact that he calls on Onan to "perform the duty of a brother-in-law" toward Tamar indicates that he has decided not to pursue the legal dissolution of his marriage agreement with Tamar's father. Once that decision is made, it is only Judah's authority as *paterfamilias* which compels its execution. Thus, Judah's decision to call for levirate marriage is optional, a matter of personal choice; but once it has been called for by Judah, it is obligatory upon his sons (and himself).[42]

It seems obvious, however, that Tamar desires a levirate for her own reasons. The strength of her desire is demonstrated by the extreme measures which she employs to be able to have a child through a levir. Verse 14 indicates that Tamar expected to be married to Shelah; yet, her seduction of Judah shows that being married was of secondary importance. Her primary concern is that she bear a child.[43] This is the means by which she would begin to

---

[40] In fact, the story gives no direct indication that there was any legal authority in the area at all, besides that of Judah himself.

[41] See Leggett, *Levirate and Goel*, pp. 37–39.

[42] Judah's declaration that Tamar is more righteous than he is in regard to their respective obligations toward Er (Belkin, "Levirate and Agnate Marriage," p. 278).

[43] "In terms of long-range security in the social structure, it is more important for a woman to become her children's mother than her husband's wife." S. Niditch, "The Wronged Woman Righted: An Analysis of Genesis 38,"

attain her own goals. Not just any father would do, though. She specifically sets out to seduce Judah, and no one else. Why? Two "wishes" are granted by such an action: the meeting of her physical needs until her children are grown, and personal vindication.

There is no mention made of meeting Tamar's physical needs in the story, but the overwhelming evidence of the plight of widows in such a situation indicates that the concern would be a given.[44] The ostensible impetus behind this desire would have been loyalty toward her first husband,[45] but there probably were other considerations as well. An important issue in understanding her viewpoint is Tamar's status throughout the story. The evidence is ambiguous.[46] In verse 9 she is approached by Onan as "his brother's wife" (see below); yet, in v 14, she is waiting to be given "in marriage" to Shelah. Perhaps she is thought of as "betrothed" to Shelah, because of his young age.[47] She is living in her father's house, yet she is obviously desirous to be out of his house and back in the house of Judah. It is possible that she is considered an embarrassment or at least a liability in her father's house.[48] Even though enough time has passed for Shelah to become "grown up," she still wears the clothing of a widow (vv 12–14). She is discouraging other potential suitors by doing so, obviously "saving herself" for Shelah; yet she remains in her father's house. The

---

HTR 72 (1979) 145. Cp. Belkin, "Levirate and Agnate Marriage," p. 283; George Coats, "Widow's Rights: A Crux in the Structure of Genesis 38," *CBQ* 34 (1972) 463–66. A good illustration of this is provided by 2 Kgs 4:11–37.

[44] F. C. Fensham, "Widow, Orphan, and the Poor in Ancient Near Eastern Legal and Wisdom Literature," *JNES* 21 (1962) 129–39.

[45] Pedersen, *Israel* I–II, pp. 79–80.

[46] A debate between the schools of Hillel and Shammai over this issue was never resolved (Belkin, "Levirate and Agnate Marriage," pp. 305–18).

[47] Belkin ("Levirate and Agnate Marriage," pp. 279–80) says that Tamar's marriage to Er had not been dissolved when she returned to her father's house. This would imply that she was still considered Er's wife when Onan went to her. Cp. Coats, "Widow's Rights," p. 463. The fact that she is accused of "harlotry" rather than "adultery" (cp. Deut 22:21) might imply that she is not thought of as a married woman; but additional study is needed to evaluate that.

[48] Niditch labels such a woman "a sociological misfit," who needs a levirate relationship to reaffirm her place within her husband's family ("Wronged Woman Righted," pp. 146–48).

financial implications of this arrangement on Tamar and her father are unclear, but it is likely that this was not what either of them preferred in that respect.[49] Also, a person (potential suitor?) observing this situation who does not have the vantage point of the "omniscient narrator" might assume that the deaths of Er and Onan and the reluctance of Judah regarding Shelah were all somehow Tamar's fault. It is likely, then, that Tamar is motivated not only by loyalty, but by an apprehension about her own welfare as an unmarried—and possibly cursed[50]—adult woman. By seducing Judah and having a child by him, she will demonstrate her own blessed status before God, expose the fact that Judah's withholding of Shelah is unjust, provide "legal" offspring for her late husband, and acquire her own financial support. An arrangement initially chosen by a father concerned about socioeconomic strength is ultimately brought to fruition as a result of a widow's concerns for her own welfare and personal vindication.

Tamar's motives contrast markedly to Onan's. Her shameful-looking deception brings honor upon herself, because it furthers the cause of the family group; Onan's honorable-looking deception brings shame and divine wrath down upon himself, because it reflects a self-centeredness that would be frowned upon in the community. Onan would have appeared to be doing the honorable thing by going in to Tamar, because it would then be his word against hers that he had actually performed his levirate duty.[51] Her "failure" to bear a child for her dead husband could be seen as just that: her failure. The deceptiveness of Onan's act goes a long way toward explaining God's reaction. No other human could know the truth of what had transpired, so God alone could mete out justice.

But that is only a partial explanation. Onan's action is wrong not simply because it is deceptive; it also betrays a "hateful"

---

[49] MAL A¶25 stipulates that a woman in Tamar's situation is expected to return her dead husband's marriage gifts to her brothers-in-law. Apparently this was a legally complex situation, because there are several other Middle Assyrian laws which begin with the premise, "If a [married] woman is residing in her own father's house..." (¶¶26–27, 32–33, 36, 38).

[50] It is "poetic justice" that she uses shameful means to restore her honor.

[51] T. and D. Thompson, "Some Legal Problems," pp. 93–94; L. Mars, "What Was Onan's Crime?" *CompStudSocHist* 26 (1984) 435–37.

attitude toward his dead brother.[52] In other words, his action demonstrates a blatant disregard for the love which should exist between brothers.

> The point which emerges clearly from the story is that levirate proclaims the separate identity of individual siblings and attempts, ...by virtue of the moral bonds between them, to maintain and preserve the individual identity of one beyond his normal life span by the sacrifice of at least part of the individuality of the other. It is this *self*-sacrifice so that another may "live" which Onan rejects and which constitutes the heart of levirate.[53]

There is then, an inherently personal animosity suggested by a refusal to serve as a levir. The perpetuation of a man's "name" meant sustaining his very being; it meant maintaining the existence of his soul, in some sense. "In the name lies the whole substance of the man's soul; if it is killed, then there is only absolute emptiness."[54] The man who refuses to perform this duty for his own brother is robbing him of his most important quality, in the minds of his peers. This refusal would have been perceived as a sign of great selfishness. Such selfishness strikes at the heart of the natural covenantal bond which is essential to group cohesion in kinship societies.[55]

In this, then, we see that the story exposes a very personal struggle, a struggle between Onan's base self-interests and a

[52] Mars argues "that Onan's crime was not coitus interruptus but was in fact murder" ("What Was Onan's Crime?" pp. 435–38). A legal "equality" between "hatred" toward a brother and "murder" is suggested by Matt 5:21–26 and 1 John 3:11–18.

[53] Abrahams, "Some Aspects of Levirate," p. 167. Cp. Mars, "What Was Onan's Crime?" pp. 432–35.

[54] Pedersen, *Israel* I–II, pp. 255–56. In the same context, Pedersen writes, "The extermination of the name is the strongest expression of annihilation... Nothing has such an effect in Israel as the danger that the name may be exterminated."

De Vaux (*Ancient Israel*, p. 166) notes that a part of the reason for the strong desire to maintain one's inheritance was the need to retain the family tomb; see Burrows, "Ancient Oriental Background," p. 2.

[55] "The phrase 'Mind your own business' has a much deeper meaning than just an impolite reproach. It contradicts the entire concept of the collective responsibility structure of the co-liable unit" (Ginat, *Blood Disputes*, p. 94; cp. Davies, "Inheritance Rights," pp. 257–60).

highly-honored ideal of making the welfare of the broader group one's top priority. Tamar's actions are ultimately viewed as "righteous" because she endures the shame of prostitution for the good of the family; Onan's actions are "displeasing in the sight of the Lord" because they are self-serving at the expense of the group. This struggle epitomizes the dilemma faced by members of kinship-based communities in making many of their decisions about an appropriate course of action. "By its very nature and operation [levirate marriage] pits motives of kinship, loyalty and piety against enduring self-interest and selfishness."[56] In Israelite thought, this is reinforced theologically, as Yahweh himself calls on individuals to place the welfare of the group before their own. Onan is loathe to do this, yet he wants to receive the honor due to one who has. This is another significant part of the explanation for Yahweh's strong reaction to Onan's deception.

A more specific motivation for Onan's refusal to perform his levirate duties is somewhat elusive. The text simply says that "Onan knew that the offspring would not be his" (v 9). It is rightfully assumed that there are economic implications to this, that bearing "offspring" for Er would somehow affect Onan's economic well-being and his inheritance. The exact nature of these consequences is not clear, though. It could be that Er's share of the inheritance would fall to Onan, that he would get the eldest brother's share plus his own, if Er had no offspring.[57] It could be that the inheritance would now be split two ways (between Onan and Shelah) rather than three, with Onan getting the double-share of the eldest son; but there is no hint that Shelah might have benefited from Onan's deception. It is unclear whether all of Tamar's offspring would belong to Er, or just the firstborn. The latter might be suggested by Deut 25:6, but no such distinction is made between the twins who are born. If all of Tamar's children are regarded as Judah's offspring, then this would require Onan to have (and support) two wives, two families.[58] The financial

---

[56] Brichto, "Kin, Cult, Land," p. 17; cp. Belkin, "Levirate and Agnate Marriage," p. 279; Manor, "Brief History," pp. 135–36; Mars, "What Was Onan's Crime?" pp. 429–38.

[57] T. and D. Thompson, "Some Legal Problems," pp. 93–94; Brichto, "Kin, Cult, Land," p. 16.

[58] Neufeld, *Ancient Hebrew Marriage Laws*, p. 49.

burden (and psychological toll; see Abraham's family) of such a situation might have seemed too daunting to this young man. Whatever his reservations, Onan refuses to carry out his brotherly obligations apparently to further his own interests, bringing divine disapproval upon himself.[59] In contrast, Tamar endures personal humiliation for the sake of Er's "name" and is declared righteous. Together, they display the competing interests that probably existed any time such a situation arose.

While the adduced motives behind the actions of Judah, Onan, and Tamar help to suggest a reasonable understanding of the "pros and cons" of levirate marriage, the ultimate effects of their actions raise a few additional questions about the execution of the custom. A central question concerns Judah's right even to function as a levir for his dead son.[60] There are several examples from present-day societies of a widow's father-in-law serving as the levirate on behalf of his dead son (see above), and HL ¶193 acknowledges the same among the Hittites. This possibility is not mentioned in the Deuteronomic levirate law, however, prompting many commentators to conclude that this story reflects an earlier stage in Israel's legal history, when a broader circle of the deceased's relatives could serve as his levir. Ultimately, however, additional examples are needed to confirm or refute this conclusion.

Related questions remain regarding Tamar's fate following the births of Perez and Zerah. She had been living with her own father since the death of Onan, but it is doubtful that she continued to do so after they are born. The genealogical evidence suggests that she and her children were raised in Judah's house. Nothing is said, though, about her subsequent legal status. It seems most likely that she lived in Judah's house as his daughter-in-law. The note that Judah "did not lie with her again" would

---

[59] For additional proposals, see Leggett, *Levirate and Goel*, pp. 30–31 n. 5.

[60] Most regard this as a "levirate relationship" that falls short of being a marriage. See von Rad, *Genesis*, p. 356; Belkin, "Levirate and Agnate Marriage," p. 279; Coats, "Widow's Rights," pp. 461–66; Manor, "Brief History," p. 135. Leggett hints that it might be inaccurate to designate this a levirate relationship at all (*Levirate and Goel*, pp. 35–37). If he is correct, then we would have to conclude that there was another custom in Israel that fulfilled precisely the same function as a levirate relationship: it perpetuated the name of a dead man through his widow's offspring.

THE LEVIRATE LAW

seem pointless *unless* she was living in his house. Also, the genealogical note in 1 Chr 2:4 refers to her as his daughter-in-law.[61]

Additional clarity is achieved by considering the fact that no mention is made of Onan's own need for "offspring" in this story. Judah instructs Onan "to raise up offspring for your brother" (v 9). The same concern is not expressed following Onan's death; no steps are taken to "raise up offspring" for him. What makes his situation different? It is not the fact that Onan's death is the result of divine wrath, for the same was true in Er's case. The difference between Er and Onan is that Er had a wife when he died.[62] It is possible that Onan was married to Tamar, but that she was not his "wife;" that is, Tamar is married to Onan but is considered Er's wife (see n. 47). Onan is merely a surrogate for his dead brother. Just as "the offspring would not be his" (legally speaking), Tamar was not "his." Yet he would still be responsible to provide for her and "the offspring" as any husband/father should provide for his family. This helps to explain why any brother might hesitate before he entered into a levirate marriage.

This raises a final question about what light Judah's genealogical record sheds on our understanding of Israelite levirate. The three genealogical passages mentioning Judah's family (Gen 46:12; Num 26:19–22; 1 Chr 2:3–6) list Perez and Zerah as sons of Judah and (half-)brothers to Er, Onan, and Shelah. They also add that Er and Onan died in Canaan (that they did not move with Jacob's family to Egypt). The texts do not explain the implications of this in terms of inheritance and/or the "name" of the deceased or that Perez and Zerah were technically

[61] The same genealogical texts mention a lineage for Shelah. This implies that he married another woman later. It is likely that Judah's relations with Tamar would have made her previously-anticipated marriage to Shelah incestuous (but see Manor, "Brief History," p. 135).

[62] In the other levirate passages, concern is expressed over the "name" of the deceased. The present line of thinking implies that an Israelite man did not have his own "name" until he was married. I have not worked out the implications of such an hypothesis, though. I would guess that the acquisition of a "name" is somehow tied to the apportionment of an inheritance by a father as part of his son's marriage; but we would need specific examples to confirm this. See below, on Ruth 4.

the "offspring" of Er.[63] The names of Er and Onan are still mentioned in the genealogies, even though they have no heirs. Does this mean that their "names" have been perpetuated? We do not know. As for inheritance, analogies suggest that Perez and Zerah could have been considered sons of both Er and Judah until they chose which was to be their true "father." Or it could be that they replaced Er as heirs of an inheritance from Judah. The biblical texts do not clarify this point. Without additional information, it is impossible to draw any firm conclusions.

Ruth 4:1–17

The story of Ruth and Boaz shares some important characteristics with that of Tamar and Judah. In both stories, an Israelite man dies, leaving a childless non-Israelite widow behind. In both stories, the young widow uses "questionable" means to get a new husband from among her first husband's kinsmen. In both stories, someone more distant than a brother fathers offspring through the widow on behalf of the deceased, even though someone more closely related is still alive. Characters in the later story even refer back to the Tamar-Judah story in the process of pronouncing a blessing over Ruth and Boaz, thereby highlighting the thematic connections between the two couples.[64]

There are also some significant differences between the two stories which need to be evaluated. The most significant is that the root בם׳ does not appear in reference to the Ruth- Boaz marriage (see Gen 38:8–9; Deut 25:5, 7, 9). Instead, the role played by Naomi's kinsman and Boaz is referred to as "redeemer" (גאל; see Ruth 3:9, 12, 13; 4:4, 6–8, 14). This has led some to argue that the Ruth-Boaz marriage is not "levirate marriage."[65] I will address this again in the light of the preceding surveys. A couple

---

[63] See Mars, "What Was Onan's Crime?" p. 438.

[64] See Burrows, "Levirate Marriage in Israel," p. 23; Niditch, "Wronged Woman Righted," p. 147.

[65] See, e.g., Driver, *Deuteronomy*, pp. 284–85; Belkin, "Levirate and Agnate Marriage," pp. 284–88; Gordis, "Love, Marriage, and Business," pp. 246–52; Beattie, "Book of Ruth," p. 265; J. M. Sasson, "The Issue of *Ge'ullah* in *Ruth*," *JSOT* 5 (1978) 52–64, esp. p. 64 n. 2; Manor, "Brief History," pp. 137–38; and references in Leggett, *Levirate and Goel*, p. 5.

of textual problems have muddied the waters even more. Other issues impinging on one's interpretation of this story arise mainly from uncertainties about Naomi's authority and powers in relation to the property of her own late husband. Finally, the role played by city elders in such a case is explicitly mentioned in Ruth 4. That information will help us more directly in our investigation of the role of the elders in Deut 25:5–10.

Several aspects of the story of Boaz and Ruth can be better elucidated with the help of comparative anthropology. Particular pieces of the story most directly touch on questions related to levirate marriage and related practices. The first, which in some ways foreshadows the ending, comes in Ruth 1:11. The widowed Naomi mentions the possibility of yet bearing sons who could become husbands for her widowed daughters-in-law. The fact that she mentions this indicates that it would be allowed by custom/law. The reason why it is not a possibility is that (a) she has no husband to father such a child, and/or (b) she herself is past the age of bearing children. This shows that the Israelites accepted at some period in their history the practice mentioned in Assyrian law (and found in many present-day societies) of having a widow marry her husband's son (by another wife) as a form of levirate.[66] This is the first hint in this story that the goals of a levirate union could be accomplished through a male relative other than a brother of the deceased.

The next hints of a possible levirate arrangement appear in Ruth 3. Naomi initiates the process by suggesting that she should find a home for Ruth (3:1). This most typically would mean becoming a wife (cp. 1:9).[67] This task would normally have fallen to Ruth's father-in-law or her own father. The former, of course, is already dead, and Ruth has abandoned her ties to the latter, who lives in a different land. Boaz's response to Ruth shows that he understands her advances as leading toward marriage. In particular, his comment that she could have gone after younger

---

[66] For opposing interpretations of Naomi's words, see Leggett, *Levirate and Goel*, pp. 174–79; Beattie, "Book of Ruth," pp. 264–65.

[67] Brichto, "Kin, Cult, Land," pp. 13–14; Leggett, *Levirate and Goel*, pp. 189–90.

men and that they could be "poor or rich" (3:10) indicates that she
is seeking more than simple redemption of property.[68]
The fact that Naomi suggests that Ruth approach Boaz rather
than the closer kinsman reflects, in my mind, the fact that a
widow had some say in "acquiring" a levir.[69] Boaz's own response
(3:10–13) furthers this impression in two ways. He acknowledges
that there is a nearer kinsman who must be given the option first
(for reasons of honor?), yet he does not in any way deny that Ruth
has the right to request that Boaz become her husband.[70] Another
way in which Boaz indicates that Ruth has some say in the matter
is the fact that Ruth turns to him rather than some younger
man.[71] The survey of analogous societies given above indicates
that it is common for a widow to look to her late husband's
younger relatives to serve as a levir, primarily because a younger
man can be expected to provide support for a widow for more years
than could an older man. This clarifies an important dimension to
Boaz's comment in v 10: "May you be blessed by the Lord, my
daughter; you have made this last kindness greater than the first,
in that you have not gone after young men, whether poor or rich."
It would have been more natural for her to show her "kindness"
(again revealing her choice in the matter) to a poor young man
rather than Boaz; with Boaz, Ruth runs a greater risk of being

---

[68] Leggett, *Levirate and Goel*, pp. 193–201; Th. C. Vriezen, "Two Old
Cruces," *OTS* 5 (1948) 86; F. W. Bush, *Ruth, Esther* (WBC; Dallas: Word
Books, 1996), pp. 166–69.

[69] Leggett, *Levirate and Goel*, pp. 195–96, 206. Coats ("Widow's Rights,"
pp. 464–65) argues that Naomi assists Ruth here with the sole intent of
providing a man by whom Ruth could conceive a child, that there was no
guarantee that marriage would follow. It is implausible, though, that a widow
would not think beyond the stage of conception. It would have been very
difficult to live as a woman with a child without a man to provide a house and
sustenance. Certainly, other arrangements besides marriage might be
sufficient; but to imply (as Coats does) that a widow was only concerned
about becoming pregnant does not do justice to the whole picture.

[70] Belkin, "Levirate and Agnate Marriage," p. 287. She does not have the
final say, because the kinsman could have chosen to take Ruth in marriage.
This simply shows that she could let her wishes be known.

[71] It is likely that the kinsman is younger than Boaz. If so, that might
help explain his reluctance to take on levirate responsibilities. A younger
man probably would have still been concerned about developing his own
financial stability.

widowed again before her children are old enough to provide for her, and losing Boaz's wealth in trying to survive. Her willingness to rely on an older man demonstrates the same willingness to take a chance for others as she displayed toward Naomi. This is expressed by Boaz in his blessing.

The story quickly moves to its climax, as Boaz calls together the local elders and other leading citizens to negotiate for the inheritance of Elimelech and the hand of Ruth. This scene is occasionally cited as a classic example of an Israelite legal proceeding,[72] even though there have been numerous little debates over the exact interpretation of various details. One of the more notable of these has been the debate over the classification of the marriage that Boaz arranges. The majority of interpreters assume that the marriage is levirate. This has been challenged at times, primarily because of the absence of any use of the root יבם in reference to the marriage, coupled with the fact that the function Boaz assumes from the nearer kinsman is referred to as "redeemer" (גאל; 3:12; 4:1, 3, 6, 8), whose job it is to "redeem" (גאל) Ruth (3:13; cp. 4:4, 6, 7). For this reason, it has sometimes been called a "redeemer-marriage" (for which there are no exact parallels), or simply the second marriage of a childless widow. There is the additional argument that the levirate law mentions only a brother serving as levir, while Boaz is a more distant relative.[73] The evidence provided in the preceding surveys shows that such a restriction would constitute a narrower understanding

---

[72] See Köhler, *Hebrew Man*, pp. 128–29; Evans, "Ancient Mesopotamian Assemblies," pp. 2–3; Boecker, *Law*, pp. 31–33.

[73] Burrows, "Levirate Marriage in Israel," p. 23; idem, "Marriage of Boaz and Ruth," p. 445; L. M. Epstein, *Marriage Laws in the Bible and the Talmud* (Cambridge: Harvard University, 1942), pp. 85–88; Beattie, "Book of Ruth," pp. 260–67; Gordis, "Love, Marriage, and Business," pp. 246–48; but see Leggett, *Levirate and Goel*, pp. 193–201; Richter, "Zum Levirat," pp. 123–26; Théo R. Schneider, "Translating Ruth 4.1–10 among the Tsonga People," *BibTr* 33 (1982) 301–302.

Jack Sasson proposes a slightly different solution. He suggests that redemption pertains only to what the kinsman or Boaz does for Naomi, while the marriage of Ruth is a completely separate concern. Sasson, "Issue of *Ge'ullah*," pp. 52–64. The greatest weakness (acknowledged by Sasson, p. 58) to this proposal is that Bcaz pledges to act as a redeemer for Ruth (3:13). See also D. R. G. Beattie, "Redemption in Ruth, and Related Matters: A Response to Jack M. Sasson," *JSOT* 5 (1978) 65–68.

of levirate marriage than is held in most societies in which the levirate is used, where almost any close male relative is eligible to serve as a levir on behalf of the deceased. The more important criterion for designating a marriage as "levirate," in the minds of modern researchers, is the placement of the couple's offspring in the descent lines. Boaz's stated goal in the marriage is "to restore/perpetuate the name of the dead in his inheritance, that the name of the dead may not be cut off..." (4:5, 10; cp. Deut 25:6, 7). This fits precisely the standard definition of levirate marriage.[74]

One must still address the fact that the writer consistently refers to the role to be played by Boaz as "redeemer" (גאל). This might imply that he and his audience distinguished between what Boaz does in marrying Ruth and what a "levir" (יבם) did. The most common proposal is that they distinguished between marriages involving a "levir" and marriages involving a "redeemer" (i.e., a brother or more distant relative; see Lev 25:48–49). Dale Manor has proposed that it is a matter of primacy. In levirate marriage, the widow is the primary concern and the property is secondary; in redeemer marriage, the reverse is true.[75] This is based primarily on the fact that the negotiations between Boaz and the other kinsman begin with the property and then move to Ruth. This basis is too narrow to confirm this proposal. I would suggest that, if there is any significant distinction between redemption and levirate,[76] it might be a sequential one. The laws on "redemption" (Lev 25:25–55) explain what is to happen after

---

[74] Belkin, "Levirate and Agnate Marriage," pp. 285–86; Brichto, "Kin, Cult, Land," p. 12 n. 16; Richter, "Zum Levirat," p. 125. For oppsoing arguments, see Bush, *Ruth, Esther*, pp. 221–27.

[75] Manor, "Brief History," p. 138. Beattie cites a similar opinion espoused by the medieval Qaraite, Salmon ben Yeroham. He held that יבם applies to a man's rights over a widow only, while גאל applied to widows and property together ("Book of Ruth," p. 259).

[76] Several see redemption and levirate as similar or complementary practices. See Neufeld, *Ancient Hebrew Marriage Laws*, pp. 37–39; de Vaux, *Ancient Israel*, pp. 38, 166; Benjamin, *Deuteronomy and City Life*, p. 247. Schneider, "Translating, Ruth 4.1–10," pp. 302–308; Manor, "Brief History," pp. 137–38; R. L. Hubbard, Jr., *The Book of Ruth* (NICOT; Grand Rapids: Eerdmans, 1988), pp. 238–47; Davies, "Inheritance Rights," pp. 257–61; R. Westbrook, *Property and the Family in Biblical Law* (JSOTS 113; Sheffield: Sheffield Academic, 1991), pp. 63–68.

property has been sold or a person has become indentured to another family. Of special significance here is the stipulation in Lev 25:47–49:

> If a stranger or a sojourner with you becomes rich, and your brother beside him becomes poor and sells himself to the stranger or sojourner with you, or to a member of the stranger's family, then after he is sold he may be redeemed; one of his brothers may redeem him, or his uncle, or his cousin may redeem him, or a near kinsman belonging to his family may redeem him; or if he grows rich he may redeem himself.

Redemption is a way for one family to regain control of something or someone which/who was sold to another family. Perhaps the term גאל is used in the story of Ruth because the property has already been sold to an outsider (see below). In contrast, a simple levirate marriage involves the direct transfer of "ownership" and responsibilities from one kinsman to another, without the intermediate transfer to another family. If this is correct, then the transaction negotiated in Ruth 4 is designated גאילה because of how it fits into an overall sequence of transactions; it reverses a prior transfer of ownership between families. There are also a couple of "wrinkles" in this situation because a foreign childless widow is involved. They will be addressed shortly.

Like any other proposed explanation of what transpires in Ruth 4, this one requires that we supplement the information actually given in the text with what is, at best, only inferred. The biggest hurdle to overcome is the virtual silence in the text on the prior transaction which redemption would reverse. This problem has been raised in a slightly different way in several previous investigations regarding Ruth 4:3. Boaz begins formal proceedings by stating that Naomi "has sold the portion of the field which belonged to our brother Elimelech." Numerous questions arise from this statement. Has the field already been sold, or is Naomi simply in the process of selling it? What had happened with this field during the family's ten-year absence? Was Naomi the owner of the field, or its trustee on Elimelech's behalf? Why did Ruth glean in Boaz's field if Naomi possessed a field of her own? There are no clear-cut answers to these questions. What follows is but an educated guess.[77]

There are at least two aspects of Naomi's situation with parallels in the Hebrew Bible. The "malelessness" of her family is similar to that of the daughters of Zelophehad, who inherited their father's property when he died and left no male heirs (Num 27:1–11; 36:1–12). The problem then becomes providing male heirs for subsequent generations who can work the land, which the daughters of Zelophehad were able to do through marriage. This implies, though, that females could control (own? hold in trust?) property in Israel.[78] The other parallel exists in the case of the Shunammite woman in the stories of Elisha. Her family abandons their property during a famine, and the crown claims ownership. Upon her return, the king does the righteous thing and restores the property to the widow and her son (2 Kgs 8:1–6). The king refers to the property as "her house and her field" (v 3). Either the Shunammite and her husband had been living with her family on property given to her as a dowry, or widows naturally came into possession of their husband's property when he died and their children were still minors.[79] Naomi is in a worse predicament than those women because she is unable to bear any more sons. She has no heirs for whom she can simply hold the property. This forces her to sell it instead.

The differences that would have existed in a pre-state system can account for other differences between the Shunammite's

---

[77] The following proposal parallels in many ways the interpretation of Westbrook, *Property*, pp. 63–68. The primary differences involve Naomi's rights concerning land and the significance of Ruth's foreign status.

[78] There are varying opinions about whether the widow inherited and owned the property, or simply held it on her husband's behalf. See Burrows, "Marriage of Boaz and Ruth," p. 448; Neufeld, *Ancient Hebrew Marriage Laws*, pp. 240–41; Rowley, "Marriage of Ruth," p. 184; Brichto, "Kin, Cult, Land," p. 18; Leggett, *Levirate and Goel*, pp. 212–18; Gordis, "Love, Marriage, and Business," pp. 255–59; Beattie, "Book of Ruth," pp. 254–56; Z. Ben-Barak, "Inheritance by Daughters in the Ancient Near East," *JSS* 25 (1980) 22–33; Davies, "Inheritance Rights," pp. 138–39; S. Niditch, "Legends of Heroes and Heroines," in *The Hebrew Bible and Its Modern Interpreters*, ed. D. A. Knight and G. M. Tucker (Philadelphia: Fortress Press; Chico, CA: Scholars Press, 1985), p. 452; Westbrook, *Property*, pp. 64–65.

[79] See Burrows, "Marriage of Boaz and Ruth," p. 448; Beattie, "Book of Ruth," p. 256.

situation and Naomi's. It is likely that Elimelech's kinsmen "held" his land,[80] that this was known by the Bethlehem elders, and that the land was granted to Naomi (in the absence of any male family members) upon her return. The fact that Ruth still has to glean elsewhere is not surprising. She and Naomi apparently return to Bethlehem near harvest-time, so they could not have planted a crop until the following season. If there had not been enough men in the family to work that particular field the previous season, the field would have lain fallow. Naomi could have sold the field any time after her return, apparently to another family which did have the means and manpower to work it in the near future.

Like any other property that passed from one family to another, Elimelech's land could be redeemed by one of his relatives. This could happen even several years after the initial sale, and the new owner apparently could not refuse the redemption. For this reason, it is quite plausible to translate the verb מָכְרָה ("has sold") in Ruth 4:3 as a simple past or perfect tense verb. It is not necessary to assume that Naomi is only in the process of selling;[81] in fact, the use of the same verb tense in the redemption laws makes the simple past or perfect the most likely rendering of the verb.[82]

At the prompting of Ruth, Boaz now steps forward to press for redemption in a very honorable way. He expresses his own resolve to redeem, but he first allows the nearer kinsman the privilege of doing so himself. It is harvest-time, and we can assume that each was best able to make such a purchase at that time of the year. The kinsman, who would normally have been expected by the

---

[80] Burrows, "Marriage of Boaz and Ruth," p. 447; H. H. Rowley, "The Marriage of Ruth," *HTR* 40 (1947) 88.

[81] So Leggett, *Levirate and Goel*, pp. 89, 218–22; Gordis, "Love, Marriage, and Business," pp. 255–56; Hubbard, *Book of Ruth*, p. 239; Bush, *Ruth, Esther*, pp. 211–15.

[82] Cp. Westbrook, *Property*, pp. 65–67; Brichto, "Kin, Cult, Land," pp. 14–15. Brichto believes that the field was sold by Elimelech prior to his moving to Moab. This does not explain, however, why Naomi is the one credited with selling the field.

Beattie ("Book of Ruth," pp. 257–58) raises the issue of "absolute rights" of ownership in cases of redemption. The (literally) bigger question left unanswered is the relationship between an individual's ownership of property, claims held by one's family, and the idea of clan or tribal domain.

family to make such a redemption, is now prodded into action by Boaz, and he pledges to do so.

It is at this point (Ruth 4:5) that the most puzzling aspect of the negotiations surface—Ruth's relationship to the field in question. Part of the problem is reflected in two textual variants in this verse, but it probably is complicated by Ruth's foreign status. The first variant raises the possibility that Ruth is a co-owner with Naomi of the field. The MT reading has Boaz saying, "On the day you buy the field from the hand of Naomi and from Ruth the Moabite, then [also] the wife of the dead man you will buy..." There are two reasons for rejecting this reading in favor of the reading of the Vulgate ("...from the hand of Naomi, then Ruth the Moabite, the wife of the dead man, you also buy..."). First, the change in prepositions ("from the hand of Naomi" to "from Ruth") seems awkward. Second, the final agreement made before witnesses in 4:9–10 unequivocally states that Boaz is acquiring both the field and Ruth "from the hand of Naomi."[83]

This still leaves unanswered the question of the relationship between Ruth and the field.[84] Some regard redemption of property and levirate marriage as completely separate matters; others conclude that Ruth is somehow part of the "property" which is to be redeemed.[85] It is my opinion that the answer varies, depending on the "purchaser." Naomi's initial sale of the property to an "outsider" would not have included Ruth, because an outsider would not be acting out of any sense of obligation toward his family. It is strictly a financial transaction.[86] For an outsider to

---

[83] See Campbell, *Ruth*, p. 146; E. W. Davies, "Ruth 4:5 and the Duties of the *go'el*," *VT* 33 (1983) 234 n. 2; Bush, *Ruth, Esther*, pp. 215–19.

[84] See Leggett, *Levirate and Goel*, pp. 222–25 for further references.

[85] Burrows, "Marriage of Boaz and Ruth," p. 449; Leggett, *Levirate and Goel*, pp. 225–29; Gordis, "Love, Marriage, and Business," p. 248; Hubbard, *Book of Ruth*, pp. 243–45.

Personally, I dislike the mercantile language of this episode, as it applies to Ruth. I use it because of the use of the term "buy, purchase" throughout the story. This probably reflects the fact that the Western sense of "buy" is narrower than what the term קנה ("buy") means to imply. See the very helpful discussion of this in Schneider, "Translating Ruth 4.1–10," pp. 301–308; cp. D. Weiss, "The Use of QNY in Connection with Marriage," *HTR* 57 (1964) 244–48.

[86] The redemption laws in Leviticus are currently placed in the broader context of the Jubilee laws, which call for the eventual remanding of the

"purchase" the property and Ruth together would be to reduce the widow to the level of foreign slave. The redemption of property by a kinsman, however, is motivated primarily by a sense of obligation to one's broader family, as it is with levirate obligations. A kinsman could not do one and ignore the other, because the same motivation lies behind both.[87] This is what Boaz raises with the kinsman in v 5: that his sense of obligation to redeem the field of Elimelech should also compel him to take Ruth in levirate.

Now the need to address the second textual variant surfaces. According to the Kethibh-reading, Boaz here reveals his own desire to marry Ruth.[88] This reading does not fit the overall flow of thought very well, though. It creates a contrast between an action by the kinsman and a reaction by Boaz, suggesting that Boaz's reaction would pose something of a threat to the kinsman. "On the day that *you* purchase the field from the hand of Naomi, *I* will purchase Ruth... to raise up the name of the dead man on his inheritance." The conclusion that one would have to draw is that the kinsman would purchase the field, but then he would have to hand it over to Boaz without compensation for the sake of Ruth and Mahlon. One problem with this is it assumes that the prior rights of the kinsman apply to his right to redeem the field of the

property to its original owner's family. This would lead to the conclusion that the purchase of another family's field amounted to little more than a lease. It is generally conceded that the Jubilee laws are a late innovation. It is possible, however, that the redemption sections of these laws had existed for many years before they were overlaid with the Jubilee regulations.

[87] Leggett (*Levirate and Goel*, pp. 240–49) discusses similar proposals by B. Wambacq ("Le Mariage de Ruth," in *Melanges Eugène Tisserant*, 1, Rome, 1964, pp. 449–59), P. Cruveilhier ("Le lévirat chez les Hébreux et chez les Assyriens," *RB* 34 [1925] 524–26), and others. Wambacq argues that Ruth's status as a childless widow makes this a special case. Ordinarily, property and widow could be handled separately; but when the widow was childless, then they had to be handled jointly. It seems likely to me, however, that the kinsman would have already known this. More attractive is Cruveilhier's proposal that one's "name" was perpetuated in a combination of property and offspring. For similar views, see the references mentioned by Leggett, *Levirate and Goel*, p. 244 n. 106, and p. 246 n. 109.

[88] A few accept the Kethibh-reading, but the majority emend to the Qere-reading. For the former, see D. R. G. Beattie, "Kethibh and Qere in Ruth IV 5," *VT* 21 (1971) 490–94; Vriezen, "Two Old Cruces," pp. 80–88. For a careful refutation of these proposals, see Leggett, *Levirate and Goel*, pp. 229–37. Cp. Davies, "Ruth 4:5," p. 232; Campbell, *Ruth*, p. 146.

deceased, but not to his right to marry the widow of the deceased. This is impractical, if the marriage of the widow automatically gives her new husband ownership of the property. Another problem with this rendering is the temporal aspect of it. It implies that Boaz will not take Ruth until the kinsman purchases the field; but then, "on that day," he will assume the role of the levirate. The preferred reading, then, is the Qere-reading ("On the day you purchase the field..., you also purchase Ruth..."). This reveals Boaz's intention! to hold his kinsman responsible for taking care of Ruth.

There are some hints throughout the story to suggest that Ruth's status as a foreigner adds a special dimension to the story.[89] Her late husband's property (technically subsumed within Elimelech's) has been sold to someone outside Elimelech's family, who has no obligation to help her.[90] A typical widow in such a situation would return to her own house for protection and sustenance. But Ruth is a foreigner, dependent on the benevolence of her impoverished mother-in-law and her mother-in-law's family by marriage. Under the existing circumstances, Ruth can expect to have to go to a man outside Elimelech's family as a widowed foreigner, and as a woman who brings no dowry with her. Her prospects are indeed bleak.[91]

It is not clear how Ruth is perceived, even by those within the family. It is possible, in my opinion, that the kinsman in the story holds the view (with others in his family) that levirate obligations do not necessarily apply in this case, because the widow is a foreigner. As long as no one raises the issue, there could be an

---

[89] Leggett, *Levirate and Goel*, pp. 205–208; D. N. Fewell and D. M. Gunn, "'A Son is Born to Naomi!': Literary Allusions and Interpolation in the Book of Ruth," *JSOT* 40 (1988) 103–107; Hubbard, *Book of Ruth*, pp. 245–46, esp. n. 52; see also the comments of Cassel and Lange, quoted by Leggett, *Levirate and Goel*, p. 250 n. 125.

[90] This is not undermined by Boaz's statement that he has bought the property of Elimelech and his sons "from the hand of Naomi" (vv 5, 9). As in other cases of redemption, she continues to hold an ultimate claim to the property on behalf of the family, even though she has "sold" it to someone outside the family.

[91] Naomi's own situation is not much better. Since she has sold the field, she will soon become totally dependent on the good graces of her late-husband's relatives. They would be obligated to provide for her, and she has little left to offer in the way of compensation.

implicit agreement that those obligations can be ignored. This is why he does not initially raise the issue of Ruth when Boaz mentions the property. It is only when Boaz links performance of the duties of a levirate ("restore the name of the dead man to his inheritance") to redemption that the kinsman acknowledges (and then declines to fulfill) those obligations.[92] That Boaz might stand out from others in his family in this way is implied by the way he views Ruth at their first meeting. A servant first introduces her to him, referring to Ruth as "the Moabite maiden, who came back with Naomi from the country of Moab" (2:6). She is not designated as "the widow of Mahlon" or in some other way that would indicate her ties to the family. This classification of her could have been shared by others in the community. Even Ruth refers to herself in this way, saying to Boaz, "Why have I found favor in your eyes, that you should take notice of me, when I am a foreigner?" Boaz's comments reveal a different estimation of her. To him, she is the daughter-in-law of an Israelite woman, the widow of an Israelite man, who has left her native people and "taken refuge" under the "wings" of Israel's God (2:11–12).[93] She

---

[92] Leggett assumes that the kinsman actually was ignorant of the need to include Ruth (*Levirate and Goel*, pp. 249–50; cp. Belkin, "Levirate and Agnate Marriage," p. 285). Others reject this assumption (see Ruth 3:11; T. and D. Thompson, "Some Legal Problems," p. 98; Westbrook, *Property*, pp. 66–67). Beattie's retention of the Kethibh in 4:5 ("I will buy Ruth...") is driven primarily by the assumption that the kinsman should have known of his obligation to marry Ruth, without having to be told by Boaz ("Kethibh and Qere," p. 492; idem, "Book of Ruth," pp. 262–63). The current explanation removes that assumption. To do the one (redeem the property) and not the other (perpetuate the name of the deceased) would amount to the same sort of selfishness displayed by Onan.

Davies ("Ruth 4:5," pp. 233–34) proposes that the kinsman thought that marriage to Naomi, not Ruth, would accompany the redemption of the property. He would be willing to do this, because he could expect Naomi to die without bearing children, in which case the kinsman would gain full ownership of Elimelech's property. The problem with this proposal is that it ignores the fact that the field is being bought from Naomi.

[93] This is probably part of the reason that Naomi specifically instructs Ruth to look to Boaz when she wants to find her a good home (3:1). Other men would look upon her as a foreigner, while Boaz views her as the widow of an Israelite. For a different interpretation, see Fewell and Gunn, "'A Son is Born to Naomi!'" p. 106.

is, in his mind, to be treated as an Israelite widow would be treated.

These considerations make more understandable the kinsman's initial acceptance but eventual rejection of his redeemer obligations. He is willing to fulfill those obligations as long as the end result is economic gain for himself. His reluctance to carry out those responsibilities with the prospect of realizing no direct financial benefits is not surprising.[94] Two additional considerations might make his reluctance more acceptable to the family. First, there is another relative (Boaz) who has already expressed his own willingness to take on this potentially detrimental obligation.[95] Second, the foreign status of the widow is devoid of any inter-familial benefit that the family might have enjoyed from his marriage to a woman from a local family. Mahlon entered into the original marriage in part to improve his own status as a sojourner; no such benefit awaits one who marries Ruth now.[96]

This brings us to the act of withdrawing the sandal, which formalizes the agreement between Boaz and the kinsman.[97] The narrator introduces this scene as an act which regularly occurred in cases of "redemption and exchange" (עַל־הַגְּאֻלָּה וְעַל־הַתְּמוּרָה; v

---

[94] The financial drawbacks to levirate marriage which were noted in the case of Onan (Genesis 38) would inhere with the levirate here. See Burrows, "Marriage of Boaz and Ruth," p. 452; Belkin, "Levirate and Agnate Marriage," p. 286; Brichto, "Kin, Cult, Land," pp. 15–16; Hubbard, *Book of Ruth*, pp. 246–47; Davies, "Inheritance Rights," p. 260; Beattie, "Book of Ruth," p. 261; Westbrook, *Property*, p. 67.

[95] "The fact that Boaz, before the *go'el* refused, had already offered to take upon himself the responsibility, may well be in itself sufficient to explain the apparent lack of obligation" [on the part of the closer relative]. T. and D. Thompson, "Some Legal Problems," p. 81 n. 1. Cp. Belkin, "Levirate and Agnate Marriage," p. 287.

[96] It is also possible that Boaz is providing his kinsman with a way of saving face in the family. He might simply be allowing the kinsman the chance to express his willingness to help the cause of the family by redeeming the field that has been sold. They would then not think so harshly of him for being unwilling to take on the extra burden of supporting a childless widow as well.

[97] The LXX includes an additional clause at the end of v 8, indicating that the kinsman handed the sandal to Boaz. Apparently, וַיִּתֶּן לוֹ ("and gave it to him") was lost from the MT by haplography. See Campbell, *Ruth*, pp. 140–54, for this and other variants in the text.

7).[98] A similar action is prescribed in Deut 25:9–10, but with a significantly different intent. This has raised some questions about how the two are related, if at all.[99] There are at least three differences between the actions, as they are described: (1) the verb used to denote the withdrawing of the sandal is different in the two passages (חלץ in Deut 25:9, שלף here); (2) in the levirate law, the widow draws off the sandal, while the "seller" (the kinsman here) normally pulls off his own sandal; and, (3) the ceremony in Deut 25:9–10 is intended as a remonstrance of the unwilling levir, while this one seems totally neutral regarding any evaluation of the participants. These differences suggest that the two acts are not to be regarded as identical. The fact, however, that both involve authority over property (on the property aspect of the levirate law, see below) and the removal of a sandal does indicate that they probably are related to each other in some way.

This prompts the question about which came first, about which is the more typical ceremony and which is the variant. If one assumes that Deut 25:9–10 describes the typical ceremony, there could be several explanations for the lack of any opprobrium in the

---

[98] Brichto understands this as a hendiadys ("the transfer of the right to redemption"), with a very limited application ("Kin, Cult, Land," p. 18; cp. Burrows, "Levirate Marriage," p. 30). The admitted paucity of evidence of such transactions prohibits certainty on the matter, but I agree with the overall tenor of such a conclusion. One curious aspect of the story is the omission of any reference to the person to whom Naomi had first sold the field. I assume that this is so because (1) he cannot stand in the way of the redemption, and (2) Boaz is simply acquiring the right to redeem (Westbrook, *Property*, p. 68). The interim owner of the property is not involved at this stage, because the actual redemption transaction takes place at another time. As Schneider notes, no mention is made of money passing hands. Boaz is not buying a commodity, but rather the obligation/right to show "the gentlemanly care, the protection, the responsible action" toward Ruth ("Translating Ruth 4.1–10," p. 308).

[99] Burrows, "Levirate Marriage," p. 30; G. Evans, "'Gates' and 'Streets': Urban Institutions in Old Testament Times," *JRelHist* 2 (1962) 10; Brichto, "Kin, Cult, Land," p. 19; Phillips, *Deuteronomy*, p. 169; Leggett, *Levirate and Goel*, p. 253; Gordis, "Love, Marriage, and Business," pp. 247–48; Carmichael, "A Ceremonial Crux," pp. 323–24; Manor, "Brief History," p. 133; Niditch, "Legends of Heroes and Heroines," p. 453; Levinson, "Calum M. Carmichael's Approach," pp. 248–49.

ceremony in Ruth.[100] The narrator's introductory remark indicates, however, that neutrality was the normal intent of this ceremony, that it was simply a symbolic way of indicating that a transfer of property ownership had been finalized (cp. Pss 60:8; 108:9). This makes it more likely that the ceremony in the levirate law is a variation on a common practice, rather than the reverse. Therefore, in my discussion of Deut 25:5–10, I will consider what makes the use of the sandal in the case of the unwilling levirate different, and why the differences in the action there reflect negatively on the one whose sandal is removed.

One other matter to consider is the stated goal of Boaz's actions: "to maintain the name of the dead man upon his inheritance" (לְהָקִים שֵׁם־הַמֵּת עַל־נַחֲלָתוֹ; 4:5, 10), that it not be "cut off (יִכָּרֵת) from among his brothers and from the gate of his place" (v 10).[101] The context in which these expressions are used provides a little more clarification for our understanding of them (cp. Gen 38:8). Boaz declares that he has acquired "all which belonged to Elimelech and all which belonged to Chilion and Mahlon" (Ruth 4:9). Since Mahlon carries on Elimelech's "name" as his son, the one who "perpetuates the name" of Mahlon through offspring also carries the name of Elimelech.[102] The women of the community say, "A son has been born to Naomi" (Ruth 4:17). This statement makes it seem as if Boaz is serving as a levirate on Elimelech's behalf, which we know is not literally the case. In the genealogy at the end of the book, no mention is made of Elimelech or either of his sons. Instead, the descent line is traced through Boaz and his own blood line. What this suggests is that "perpetuating the name of the dead man" refers to maintaining his inheritance in his family—not his actual name in the lineage—even though he died without offspring of his own to

---

[100] These would include (a) the fact that this is a "redemption" (the undoing of a previous sale). Other proposals could include (b) the fact that someone else has already volunteered to perform the redemption; (c) the fact that the kinsman had already expressed his willingness to redeem the land; or (d) the fact that a foreign widow is involved could have reduced or eliminated any sense of disapproval by the family.

[101] See the more detailed discussion of Bush, *Ruth, Esther*, pp. 219–21.

[102] In a sense, Obed carries on the "names" of Elimelech and his sons and the "name" of Boaz. T. and D. Thompson, "Some Legal Problems," pp. 98–99.

inherit it from him. [103] This helps the broader family economically by maintaining the economic stability of a part of the group. It also prevents anyone from attaching blame to the dead man or his dependents for weakening the family.

The Elders in Ruth 4

The agreement between Boaz and the kinsman is reached in the presence of elders and others "in the gate."[104] Their participation gives us some insight into ways in which authority over property was recognized and monitored in Israel.[105] They do not initiate or try to influence either side in this situation. They gather at Boaz's initiative, not their own. There is no indication that they had raised this issue with anyone involved. This again suggests that the exercise of one's redeemer (or levirate) function is strictly optional; it is a right, not an absolute obligation.

It is helpful at this juncture to consider the role of witnesses from a sociological standpoint (see also Chapter 2). Members of an agricultural society often derive their personal economic strength from the possession and use of land. A primary basis for the power of the elders in local communities in such societies is acquired through the overseeing of land transfers. They directly influence local power structures in this role.[106] They maintain and

---

[103] Belkin, "Levirate and Agnate Marriage," pp. 285–86; Brichto, "Kin, Cult, Land," pp. 22–24; T. and D. Thompson, "Some Legal Problems," pp. 79, 84–88; Davies, "Inheritance Rights," pp. 141–42; Westbrook, *Property*, pp. 63–64. In Num 27:4, the "name" of Zelophehad is mentioned synonymously with "possession," in reference to inherited land.

[104] There is some flexibility in the designations here. At the beginning, Boaz is said to take "ten men from the elders of the city" to hear the negotiations (4:2). He calls on the kinsman to declare his intention to redeem "before those sitting [here] and before the elders of my people" (4:4). Later, he appeals to "the elders and all the people to act as witnesses" (4:9). Then, "all the people who were in the gate and the elders" respond in confirmation at the conclusion of the transaction (4:11).

[105] See Chapter 2 (esp. n. 82) on "witnesses" in the ancient Near East. Also G. M. Tucker, "Witnesses and 'Dates' in Israelite Contracts," *CBQ* 28 (1966) 42–45; Hubbard, *Book of Ruth*, pp. 235–36.

[106] An effective strategy by which state governments undermine the influence of indigenous leaders is to strip those leaders of their control over

strengthen their influence by serving as witnesses to business transactions (including marriages) involving land, effectively necessitating their participation in and approval of such transactions. Transactions completed without their assistance run the risk of being considered invalid by the general population.

An excellent study of the role of witnesses is provided by David Parkin.[107] He investigates how that role evolves as a people (the Giriama of southeastern Kenya), whose economy has traditionally been redistributional, is affected by capitalism. "Homestead heads"/"elders" serve as witnesses because they are considered the most reliable persons to consult in matters involving claims going back several years. The person acquiring property must have the approval of the community in general. In cases of inheritance, the witnesses insure that the heir is a legitimate one. In cases involving inter-family purchases (often the result of abandonment or mortgage), the elders are sought as witnesses to gain the acceptance of the community at large. The parties involved in such transactions feel indebted to the elders for their cooperation. Thus, the elders maintain control, even as the social landscape of the community is altered. The elders also possess certain controlling mechanisms, which they can invoke, if someone is pursuing personal gain in a manner which the elders deem to be detrimental to the community as a whole.[108] In all this, the elders try to insure that persons participating in land transactions have to gain their approval and help to succeed.[109]

Boaz chooses some—but not all—of the city's elders to serve as witnesses (4:2). We can surmise that the ones he chooses are

---

land transactions. See, e.g., Fernea, *Shaykh and Effendi*, pp. 150–53; Amanolahi-Baharvand, "Baharvand," pp. 209–24.

[107] *Palms, Wine, and Witnesses*, esp. pp. 7–16.

[108] Among the Giriama, these mechanisms are religious (see Deut 25:7–10). Younger entrepreneurs in the community have started getting around this by adopting a different religion (Parkin, *Palms, Wine, and Witnesses*, pp. 37–46).

[109] Parkin, *Palms, Wine, and Witnesses*, pp. 28–29. This situation is a bit more complex than it sounds at first. The elders also think of their own personal interests, and will sometimes allow an individual to obtain greater holdings than others. Their hope is that the wealthier individual will remember the elder's helpfulness, thereby "owing" something to him in return. The battle within an elder between looking out for his own interests and looking out for the interests of the community is a constant one.

members of his family group, because he refers to them as "elders of my people" (עַמִּי זִקְנֵי; v 4). This indicates that this matter concerns the broader lineage group of which Boaz is a member. Specifically, it entails the transfer of the right of redemption (and consequently, levirate) from one member of the group to another (see n. 34). The role of the elders as witnesses demonstrates and reaffirms their positions as leaders of the lineage group. Conversely, it demonstrates Boaz's recognition of their authority and influence. His position as a male head of household—and the place of that household in the clan—is understood in a significant way in relation to these individuals. They verify the agreement and affirm all those directly involved (Boaz, the kinsman, Naomi, and Ruth).

Other individuals ("the people who were in the gate," vv 9, 11) also are present to serve as witnesses in this story. There are several persons to which this could refer. The reasons for the participation of each would be significant, if they could be confirmed. Their mere presence indicates that this matter ultimately involves other families in the community. Their primary goal is to maintain an equilibrium and harmony among the various segments of the community. These "people" could include elders of other family groups, in particular, the family of the man from whom the property is being redeemed. They would probably need to be present in the second stage of these proceedings as well, when the property is actually redeemed. There could be other individuals, beside elders, who want to use this occasion as an opportunity to gain information which will translate into influence for themselves in the future. For example, there might be a military leader among them who is wishing to widen his sphere of influence, or a priest who is strengthening his ties to this lineage group (see Isa 8:1–2). Also, some of them probably were "elders in training." These would have been younger men who were learning the proper way to handle such transactions by hands-on experience. Moreover, they would have been witnessing to the transaction so that, when they became elders, they would have some prerequisite knowledge of landholdings necessary for the job.[110] In this particular case, the witnesses do more than pledge to verify the transaction; they also pronounce a divine blessing over Ruth and Boaz (vv 11–12).[111] This indicates several things about the community's "official position" on the impending marriage. First, it demonstrates their full acceptance of Ruth as a member of the community. Any who might question her status would now be going against the sentiments of the community leaders. The blessing also formalizes their approval of Boaz's actions on her behalf. This implicitly reaffirms the community's high estimation of anyone who might choose to perform a similar function in the future. They recognize that redemption and levirate are functions which can affect the levir or redeemer in a detrimental way, which in itself can have adverse effects on the broader family group. Yet they also believe there are potential benefits for the community in such an arrangement, and the blessing expresses their appreciation to the redeemer/levir for his willingness to take this risk. Finally, by invoking Yahweh, they express their belief that Boaz is doing something that Yahweh himself supports. The invoking of Tamar and the "houses" which are descended from her (4:12) furthers this, as it would call up for the audience thoughts of Yahweh's disapproval of Onan and his tacit approval of Tamar (expressed by Judah). The sense of connectedness between past and present generations evoked by this blessing is an attitude commonly promoted by elders.

---

[110] A parallel to the story in Ruth 4:1–12 is Jeremiah's redemption of his cousin's field (Jer 32:6–15). This transaction is conducted before "witnesses" (Jer 32:10, 12). Based on ancient Near Eastern parallels, it is logical to assume that some, if not all, of these "witnesses" are elders of the community. See n. 104, above.

[111] There is a minor textual variant in v 11. The reading of the LXX transposes הַזְּקֵנִים and עֵדִים, further requiring the repetition of וַיֹּאמְרוּ. Either reading is possible. In the LXX's reading, it is understood that the elders are among the "witnesses" who sit in the gate. Then the text specifies that it is the elders who pronounce the blessing. The reading of the MT implies that all in the gate pronounced the blessing on Boaz. Even if this was the case, it is likely that elders actually vocalized the blessing on behalf of all those present.

PRELIMINARY CONCLUSIONS

The materials considered thus far show some commonalities in tandem with flexibility in the utilization of levirate relationships. It is to be expected that the inclusion of other societies would reveal other variations, but I would not expect them to be substantially different from what has already been described here. What follows is a summary of findings which seem most pertinent to consider when we turn to look at the levirate law in Deut 25:5–10.

(1) There are no societies among those surveyed in which the levirate is an absolute mandate; it is optional. It is a custom or traditional practice used because it "makes sense" to those involved. Some peoples "allow" it, some "prefer" it, some "expect" it. In none of the societies examined is it mandated by law from a central state structure upon the local populations. The levir is obligated morally, not legally, and only to the extent that the dead man's family insists upon it. The cuneiform examples appear within the broader context of the economic needs of "at-risk widows," where they constitute one of several possible ways of providing for a widow. The instances reported in the Hebrew Bible (Genesis 38; Ruth 4) arise when they are called for by a responsible male figure, but no reference is made to legal mandate in either instance.

(2) The field of "candidates" from which a levir comes is constrained by two considerations. On one side are concerns about incest. Ironically, it is often those with the strictest incest taboos who are most likely to expect a levirate arrangement between a widow and a male in-law who previously had been strictly forbidden to her. On the other side, the "true" levirate serves the purpose of perpetuating the line of the deceased in terms of inheritance and social placement; so, the levir must be a close enough kin to be willing and economically "qualified" (in the eyes of his neighbors) to accomplish this purpose. The role most commonly falls to a brother of the deceased, a half-brother, his father, or a son by another wife; but an uncle, cousin, or slightly more distant relative can also be a levir in many cases. The two biblical examples show that the closest male relative is assumed

to be the one who will serve as the levir, but in both cases someone slightly more distant actually fills the role.

(3) The widow commonly has some say in whom she will marry in levirate. Her in-laws might restrict the "field of candidates" somewhat, but the final decision is most often left in the hands of the widow herself. Several cuneiform laws mention a widow's right to marry whomever she wishes. The only exception to this is when the man dies during the betrothal period. In that case, the bride's father has the right to accept a "replacement" groom or look elsewhere. Each biblical example shows the widow exercising some of her own initiative in finding and marrying someone to act as a levir.[112]

(4) There are three intertwining motivations for the levirate, two economic and one social. The social motivation has to do with a man's "name" or "memory" being preserved among descendants. One finds this motivation mentioned less often than the economic ones, which are virtually universal among societies in which one finds the levirate practiced. The economic motivations are immediate and long-term, narrow and broad. The immediate and narrow motivation is manifested in concern for the welfare of the widow and any children she already has. The long-term and broad motivation arises from a desire to perpetuate the economic benefits provided by the dead man to his kinsmen while he was still alive after his death. This translates into measures taken to preserve a family inheritance. Cuneiform laws explicitly mention only a concern for a widow and her children, although economic

---

[112] The silence of some biblical texts concerning levirate relationships might also betray the optional nature of such situations. Abigail (1 Samuel 25) is widowed at the sudden death of Nabal. There is no mention of children from that marriage, yet no mention is made of a possible levirate marriage either; and she marries outside the family (to David). One wonders what became of Nabal's obviously significant landholdings. More to the point being considered here, when David writes to Abigail, asking for her in marriage, the invitation is received and answered by Abigail herself; no consultation with a male in Nabal's family is recorded. This might imply that she had the right to make her own choice in the matter, but more of her particular circumstances would have to be known in order to reach any firm conclusion. The same is true of Bathsheba's marriage to David, although her pregnancy probably eliminated all other options. Other widows who are identified are supported by their sons and a benevolent king (2 Sam 14:4–7; 2 Kgs 4:11–37; 8:1–6).

effects on the broader family are sometimes implied. The biblical examples reflect all three motivations in one way or another.

INTERPRETATION OF DEUT 25:5–10

It is widely held that a significant change in the practice of the levirate effected by this law is the restriction of possible levirs to one's blood brothers. This conclusion is based on the assumption that the law intends to be comprehensive in its treatment of the matter. However, I find no other examples of the levirate being applied in such a restricted way. There are no examples of it being so restricted among contemporary societies; it is not so restricted in cuneiform law; it is not so restricted in any other biblical story.[113] Therefore, it would seem more natural to adopt a different assumptive point of view.

The approach I would recommend is, again, that set forth by Raymond Westbrook, described in preceding chapters. He calls for interpreting biblical laws (like others) as part of a broad stream of legal prescriptions, commonly known by scribes and legal officials of the ancient Near East. In other words, this law is to be read as part of an on-going legal conversation regarding levirate marriage and similar practices.

Parts of the bigger picture of levirate marriage are filled in most clearly by other biblical passages, while cuneiform laws and contemporary societies merely suggest other possible pieces. The pieces supplied by the biblical examples primarily show that a kinsman other than the dead man's brother could serve as a levir. It seems plausible that the list of possible "candidates" is the same as that for a redeemer (Lev 25:47–49). The biblical examples indicate that the primary purposes in using the levirate are to provide financial security for the widow and to maintain the dead

---

[113] Most early Jewish interpreters did not consider the possibility of any except a blood brother serving as levir. The only flexibility they allowed was in the number of brothers that might be eligible, concluding that the willingness of any brother to serve as a levirate relieved all others of any obligation (*m. Yeb.* 4:5). See Belkin, "Levirate and Agnate Marriage," pp. 281, 288–90; cp. Matt 22:23–33; Mk 12:18–27; Lk 20:27–38.

man's inheritance in his family. The former is the primary motivation for a widow's pursuit of a levirate arrangement, while the latter is the primary concern of the levir. There are also indications that entering into a levirate marriage was a right or option rather than a legal obligation. It incurred a financial hardship on the levir, and the widow's own needs might be met by another (unrelated) man (Abigail and Bathsheba are examples of this). Either one might choose not to enter a levirate marriage for these individual reasons, but consideration for the dead man's broader family prodded both toward marriage. The extra-biblical materials reveal that there probably were additional concerns regarding the financial agreements (bridewealth, dowry, etc.) made in connection with the initial wedding. Those are not mentioned in this law, but it is likely that they were of concern in actual cases of levirate.

The levirate law falls into two parts, a main law (vv 5–6) and a corollary (vv 7–10).

> If brothers live together, and one of them dies and has no son, the wife of the dead man shall not be married outside to a stranger; her husband's brother shall go to her, and he shall take her to be his wife, and he shall perform the duty of a husband's brother to her. And the firstborn whom she bears shall stand on the name of his dead brother, and his name shall not be blotted out from Israel.
>
> And if the man does not wish to take his brother's wife, then his brother's wife shall go up to the gate to the elders, and she shall say, "My husband's brother refuses to raise up a name for his brother in Israel; he is not willing to perform the duty of a husband's brother." And the elders of his city shall call to him, and they shall speak to him. And he shall stand and say, "I do not wish to take her." Then his brother's wife shall come near to him in the sight of the elders, and she shall pull off his sandal from his foot, and she shall spit in his face. And she shall answer and say, "Thus shall it be done to the man who does not build the house of his brother." And his name shall be called in Israel, "The house of the sandal that was pulled off."

The main law sets forth three circumstances which make this a special case, a case in which the dead man's brother alone can fulfill the levirate function: (1) the brothers have not yet divided the paternal estate, (2) there are no children, and (3) the widow has indicated her intention to marry an outsider.[114] Interpretation of this law has been misguided, in my opinion, by a tendency to adopt the unwarranted assumption that the law intends to be comprehensive.[115] This is most noticeable in the widespread belief that the law intends to restrict the right of levirate in any situation to brothers only ("If brothers live together...").[116] The only flexibility on this point is provided by a minority of interpreters who read "brother" as denoting "clan brother" rather than just "blood brother."[117] This interpretation seems unlikely, however, because of the overall context. To say that clan brothers "live together" would merely mean that they reside in the same community;[118] but that would be a very common occurrence, and a widow would have several "brothers" of

---

[114] Several details which would help modern readers to interpret the law with greater confidence are left out. There is no reference to the brothers' father or the widow's father, nor to other brothers. The marital status of the reluctant brother is not mentioned. The status of any offspring after the "firstborn" is not addressed. There is no indication as to what might happen to any of the participants subsequent to the conclusion of the proceedings mentioned in the corollary section. I will keep speculation on these matters to a minimum.

[115] "The assumption is that Deuteronomy 25 contains a comprehensive account of the law of levirate. Thus any detail in the other sources [Genesis 38, Ruth 4] which is not mentioned in Deuteronomy is in conflict with it. In terms of ancient Near Eastern law this is not a valid assumption." Westbrook, *Property*, p. 71. T. and D. Thompson ("Some Legal Problems," pp. 79–99) also argue against assuming that this law is comprehensive, yet I disagree with their conclusion that it "gives only the general and ordinary circumstances of the custom" (p. 88). Rather, it assumes knowledge of "the general and ordinary circumstances" and deals with a special set of circumstances.

[116] Driver, *Deuteronomy*, p. 281; Neufeld, *Ancient Hebrew Marriage Laws*, pp. 34, 40–41; Beattie, "Book of Ruth," pp. 260–62; Gordis, "Love, Marriage, and Business," pp. 249–50; Manor, "Brief History," p. 132.

[117] Pedersen, *Israel* I–II, pp. 78, 508. There is an ancient tradition behind this, as Samaritans and Jewish Qaraites interpreted "brothers" as a reference to clan-mates. See Belkin, "Levirate and Agnate Marriage," pp. 280–81; Leggett, *Levirate and Goel*, p. 42 n. 29.

[118] Some rabbinic interpreters understood this temporally as well, that the law excluded a yet-to-be-born brother from later serving as a levir. See Belkin, "Levirate and Agnate Marriage," pp. 281–82; Leggett, *Levirate and Goel*, p. 42 n. 30.

this sort who might serve as her levir. The corollary law would make little sense, though, because it would, in effect, single out one clan brother (which one?), require him alone to marry the dead man's widow, and then disgrace him for refusing to do so. The opprobrium associated with the brother's refusal belies closer blood-ties and a narrower pool than that. It makes better sense to assume that these are blood brothers, living side-by-side in an extended family compound.[119]

Similarities in cuneiform law support the sense that this law refers to blood brothers. The circumstance of brothers who "live together" has its antecedents in laws concerning the dividing of a man's estate/inheritance among his children following his death[120] (MAL A¶25; cp. MAL B¶1 and O¶3; LL ¶21–22, 31–32; LH ¶¶165–167, 170–174, 176–184). These laws indicate that a paternal estate could be divided among a man's sons by the man himself before his death, or his sons could divide it among themselves after his death. The majority of the laws deal with the fair execution of this matter in the latter instance. The central concerns underlying these cuneiform laws are (a) that the parts of the paternal estate which are not allocated to specific family members prior to the man's death be equitably divided after his death, and (b) that the estate not be transferred to someone outside the family after his death.[121] The goal is to see that the man's dependents are taken care of (as well as the deceased could insure) and that any negative effects on the man's broader family are minimized. As we have seen, these are common goals of levirate relationships, and it is likely they are the goals of the Deuteronomic levirate law. The opening clause (Deut 25:5) indicates that the paternal estate has remained undivided since the father's death,[122] and now one of the sons has died without

---

[119] B. Halpern, "Jerusalem and the Lineages in the Seventh Century BCE: Kinship and the Rise of Individual Moral Liability," in *Law and Ideology in Monarchic Israel*, ed. B. Halpern and D. W. Hobson (JSOTS 124; Sheffield: Sheffield Academic, 1991), p. 51.

[120] T. and D. Thompson, "Some Legal Problems," pp. 89–90; Pressler, *View of Women*, p. 64. For some examples from Emar, see Eugen J. Pentiuc, "West Semitic Terms in Akkadian Texts from Emar," *JNES* 58 (1999) 84–86.

[121] See Huehnergard, "Some Biblical Notes," pp. 431–32.

[122] Davies, "Inheritance Rights," pp. 264–65; Manor, "Levirate Marriage," p. 132. The levirate law does not mention the dead man's father, which could

leaving an heir of his own.[123] It would not be surprising to find that the concerns of the law are the proper distribution of an inheritance and the prevention of the transfer of ownership to an outsider.

The "threat" in the primary law is posed by the widow. The concern is that the circumstances given in the first half of the verse will prompt her to marry "a stranger" (זר אִישׁ). The possibility that the widow's marriage to a "stranger" is imminent is less obvious, but I think it makes the best sense of the law as a whole.[124] Interpreters usually assume that this is nothing more than a general possibility. Two considerations point toward a different conclusion, though. The first is that the law envisions only two options for the widow. She can marry a "stranger," or she can marry her brother-in-law. The possibility that she could marry a slightly more distant kinsman is not entertained, even though there are examples of that option being used in Israel, thereby accomplishing the same goal ("to maintain the name of the dead man") as is desired in this law (Gen 38:8; Ruth 4:5, 10). So why is this third possibility not mentioned? I would contend it is because the law wishes to indicate that the widow is already seriously considering marriage to a particular "stranger."

The other consideration which suggests that marriage to an outsider is imminent is intertwined with the nature of the "threat" which drives the action along in this law, a threat which comes to concern the community as a whole (vv 7–10).[125] The community is concerned not because the widow will be left forever destitute. She is almost certainly young and could marry someone else to provide

---

likely signal that he too is dead. See Leggett, *Levirate and Goel*, pp. 45–48, for discussion of whether the father has died.

[123] Driver, *Deuteronomy*, p. 282; von Rad, *Deuteronomy*, pp. 154–55; T. and D. Thompson, "Some Legal Problems," pp. 89–90.

[124] On "stranger," see Huehnergard, "Some Biblical Notes," pp. 431–33. Huehnergard's evidence includes examples of a widow being declared an heir, in the absence of any male heir. However, the right to inherit is reneged if the widow marries a "stranger." My line of argument assumes that such wills would be the exception to the rule.

[125] In contrast to the story in Genesis 38, there is apparently no father here with the authority to "command" the brother-in-law (or any male kinsman) to take the widow in marriage. That he would have done so is virtually certain, because the loss of his son's "name" would diminish his own.

for her. Even if she does not, other laws in the D Code provide ways for her needs to be met by the community.[126] The community is concerned not simply because the surviving brother might absorb the dead man's inheritance into his own. That would yield a similar outcome in terms of property as levirate marriage would have: the property would be retained within the holdings of the dead man's family.[127] The community and its elders are most concerned if the case will eventually lead to a transfer of property from one family to another. That concern is most pronounced in this case if there is a strong expectation that the widow plans to look shortly to marriage to an outsider.[128] There would be no reason to humiliate her brother-in-law if she is contemplating marriage to another kinsman, through whom she could also perpetuate her husband's name, nor would there be if she is going to remain unmarried.

This law makes it clear that marriage is the accepted mode for providing an heir for the dead man ("her brother-in-law shall go to her, and he shall take her to himself for a wife"; v 5b). We have already seen that the same is expected in the case of Ruth, and that it is probably expected in the case of Tamar. This shows a basic consistency in the levirate custom in Israel. It does not necessarily indicate a shift in "policy" from the practice in Tamar's day, however, unless again one assumes that the law intends to be comprehensive and implicitly prohibits the legitimacy of an heir in another situation like that involving Judah.

What I am suggesting, then, is that the primary law (vv 5–6) envisions a situation which raised the custom of levirate marriage

---

[126] There are not two independent commands in v 5, one for the widow and an entirely separate one for her brother-in-law. In other words, the widow is not prohibited from marrying someone else no matter what her brother-in-law decides. The two go hand-in-hand. The obligation upon him is to be fulfilled *instead of* her marrying an outsider. If he does not fulfill his obligation, then she is freed from her prohibition.

[127] The concerns raised in this regard in the case of Onan are not raised by city elders, but by God. The community certainly would have taken note of such an attitude and thought less of Onan for it, but it would not have changed the economic balance between Judah's family and the rest of the community, because they were already outsiders.

[128] The concern also assumes that the dead man's inheritance goes with the widow to whomever she marries or to their offspring. See below, on "raising the name" of the dead man.

from an option to a matter of some urgency. The levirate was an option in Israel, as in other ancient Near Eastern nations, which might be employed anytime that a man died; but under certain circumstances, failure to enter into a levirate relationship had more extreme results than usual. Those circumstances were that a man had died without having children to whom he could pass on his inheritance. Further, there existed the very real possibility that that inheritance would be passed through his widow to another family, thereby disrupting a line of inheritance which had been maintained for several generations. And no one from the family has stepped forward to prevent this from happening. Under these circumstances, this law changes the right of levirate marriage into an obligation for the male most closely related to the dead man, his brother.

A minor question arises from the beginning phrase in v 6 ("And the firstborn whom she bears..."). The text mentions only the firstborn son of the levirate in reference to the "name" of the dead man. This might indicate that additional children would be considered heirs of the levir, not the dead man.[129] This would constitute a small variation from MAL A¶28, which stipulates that, if an unborn child's father dies and the mother remarries, the child still inherits from the man who sired him, not from the one who raised him. Unfortunately, the absence of actual examples prevents one from drawing a definite conclusion.

More significant is the sense of the expression, "(the firstborn...) shall stand on the name (עַל־שֵׁם יָקוּם) of his (the levir's) dead brother."[130] The construction עַל־שֵׁם is most often used with the verb קָרָא, meaning "to call according to the name of" (Gen 48:26; Deut 3:14; 2 Sam 18:18; 1 Kgs 16:24; Ezra 2:61; Neh 7:63; Esth 9:26). The expression in Deut 25:6 is unique. Slightly more common is the causative form of the phrase (הֵקִים שֵׁם; "to maintain a name, cause a name to stand"), which occurs in v 7.

---

[129] Belkin, "Levirate and Agnate Marriage," p. 288. Benjamin argues that the widow was to be celibate after bearing one child for her late husband (*Deuteronomy and City Life*, p. 246).

[130] This is a very literal translation of the idiom (cp. Driver, *Deuteronomy*, p. 283). Leggett translates the phrase, "shall succeed to the name of his brother" (*Levirate and Goel*, pp. 48–55). This captures the sense well. See also Brichto, "Kin, Cult, Land," pp. 21–32.

There, and in the other passages already mentioned (Gen 38:8; Ruth 4:5, 10), the subject is the levir. The child born of a levirate union "stands on the name" of the one who died; the levir "causes the name (of the dead man) to stand" (םֵשׁ םיִקֵה; so in Deut 25:7). Our discussion of Ruth 4 showed that the causative form of the expression has to do with inheritance. That the active form also has to do primarily with inheritance is confirmed by the antithetic final clause of the verse, "and his name shall not be blotted out (הֶחָמִּי) from Israel." The clearest explication of this clause occurs in Deut 29:15–27 (16–28, EV). In these verses, Moses tells how God will punish the apostate. In 29:19, he says the "anger of the Lord and his jealousy would smoke against that man, and the curses written in this book would settle upon him, and the Lord would blot out his name from under heaven." The wording is only slightly changed in 29:26–27, when the punishment is explained to an inquirer. "It is because they forsook the covenant of the Lord... Therefore, the anger of the Lord was kindled against this land, bringing upon it all the curses written in this book; and the Lord uprooted them from their land in anger and fury and great wrath, and cast them into another land."[131] This author does not see "blotting out the name" as a reference to the death of the individual and all his family so much as depriving that person of his land (inheritance).[132] The same thought is then expressed in 25:9, where the widow describes the unwilling levir as "a man who will not build up the house of his brother." The term "house" connotes both lineage and property.

These observations indicate that a primary concern of the entire law is the fate of the dead man's inheritance. The perpetuation of someone's "name" entails providing progeny as a means to maintaining a man's inheritance, which in turn is a

---

[131] It is true that this is from Dtr, and thus later than the law in Deut 25:6 (cp. 1 Kgs 9:6–9; Jer 22:8–9). Still, it is, at the least, an early interpretation of the phrase, meriting primary consideration when one is trying to determine the phrase's meaning in this prior passage.

[132] So Manor, "Brief History," p. 132. At least one *kudurru*-inscription from Assyria links property directly to offspring: "May he [Ninib] tear out his boundary stone, destroy his name, his seed, his offspring, his descendants from the mouth of men, and may he not let him have a son and a pourer of water." Quoted by Henry Schaeffer, *The Social Legislation of the Primitive Semites* (London: Oxford, 1915), p. 49. Cp. Brichto, "Kin, Cult, Land," p. 26.

manifestation of his personhood. These various aspects were inseparable in the Israelite mind.[133] The stated purpose of levirate marriage is to "maintain the name" (v 7) or "build up the house" (v 9) of one whose death could mark the end of his line. This is not to claim that the law is unconcerned about the welfare of the widow; she will be provided for through her husband's property, worked by the child she bears.[134] But the law is focusing on the implications of this situation for the extended family, and then for the broader community. The actions of two people threaten the preceding socioeconomic balance in the community that is represented in the ownership and use of the property. In the primary law, a "threat" is posed by the widow, whose marriage to a stranger would apparently entail the transfer of property rights as well. This is averted through levirate marriage. A second "threat" is posed by the levir, and it is addressed in the corollary law.

The major theme of the corollary law is the brother's refusal to assume his levirate responsibilities. The narrator begins this section with the statement that the brother does not "wish[135] to take his brother's wife" (v 7a), and the same is later repeated by the brother himself (v 8b). In the interim, the widow formally charges that the brother "is not willing" (לא אבה) to marry her in levirate (v 7b), and later, that the termination of her husband's house is the brother's fault (v 9b). The sequence in the proceedings serves to remove any blame from the widow and place it entirely on the shoulders of the brother. The widow brings formal charges against him in the presence of the city elders (v 7b); they themselves try to persuade him to take on his levirate duties, but

---

[133] Pedersen, *Israel* I–II, pp. 78–96; Belkin, "Levirate and Agnate Marriage," p. 292; T. and D. Thompson, "Some Legal Problems," pp. 84–88, 90, 96; Leggett, *Levirate and Goel*, pp. 49–54; Gertz, *Die Gerichtsorganisation*, p. 205; Halpern, "Jerusalem and the Lineages," p. 57. Ginat (*Blood Disputes*, pp. 44–45) writes that, in the case of homicide, the manslayer's family will sometimes give an unmarried female relative to the victim's closest kin to bear a male offspring, thereby compensating the victim's family for their loss. This, too, is "maintaining a man's name." Again see Cunnison, *Luapula Peoples*, p. 98.

[134] Belkin, "Levirate and Agnate Marriage," p. 288.

[135] The verb חפץ often carries a connotation of "pleasure" or "delight." See Gertz, *Die Gerichtsorganisation*, p. 204.

he still refuses (v 8); and the widow's scathing rebuke is performed "before the eyes of the elders" (v 9).

The exact reason for the levir's unwillingness to marry his brother's widow is not given.[136] The reason for Onan's unwillingness ("the offspring would not be his") and the reason for the unwillingness of the Boaz's kinsman ("lest I harm my own inheritance") are not necessarily the same, although they probably reflect similar (financial) considerations. Either of those reasons could explain a brother's unwillingness to marry in levirate, and there could be other reasons. It is generally held that the brother is motivated primarily by such financial considerations, that he expects eventually to inherit his dead brother's portion of the estate (see the speculations suggested in Onan's case as possibilities), and that the future benefits of that outweigh any negative consequences he might suffer as a result of his current decision. This is certainly possible, but I give reasons below for considering another understanding of the law. Whatever specific reason there might have been, the law here states in very general terms that the brother is simply unwilling to marry the widow. It apparently was not deemed necessary to provide a specific reason, probably because any reason would yield the same result.

The widow's accusation (v 7b) puts the spotlight on what the brother's actions reveal about his attitude toward the dead man more than about his feelings toward the widow. He "refuses" to sustain his brother's "name;" he does not "build the house of his brother." Renunciation of his levirate duties for any reason connotes, to some degree, a sort of "hatred" toward the dead man, as discussed in the case of Onan. The brother is placing his own interests above those of his extended family, putting the individual above the group. The humiliation the brother endures (vv 9–10) takes place in front of the elders, indicating a community-wide disapproval of his unwillingness. The strength of the group is dependent on the willingness of its individual members to sacrifice their individual desires for the benefit of the group. To ignore the attitude of the unwilling levir is tantamount to undermining the spirit of group strength.

---

[136] For discussions of past suggestions, see Davies, "Inheritance Rights," pp. 257–60; and Beattie, "The Book of Ruth," p. 261.

The underlying selfishness of the brother is contrasted to the widow's attitude. She apparently has an opportunity to go to a "stranger" whom she must feel will support her well; however, she here indicates her willingness to forego that option for the sake of her late husband and his family. She does not go to the other man without first appealing to her brother-in-law to do his part for the good of the group.[137] She gives a lower priority to the considerations that have led her to contemplate a marriage to a stranger, and a higher priority to the welfare of the group. In so doing, she shows that she has a greater loyalty for her husband's family than the brother does. She is more honorable than he.

The present interpretation sees two principle reasons for the involvement of elders, one social and one notarial. The social concerns would have been more acutely felt by family members, and it would not be surprising if they had been addressed by lineage heads only, perhaps even in a less formal way. On the other hand, such selfishness strikes at the heart of community cohesion, which the elders would hold very dear. The notarial role must fall to the elders of the broader community, because subsequent transactions involving this property would involve persons outside the dead man's own family.

The social aspect of the elders' role has been mentioned already, but further comment is warranted. These are elders of the city, representing several lineage groups in the community and not just the group of which the brother-in-law is a member (cp. "elders of my people" in Ruth 4:4). The absence of any reference to these elders in the primary law is not necessarily significant, but their presence in the corollary law, when the brother-in-law refuses to perform his levirate duties, might suggest that the case changes from a family matter (vv 5–6) to a community matter (vv 7–10).[138] His refusal reflects the selfish individualism that runs counter to and undermines the group cohesion which community elders so diligently work to develop. A

---

[137] See Leggett, *Levirate and Goel*, p. 57.

[138] Phillips (*Deuteronomy*, pp. 168–69) sees a shift from a personal family forum, in Genesis 38, to a more public municipal forum, in Deut 25:5–10 and Ruth 4. One should also consider the "stranger" status of Judah's family, as well as the absence in that story of any hint that Tamar might be considering marriage to anyone else.

man who is unwilling to help his own brother will be even less trustworthy in his relationships with more distant relatives and neighbors. The community is naturally wary of such individuals.[139] The role of the elders at this point is to encourage a greater sense of responsibility toward the group, to try to change the attitude of the brother-in-law.

The elders turn to their power of persuasion to address the brother's attitude. They "speak to him" (v 8a). Again, the writer does not specify what is said, because that would vary from community to community and from instance to instance. But this is one of their most commonly-used weapons.[140] Analogies from contemporary societies suggest that they would probably bring up the kinds of things we have seen throughout this study of elders. They would acknowledge the financial burden involved in a levirate marriage and their understanding of the brother's reluctance to enter into it; but they would also speak about the importance to the community of having those among them who fulfill unwanted familial obligations; they would discuss the situation of widows and the honor involved in providing for them; they would remind the brother of "heroes" like Boaz; they would speak about how his unwillingness will be perceived by the community, and how that might affect his relations with others in the future. They would try to convince him that, "in the bigger picture," it would be in his own best interests to perform his

---

. [139] Susan Niditch gives a slightly different rationale. She contends that, "Through his levirate duty, a male again helps society to avoid a sociological misfit, the young childless widow." Niditch, "Wronged Woman Righted," p. 146; cp. Mars, "What Was Onan's Crime?" p. 434. This too would constitute something which would be discouraged in the community.

[140] There are numerous examples of elders using opprobrium as a way of influencing community members into fulfilling their obligations to one another. See, e.g., Ginat, *Blood Disputes*, pp. 90–113, esp. pp. 96, 99, 103, 109, 113. "Bedouin and rural Arabs are 'shame cultures' in the sense that 'individuals are controlled by public threats to personal reputation and honor. Public shame reflects not only on the individual, but on his family and kin.'" (Ginat, *Blood Disputes*, p. 113; quoting from N. Abercrombie, S. Hill, and B. S. Turner, *Dictionary of Sociology* [Harmondsworth: Penguin, 1984], p. 190). Cp. A. Kuper, "Kgalagari Lekgota," p. 89; Lyn M. Bechtel, "Shame as a Sanction of Social Control in Biblical Israel: Judicial, Political, and Social Shaming," *JSOT* 49 (1991) 47–76.

levirate duties.[141] Their effectiveness would have depended on the amount of respect accorded them by their community and the strength of kinship ties there.[142]

The brother-in-law formally rejects the elders' words (v 8b), and this leads to a reprimand in the form of *khalitsah*, which the elders witness and "notarize" (v 9). The disparaging "name" that is given to him (v 10) places a quasi-official seal on that ceremony. The opprobrium attached to this ceremony diminished over the centuries, so that the rabbis eventually were able to prefer *khalitsah* to the fulfillment of levirate duties in most cases. I will try to show why this later development probably misrepresents the original intent of the ceremony.

The similarities between *khalitsah* and the removal of the sandal in Ruth 4 have attracted much interest. Some see these as the same ceremony practiced at different times, some believe they are totally unrelated, and many fall somewhere in between (see above, on Ruth 4).[143] The author in Ruth 4 introduces the action there as if it were the common practice. If we accept that as a premise, then this instance stands out as a variation on that common practice. There are three differences in the description in Deut 25:9, in comparison with the action described in Ruth 4: (a) the verb for "remove" is שָׁלַף in Ruth 4 and חָלַץ here;[144] (b) in

---

[141] Leggett (*Levirate and Goel*, pp. 58–59 n. 71) quotes David Daube regarding this action. "No doubt a man branded as 'he that hath his shoe loosed' was avoided by the better citizens, excluded from higher offices and not much trusted in any business transactions... A breach of trust by one brother vis-à-vis the other, even if it does not amount to a proper crime, is a grave moral offense. It deserves public censure; ...hence the public degradation of the faithless consors in Deuteronomy." (D. Daube, "Consortium," in *Neotestimentica et Semitica, Studies in Honor of Matthew Black*, 1969, pp. 78–81.)

[142] Davies, "Inheritance Rights," p. 261; Benjamin, *Deuteronomy and City Life*, pp. 250–51; Bechtel, "Shame," pp. 47–48, 55–67; cp. Ginat, *Blood Disputes*, pp. 96, 110–12, 125, 152–55.

[143] Evans, "'Gates' and 'Streets,'" p. 10; T. and D. Thompson, "Some Legal Problems," pp. 90–92; Burrows, "Levirate Marriage," p. 30; Brichto, "Kin, Cult, Land," pp. 19–20; Leggett, *Levirate and Goel*, pp. 58–62; Gordis, "Love, Marriage, and Business," pp. 247–48; Mayes, *Deuteronomy*, p. 329; Braulik, *Deuteronomium II*, p. 188; Gertz, *Die Gerichtsorganisation*, pp. 199–201.

[144] There is no apparent difference in the meanings of the two terms; they are merely synonyms. If there were different connotations attached to the two, those were because of the actions which came to accompany each. The

Ruth 4, the "seller" removes his own shoe; in Deut 25:9, the widow
removes her brother-in-law's shoe; and (c) there is no disapproval
attached to removing one's sandal in Ruth 4, while Deut 25:9 calls
for the widow also to spit in her brother-in-law's face and to give
him a public reprimand.

If we assume that the transfer of the sandal indicated the
transfer of certain legal rights (see on Ruth 4:7), then we should
consider the widow's involvement and actions in Deut 25:9 as
signifying particular differences. It is obvious that the "name" the
brother-in-law receives in v 10 implies shame. On the other hand,
there is no hint that the kinsman's refusal in Ruth 4 resulted in
any shame for him. So, what is the reason for the shame in Deut
25:9–10? The shame could be because the man is having certain
rights "forcibly" removed. He is not "willingly" handing them over
as the kinsman did in Ruth 4; he is having his rights removed by
someone else. It could also be that the shame is associated with
the fact that a woman (not some other man) takes away these
rights. Without having to go to Carmichael's sexual symbolism,[145]
one can still understand how, given the cultural ideas surrounding
gender, having a female deprive a male of one of his rights would
bring shame upon the male.

There are related questions as to what rights the brother-in-law
is giving up in this ceremony. The widow might be symbolically
removing from her brother-in-law his right to take her as a
wife.[146] The reservation I have with this is that the case in Ruth 4
involves rights over property, not rights over persons. It seems
more likely that the *khalitsah* is indicating that the brother-in-
law's refusal to marry the widow results in the loss of his rights to

---

verb שׁלף is most commonly used to denote the drawing out of a sword from
its sheath. There is one other instance in which חלץ is used to refer to
removing one's shoes (Isa 20:2). This is the only evidence that that term
might have been the more common one for this particular action, but we
really cannot be certain of this. In any case, neither suggests an inherent
nuance that would add any insight into why it is used in this context.

[145] Carmichael, "Ceremonial Crux," pp. 321–36.

[146] Driver, *Deuteronomy*, pp. 281, 283; de Vaux, *Ancient Israel*, p. 169;
Neufeld, *Ancient Hebrew Marriage Laws*, p. 42; Leggett, *Levirate and Goel*,
pp. 60–62; Manor, "Brief History," p. 133.

joint ownership of the property with his brother.[147] This assumes the significance of one stated fact: the brothers were living together when one died, which I understand to mean that they had not yet divided the paternal estate.

What then happens to the dead man's property rights (from a legal standpoint) can be disputed. It is likely that, if neither brother were married, the rights which had been jointly held by the two brothers would have fallen entirely to the surviving brother. This all changes, however, because one is married. Once he married, it would have been understood that a portion of this jointly-held property was being used to provide for his wife, and that it eventually would have been used to provide for any future offspring, who would "maintain his name." One would expect these obligations to be maintained by the closest male kin. But the brother-in-law now declares that he intends to discontinue providing for the woman, and that he refuses to insure that his brother's "name" be maintained. Because he rejects those responsibilities, he can no longer hold on to any joint claim to the rights over that portion of the property (cp. Ruth 4:5). I would assume, then, that the brother-in-law is having to relinquish his rights over part of the estate to the widow. One could also start from a point one step removed from that. It could be that the widow had already been holding those property rights jointly with her brother-in-law since her husband's death, that she was acting on her husband's behalf. The *khalitsah* might then indicate that the brother-in-law is relinquishing his claims to the portion of the property, that the estate is being divided permanently, that the widow now has full rights over her husband's portion, and that she can take that property with her into marriage with another man.[148]

---

[147] Phillips says that the *khalitsah* forces the brother-in-law to take on responsibility for his brother's property against his wishes. (*Deuteronomy*, p. 169) Unless this automatically includes marrying the widow, I would see no inducement in this.

[148] The exact legal situation is unclear. I have discussed earlier the possibility that a widow could come to own her husband's property or hold it in trust (see on Ruth 4:3, above). As in Ruth's case, it could be that the malelessness of the nuclear family gives the widow special rights. "[Deut 25:6] suggests that, to preserve the son's inheritance, the widow may

The elders function as notaries in the biblical levirate law, according to this line of reasoning.[149] As in the story of Ruth and Boaz, they serve as witnesses. They affirm the legitimacy of the transaction, and they stand ready to verify it at a later date. Their participation might be attributable simply to the absence of the brothers' father. It could be that, when a father died without having divided the paternal estate himself, the civic leaders assumed that role in his stead.[150] One wonders, though, why this could not have been done by the heads of the extended family instead of bringing it before the city elders. Perhaps all property transactions—even those among family members—had to be notarized by the elders of the city.[151] It is also possible that the participation of the city elders indicates an anticipation that the property will be taken from one family and given to another when the widow remarries. If that is the case, the present proceedings are setting the stage for a future transaction involving the transfer of property to the "stranger" that the widow marries. That is a more serious matter, and certainly would require the elders' participation.

The spitting and the application of a derogatory name would seem justified in either case, but more so in the latter. They indicate that the brother has renounced his rights for reasons that are considered shameful. His reputation is marred as a result of his own selfishness.[152] The giving of this shameful name reflects an ironic twist to the outcome of the proceedings. The brother is being shamed for refusing to "maintain the name of his brother." The result is that his own "name" is now made disreputable. Similarly, he is branded as someone who would not "build the house of his brother." The result is that he establishes his own "house," albeit a shameful one.[153]

---

typically have remained in possession of her husband's house..." Halpern, "Jerusalem and the Lineages," p. 51.

[149] See Driver, *Deuteronomy*, p. 283; Benjamin, *Deuteronomy and City Life*, p. 250.

[150] Braulik, *Deuteronomium II*, p. 188.

[151] See Cunnison, *Luapula Peoples*, p. 96; Holy, *Neighbours and Kinsmen*, p. 126.

[152] Leggett, *Levirate and Goel*, pp. 58–62.

[153] "...the principle to which the *yebhamah* appealed in this denunciation was in essence an extension of the law of equal retribution characteristic of

The fact that he is given the name of a shamed "house" also suggests something far more drastic for the unwilling brother. If the name reflects reality, we should conclude that the brother is now separating from his father's "house" and establishing his own. Most of his relatives would not want to associate themselves with him (why should they expect any greater loyalty toward them?), and so he would be relatively isolated. The "hatred" toward his brother which his refusal displayed is now seen as "hatred" for his entire family. As Pedersen says, the unwilling brother-in-law is "a marked man, and he and his house forever must suffer under it... He cannot any more be looked upon as a normal citizen among his people."[154]

One other point of speculation must be addressed before drawing conclusions about interpreting the law in its present shape. This has to do with what one assumes will happen after v 10. One man has died, leaving a widow and no children; his widow and the city elders have tried unsuccessfully to get his brother to assume responsibility for her and for maintaining the dead man's "name" (lineage and property) in the community; as a result of his refusal, the brother has been effectively ostracized and separated from his extended family. Apparently, nothing else can be done to maintain the dead man's "name." But what will become of his widow and brother?

The usual interpretation would lead one to conclude that the widow is essentially abandoned.[155] The brother-in-law has received "an official reprimand," but he still gets the entire paternal estate.[156] The widow is left solely with the satisfaction of having publicly humiliated him. She must now find some other means of support, either through her own family and/or through

---

the Mosaic code (that is, 'eye for eye, tooth for tooth')." Manor, "Brief History," p. 134. See Braulik, *Deuteronomium II*, p. 186; Gertz, *Die Gerichtsorganisation*, pp. 194–95.

[154] Pedersen, *Israel* I–II, pp. 77–78; cp. Driver, *Deuteronomy*, p. 284.

[155] Mayes, *Deuteronomy*, p. 329.

[156] Davies believes that the property would revert to the father's house. ("Inheritance Rights," pp. 262–63) Still, the widow is abandoned, and there is no real reason for the family to pressure the brother-in-law to fulfill his levirate obligations. Any negative effects based on association with the brother-in-law are balanced by the acquisition of additional land for certain individuals.

marriage to a stranger. The brother-in-law would be left with more property, but also with the stigma of having turned against his own brother. He would be somewhat isolated from his own family, and he probably would have created some hard feelings between his family and the family of the widow. Surely that would have a detrimental economic effect on the brother-in-law.

The present reconstruction raises some doubts regarding such interpretations. One has to wonder, for example, how the assumed outcome would appear more attractive to the brother than the prospect of having to sacrifice some of his resources in marrying the widow and raising his brother's offspring. At least in the latter case he might be able to turn to his extended family for help. If he spurns his familial responsibilities and is ostracized, the possibility of assistance is virtually eliminated. His primary motivation would seem to be some vindictive desire to "blot out the name" of his brother.

It is also possible that something more drastic will follow these proceedings. First, the law seems to assume that the widow will now marry a stranger.[157] Second, if it is true that the widow will take with her the rights to her husband's property, then in addition to the consequences already mentioned regarding inter-familial relations, there will also be the intrusion of a "stranger" into the family's land.[158] This gives an even stronger reason for the brother to perform his levirate duties, and a stronger reason for the city elders to try to persuade him to do so.[159] By furthering a shift in property holdings, the brother-in-law is tearing at the social fabric of the entire community.

---

[157] Manor, "Brief History," p. 133.

[158] Burckhardt's description of levirate marriage among the Bedouin is very suggestive. "If a young man leaves a widow, his brother generally offers to marry her; custom does not oblige him or her to make this match, nor can he prevent her from marrying another man. It seldom happens, however, that she refuses; for by such an union the family property is kept together." (Quoted by Rowley, "The Marriage of Ruth," p. 178) This implies that the family property would be split up, if she married an "outsider."

[159] Davies believes that widows did not inherit their husband's property *because* it might pass to someone else. "Inheritance Rights," p. 263.

THE LEVIRATE LAW AND THE D CODE

The role played by the city elders indicates how the levirate law intends to promote inter-lineage and community-wide harmony. As with other laws previously discussed, there have been recent attempts to interpret this as a law which elevates the interests of the nuclear family above the interests of the wider group. It "is another law that is concerned with preserving the nuclear unit."[160] The law does seek to preserve a nuclear unit, but it does so for the sake of the extended family. The final outcome of the situation described in the law is the creation of a new nuclear family, led by the unwilling brother-in-law. But this development is opposed by the elders; it is what they are trying to prevent. It shows a lack of loyalty on the part of the brother-in-law to the wider group of which he is a part; so, their words to him suggest their support of such loyalty. The stigma and humiliation that are placed on the unwilling brother-in-law are intended as inducements to get him to honor the group's interests above his own self-interests. Furthermore, the notarial role played by the elders in this law prepares them to do so again in the near future. It gives them the ability to facilitate a smooth and peaceful transition of property rights when the widow remarries, minimizing the potential for inter-familial squabbles which could disrupt community life.

The law originates in Israel prior to the composition of the D Code, and its incorporation into the D Code shows that the Code's authors support traditional lineage structures and the ideals upon which they were founded in local affairs. The original intent of the law was to promote familial/clan loyalty by embracing a custom which placed the interests of the group above the interests of individuals. The elders' words encourage a spirit of moral responsibility to the broader group; fulfilling their notarial functions promotes inter-familial harmony in times of potential economic instability. The fact that the law is incorporated into the

---

[160] Steinberg, "Deuteronomic Law Code," p. 165. The reason for such an emphasis, it is argued, is that strengthening the nuclear family creates allies for the central government in its power struggles with traditional clan groups. See Chapters 4 and 5 for discussion. In this case, Steinberg is reviving an old line of interpretation which goes back at least to Koschaker. See Burrows, "Levirate Marriage," p. 32, for discussion.

302   THE ELDERS OF THE CITY

D Code apparently unchanged shows that its compilers wanted to perpetuate that traditional spirit of clan loyalty and inter-familial cooperation in the Israelite society of their day, not undermine it. They strive to promote moral integrity and lineage solidarity (by encouraging a man to fulfill his obligations to a dead brother and his widow) and community harmony (by overseeing land transfers).

CONCLUSIONS

Levirate marriage is a custom found in many kinship-based societies, both ancient and contemporary. It serves to protect the welfare of widows in economic environments which naturally place them at risk. It also provides a way for inherited property rights to be maintained within a lineage. This is particularly important when a young man dies before he has fathered any children. In turn, the maintenance of property rights provides economic stability for the broader community. Still, levirate marriage usually is an option rather than a strict obligation. As such, it stands as a test for a widow and her potential levir, pitting their self-interests against their sense of obligation to the dead man's extended family.

The biblical stories of Judah and Tamar (Genesis 38) and Boaz and Ruth (Ruth 4) provide concrete examples of levirate marriage in ancient Israel. These show that the levir could be any close male relative of the man who dies, although preference is given to those most closely related. Also, they show that marriage in levirate was to some degree optional. The Onan episode demonstrates the belief that the custom was divinely affirmed. It is administered by the dead man's father (in Genesis 38) or community leaders (in Ruth 4).

It has been common for tradition historians to propose an evolutionary link from these stories to the levirate law. The most common proposals place the levirate law either at the end of this evolution or in the middle, dependent on one's view of the date of the Book of Ruth. A primary element in this discussion is the range of male in-laws to whom a widow might turn to serve as a levir. Since only brothers of the deceased are mentioned in the law while other relatives serve as a levir in the narrative examples, it is usually claimed that the law intends to restrict the levirate to those brothers. The proposal made here is that marriage in levirate was always thought of as a right or an option in ancient Israel (as it was among neighboring peoples), but that the levirate law of Deut 25:5–10 gives a conglomeration of special circumstances (adult brothers living on an undivided paternal estate, the absence of any children, and the possibility of the widow marrying a "stranger") in which levirate marriage becomes an obligation. This interpretation eliminates the need for placing the law on an evolutionary continuum. It represents an exception, not the general rule. The circumstances it assumes could have existed at almost any time in Israel's history.[161] Nevertheless, in the process, it reveals motivations and tensions common to any instance of the custom. These include concerns for the welfare of the widow, social and economic responsibilities to one's family (the dead man's "name"), the significance of inter-familial economic relations, and the tension between individual and group concerns.

As the law unfolds, it gives more and more significant "motivations" for a brother-in-law to fulfill his levirate responsibilities. The initial concern is raised by the widow's apparent consideration to marry a "stranger" (v 5a). This shifts the focus to the brother-in-law, who is to marry her instead, for the sake of his brother (vv 5b–6). His reluctance to do so prompts the widow to accuse him publicly of his lack of loyalty to his late brother (v 7). The city elders then confront him to try to persuade him to marry the widow (v 8a). If he still refuses (v 8b), he is apparently stripped of any claims he might hold to his brother's share of the estate, he is publicly humiliated and reproached, and he is shamed and socially isolated by the community (vv 9–10).

The elders of the city play a significant role in the corollary case of this law. They are perhaps uninvolved in the main case (25:5–6), because the situation would initially be a family matter, and it would remain so if the brother-in-law fulfilled his levirate responsibilities. Once he refuses to do so (v 7), it becomes a community matter, and so it is brought before the city elders.

---

[161] Cp. Gertz, *Die Gerichtsorganisation*, pp. 197–204.

They address the situation for two reasons. First, they affirm the brother-in-law's moral responsibility to his dead brother and his widow. Someone who is unwilling to honor his personal obligations threatens the spirit of mutual cooperation which binds together their community. The elders speak to him for the good of the entire community, using their powerful tools of persuasion in an attempt to change his mind. If they are unsuccessful in this endeavor (v 8), they then serve in a notarial role to oversee the settlement of legal questions regarding the dead man's property (v 9). Exactly what this entails would vary, but it seems to culminate in the full transfer of the dead man's property rights to his widow (and her next husband). Such transactions typically are handled by elders, because they involve more than one family and have long-term consequences for those families (and others in the community). In all this, their primary concern is the welfare of the whole community; their concern for the dead man and his family derives from that broader concern.

The levirate law is a good example of how supposedly private matters can have public implications and repercussions. It appeals to the moral integrity of individuals in the community for the purpose of maintaining the harmony and cooperative strength of the community as a whole. We have discerned this as an underlying goal in each of the other laws investigated in this study. It probably is for this reason that the law has been incorporated without any recognizable alterations into the D Code; it serves well the purposes of the redactors in its existing form. And as in those other laws, city elders lead the way in encouraging members of their community to consider of utmost importance the moral integrity and social solidarity of their community.

Chapter 8
General Conclusions

The scope of this study has intentionally been rather restricted. I have tried to remain focused on but five laws which actually mention elders (others might assume the participation of elders), all contained within one section of the Book of Deuteronomy. Excursions beyond those laws have been conducted primarily for the purpose of illuminating some aspect of one or more of them. Thus, we are looking at a partial picture of elders, viewed from a narrow literary perspective. Similar investigations of other passages mentioning elders are needed to fill out the picture.

Nevertheless, the lens of cross-cultural comparison has brought this portion of the picture into clearer focus, thereby offsetting some of the drawbacks inherent in such a narrow study. More extensive comparisons are possible for some situations than others (compare the amount of data available concerning murder or adultery with those related to intra-familial discipline of habitual wrongdoers); yet, the interpretation of each passage is aided by this approach. This approach is particularly helpful in reminding us that each biblical law represents only one response among many possible responses to a given situation. Moreover, comparisons within the biblical canon itself suggest that other responses found in analogous societies might also have been employed in Israel. Biblical scholars have long been aware of these differences, and they have usually employed diachronic explanations to resolve them. This approach reveals that some synchronic explanations are also possible.

These considerations spill over into questions about the nature of biblical law. Many have assumed that the laws are intended to be read as exhaustive absolutes. For example, laws which call for the stoning of an offender are read rigidly, as if no other response to the specified offense is to be allowed, even though other biblical texts relate instances in which other responses were given. The typical way of dealing with these "conflicting" data has been to develop a diachronic reconstruction that explains these as cultural shifts, usually involving some conflict between traditional adjudicative practices and those accompanying the rise of a centralized state. A cross-cultural approach suggests that we should expect there to be exceptions, that adjudicators were probably expected to demonstrate some latitude. Members of kinship-based societies are never rigid in their implementation of legal prescriptions (written or oral), because there is always a history of flexibility in dealing with these situations. This flexibility is actually reflected in the differences one finds among the various law codes of the ancient Near East. It appears that none of those codes was intended to be comprehensive; rather, they were intended to be read in the light of the other codes and/or a sort of "common law," known to some degree by those throughout the region who served in judicial capacities. This is why there were "judges" in the ancient Near East. They had to be wise in order to exercise appropriate flexibility (dare we say "justice"?) in the enforcement of laws and traditions. A part of this wisdom would have come from experience with legal practices and norms common to the region. The same sort of wisdom and flexibility naturally would have been expected of Israel's elders and judges, if they are at all like local adjudicators in contemporary kinship-based societies. The Deuteronomic laws probably were written with that understanding in mind, and they should be read accordingly.

SUMMARY OF FINDINGS REGARDING
CITY ELDERS IN DEUTERONOMY

The analyses presented here suggest some fundamental ideas pertaining to the roles played by city elders in Israel. First, such leaders perform a variety of functions: judicial (19:1–13; 22:13–21), notarial (21:18–21; 25:5–10), representative (19:1–13; 21:1–9), and cultic (21:1–9). Attempts to isolate these functions into distinct categories seem counter-productive to the enterprise of understanding the roles of city elders in Israelite society. These functions apparently overlapped in the minds of ancient Israelites, as they do among contemporary kinship-based groups. For example, elders are expected to serve both as adjudicators and as witnesses (to previous transactions) in the same legal proceedings. What would seem like a "conflict of interest" to Western readers is accepted as "natural" by members of those communities.

Second, the power and authority of elders are essentially limited to the local community. They do not exercise their power and authority in any way which would suggest that elders enjoyed a higher class status than other members of their community. They are simply the recognized leaders of a group of equals. Nor is their authority absolute. In cases which prove to be beyond a group of elders' ability to resolve, other adjudicators become involved (see Chapter 2 and Deut 17:8–13; 21:1–9). Whenever a situation extends beyond the boundaries of their community, they function primarily as the representatives of that community, often in cooperation with other functionaries (see Deut 21:1–9; cp. Deut 19:1–13; Num 35:9–34; Josh 20:1–6).

Third, local elders basically work for reconciliation of a social rift, motivated by two primary considerations: the moral integrity of their community (which ultimately means its relationship with Yahweh), and the social/economic solidarity of their community. Both of these are threatened by the offense addressed in each law, and so both would have been of concern in each law from its inception. The asylum-law (Deut 19:1–13) equips the elders to preserve more easily the moral status of their community by affirming their efforts to insure the execution of one guilty of premeditated murder and by working to prevent the "shedding of innocent blood." It also promotes community solidarity by

including measures which would inhibit the development of a
feud. The elders primarily affirm the moral integrity of their
community in the case of the unidentified murder victim (Deut
21:1–9); but they also reflect the unity of their town by being able
to represent the entire group in their statement. A rebellious son
represents the antithesis of an Israelite community's moral
standards and must be reformed or removed; but he also
threatens its unity by creating friction between his family and
others around it. The law in Deut 21:18–21 affirms the elders'
efforts to inhibit such developments. Similarly, the case of the
wrongfully-accused bride exposes a potential rift between two
families (Deut 22:13–19), and so the law calls on the elders to
move to prevent it. Its corollary (Deut 22:20–21) demonstrates the
severity with which a legitimate accusation of promiscuity is to be
handled in order to maintain a community's moral integrity. If
they do not, that integrity is impugned and bitter feelings between
the two families are fueled. The levirate law (Deut 25:5–10) shows
how elders would encourage one's moral obligations to one's
immediate family, by calling on them to "speak" with the reluctant
levir. At the same time, they are prepared to work toward
preserving community-wide peace, should those efforts fail and
the economic fracturing of a family ensue, by bearing witness to
the levir's humiliation and the removal of his rights over the dead
man's property.

THE ELDERS-LAWS AND THE D CODE

Four of the five elders-laws display evidence of
Deuteronom(ist)ic expansion; only the levirate law (Deut 25:5–10)
remained unchanged. Interestingly, consideration for the moral
integrity and social solidarity of the community are made more
explicit in these Deuteronom(ist)ic additions. This does not mean,
however, that the redactors were seeking to introduce these.
notions into the laws. The cross-cultural analyses conducted here
show that these notions would have been understood naturally in
the social context of Israelite communities. Rather, the more
explicit statement of these notions indicates that the redactors

wished to affirm and perpetuate them, but then also adapt them to a national perspective. Thus, the redactors do not significantly alter the basic intent of the pre-existing laws in this process; instead, they affirm and reinforce that intent. Overall, one finds that notions expressed in the Deuteronom(ist)ic expansions which are more "at home" in a single community are now being expanded to the level of the nation, as if the nation is to be thought of as a single community.

A basic principle underlying these laws at every level of redaction is that an individual's (or a single family's) actions affect the entire community. Their actions threaten the moral integrity and the solidarity of the local community. This is true of each elders-law, and ultimately is the reason why the elders are involved. They are working in these situations for the good of the community. The redactors of these laws primarily expand this notion by implying that the community's response (or non-response) to the situations addressed in the laws affects the entire nation. One sees this most clearly in the use of the purge-formula and other concluding Deuteronom(ist)ic expansions (Deut 19:13; 21:9, 21; 22:21). Proper adjudication originally would have been the concern solely of the local community; now it is of concern to the entire nation of Israel. By purging evil from the local community, the people purge evil from the entire nation.

This expanded perspective is a natural consequence of cult centralization, because such centralization carries with it a centralizing of religious traditions. Limiting worship to one place means that all Israelite communities will come together to celebrate a common tradition of divine land grant. This tradition reinforces and unifies those communities in their understanding of how the moral integrity of their own community is threatened by certain actions. Similarly, cult centralization could have transformed ideas about the significance of rifts between families. Other laws in the Deuteronomic Code call for members of all communities to come together at the one central place to worship (see 16:1–17). It seems that such gatherings previously took place at the local level (cp. 1 Sam 16:1–5; 20:6). What once had symbolized local unity and harmony now is to take place on a national scale. Again, the idea of "community" is being expanded. A logical result of this change might be that local rifts could be seen to have national consequences. By the same token, it would be just as natural to appeal to the ideas which had traditionally been brought forward at the local level to combat local rifts in an attempt to promote the same goals of harmony and moral integrity at the national level (see 13:7–19).

Other Deuteronom(ist)ic additions in the asylum law (19:1, 2b–3a, 6–10) arise for similar reasons. The pre-Deuteronomic core is concerned with upholding the honor of the families involved and the overall integrity of the local community. The portions added by the redactor(s) supplement those concerns with the notion of divine land grant, by emphasizing that disproportionate retaliation ("shedding innocent blood" in the name of blood-vengenance) is a sacral offense. Cult centralization undercuts the religious basis for the designation of most cities as asylum-cities, which could have threatened to eliminate this function from them. This law removes that threat by perpetuating the same asylum function to them, in spite of cult centralization. Other traditions take this process a step further by specifying the locations of these asylum-cities (Deut 4:41–43; Joshua 20).

The secondary layer to the law in Deut 21:1–9 also presents the notion of divine land grant as that which underlies concerns about pollution of the land. The only expansion in that law which does not fall into these categories is the rationale for the participation of Levitical priests in v 5. It appears to be based on Deuteronom(ist)ic prescriptions given elsewhere (see 17:8–13), but it could be attributable to a later, non-deuteronomistic hand.

These conclusions suggest a great degree of continuity between the pre-Deuteronomic elders-laws and the laws in their present form. Their inclusion in the D Code suggests that the Deuteronomic lawgiver does not intend to undermine traditional local power structures and ideas. In fact, it seems that these laws were included in the present law code because they already contained ideas and institutions which the redactors wished to endorse and promote. In addition, the expansion of the perspective from the local level to the national level (seen clearly in the redactional supplements) was already present in the pre-Deuteronomic layers of some laws (see the discussions of the references to "Israel" in 21:8; 22:19; and 25:10).

This impression of continuity runs counter to the conclusions of some recent studies on the effects that the Deuteronomic laws had on life in Israelite communities. Those studies argue that these laws intend to promote allegiance to one's nuclear family at the expense of the broader community. This is seen as a means of affording greater power to the central authorities. I have argued in the opposite direction. The pre-Deuteronomic laws promote the welfare of the community over the self-interests of individuals and individual families. Deuteronom(ist)ic redactions of these laws primarily expand this concern for the welfare of the community further outward, tying the welfare of the nation to the welfare of each of its communities. Moreover, the old mechanisms for promoting the welfare of the community (adjudication by city elders and other local functionaries) are not displaced in this process; rather, they are affirmed.

This leaves one other issue to be considered, one which I have avoided for the most part: the historical provenance of these laws. Most of the laws give little direct help in addressing this issue. They all give the general impression that the communities in which these laws are to be implemented exist in a politically-independent Israel; there are no concerns about non-Israelite interference. It seems more likely that laws presented in this assumptive frame would originate in pre-exilic Israel, where such a situation would be a reality, rather than in an exilic or post-exilic milieu, where independence is never more than an ideal. The fact that this impression persists and is furthered in the Deuteronom(ist)ic layers suggests that they too are pre-exilic. This is most pronounced in the asylum-law, which is redactionally the most complex of these laws. The secondary layers of the asylum-law assume cult centralization and (subsequent?) territorial expansion. The latter most likely reflects expansion under the leadership of Josiah (see on 19:8–10). The former could be a development either of the Josianic or Hezekianic regimes.

The strictly local perspective of the pre-Deuteronomic layers of the laws probably reflects a place of origin in contrast to that of the redacted laws. That prior perspective is distanced in some sense (geographically, politically) from any central power structures. It is tempting to associate these to some extent with disenfranchised local populations from the North who fled south in the wake of Assyrian incursions, or with groups such as "the people of the land" in the South. These are only preliminary suggestions, however, which would have to be clarified by similar investigations of other laws.

BIBLIOGRAPHY

BIBLICAL AND ANCIENT NEAR EASTERN STUDIES

Albright, W. F. "The Judicial Reform of Jehoshaphat." In *Alexander Marx Jubilee Volume*, pp. 61–82. Ed. Saul Lieberman. New York: Jewish Publication Society, 1950.

―――. "The List of Levitic Cities." In *Louis Ginzberg Jubilee Volume*, pp. 49–73. Ed. S. Lieberman, *et al*. New York: American Academy for Jewish Research, 1946.

Alt, Albrecht. *Kleine Schriften zur Geschichte des Volkes Israel*. 3 Volumes. Munich: C. E. Beck, 1953–59.

Arnaud, D. *Emar VI: Tome 3, Textes sumériens et accadiens: Texte*. Paris, 1986.

Aufrecht, Walter E. "Genealogy and History in Ancient Israel." In *Ascribe to the Lord: Biblical and Other Studies in Memory of Peter C. Craigie*, pp. 205–35. Ed. L. Eslinger and G. Taylor. JSOTS 67; Sheffield: Sheffield Academic, 1988.

Auld, A. G. "Cities of Refuge in Israelite Tradition." *Journal for the Study of the Old Testament* 10 (1978) 26–40.

―――. "The 'Levitical Cities': Texts and History." *Zeitschrift für die alttestamentliche Wissenschaft* 91 (1979) 194–206.

Bayliss, M. "The Cult of Dead Kin in Assyria and Babylonia." *Iraq* 35 (1973) 115–25.

Beattie, D. R. G. "The Book of Ruth as Evidence for Israelite Legal Practice." *Vetus Testamentum* 24 (1974) 251–67.

―――. "Kethibh and Qere in Ruth IV 5." *Vetus Testamentum* 21 (1971) 490–94.

313

———. "Redemption in Ruth, and Related Matters: A Response to Jack M. Sasson." *Journal for the Study of the Old Testament* 5 (1978) 65–68.

Bechtel, Lyn M. "Shame as a Sanction of Social Control in Biblical Israel: Judicial, Political, and Social Shaming." *Journal for the Study of the Old Testament* 49 (1991) 47–76.

Belkin, Samuel. "Levirate and Agnate Marriage in Rabbinic and Cognate Literature." *Jewish Quarterly Review* 60 (1970) 275–329.

Bellefontaine, Elizabeth. "Deuteronomy 21:18–21: Reviewing the Case of the Rebellious Son." *Journal for the Study of the Old Testament* 13 (1979) 13–31.

Ben-Barak, Zafrira. "Inheritance by Daughters in the Ancient Near East." *Journal of Semitic Studies* 25 (1980) 22–33.

Benjamin, Don C. *Deuteronomy and City Life*. Lanham, MD: University Press of America, 1983.

Berg, Horstklaus. "Die 'Ältesten Israels' im Alten Testament." Diss. theol., Hamburg, 1959.

Berry, G. R. "The Code Found in the Temple." *Journal of Biblical Literature* 39 (1920) 44–51.

Bewer, J. A. "The Ge'ullah in the Book of Ruth." *American Journal of Semitic Languages* 19 (1903) 143–48.

———. *The Literature of the Old Testament*. 3rd edition. New York/London: Columbia University, 1922/1962.

Blenkinsopp, Joseph. "Deuteronomy and the Politics of Post-Mortem Existence." *Vetus Testamentum* 45 (1995) 1–16.

Boecker, Hans Jochen. *Law and the Administration of Justice in the Old Testament and Ancient East*. Trans. J. Mosier. Minneapolis: Augsburg, 1980.

Boling, Robert. *Joshua*. AB; New York: Doubleday, 1982.

Bornkamm, G. S.v. "πρεσβυς," *Theological Dictionary of the New Testament*. Volume VI, pp. 651–80. Ed. G. Kittel and G. Friedrich. Trans. and ed. G. W. Bromiley. Grand Rapids: Eerdmans, 1968.

Bovati, P. *Re-Establishing Justice: Legal Terms, Concepts and Procedures in the Hebrew Bible*. Trans. M. J. Smith. JSOTS 105; Sheffield: JSOT, 1994.

Braulik, Georg. *Deuteronomium II, 16,18–34,12*. Würzburg: Echter, 1992.

———. "Zur Abfolge der Gesetze in Deuteronomium 16,18–21,23. Weitere Beobachtungen." *Biblica* 69 (1988) 63–92.

Brichto, Herbert C. "Kin, Cult, Land and Afterlife—A Biblical Complex." *Hebrew Union College Annual* 44 (1973) 1–54.

Broshi, Magen. "The Expansion of Jerusalem in the Reigns of Hezekiah and Manasseh." *Israel Exploration Journal* 24 (1974) 21–26.

Buchholz, J. *Die Ältesten Israels im Deuteronomium*. GTA 36; Göttingen: Vandenhoeck & Ruprecht, 1988.

Burrows, Millar. "The Ancient Oriental Background of Hebrew Levirate Marriage." *Bulletin of the American Schools of Oriental Research* 77 (1940) 2–15.

———. "Levirate Marriage in Israel." *Journal of Biblical Literature* 59 (1940) 23–33.

———. "The Marriage of Ruth and Boaz." *Journal of Biblical Literature* 59 (1940) 445–54.

Bush, Frederic W. *Ruth, Esther*. WBC 9; Dallas: Word Books, 1996.

Buss, Martin J. "The Distinction between Civil and Criminal Law in Ancient Israel." *Proceedings of the Sixth World Congress on Jewish Studies, 1973*. Volume I, pp. 51–62. Jerusalem: Jerusalem Academic, 1977.

Callaway, P. R. "Deut 21:18–21: Proverbial Wisdom and Law." *Journal of Biblical Literature* 103 (1984) 341–52.

Campbell, Edward F., Jr. *Ruth*. AB; Garden City: Doubleday, 1975.

Carmichael, Calum M. "A Ceremonial Crux: Removing a Man's Sandal as a Female Gesture of Contempt." *Journal of Biblical Literature* 96 (1977) 321–36.

———. *The Laws of Deuteronomy*. Ithaca: Cornell University, 1974.

Causse, A. *Du groupe ethnique à la communauté religieuse: le problème sociologique de la religion d'Israël*. Paris: F. Alcan, 1937.

Coats, George. "Widow's Rights: A Crux in the Structure of Genesis 38." *Catholic Biblical Quarterly* 34 (1972) 461–66.

Conrad, J. S.v. "זקן," *Theological Dictionary of the Old Testament*. Volume IV, pp. 122–31. Ed. G. J. Botterweck and H. Ringgren. Trans. David E. Green. Grand Rapids: Eerdmans, 1980.

Cross, F. M. "Reuben, First-Born of Jacob." *Zeitschrift für die alttestamentliche Wissenschaft, Supplemental Volume* 100 (1988) 46–65.

Crüsemann, F. *Der Widerstand gegen das Königtum. Die antiköniglichen Texte des Alten Testamentumes und der Kampf um den frühen israelitischen Staat*. WMANT 49; Neukirchen-Vluyn: Neukirchener, 1978.

Dandamayev, M. A. "The Neo-Babylonian Elders." In *Societies and Languages of the Ancient Near East: Studies in Honour of I. M. Diakanoff*, pp. 38–41. Warminster: Aris and Phillips, 1982.

David, M. "Die Bestimmung über die Asylstädte." *Oudtestamentische Studiën* 9 (1951) 30–48.

Davies, E. W. "Inheritance Rights and Hebrew Levirate Marriage." *Vetus Testamentum* 31 (1981) 138–44, 257–68.

———. "Ruth 4:5 and the Duties of the *go'el*." *Vetus Testamentum* 33 (1983) 231–34.

Davies, G. H. "Elder in the OT." *The Interpreter's Dictionary of the Bible*. Volume II, pp. 72–73. Ed. G. A. Buttrick, *et al*. Nashville: Abingdon, 1962.

Dearman, J. Andrew. "The Levitical Cities of Reuben and Moabite Toponymy." *Bulletin of the American Schools of Oriental Research* 276 (1989) 55–66.

Dempster, S. "The Deuteronomic Formula KI YIMMATSE' in the Light of Biblical and Ancient Near Eastern Law: An Evaluation of David Daube's Theory." *Revue Biblique* 91 (1984) 188–211.

Diakonoff, I. M. "Extended Families in Babylonian Ur." *Zeitschrift für Assyriologie* 75 (1985) 47–65.

Dion, Paul. "The Greek Version of Deut 21:1–9 and Its Variants: a Record of Early Exegesis." In *De Septuaginta: Studies in Honour of John William Wevers on His 65th Birthday*, pp. 151–60. Ed. A. Pietersma and C. Cox. Mississauga, Ont: Benben Publ., 1984.

Donner, H. "The Separate States of Israel and Judah." In *Israelite and Judaean History*. Ed. J. H. Hayes and J. M. Miller. OTL; Philadelphia: Westminster, 1977.

Driver, S. R. *A Critical and Exegetical Commentary on Deuteronomy*. ICC; New York: Charles Scribner's Sons, 1895.

Dus, Jan. "Die 'Ältesten Israels.'" *Communio Viatorum* 3 (1960) 232–42.

Eissfeldt, Otto. "Der geschichtliche Hintergrund der Erzählung von Gibeas Schandtat (Richter 19–21)." *Kleine Schriften* II, pp. 64–80. Ed. R. Sellheim and F. Maass. Tübingen: J. C. B. Mohr, 1953.

―――. *The Old Testament, An Introduction*. 3rd Edition. Trans. P. R. Ackroyd. New York: Harper & Row, 1965.

Epstein, L. M. *Marriage Laws in the Bible and the Talmud*. Cambridge: Harvard University, 1942.

―――. *Sex Laws and Customs in Judaism*. New York: Ktav, 1948.

Evans, G. "Ancient Mesopotamian Assemblies." *Journal of the American Oriental Society* 78 (1958) 1–11.

―――. "Ancient Mesopotamian Assemblies—an addendum." *Journal of the American Oriental Society* 78 (1958) 114–15.

―――. "'Gates' and 'Streets': Urban Institutions in Old Testament Times." *Journal of Religious History* 2 (1962) 1–12.

Fensham, F. C. "Widow, Orphan, and the Poor in Ancient Near Eastern Legal and Wisdom Literature." *Journal of Near Eastern Studies* 21 (1962) 129–39.

Fewell, Danna N., and David M. Gunn. "'A Son is Born to Naomi!': Literary Allusions and Interpolation in the Book of Ruth." *Journal for the Study of the Old Testament* 40 (1988) 99–108.

Fiensy, D. "Using the Nuer Culture of Africa in Understanding the Old Testament: An Evaluation." *Journal for the Study of the Old Testament* 38 (1987) 73–83.

Finkelstein, Israel. *The Archaeology of the Israelite Settlement*. Trans. D. Saltz. Jerusalem: Israel Exploration Society, 1988.

Finkelstein, J. J. "On Some Recent Studies in Cuneiform Law." *Journal of the American Oriental Society* 90 (1970) 243–56.

―――. "Sex Offenses in Sumerian Laws." *Journal of the American Oriental Society* 86 (1966) 355–72.

Fleishman, J. "Offences against Parents Punishable by Death: Towards a Socio-Legal Interpretation of Ex. 21:15, 17." *The Jewish Law Annual* 10 (1992) 7–37.

Fleming, Daniel E. *The Installation of Baal's High Priestess at Emar: A Window on Ancient Syrian Religion.* HSM; Atlanta: Scholars, 1992.

Freedman, David Noel. S.v., "Ältester," *Biblisch-Historisches Handwörterbuch* I, pp. 76–77. Ed. Bo Reicke and L. Rost. Göttingen: Vandenhoeck and Ruprecht, 1966.

Frick, Frank. *The Formation of the State in Ancient Israel: A Survey of Models and Theories.* Sheffield: Almond, 1985.

Frymer-Kensky, Tikva. "Law and Philosophy: The Case of Sex in the Bible." *Semeia* 45 (1989) 89–102.

———. "The Strange Case of the Suspected Sotah (Numbers v 11–31)." *Vetus Testamentum* 34 (1984) 11–26.

Gelb, I. J. "*SHIBUT KUSHURRA'IM*, 'Witnesses of the Indemnity.'" *Journal of Near Eastern Studies* 43 (1984) 263–74.

Gerbrandt, Gerald E. *Kingship According to the Deuteronomistic History.* SBLDS 87; Atlanta: Scholars, 1986.

Gertz, Jan Christian. *Die Gerichtsorganisation Israels im deuteronomischen Gesetz.* FRLANT 165; Göttingen: Vandenhoeck & Ruprecht, 1993.

Gibson, M. "Introduction." In *The Organization of Power: Aspects of Bureaucracy in the Ancient Near East*, pp. 1–5. Ed. M. Gibson and R. D. Biggs. SAOC, No. 46; Chicago: Oriental Institute, 1987.

Good, E. M. "Capital Punishment and Its Alternatives in Ancient Near Eastern Law." *Stanford Law Review* 19 (1967) 947–77.

Gordis, Robert. "Democratic Origins in Ancient Israel—The Biblical 'EDAH." In *Alexander Marx Jubilee Volume*, pp. 369–88. Ed. Saul Lieberman. New York: Jewish Publication Society, 1950.

———. "Love, Marriage, and Business in the Book of Ruth: A Chapter in Hebrew Customary Law." In *A Light Unto My Path*, pp. 241–64. Ed. H. N. Bream, *et al.* Philadelphia: Temple University, 1974.

Gottwald, Norman. *The Tribes of Yahweh: A Sociology of the Religion of Liberated Israel, 1250–1050 B.C.E.* Maryknoll, NY: Orbis Books, 1979.

Graham, W. C. "The Modern Controversy about Deuteronomy." *Journal of Religion* 7 (1927) 396–418.

Greenberg, Moshe. "The Biblical Concept of Asylum." *Journal of Biblical Literature* 78 (1959) 125–32.

———. "Some Postulates of Biblical Criminal Law." In *Yehezkel Kaufmann Jubilee Volume*, pp. 5–28. Ed. M. Haran. Jerusalem: Magnes Press, 1960. Reprinted in *A Song of Power and the Power of Song: Essays on the Book of Deuteronomy*, pp. 283–300. Ed. D. L. Christensen; Winona Lake, IN: Eisenbrauns, 1993.

Greengus, Samuel. "The Old Babylonian Marriage Contract." *Journal of the American Oriental Society* 89 (1969) 505–32.

———. "A Textbook Case of Adultery in Ancient Mesopotamia." *Hebrew Union College Annual* 40–41 (1969/1970) 33–44.

Grosz, K. "Dowry and Brideprice in Nuzi," in *Studies on the Civilization and Culture of Nuzi and the Hurrians* (E. R. Lacheman Festschrift), pp. 161–82. Ed. M. A. Morrison and D. I. Owen. Winona Lake, IN: Eisenbrauns, 1981.

Haas, P. "'Die He Shall Surely Die': The Structure of Homicide in Biblical Law." *Semeia* 45 (1989) 67–87.

Halpern, Baruch. *The Constitution of the Monarchy.* HSM 25; Chico, CA: Scholars, 1981.

———. "Jerusalem and the Lineages in the Seventh Century BCE: Kinship and the Rise of Individual Moral Liability." In *Law and Ideology in Monarchic Israel*, pp. 1–107. Ed. B. Halpern and D. W. Hobson. JSOTS 124; Sheffield: Sheffield Academic, 1991.

Haran, M. "Studies in the Account of the Levitical Cities. I. Preliminary Considerations." *Journal of Biblical Literature* 80 (1961) 45–54, 156–65.

Heltzer, M. *The Rural Community in Ancient Ugarit.* Wiesbaden: Ludwig Reichert, 1976.

Herrmann, S. *A History of Israel in Old Testament Times.* 2nd Edition. Philadelphia: Fortress Press, 1981.

Hoffner, H. A., Jr. "Incest, Sodomy and Bestiality in the Ancient Near East." In *Orient and Occident* (FS Cyrus Gordon), pp. 81–90. AOAT 22; Neukirchen-Vluyn: Neukirchener, 1973.

Hölscher, G. "Komposition und Ursprung des Deuteronomiums." *Zeitschrift für die alttestamentliche Wissenschaft* 40 (1922) 161–255.

Hooke, S. H. "The Theory and Practice of Substitution." *Vetus Testamentum* 2 (1952) 2–17.

Hoppe, Leslie J. "Elders and Deuteronomy." *Église et théologie* 14 (1983) 259–72.

———. "The Origins of Deuteronomy." Ann Arbor, MI: University Microfilms, 1978.

Hubbard, Robert L., Jr. *The Book of Ruth.* NICOT; Grand Rapids: Eerdmans, 1988.

Huehnergard, John. "Biblical Notes on Some New Akkadian Texts from Emar (Syria)." *Catholic Biblical Quarterly* 47 (1985) 428–34.

Jackson, B. S. "Ideas of Law and Legal Administration: A Semiotic Approach." In *The World of Ancient Israel*, pp. 185–202. Ed. R. E. Clements; Cambridge: Cambridge University, 1989.

Jacobsen, Thorkild. "An Ancient Mesopotamian Trial for Homicide." *Oriens Antiquus* 3 (1959) 130–50.

———. "Primitive Democracy in Ancient Mesopotamia." *Journal of Near Eastern Studies* 2 (1943) 159–72.

Jankowska, N. B. "Extended Family Commune and Civil Self-Government in Arrapha in the Fifteenth–Fourteenth Century B.C." In *Ancient Mesopotamia: Socio-Economic History*, pp. 235–52. Moscow: Nauka Publishing House, 1969; Schaan: H. R. Wohlwend, 1981.

———. "Life of the Military Élite in Arrapha." In *Studies on the Civilization and Culture of Nuzi and the Hurrians* (E. R. Lachemann FS), pp. 195–200. Ed. M. A. Morrison and D. I. Owen. Winona Lake, IN: Eisenbrauns, 1981.

Jas, R. *Neo-Assyrian Judicial Procedures.* SAAS V; Helsinki: Vammalan Kirjapaino Oy, 1996.

Jirku, A. "Drei Fälle von Haftpflicht im altorientalischen Palästina-Syrien und Deuteronomium cap. 21." *Zeitschrift für die alttestamentliche Wissenschaft* 79 (1967) 359–61.

Kenik, H. A. *Design for Kingship: The Deuteronomistic Narrative Technique in 1 Kings 3:4–15.* SBLDS 69; Chico, CA: Scholars, 1983.

Klengel, H. "Die Rolle der 'Ältesten' (LU^MESH^SHU.GI) im Kleinasien der Hethiterzeit." *Zeitschrift für Assyriologie* 57 (1965) 223–36.

———. "Zu den *shibutum* in altbabylonischer Zeit." *Orientalia* n.s. 29 (1960) 357–75.

Knierim, Rolf. "Exodus 18 und die Neuordnung der Mosaischen Gerischtsbarkeit." *Zeitschrift für die alttestamentliche Wissenschaft* 73 (1961) 146–71.

———. "The Problem of Ancient Israel's Prescriptive Legal Traditions." *Semeia* 45 (1989) 7–23.

Köhler, Ludwig. "Justice in the Gate." In *Hebrew Man*, pp. 127–34. Trans. P. Ackroyd. New York: Abingdon, 1956.

Kornfeld, W. "L'adultère dans l'orient antique." *Revue Biblique* 57 (1950) 92–109.

Kupper, J.-R. "La cité et la royaume de Mari: l'organisation urbaine à l'époque amorite." *Mari, annales de recherches interdisiplinaires* 4 (1985) 463–66.

L'Hour, J. "Une législation criminelle dans le Deutéronome." *Biblica* 44 (1963) 1–28.

Leggett, Donald A. *The Levirate and Goel Institutions in the Old Testament, with Special Attention to the Book of Ruth*. Cherry Hill, NJ: Mack, 1974.

Lemche, Niels Peter. *Early Israel*. Leiden: Brill, 1985.

Levinson, Bernard M. "Calum M. Carmichael's Approach to the Laws of Deuteronomy." *Harvard Theological Review* 83 (1990) 227–57.

———. *Deuteronomy and the Hermeneutics of Legal Innovation*. New York/Oxford: Oxford University, 1997.

Locher, Clemens. *Die Ehre einer Frau in Israel: Exegetische und rechtsvergleichende Studien zu Deuteronomium 22,13–21*. OBO 70; Göttingen: Vandenhoeck & Ruprecht, 1986.

Lohfink, Norbert. "Die Bundesurkunde des König Josias. Eine Frage an der Deuteronomiumsforschung." *Biblica* 44 (1963) 261–88, 461–98.

———. "Distribution of the Functions of Power: The Laws Concerning Public Offices in Deuteronomy 16:18–18:22." In *A Song of Power and the Power of Song: Essays on the Book of Deuteronomy*, pp. 336–52. Ed. D. L. Christensen. Winona Lake: Eisenbrauns, 1993. Originally "Die Sicherung der Wirksamkeit des Gotteswortes durch das Prinzip der Schriftlichkeit der Tora und durch das Prinzip der Gewaltenteilung nach den Ämtergesetzen des Buches Deuteronomium (Dt 16,18–18,22)." In *Testimonium Veritati: Festschrift Wilhelm Kempf.* Ed. H. Wolter. Frankfurter Theologische Studien 7; Frankfurt: Knecht, 1971. Trans. R. Walls. In *Great Themes from the Old Testament*, pp. 55–75. Chicago: Franciscan Herald, 1981.

————. "Kerygmata des Deuteronomistischen Geschichtswerks." In *Die Botschaft und die Boten. Festschrift für H. W. Wolff*, pp. 87–100. Ed. J. Jeremias and L. Perlitt; Neukirchen-Vluyn: Neukirchener, 1981.

————. "Recent Discussion on 2 Kings 22–23: The State of the Question." In *A Song of Power and the Power of Song: Essays on the Book of Deuteronomy*, pp. 36–61. Ed. D. L. Christensen. SBTS 3; Winona Lake, IN: Eisenbrauns, 1993. Trans. L. M. Maloney, from "Zur neueren Diskussion über 2 Kön 22–23." In *Das Deuteronomium: Entstehung, Gestalt und Botschaft*, pp. 24–48. Ed. N. Lohfink. BETL; Louvain: Louvain University, 1985.

Macholz, G. C. "Die Stellung des Königs in der israelitischen Gerichtsverfassung." *Zeitschrift für die alttestamentliche Wissenschaft* 84 (1972) 159–82.

————. "Zur Geschichte der Justizorganisation in Juda." *Zeitschrift für die alttestamentliche Wissenschaft* 84 (1972) 314–40.

Malamat, Abraham. "Kingship and Council in Israel and Sumer: A Parallel." *Journal of Near Eastern Studies* 22 (1963) 247–53.

Manor, Dale. "A Brief History of Levirate Marriage as It Relates to the Bible." *Restoration Quarterly* 27 (1984) 129–42.

Marcus, David. "Juvenile Delinquency in the Bible and the Ancient Near East." *Journal of the Ancient Near Eastern Society* 13 (1981) 31–52.

Mars, L. "What Was Onan's Crime?" *Comparative Studies in Social History* 26 (1984) 429–38.

Martin, J. D. "Israel as a Tribal Society." In *The World of Ancient Israel: Sociological, Anthropological and Political Perspectives*, pp. 95–117. Ed. R. E. Clements. Cambridge: Cambridge University, 1989.

Matthews, Victor H. "Entrance Ways and Threshing Floors: Legally Significant Sites in the Ancient Near East." *Fides et Historia* 19 (1987) 25–40.

————. *Pastoral Nomadism in the Mari Kingdom (ca. 1830–1760 B.C.)* ASOR Diss. Series 3; Cambridge, MA: ASOR, 1978.

————, and Don C. Benjamin. "The Elder." *The Bible Today* 30 (1992) 170–74.

Mayes, A. D. H. *Deuteronomy.* Grand Rapids: Eerdmans, 1979.

Mazar, Benjamin. "The Cities of the Priests and the Levites." *Supplements to Vetus Testamentum* 7 (1960) 193–205.

Mcbride, S. Dean, Jr. "Polity of the Covenant People: The Book of Deuteronomy." *Interpretation* 41 (1987) 229–44.

McCarter, P. Kyle. *1 Samuel.* Anchor Bible. Garden City: Doubleday, 1980.

McKeating, Henry. "The Development of the Law of Homicide in Ancient Israel." *Vetus Testamentum* 25 (1975) 46–68.

————. "Sanctions Against Adultery in Ancient Israelite Society, with Some Reflections on Methodology in the Study of Old Testament Ethics." *Journal for the Study of the Old Testament* 11 (1979) 57–72.

McKenzie, D. A. "Judicial Procedure at the Town Gate." *Vetus Testamentum* 14 (1964) 100–104.

McKenzie, J. L. "The Elders in the Old Testament." *Biblica* 40 (1959) 522–40 [= *Analecta Biblica* 10 (1959) 388–406].

McNutt, Paula M. "The Kenites, the Midianites, and the Rechabites as Marginal Mediators in Ancient Israelite Tradition." *Semeia* 67 (1994) 109–45.

————. *Reconstructing the Society of Ancient Israel.* Louisville, KY: Westminster/John Knox, 1999.

Mendelsohn, I. "Guilds in Ancient Palestine." *Bulletin of the American Schools of Oriental Research* 80 (1940) 17–21.

————. "Guilds in Babylonia and Assyria," *Journal of the American Oriental Society* 60 (1940) 68–72.

Milgrom, Jacob. "The Alleged 'Demythologization and Secularization' in Deuteronomy." *Israel Exploration Journal* 23 (1973) 156–61.

————. "Sancta Contagion or Altar/City Asylum." In *Congress Volume, Vienna 1980,* pp. 278–310. Ed. J. A. Emerton. Supplements to Vetus Testamentum 32; Leiden: E. J. Brill, 1981.

Morgenstern, J. "The Book of the Covenant, Part II." *Hebrew Union College Annual* 7 (1930) 19–258.

Neufeld, E. *Ancient Hebrew Marriage Laws, with Special References to General Semitic Laws and Customs*. London: Longmans, Green and Company, 1944.

Nicolsky, N. M. "Das Asylrecht in Israel." *Zeitschrift für die alttestamentliche Wissenschaft* 7 (1930) 146–75.

Niditch, Susan. "Legends of Heroes and Heroines." In *The Hebrew Bible and Its Modern Interpreters*, pp. 445–63. Ed. D. A. Knight and G. M. Tucker. Philadelphia: Fortress; Chico, CA: Scholars, 1985.

———. "The Wronged Woman Righted: An Analysis of Genesis 38." *Harvard Theological Review* 72 (1979) 143–49.

Niehr, Herbert. "Grundzüge der Forschung zur Gerichtsorganisation Israels." *BibZ* 31 (1987) 206–27.

Noth, Martin. *The History of Israel*, 2nd ed. New York: Harper and Row, 1960.

———. *Numbers*. Trans. J. D. Martin. OTL; London: SCM, 1968.

Otto, Eckart. "Aspects of Legal Reforms and Reformulations in Ancient Cuneiform and Israelite Law." In *Theory and Method in Biblical and Cuneiform Law: Revision, Interpolation and Development*, pp. 160–96. Ed. B. M. Levinson. Journal for the Study of the Old Testament Supplements 181; Sheffield: Sheffield Academic, 1994.

———. "Das Eherecht im Mittelassyrischen Kodex und im Deuteronomium. Tradition und Redaktion in den §§12–16 der Tafel A des Mittelassyrischen Kodex und in Dtn 22, 22–29." In *Festschrift for K. Bergerhof*, pp. 259–81. Ed. M. Dietrich and O. Loretz. AOAT 232; Kevelaer: Butzon & Bercker; Neukirchen-Vluyn: Neukirchener, 1993.

———. "Der Dekalog als Brennspiegel israelitischer Rechtsgeschichte." In *Alttestamentlicher Glaube und Biblische Theologie* (FS H. D. Preuss), pp. 59–68. Ed. J. Hausmann and H.-J. Zobel. Stuttgart: Kohlhammer, 1992.

———. "Die Einschränkung des Privatstrafrechts durch öffentliches Strafrecht in der Redaktion der Paragraphen 1–24, 50–59 des Mittelassyrischen Kodex der Tafel A (KAV 1)." *Biblische Welten. Festschrift für Martin Metzger zu seinem 65. Geburtstag*, pp. 131–66. Ed. W. Zwickel. OBO 123; Göttingen: Vandenhoeck and Ruprecht, 1993.

Patai, Rafael. "The 'Egla 'Arufa or the Expiation of the Polluted Ground." *Jewish Quarterly Review* 30 (1939) 59–69.

Patrick, Dale. *Old Testament Law*. Atlanta: John Knox, 1985.

Pedersen, Johannes. *Israel: Its Life and Culture* I–II. London: Oxford, 1926.

Pentiuc, Eugen J. "West Semitic Terms in Akkadian Texts from Emar." *Journal of Near Eastern Studies* 58 (1999) 81–96.

Pfeiffer, R. H. *Introduction to the Old Testament*. New York: Harper and Brothers, 1941.

Phillips, Anthony. *Ancient Israel's Criminal Law: A New Approach to the Decalogue*. London: Basil Blackwell, 1970.

————. "Another Look at Adultery." *Journal for the Study of the Old Testament* 20 (1981) 3–25.

————. *Deuteronomy*. CBC; Cambridge: Cambridge University, 1973.

————. "NEBALAH—a Term for Serious Disorderly and Unruly Conduct." *Vetus Testamentum* 25 (1975) 237–42.

van der Ploeg, J. "Les anciens dans l'Ancien Testament." In *Lex tua veritas. Festschrift für Hubert Junker*, pp. 175–91. Ed. H. Groß and F. Mußner. Trier: Paulinus-Verlag, 1961.

Pressler, Carolyn. *The View of Women Found in the Deuteronomic Family Laws*. BZAW 216; New York/Berlin: Walter de Gruyter, 1993.

Preuss, Horst Dietrich. *Deuteronomium*. ErFor 164; Darmstadt: Wissenschaftliche Buchgesellschaft, 1982.

von Rad, Gerhard. *Deuteronomy*. OTL; Philadelphia: Westminster, 1966.

Rainey, Anson. "Family Relations in Ugarit." *Orientalia* 34 (1965) 10–22.

Reviv, Henoch. *The Elders in Ancient Israel: A Study of a Biblical Institution*. Trans. Lucy Plitmann. Jerusalem: Magnes, 1989.

————. "The Traditions Concerning the Inception of the Legal System in Israel: Significance and Dating." *Zeitschrift für die alttestamentliche Wissenschaft* 94 (1982) 566–75.

Richter, H.-F. "Zum Levirat im Buch Ruth." *Zeitschrift für die alttestamentliche Wissenschaft* 95 (1983) 123–26.

Roeroe, Wilhelm A. "Das Ältestenamt im Alten Testament." Diss. theol., Mainz, 1976.

Rofé, A. "The Arrangement of the Laws in Deuteronomy." *Ephemerides theoligicae lovanienses* 64 (1988) 265–87.

———. "Family and Sex Laws in Deuteronomy and the Book of the Covenant." *Henoch* 9 (1987) 130–59.

———. "The History of the Cities of Refuge in Biblical Law." In *Scripta Hierosolymitana, Vol. 31: Studies in the Bible, 1986*, pp. 205–39. Ed. Sara Japhet. Jerusalem: Magnes, 1986.

Rogerson, John W. "Was Early Israel a Segmentary Society?" *Journal for the Study of the Old Testament* 36 (1986) 17–26.

Roth, Martha T. *Law Collections from Mesopotamia and Asia Minor.* SBL Writings from the Ancient World Series, 6; Atlanta, GA: Scholars, 1995.

———. "'She Will Die by the Iron Dagger': Adultery and Neo-Babylonian Marriage." *Journal of the Economic and Social History of the Orient* 31 (1988) 186–206.

Rowley, H. H. *The Servant of the Lord and Other Essays.* London: Lutterworth, 1952.

Rüterswörden, Udo. *Von der politischen Gemeinschaft zur Gemeinde: Studien zu Dt 16,18–18,22.* BBB 65; Frankfurt am Main: Athenäum, 1987.

Salmon, J. M. "Judicial Authority in Early Israel: An Historical Investigation of Old Testament Institutions." Th.D. Diss., Princeton University. Ann Arbor, MI: University Microfilms, 1968.

Sasson, Jack M. "The Issue of *Ge'ullah* in Ruth." *Journal for the Study of the Old Testament* 5 (1978) 52–64.

Schaeffer, Henry. *The Social Legislation of the Primitive Semites.* London: Oxford, 1915.

Schäfer-Lichtenberger, Christa. *Stadt und Eidgenossenschaft im Alten Testament.* BZeitschrift für die alttestamentliche Wissenschaft 156; Berlin: Walter de Gruyter, 1983.

Schneider, Théo R. "Translating Ruth 4.1–10 among the Tsonga People." *The Bible Translator* 33 (1982) 301–308.

Seesemann, Otto. "Die Ältesten im Alten Testament." Diss. phil., Leipzig, 1895.

Seitz, Gottfried. *Redaktionsgeschichtliche Studien zum Deuteronomium.* Stuttgart: Kohlhammer, 1971.

Sellin, E., and G. Fohrer. *Introduction to the Old Testament.* Trans. D. E. Green. Nashville: Abingdon, 1968.

Smith, Henry Preserved. *A Critical and Exegetical Commentary on the Books of Samuel.* ICC; Edinburgh: T. and T. Clark, 1899 (reprint ed. 1977).

Silver, D. J. "Moses Our Teacher was a King." *Jewish Law Annual* 1 (1978) 123–32.

Sonsino, Rifat. *Motive Clauses in Hebrew Law: Biblical Forms and Near Eastern Parallels.* SBLDS 45; Chico, CA: Scholars Press, 1980.

Stager, Lawrence. "The Archaeology of the Family in Ancient Israel." *Bulletin of the American Schools of Oriental Research* 260 (1985) 1–35.

Stein, Gil. "The Organizational Dynamics of Complexity in Greater Mesopotamia." In *Chiefdoms and Early States in the Near East: The Organizational Dynamics of Complexity*, pp. 11–22. Ed. G. Stein and M. S. Rothman. Monographs in World Archaeology No. 18; Madison, WI: Prehistory, 1994.

Steinberg, Naomi. "The Deuteronomic Law Code and the Politics of State Centralization." In *The Bible and the Politics of Exegesis. Essays in Honor of Norman K. Gottwald on His Sixty-Fifth Birthday*, pp. 161–70. Ed. David Jobling, P. L. Day, G. T. Sheppard. Cleveland: Pilgrim, 1991.

Steinkeller, Piotr. "The Administrative and Economic Organization of the Ur III State: The Core and the Periphery." In *The Organization of Power: Aspects of Bureaucracy in the Ancient Near East*, pp. 19–41. Ed. M. Gibson and R. D. Biggs. SAOC, No. 46; Chicago: Oriental Institute, 1987.

Stern, Ephraim. *Excavations at Tel Mevorakh (1973–1976). Part One: From the Iron Age to the Roman Period.* Qedem 9; Jerusalem: The Institute of Archaeology, The Hebrew University of Jerusalem, 1978.

Stulman, Louis. "Encroachment in Deuteronomy: An Analysis of the Social World of the D Code." *Journal of Biblical Literature* 109 (1990) 613–32.

———. "Sex and Familial Crimes in the D Code: A Witness to Mores in Transition." *Journal for the Study of the Old Testament* 53 (1992) 47–63.

Sturdy, J. *Numbers.* CBC; Cambridge: Cambridge University, 1976.

Tadmor, Hayim. "'The People' and the Kingship in Ancient Israel: The Role of Political Institutions in the Biblical Period." *Journal of World History* 11 (1968) 46–68.

———. "Traditional Institutions and the Monarchy: Social and Political Tensions in the Time of David and Solomon." In *Studies in the Period of David and Solomon, and Other Essays*, pp. 239–57. Ed. T. Ishida. Tokyo: Yamakawa-Shuppansha, 1982.

Thiel, W. *Die soziale Entwicklung Israels in vorstaatlicher Zeit*. Neukirchen-Vluyn: Neukirchener Verlag, 1980.

Thompson, J. A. *Deuteronomy*. Downers Grove, IL: Inter-Varsity, 1974.

Thompson, Thomas and Dorothy. "Some Legal Problems in the Book of Ruth." *Vetus Testamentum* 18 (1968) 79–99.

de Tillesse, G. Minette. "Sections 'tu' et sections 'vous' dans le Deutéronome." *Vetus Testamentum* 12 (1962) 29–87.

Tucker, Gene M. "Witnesses and 'Dates' in Israelite Contracts." *Catholic Biblical Quarterly* 28 (1966) 42–45.

de Vaux, Roland. *Ancient Israel: Its Life and Institutions*. Trans. J. McHugh. New York: McGraw-Hill, 1961.

Vriezen, Th. C. "Two Old Cruces." *Oudtestamentische Studien* 5 (1948) 80–88.

Weber, Max. *Ancient Judaism*. Trans. H. H. Gerth and D. Martindale. Glencoe, IL: Free, 1952.

Weinfeld, Moshe. "On 'Demythologization and Secularization' in Deuteronomy." *Israel Exploration Journal* 23 (1973) 230–33.

———. *Deuteronomy 1–11*. AB; New York: Doubleday, 1991.

———. *Deuteronomy and the Deuteronomic School*. Oxford: Clarendon, 1972.

———. "Judge and Officer in Ancient Israel and in the Ancient Near East." *Israel Oriental Studies* 7 (1977) 65–88.

———. "The Origin of Humanism in Deuteronomy." *Journal of Biblical Literature* 80 (1961) 241–47.

Weiser, Artur. *The Old Testament: Its Formation and Development*. 4th Edition. Trans. D. M. Barton. New York: Association, 1968.

Weisman, Ze'ev. "Charismatic Leaders in the Period of the Judges." *Zeitschrift für die alttestamentliche Wissenschaft* 89 (1977) 379–411.

———. "The Place of the People in the Making of Law and Judgment." In *Pomegranates and Golden Bells: Studies in Biblical, Jewish, and Near Eastern Ritual, Law, and Literature in Honor of Jacob Milgrom*, pp. 407–20. Ed. D. P. Wright, D. N. Freedman, and A. Hurvitz. Winona Lake, IN: Eisenbrauns, 1995.

Weiss, D. "The Use of QNY in Connection with Marriage." *Harvard Theological Review* 57 (1964) 244–48.

Welch, A. C. *The Code of Deuteronomy: A New Theory of Its Origin.* New York: George H. Doran, 1924.

Wellhausen, Julius. *Prolegomena zur Geschichte Israels.* 6th ed. Berlin: Walter de Gruyter, 1927.

Wenham, G. J. "*Bᵉtulah*, a Girl of Marriageable Age." *Vetus Testamentum* 22 (1972) 326–48.

———, and J. G. McConville. "Some Drafting Techniques in Some Deuteronomic Laws." *Vetus Testamentum* 30 (1980) 248–52.

Westbrook, Raymond. "Adultery in Ancient Near Eastern Law." *Revue Biblique* 97 (1990) 542–80.

———. "A Matter of Life and Death." *Journal of the Ancient Near Eastern Society* 25 (1997) 61–70.

———. *Property and the Family in Biblical Law.* JSOTS 113; Sheffield: Sheffield Academic, 1991.

Whitelam, Keith. *The Just King: Monarchical Judicial Authority in Ancient Israel.* JSOTS 12; Sheffield: JSOT, 1979.

Willis, Timothy M. "Yahweh's Elders (Isa 24,23): Senior Officials of the Divine Court." *Zeitschrift für die alttestamentliche Wissenschaft* 103 (1991) 375–85.

Wilson, Robert. *Genealogy and History in the Biblical World.* New Haven: Yale University, 1977.

———. "Israel's Judicial System in the Preexilic Period." *Jewish Quarterly Review* 74 (1983) 229–48.

Wright, D. P. "Deuteronomy 21:1–9 as a Rite of Elimination." *Catholic Biblical Quarterly* 49 (1987) 387–403.

Zevit, Ziony. "The ʿegla Ritual of Deuteronomy 21:1–9." *Journal of Biblical Literature* 95 (1976) 377–90.

SOCIOLOGICAL AND ETHNOGRAPHIC STUDIES

Abélès, M. "In Search of the Monarch: Introduction of the State among the Gamo of Ethiopia." In *Modes of Production in Africa: The Precolonial Era*, pp. 35–67. Ed. D. Crummey and C. C. Stewart. Beverly Hills, CA: Sage, 1981.

Abrahams, R. G. "Neighbourhood Organization: A Major Sub-System among the Northern Nyamwezi." *Africa* 35 (1965) 168–86.

———. *The Political Organization of the Unyamwezi*. Cambridge: Cambridge University, 1967.

———. "Some Aspects of Levirate." In *The Character of Kinship*, pp. 163–74. Ed. Jack Goody. Cambridge: Cambridge University, 1973.

Ahmed, A. S. *Social and Economic Change in the Tribal Areas [Pakistan], 1972–1976*. Karachi: Oxford University, 1977.

Amanolahi-Baharvand, S. "The Baharvand, Former Pastoralists of Iran." Ph.D. Diss., Rice University. Ann Arbor: University Microfilms, 1975.

Baroja, J. C. "Honour and Shame: A Historical Account of Several Conflicts." In *Honour and Shame: The Values of Mediterranean Society*, pp. 79–137. Ed. J. G. Peristiany. Chicago: University of Chicago, 1966.

Bascom, W. *The Yoruba of Southwestern Nigeria*. New York: Holt, Rinehart and Winston, 1969.

Beattie, John. *The Nyoro State*. Oxford: Clarendon, 1971.

Beidelman, T. O. "Chiefship in Ukaguru: The Invention of Ethnicity and Tradition in Kaguru Colonial History." *International Journal of African History* 11 (1978) 227–46.

———. *The Kaguru: A Matrilineal People of East Africa*. New York: Holt, Rinehart and Winston, 1971.

———. "Nuer Priests and Prophets: Charisma, Authority, and Power among the Nuer." In *The Translation of Culture*, pp. 375–415. Ed. T. O. Beidelman. London: Tavistock, 1971.

Binford, L. R. "Smudge Pits and Hide Smoking: The Use of Analogy in Archaeological Reasoning." *American Antiquities* 32 (1967) 1–12.

Bloch, Maurice. "Decision-Making in Councils Among the Merina of Madagascar." In *Councils in Action*, pp. 29–62. Ed. A. Richards and A. Kuper. Cambridge: Cambridge University, 1971.

Bohannan, Laura. "Political Aspects of the Tiv Social Organization." In *Tribes Without Rulers*, pp. 33–66. Ed. J. Middleton and David Tait. London: Routledge and Kegan Paul, 1958.

Bohannan, Paul. "Ethnography and Comparison in Legal Anthropology." In *Law in Culture and Society*, pp. 401–18. Ed. L. Nader. Chicago: Aldine, 1969.

Bonte, P. "Pastoral Production, Territorial Organisation and Kinship in Segmentary Lineage Systems." In *Social and Ecological Systems*, pp. 203–34. Ed. P. C. Burnham and R. F. Ellen. ASAM 18; London: Academic, 1979.

Bourdieu, Pierre. "The Sentiment of Honour in Kabyle Society." In *Honour and Shame: The Values of Mediterranean Society*, pp. 193–241. Ed. J. G. Peristiany. Chicago: University of Chicago, 1966.

Briggs, L. C. *Tribes of the Sahara*. Cambridge, MA: Harvard University, 1967.

Buckland, W. W. *A Text-Book of Roman Law from Augustus to Justinian*. Cambridge: Cambridge University, 1921.

Buxton, J. C. *Chiefs and Strangers: A Study of Political Assimilation among the Mandari*. Oxford: Clarendon, 1963.

———. "The Mandari of the Southern Sudan." In *Tribes Without Rulers*, pp. 67–96. Ed. J. Middleton and David Tait. London: Routledge and Kegan Paul, 1958.

Campbell, J. K. "Honour and the Devil." In *Honour and Shame: The Values of Mediterranean Society*, pp. 141–70. Ed. J. G. Peristiany. Chicago: University of Chicago, 1966.

Carneiro, Robert L. "A Theory of the Origins of the State." *Science* 169 (1970) 733–38.

Chem-Langhie, B. "Southern Cameroon House of Chiefs."*International Journal of African History* 16 (1983) 653–56.

Claessen, Henri J. M., and Peter Skalník, eds. *The Early State*. New York: Mouton, 1978.

Clark, E. C. *History of Roman Private Law. Part III: Regal Period*. Cambridge: Cambridge University, 1919.

Cohen, Y. A. "Ends and Means in Political Control: State Organization and the Punishment of Adultery, Incest, and Violation of Celibacy." *American Anthropologist* 71 (1969) 658–87.

Cole, Dennis P. *Nomads of the Nomads: The Al-Murrah of the Empty Quarter*. Chicago: Aldine, 1975.

Cotran, E. "Tribal Factors in the Establishment of the East African Legal Systems." In *Tradition and Transition in East Africa: Studies of the Tribal Element in the Modern Era*, pp. 127–46. Ed. P. H. Gulliver. Berkeley and Los Angeles: University of California, 1969.

Cruise O'Brien, D. B. *Saints and Politicians: Essays in the Organisation of a Senegalese Peasant Society*. Cambridge: Cambridge University, 1975.

Cunnison, Ian. *Baggara Arabs: Power and the Lineage in a Sudanese Nomad Tribe*. Oxford: Clarendon, 1966.

———. *The Luapula Peoples of Northern Rhodesia: Custom and History in Tribal Politics*. Manchester: Manchester University, 1959.

Declareuil, J. *Rome the Law-Giver*. Westport, CT: Greenwood, 1927/1970.

Deng, F. M. *The Dinka of the Sudan*. New York: Holt, Rinehart and Winston, 1972.

Dennis, B. G. *The Gbandes: A People of the Liberian Hinterland*. Chicago: Nelson-Hall Co., 1972.

Doughty, C. M. *Arabia Deserta* I. New York: Boni and Liveright, 1936.

Dresch, P. "The Positions of *shaykhs* among the Northern Tribes of Yemen." *Man* 19 (1984) 31–49.

Dyson-Hudson, N. *Karimojong Politics*. Oxford: Clarendon, 1966.

Eades, J. S. *The Yoruba Today*. Cambridge: Cambridge University, 1980.

Edel, M. M. *The Chiga of Western Uganda*. London: Dawsons of Pall Mall, 1969.

Ensminger, J. "Co-Opting the Elders: The Political Economy of State Incorporation in Africa." *American Anthropologist* 92 (1990) 662–75.

Evans-Pritchard, E. E. *Kinship and Marriage Among the Nuer*. Oxford: Clarendon, 1951.

———. *The Nuer*. Oxford: Oxford University, 1940.

Fallers, Lloyd. *The King's Men: Leadership and Status in Buganda on the Eve of Independence*. London: Oxford University, 1964.

Fernea, R. A. *Shaykh and Effendi*. Cambridge, MA: Harvard University, 1970.

Fortes, Meyer. "The Structure of Unilineal Descent Groups." *American Anthropologist* 55 (1953) 17–41.

Fox, Richard. *Urban Anthropology: Cities in Their Cultural Setting*. Englewood Cliffs, NJ: Prentice-Hall, Inc., 1977.

Garthwaite, G. R. *Khans and Shahs: A Documentary Analysis of the Bakhtiyari in Iran*. Cambridge: Cambridge University, 1983.

Gellner, E. *Saints of the Atlas*. London: Trinity, 1969.

Ginat, Joseph. *Blood Disputes among Bedouin and Rural Arabs in Israel: Revenge, Mediation, Outcasting and Family Honor*. Pittsburgh: University of Pittsburgh, 1987.

Glavanis, Kathy R. G., and Pandeli M. Glavanis. "The Sociology of Agrarian Relations in the Middle East: The Persistence of Household Production." *Current Sociology* 31,2 (1983) 1–106.

Gluckman, Max. "Concepts in the Comparative Study of Law." In *Law in Culture and Society*, pp. 349–73. Ed. L. Nader. Chicago: Aldine, 1969.

———. "Kinship and Marriage Among the Lozi of Northern Rhodesia and the Zulu of Natal." In *African Systems of Kinship and Marriage*, pp. 166–206. Ed. A. R. Radcliffe-Brown and D. Forde. London: Oxford University, 1950.

———. *Politics, Law and Ritual in Tribal Society*. Chicago: Aldine, 1965.

Godelier, Maurice. "The Concept of the 'Asiatic Mode of Production' and Marxist Models of Social Evolution." In *Relations of Production: Marxist Approaches to Economic Anthropology*, pp. 209–57. Ed. D. Seddon, Trans. H. Lackner. London: Frank Cass, 1980.

Goldberg, H. "From Shaykh to Mazkir: Structural Continuity and Organizational Change in the Leadership of a Tripolitanian Jewish Community." In *Jewish Societies in the Middle East: Community, Culture, and Authority*, pp. 137–53. Ed. Sh. Deshen and W. P. Zenner. Washington, D.C.: University Press of America, 1982.

Gough, Kathleen. "Nuer Kinship: A Re-Examination." In *The Translation of Culture*. Ed. T. O. Beidelman. London: Tavistock, 1971, pp. 79–121.

Gould, R. A. "Beyond Analogy." In *Living Archaeology*, pp. 29–47. Cambridge: Cambridge University, 1980.

Greene, S. E. "Land, Lineage and Clan in Early Anlo." *Africa* 51 (1981) 451–64.

Grossman, D. "The Bethel Hills—An Unusual Rural Development." *Israel—Land and Nature* 1,1 (1975) 24027.

Gulick, J. *Social Structure and Culture Changes in a Lebanese Village*. New York: Wenner-Gren Foundation for Anthropological Research, 1955.

Gulliver, P. H. "Case Studies of Law in Non-Western Societies: Introduction." In *Law in Culture and Society*, pp. 11–23. Ed. L. Nader; Chicago: Aldine, 1969.

Hallpike, C. R. "Some Problems in Cross-Cultural Comparison." In *The Translation of Culture*, pp. 137–38. Ed. T. O. Beidelman. London: Tavistock, 1971.

Hammond, P. B. *Yatenga: Technology in the Culture of a West African Kingdom*. New York: The Free Press, 1966.

Holy, Ladislav. *Neighbours and Kinsmen: A Study of the Berti People of Darfur*. New York: St. Martin's, 1974.

————, and J. Blacking, "Explanation through Comparison." *Journal of Comparative Family Studies* 5 (1974) 57–60.

Johnson, D. H. "Tribal Boundaries and Border Wars: Nuer-Dinka Relations in the Sobat and Zaref Valleys, c. 1860–1976." *Journal of African History* 23 (1982) 183–202.

Jolowicz, H. F. *Roman Foundations of Modern Law*. Westport, CT: Greenwood, 1957/1978.

Jones, D. S. "Traditional Authority and State Administration in Botswana." *Journal of Modern African Studies* 21,1 (1983) 133–39.

Jones, G. I. "Councils Among the Central Ibo." In *Councils in Action*, pp. 63–79. Ed. A. Richards and A. Kuper; Cambridge: Cambridge University, 1971.

Katakura, M. *Bedouin Village: A Study of a Saudi Arabian People in Transition*. Tokyo: University of Tokyo, 1977.

Khaldûn, Ibn. *The Muqaddimah: An Invitation to History*. Trans. Franz Rosenthal. Abridged Edition. Princeton: Princeton University, 1969.

Khuri, F. I. *Tribe and State in Bahrain: The Transformation of Social and Political Authority in an Arab State*. Chicago: University of Chicago, 1980.

Klima, G. J. *The Barabaig: East African Cattle-Herders*. New York: Holt, Rinehart and Winston, 1970.

Kuper, Adam. "Introduction: Council Structure and Decision-Making." In *Councils in Action*, pp. 13–26. Ed. A. Richards and A. Kuper. Cambridge: Cambridge University, 1971.

———. "The Kgalagari Lekgota." In *Councils in Action*, pp. 80–99. Ed. A. Richards and A. Kuper; Cambridge: Cambridge University, 1971.

Kuper, H. "Kinship Among the Swazi." In *African Systems of Kinship and Marriage*, pp. 86–110. Ed. A. R. Radcliffe-Brown and D. Forde. London: Oxford University, 1950.

———. *The Swazi: A South African Kingdom*. New York: Holt, Rinehart and Winston, 1963.

Lamphear, J. "Aspects of Turkana Leadership during the Era of Primary Resistance." *Journal of African History* 17 (1976) 225–43.

Lawless, Robert. "On the Segmentary Lineage." *Current Anthropology* 18 (1977) 114–15.

Lewis, B. A. *The Murle: Red Chiefs and Black Commoners*. Oxford: Clarendon, 1972.

Lindholm, C. "Kinship Structure and Political Authority: The Middle East and Central Asia." *Comparative Studies in Social History* 28 (1986) 334–55.

MacGaffey, Wyatt. *Religion and Society in Central Africa: The Bakongo of Lower Zaire*. Chicago: University of Chicago, 1986.

Mair, Lucy. *African Societies*. Cambridge: Cambridge University, 1974.

Marfoe, Leon. "The Integrative Transformation: Patterns of Sociopolitical Organization in Southern Syria." *Bulletin of the American Schools of Oriental Research* 234 (1979) 1-42.

Marx, E. *The Social Context of Violent Behaviour: A Social Anthropological Study in an Israeli Immigrant Town*. London: Routledge and Kegan Paul, 1976.

Middleton, John. "Home-Town: A Study of an Urban Centre in Southern Ghana." *Africa* 49 (1979) 246–57.

———, and David Tait. "Introduction." In *Tribes Without Rulers*, pp. 1–31. London: Routledge and Kegan Paul, 1958.

Mitchell, J. C. *The Yao Village: A Study in the Social Structure of a Nyasaland Tribe*. Manchester: Manchester University, 1966.

Moore, Sally Falk. "Comparative Studies." In *Law in Culture and Society*, pp. 337–47. Ed. L. Nader. Chicago: Aldine, 1969.

———. "Descent and Legal Position." In *Law in Culture and Society*, pp. 374–99. Ed. L. Nader; Chicago: Aldine, 1969.

Musil, Alois. *The Manners and Customs of the Rwala Bedouins*. New York: American Geographic Society, 1928.

Nadel, S. F. *The Nuba: An Anthropological Study of the Hill Tribes in Kordofan*. London: Oxford University, 1947.

Nader, Laura, ed. *Law in Culture and Society*. Chicago: Aldine, 1969.

Netting, R. McC. "Sacred Power and Centralization: Aspects of Political Adaptation in Africa." In *Population Growth: Anthropological Implications*, pp. 219–44. Ed. B. J. Spooner; Cambridge, MA: MIT, 1972.

Newman, Kathleen S. *Law and Economic Organization: A Comparative Study of Preindustrial Societies*. Cambridge: Cambridge University, 1983.

Noland, S. "Dispute Settlement and Social Organization in Two Iranian Rural Communities." *Anthropology Quarterly* 54 (1981) 190–202.

Parkin, David. *Palms, Wine, and Witnesses: Public Spirit and Private Gain in an African Farming Community*. Aylesbury: Chandler Publishing Co., 1972.

Peristiany, J. G., ed. *Honour and Shame: The Values of Mediterranean Society*. Chicago: Chicago University, 1966.

————. "Honour and Shame in a Cypriot Highland Village." In *Honour and Shame: The Values of Mediterranean Society*, pp. 173–90. Ed. J. G. Peristiany. Chicago: Chicago University, 1966.

————. "Law." In *The Institutions of Primitive Society*, pp. 39–49. Ed. E. E. Evans-Pritchard. Glencoe, IL: The Free Press, 1954.

Peters, Emrys L. "Some Structural Aspects of the Feud among the Camel-Herding Bedouin of Cyrenaica." *Africa* 37 (1967) 263–82.

Radcliffe-Brown, A. R. "Introduction." In *African Systems of Kinship and Marriage*, pp. 1–65. Ed. A. R. Radcliffe-Brown and Daryll Forde. London: Oxford University Press, 1950.

————. "Primitive Law." *Encyclopaedia of the Social Sciences*, Vol. IX, pp. 202–206. New York: Macmillan Co., 1933.

Read, M. *The Ngoni of Nyasaland*. London: Frank Cass and Co., 1970.

Richards, Audrey. "The Conciliar System of the Bemba of Northern Zambia." In *Councils in Action*, pp. 100–29. Ed. A. Richards and A. Kuper. Cambridge: Cambridge University, 1971.

————. "Introduction: The Nature of the Problem." In *Councils in Action*, pp. 1–12. Ed. A. Richards and A. Kuper. Cambridge: Cambridge University, 1971.

Roscoe, J. *The Baganda: An Account of their Native Customs and Beliefs*. New York: Barnes and Noble, 1966.

Rosenfeld, H. "Social and Economic Factors in Explanation of the Increased Rate of Endogamy in the Arab Village in Israel." In *Mediterranean Family Structures*, pp. 115–36. Ed. J. G. Peristiany. Cambridge: Cambridge University, 1976.

Sahlins, Marshall D. "The Segmentary Lineage: An Organization of Predatory Expansion." *American Anthropologist* 63 (1961) 322–45.

Salzman, P. "Does Complementary Opposition Exist?" *American Anthropologist* 80 (1978) 53–70.

————. "Ideology and Change in Middle Eastern Tribal Societies." *Man* 13 (1978) 618–37.

Schapera, I. "Kinship and Marriage among the Tswana." In *African Systems of Kinship and Marriage*, pp. 140–65. Ed. A. R. Radcliffe-Brown and D. Forde. London: Oxford University Press, 1950.

———. "Law and Justice." In *The Bantu-Speaking Tribes of South Africa: An Ethnographical Survey*, pp. 197–219. Ed. I. Schapera. London: Routledge and Kegan Paul, 1959.

———. "Political Institutions." In *The Bantu-Speaking Tribes of South Africa: An Ethnographical Survey*, pp. 173–95. Ed. I. Schapera. London: Routledge and Kegan Paul, 1959.

Sjoberg, Gideon. *The Preindustrial City*. Glencoe, IL: The Free Press, 1960.

Smith, Edwin M., and Andrew Murray Dale. *The Ila-Speaking Peoples of Northern Rhodesia*, Vol. I. New Hyde Park, NY: University Books, 1968.

Smith, William Robertson. *Kinship and Marriage in Early Arabia*. Boston: Beacon, 1885; repr. 1967.

Spencer, P. *The Samburu: A Study of Gerontocracy in a Nomadic Tribe*. London: Routledge and Kegan Paul, 1965.

Tait, David. "The Territorial Pattern and Lineage System of Konkomba." In *Tribes Without Rulers*, pp. 167–202. Ed. John Middleton and David Tait. London: Routledge and Kegan Paul, 1958.

Taubenschlag, R. *The Law of Greco-Roman Egypt in the Light of the Papyri (332 B.C.–640 A.D.)* New York: Herald Square, 1944.

Teitelbaum, Michelle. "Old Age, Midwifery, and Good Talk: Paths to Power in a West African Gerontocracy." In *Aging and Cultural Diversity: New Directions and Annotated Bibliography*, pp. 39–60. Ed. H. Strange and M. Teitelbaum. South Hadley, MA: Bergin and Garvey, 1987.

Tosh, John. *Clan Leaders and Colonial Chiefs in Lango: The Political History of an East African Stateless Society, c. 1800–1839*. Oxford: Clarendon, 1978.

Tuden, A. "Leadership and the Decision-Making Process." In *Political Anthropology*, pp. 275–83. Ed. M. J. Swartz *et al*. Chicago: Aldine, 1966.

Tymowski, M. "The Evolution of Primitive Political Organization from Extended Family to Early State." In *Development and Decline: The Development of Sociopolitical Organization*, pp. 183–95. Ed. H. J. M. Claessen, P. van de Velde, and M. E. Smith. South Hadley, MA: Bergin and Garvey, 1985.

van Velzen, J. *The Politics of Kinship: A Study in Social Manipulation among the Lakeside Tonga of Malawi*. Manchester: Manchester University, 1971.

Verdier, R. "The Ontology of the Judicial Thought of the Kabrè of Northern Togo." In *Law in Culture and Society*, pp. 141–46. Ed. L. Nader. Chicago: Aldine, 1969.

Wagner, Gunter. "The Political Organization of the Bantu of Kavirondo." In *African Political Systems*, pp. 196–236. Ed. M. Fortes and E. E. Evans-Pritchard. London: Oxford University, 1940.

Watson, A. *The Law of the Ancient Romans*. Dallas: SMU, 1970.

Watson, Patty Jo. "The Idea of Ethnoarchaeology: Notes and Comments." In *Ethnoarchaeology: Implications of Ethnography for Archaeology*, pp. 277–88. Ed. C. Kramer. New York: Columbia University, 1979.

———. "The Theory and Practice of Ethnoarchaeology with Special Reference to the Near East." *Paléorient* 6 (1980) 55–64.

Weber, Max. *Ancient Judaism*. Trans. H. H. Gerth and D. Martindale. Glencoe, IL: The Free Press, 1952.

———. *The City*. Trans. and Ed. D. Martindale and G. Neuwirth. New York: The Free Press, 1958.

Winans, E. V. *Shambala: The Constitution of a Traditional State*. Berkeley and Los Angeles: University of California, 1962.

Winter, E. "The Aboriginal Political Structure of Bwamba." In *Tribes Without Rulers*, pp. 136–66. Ed. J. Middleton and David Tait. London: Routledge and Kegan Paul, 1958.

Zeid, A. A. M. "Honour and Shame among the Bedouins of Egypt." In *Honour and Shame: The Values of Mediterranean Society*, pp. 245–59. Ed. J. G. Peristiany. Chicago: University of Chicago, 1966.

Author Index

SCRIPTURE INDEX

Leviticus

4:13	126
4:13–21	157
18:6	207, 226
18:6–19	208
18:14	226
18:16	251
18:18	252
18:19	226
18:20	208
18:22	208
18:23	208
18:24–28	209
18:24–30	208
18:29	208
19:20–22	208
19:32	8
20:9	171–72
20:10	208
20:11–12	208
20:13	208
20:14	208
20:15–16	208
20:16	226
20:17–21	208
20:18	208
20:20–21	208
20:21	251
24:14–16	126
25:25–55	266
25:47–49	267, 283
25:47–55	138
25:48–49	266

Numbers

5:11–31	163, 207–209
11:10–30	35, 38
16:5	126
16:6	126
16:11	126
16:16	126
16:40	126
26:9–10	126
26:19–22	254, 261
27:3	126
27:4	277
27:1–11	251, 268
35	111, 118–19, 121, 124, 126, 128–30

35:1–8	121
35:6	89, 111, 113, 130
35:9–34	89, 111, 119, 121, 125, 128–30, 307
35:10–11	130
35:10–15	89, 113
35:11	89, 127
35:13–15	121, 130
35:16	127
35:16–21	119
35:22–25	126–27
35:22–28	119
35:25–28	89, 113
35:31–32	119
35:32	89, 113
35:33–34	158
36:1–12	251, 268

Deuteronomy

1:9–18	35, 38–40, 84
1:15	84
1:27	153
2:21	116
3:14	289
3:18	149
4:3	149
4:20	153
4:36	170
4:37	153
4:40	158
4:41–43	89, 111, 113–15, 118–19, 121–22, 124–25, 129–30, 161, 310
4:42	89, 113, 127
5:6	153
5:15	115, 153
5:16	116, 158, 171–72
5:18	207
5:29	116, 158
5:33	116, 158
6:3	116, 158
6:12	153
6:18	116, 149, 158
6:21	153
6:23	153
7:8	149, 152
7:16	183
8:5	170
8:14	153

INDEX 353